Knowledge Across Cultures

CERC Studies in Comparative Education

1. Mark Bray & W.O. Lee (eds.) (2001): *Education and Political Transition: Themes and Experiences in East Asia*. Second edition. ISBN 962-8093-84-3. 228pp. HK$200 / US$32.

2. Mark Bray & W.O. Lee (eds.) (1997): *Education and Political Transition: Implications of Hong Kong's Change of Sovereignty*. ISBN 962-8093-90-8. 169pp. HK$100 / US$20.

3. Philip G. Altbach (1998): *Comparative Higher Education: Knowledge, the University, and Development*. ISBN 962-8093-88-6. 312pp. HK$180 / US$30.

4. Zhang Weiyuan (1998): *Young People and Careers: A Comparative Study of Careers Guidance in Hong Kong, Shanghai and Edinburgh*. ISBN 962-8093-89-4. 160pp. HK$180 / US$30.

5. Harold Noah & Max A. Eckstein (1998): *Doing Comparative Education: Three Decades of Collaboration*. ISBN 962-8093-87-8. 356pp. HK$250 / US$38.

6. T. Neville Postlethwaite (1999): *International Studies of Educational Achievement: Methodological Issues*. ISBN 962-8093-86-X. 86pp. HK$100 / US$20.

7. Mark Bray & Ramsey Koo (eds.) (1999): *Education and Society in Hong Kong and Macau: Comparative Perspectives on Continuity and Change*. ISBN 962-8093-82-7. 286pp. HK$200 / US$32.

8. Thomas Clayton (2000): *Education and the Politics of Language: Hegemony and Pragmatism in Cambodia, 1979-1989*. ISBN 962-8093-83-5. 243pp. HK$200 / US$32.

9. Gu Mingyuan (2001): *Education in China and Abroad: Perspectives from a Lifetime in Comparative Education*. ISBN 962-8093-70-3. 252pp. HK$200 / US$32.

10. William K. Cummings, Maria Teresa Tatto & John Hawkins (eds.) (2001): *Values Education for Dynamic Societies: Individualism or Collectivism*. ISBN 962-8093-71-1. 260pp. HK$200 / US$32.

11. Ruth Hayhoe & Julia Pan (eds.) (2001): *Knowledge Across Cultures: A Contribution to Dialogue Among Civilizations*. ISBN 962-8093-73-8. 391pp. HK$250 / US$38.

Other books published by CERC

1. Mark Bray & R. Murray Thomas (eds.) (1998): *Financing of Education in Indonesia*. ISBN 971-561-172-9. 133pp. HK$140 / US$20.

2. David A. Watkins & John B. Biggs (eds.) (1996, reprinted 1999): *The Chinese Learner: Cultural, Psychological and Contextual Influences*. ISBN 0-86431-182-6. 285pp. HK$200 / US$32.

3. Ruth Hayhoe (1999): *China's Universities 1895-1995: A Century of Cultural Conflict*. ISBN 962-8093-81-9. 299pp. HK$200 / US$32.

4. David A. Watkins & John B. Biggs (eds.) (2001): *Teaching the Chinese Learner: Psychological and Pedagogical Perspectives*. ISBN 962-8093-72-X. 306pp. HK$200 / US$32.

Order through bookstores or from:

Comparative Education Research Centre
The University of Hong Kong
Pokfulam Road, Hong Kong, China

Fax: (852) 2517 4737
E-mail: cerc@hkusub.hku.hk
Website: www.hku.hk/cerc

The list prices above are applicable for order from CERC, and include sea mail postage; add US$5 per copy for air mail.

CERC Studies in Comparative Education 11

Knowledge Across Cultures:

A Contribution to Dialogue Among Civilizations

Ruth Hayhoe and Julia Pan
Editors

Comparative Education Research Centre
The University of Hong Kong

First published 2001
Comparative Education Research Centre
The University of Hong Kong
Pokfulam Road, Hong Kong, China

© Comparative Education Research Centre 2001

ISBN 962 8093 73 8

Typesetting and layout by Doreen Cheng.

The cover design for this book has been adapted from an oil painting, created by the Chinese artist, He Gong, especially for the 1992 Conference on "Knowledge Across Cultures" in Toronto. He Gong teaches in Sichuan University's Fine Art Department in Chengdu, China, as well as working as an artist in the United States.

Contents

Part V: China's Influences Past, Present and Future

List of Acronyms

AD	Anno Domini
AIHEC	American Indian Higher Education Consortium
BAICE	British Association for International and Comparative Education
BC	Before Christ
BCCI	Bank of Credit and Commerce International
BCE	Before the Common Era
BEMS	Board of Extra Mural Studies (India)
CBC	Canadian Broadcasting Corporation
CE	Common Era
CERC	Comparative Education Research Centre (The University of Hong Kong)
CESHK	Comparative Education Society of Hong Kong
CGIAR	Consultative Group in International Agricultural Research
CIDA	Canadian International Development Agency
CIES	Comparative and International Education Society (USA)
CIESC	Comparative and International Education Society of Canada
CIMMYT	International Maize and Wheat Improvement Centre (Mexico)
CIS	Centre for Integrated Systems (Stanford University, USA)
DAAD	Deutscher Akademischer Austauschdienst (German Academic Exchange Service)
DACEE	Department of Adult and Continuing Education and Extension (India)
DIC	Diploma of Imperial College (London, England)
EFA	Education for All
GATT	General Agreement on Trade and Tariffs
GNP	Gross National Product
HEI	Higher Education Institution
IAEA	International Atomic Energy Association
ICGEP	International Centres for Genetic Engineering and Biotechnology (Delhi, India and Trieste, Italy)
ICIPE	International Centre for Insect Physiology and Ecology (Kenya)
ICTP	International Centre for Theoretical Physics (Trieste, Italy)
IDA	International Development Association
IDB	Inter-American Development Bank
IDRC	International Development Research Centre (Canada)
IMF	International Monetary Fund
INAC	Indian and Northern Affairs Canada
IRRI	International Rice Research Institute (Philippines)
NEST	International Foundation for the Promotion of New and Emerging Sciences and Technologies

NGO	Non-Governmental Organization
NIC	Newly Industrializing Country
NMP	Net Material Product
NOS	National Open School (India)
NSS	National Service Scheme (India)
NVIT	Nicola Valley Institute of Technology (British Columbia, Canada)
ODA	Overseas Development Agency (United Kingdom)
OECD	Organization for Economic Cooperation and Development
OISE	Ontario Institute for Studies in Education
R, D & I	Research, Development and Implementation
R & D	Research and Development
SAREC	Swedish Agency for Research Cooperation with Developing Countries
TWAS	Third World Academy of Sciences
UBC	University of British Columbia (Canada)
UGC	University Grants Commission (India)
UK	United Kingdom
UN	United Nations
UNDP	United Nations Development Program
UNESCO	United Nations Educational, Scientific and Cultural Organization
UNICEF	United Nations Children's Fund
UNIDO	United Nations Industrial Development Organization
UNU	United Nations University
USA	United States of America
USAID	United States Agency for International Development
USSR	Union of Soviet Socialist Republics
WCCES	World Council of Comparative Education Societies
X-CED	Cross-Cultural Education Department (Alaska, USA)

Foreword

Mark Bray[1]

A major element in the mission of the Comparative Education Research Centre (CERC) of the University of Hong Kong is to act as a bridge between East and West. This book, the 11th in the series 'CERC Studies in Comparative Education', is a major contribution to achievement of that mission. The book is a work of striking breadth and profound depth which CERC is proud to publish.

The careers of the book's two editors in some respects exemplify the flow of knowledge and scholarly insight between East and West. Ruth Hayhoe was born in Canada and studied in that country, in the United Kingdom and in Hong Kong. Much of her professional career has focused on links between education and culture in China. She has edited, in some cases solely and in other cases in collaboration with colleagues, a number of well-received books in the field.[2] She has also written two seminal books on China's universities, the first of which, *China's Universities and the Open Door*, appeared in 1989; and the second of which, *China's Universities 1895-1995: A Century of Cultural Conflict,* was published in second printing by CERC in 1999.[3] Julia Pan, by contrast, was born and educated in Shanghai, China, did her graduate studies in Canada, and now teaches at the Ontario Institute for Studies in Education at the University of Toronto. Among her previous collaborative works with Ruth Hayhoe has been a book which is related to the present one, on East-West dialogue in knowledge and higher education.[4] Julia Pan has also directed and managed two major projects supported by the Canadian International Development Agency to promote collaboration between Canadian and Chinese scholars.

The editors explain in their Introduction that the book has a long history. It is the product of a series of initiatives which have brought together scholars from three major civilizations on the Eastern side of the globe – Chinese, Indian and Arabic – to

---

[1]Director, Comparative Education Research Centre, The University of Hong Kong.
[2]See for example: Ruth Hayhoe and Marianne Bastid (eds.) *China's Education and the Industrialized World: Studies in Cultural Transfer* (Armonk, New York: M.E. Sharpe, 1987); Ruth Hayhoe (ed.) *Education and Modernization: The Chinese Experience* (Oxford: Pergamon Press, 1992); Glen Peterson, Ruth Hayhoe and Yongling Lu (eds.), *Education, Culture, and Identity in Twentieth-Century China* (Ann Arbor: The University of Michigan Press, 2001).
[3]Ruth Hayhoe, *China's Universities and the Open Door* (Armonk, New York: M.E. Sharpe; and Toronto: OISE Press, 1989); R. Hayhoe, *China's Universities 1895-1995: A Century of Cultural Conflict* (New York, Garland Publishing, 1996; and Hong Kong, Comparative Education Research Centre, The University of Hong Kong, 1999).
[4]Ruth Hayhoe and Julia Pan (eds.) *East-West Dialogue in Knowledge and Higher Education* (Armonk, New York: M.E. Sharpe, 1996).

vii

share with one another and with scholars from North America and Europe some of the contributions of their longstanding civilizations to scientific and social knowledge. The first edition of this book was published in 1993, but went out of print in 1996.[5] The present book is a substantially-revised second edition. It contains a completely new Introduction, a new chapter by the senior editor, and updating of the majority of other chapters.

The contents pages reveal a very distinguished set of contributors. They include Abdus Salam, the first Pakistani scientist to win a Nobel Prize, and Ali A. Mazrui, the renowned African commentator on cultural and civilizational interactions around the world.[6] Other authors include prominent academics from China, Europe, India, the Middle East, North Africa, and North America. Each contributor brings perspectives which, both individually and together, significantly advance understanding of the topic.

Some dimensions of the book can be linked to the work of Samuel Huntington, who has written about the "Clash of Civilisations".[7] The conference which laid the foundations for the present volume was held one year before publication of Huntington's 1993 article, which gained widespread attention in the aftermath of the collapse of the Soviet Union and the end of the Cold War. This book follows up on many of the themes that emerged at that time, with a decade of hindsight since those events. The new world order has radically reshaped the field Comparative Education as well as other domains of study.[8] Thus, the book is on the one hand firmly grounded in analysis of centuries of history, and on the other hand well-positioned to identify new dimensions for dialogue at the opening of the new millennium.

When this Foreword was being written, Ruth Hayhoe was coming to the end of an appointment as the second Director of the Hong Kong Institute of Education. She took this post in September 1997, shortly after the reversion of Hong Kong's sovereignty from the United Kingdom to China in July 1997. Her selection for the position was widely acclaimed as an inspired choice, precisely because of her demonstrated abilities in bringing together civilizations. Fluent in English, Cantonese and Putonghua, she is able to bridge cultures at a personal as well as intellectual level. Ruth

---

[5]Ruth Hayhoe with Hilda Briks, Andrew Gordon, Ray Kybartas, Jane Moes de Münich, Frank Moody, Julia Pan, Edward Synowski, Lorraine Wilson, Ian Winchester and Wenhui Zhong (eds.), *Knowledge Across Cultures: Universities East and West* (Wuhan: Hubei Education Press, and Toronto: OISE Press, 1993).

[6]See for example: Ali A. Mazrui, *A World Federation of Cultures: An African Perspective* (New York: Free Press, 1976); Ali A. Mazrui, *Political Values and the Educated Class in Africa* (London: Heinemann, 1978); Isidore Okpewho, Carole Boyce Davies and Ali A. Mazrui (eds.), *The African Diaspora: African Origins and New World Identities* (Bloomington: Indiana University Press, 1999).

[7]Samuel P. Huntington, "The Clash of Civilizations?", in *Foreign Affairs*, Vol. 72, No. 3, 1993; Samuel P. Huntington, *The Clash of Civilizations and the Remaking of World Order* (New York: Simon and Schuster, 1997).

[8]Robert Arnove and Carlos Alberto Torres (eds.), *Comparative Education: The Dialectic of the Local and the Global* (Lanham MD: Rowman and Littlefield, 1999); Michael Crossley and Peter Jarvis (eds.) *Comparative Education for the Twenty-first Century.* Special issue of *Comparative Education*, Vol.36, No.3, 2000.

Hayhoe had previously lived and worked in Hong Kong as well as in mainland China. She herself described the pull back to Hong Kong in 1997 as "irresistible" because of her perception that Hong Kong would be in a key position to introduce elements of Chinese culture and civilization to the global community. This book is in a sense an embodiment of that notion.

Ruth Hayhoe is also a major figure in Comparative Education. During her period of office in the Hong Kong Institute of Education, she became President of the US-based Comparative & International Education Society (CIES). She is also a member of the Comparative Education Society of Hong Kong (CESHK), the Comparative & International Education Society of Canada (CIESC), and the British Association of International & Comparative Education (BAICE), and has actively supported the World Council of Comparative Education Societies (WCCES). Ruth Hayhoe will continue her contributions to the field for many years to come; and CERC is delighted to be a vehicle for bringing the insights by Ruth Hayhoe, Julia Pan and the 27 other contributors to the present book into the public domain.

Notes on Contributors

Zahra Al Zeera has focused her research on alternative paradigms and alternative research methods as well as Islamic holistic education. She is the author of *Wholeness and Holiness in Education: An Islamic Perspective*, published in 2001. She was a Professor in the Faculty of Education, University of Bahrain. She was also a Visiting Professor for one year at University of Toronto, where she had earlier completed her doctorate. She is currently President of MIDAD, Educational Consulting.

Philip G. Altbach is J. Donald Monan SJ Professor of Higher Education and Director of the Center for International Higher Education at Boston College in the USA. He is editor of the *Review of Higher Education*, and also of *International Higher Education: An Encyclopedia* (1991). He is author of *Comparative Higher Education* (1998), *Student Politics in America* (1971) and many other books.

Fatemeh Bagherian was a graduate student majoring in Social Psychology at Carleton University, Ottawa, at the time of writing this chapter. She obtained her B.A. in Psychology at Alzahra University in Tehran, Iran in 1979.

Ray Barnhardt is a Professor of Cross-cultural Education and Rural Development in the College of Rural Alaska at the University of Alaska Fairbanks, where he has been involved in teaching and research related to Native education issues since 1970.

J. Len Berggren is a Professor of Mathematics at Simon Fraser University. His published books include *Mathematics in Medieval Islam* (1986), *Euclid's Phaenomena: A Translation and Study of a Hellenistic Work in Spherical Astronomy* (1996) with R.S.D. Thomas; *Pi: A Source Book* (2nd edition) with Jon and Peter Borwein (2000), and *Ptolemy's Geography: An annotated translation of the theoretical chapters* (2000). He is a member of the editorial boards of *Archive for the History of Exact Science* and *Historia Mathematica*.

Gregory Blue a Professor of History at the University of Victoria, Victoria, Canada. Dr. Blue's expertise is in Chinese history and, in particular, traditional China in Western social thought. He is the author of *Transformation of the World*, Vol. 17, *Science and Technology* (1981), and editor of *Memory at the Margins: World History and Anthropology* (1995), *China and Historical Capitalism* (1999), *Statecraft and Intellectual Culture in the Late Ming* (2001) and *Colonialism and the Modern World Order* (2001).

Ralph Croizier is Professor Emeritus at the University of Victoria and President of the World History Association. His principal research interests have to do with transcultural developments in modern art, principally between China and the West. He has published several books including *Art and Revolution in Modern China: The Lingnan (Cantonese) School of Painting, 1906-1951* (1988).

Earl Drake is currently Adjunct Professor at the David Lam Centre for International Communication at Simon Fraser University and Director, China Council for International Cooperation on Environment and Development. Professor Drake has had an extensive career in the Canadian diplomatic service having served as Ambassador to the People's Republic of China and as Ambassador to Indonesia. Other postings include various positions in The World Bank, the Canadian International Development Agency, and the OECD.

Ursula M. Franklin is an experimental physicist and University Professor Emeritus at the University of Toronto. She is a Companion of the Order of Canada, a Fellow of the Royal Society of Canada and a former board member of the National Research Council and the Science Council of Canada. In addition to her substantial research into the structure and properties of materials, Professor Franklin has taught, published and lectured on the social impact of technology and on women's issues, peace and human rights. She has been awarded honorary doctoral degrees by more than ten Canadian universities.

Ruth Hayhoe is Director of the Hong Kong Institute of Education. Author of *China's Universities and the Open Door* (1989) and *China's Universities 1895-1995: A Century of Cultural Conflict* (1996), she has focused her interest on China's educational and cultural relations with the Western world over a long period of time.

Ji Shuli is a Professor at the Institute of Philosophy at the Shanghai Academy of Social Sciences. His research interests include the philosophy of science and the cultural comparison between China and the West. His books include *Beyond the Boundary of Science: From Philosophy of Science to Culture of Science* (1990), and *The Evolution of Scientific Knowledge: Selections from Popper's Philosophy of Science* (editor) (1987). His professional activities include his work as a co-director of UNESCO's *History of Scientific and Cultural Development of Mankind.*

Verna J. Kirkness, Professor Emerita of the University of British Columbia, has spent her lifetime advancing aboriginal education in Canada and abroad. Her publications include six books and numerous articles that have been published in academic journals in several countries. She has received many awards in recognition of her work. These include three honorary doctorates, Canadian Educator of the Year (1990), the National Aboriginal Achievement Award and the Order of Canada. Verna is of Cree heritage and is a member of the Fisher River First Nation.

Li Bingde is the former President of Northwest Normal University in Lanzhou, China. After doing graduate studies at Yanjing University in Beijing, he taught at Henan University, then spent three years as a visiting scholar at the Universities of Lausanne and Geneva in Switzerland and the University of Paris in France between 1947 and 1950. Professor Li's books, *Teaching Theory* and *The Methodology of Scientific Research in Education,* are used in educational institutions throughout China.

Li Manli has a Ph.D. from Peking University, and is Associate Professor at the Institute of Education, Tsinghua University, Beijing, China. Dr. Li's areas of expertise are in educational administration and policy, comparative education and curriculum and teaching.

Lu Jie is a Professor of Philosophy and Sociology of Education at Nanjing Normal University, China. Professor Lu's academic interests include pedagogical, sociological, cultural and philosophical aspects of education.

Ma Kanwen is a Research Fellow at the Institute for the History of Medicine and Medical Literature at the China Academy of Traditional Chinese Medicine, Beijing, China. He is also a Senior Research Fellow in the Department of Sociology Applied to Medicine at the London Hospital Medical College, U.K. His areas of expertise include the history of Chinese and Western medicine as well as the exchange of medical knowledge between China and other countries. He has published widely and collaborated in the compilation of the *Concise Dictionary of Traditional Chinese Medical Terms* (1979).

Alamin M. Mazrui is Associate Professor of Comparative Cultural Studies in the Department of African-American and African Studies, the Ohio State University, Columbus. Trained at Stanford University in California, Dr. Mazrui has published six books in both English and Kiswahili, the latest of which is *The Power of Babel: Language and Governance in the African Experience* (1998) – co-authored with Ali A. Mazrui. Alamin Mazrui is also a well-known human rights activist in Kenya.

Ali A. Mazrui is the Albert Schweitzer Professor in the Humanities and Director of the Institute of Global Cultural Studies at Binghamton University, State University of New York. He is also Albert Luthuli Professor-at-Large in the Humanities and Development Studies at the University of Jos in Nigeria. He is Andrew D. White Professor-at-Large Emeritus and Senior Scholar in Africana Studies at Cornell University. He is Ibn Khaldun Professor-at-Large, School of Islamic and Social Sciences, Leesburg, Virginia and Walter Rodney Professor at the University of Guyana, Georgetown, Guyana. His research interests include African politics, international political culture and North-South relations.

Renuka Narang is the Director of the Department of Adult and Continuing Education and Extension, University of Mumbai (Bombay). A central concern in Dr. Narang's professional work is the issue of social justice, particularly for women. She has been active in bringing innovation and change to the Indian education system with respect to the establishment of Extension as the Third Dimension of the university system and in making the university an adult learner friendly institution.

Julia Pan is a Senior Researcher in the Department of Theory and Policy Studies in Education of the Ontario Institute for Studies in Education of the University of Toronto, where she also teaches. She has led and managed two major projects of educational and research cooperation with normal universities in China, supported by the Canadian International Development Agency.

Samiha Sidhom Peterson is a Professor of Sociology at St. Olaf College, Minnesota. Since 1989, she has been a consultant to the Minister of Education in Egypt, and has assisted in the development of policy through research projects and position papers, liaisons and negotiations with international agencies, and liaisons with senior ministry officials responsible for educational reform. She has also worked with the United Nations Council on equality for women.

Abdul Rahman was Founder-Director of the National Institute of Science, Technology and Development Studies. He is a Fellow of the Operational Research Society of India and of the International Science Policy Foundation (UK) as well as President, Asia Branch. He is also a member of the International Academy of History of Science, Paris, and of the Academy of Science, Berlin. Professor Rahman's broad involvement in international consulting and research work has taken him to projects in Iraq, Kuwait, Brazil, China, and Japan.

Majid Rahnema was Senior Lester Pearson Fellow at the Canadian International Research Centre in the late 1980s and early 1990s. At the time of writing this chapter, he was working on a book entitled "The Archeology of Poverty". Dr. Rahnema holds a doctorate in law from the Sorbonne. He has had a distinguished career in the Iranian Foreign Service, and has held teaching positions at numerous universities including McGill, Stanford, Harvard, and the United Nations University (Tokyo).

Pinayur (Raja) Rajagopal was educated at the Universities of Madras (India) and Cambridge (England). He has been at York University in Toronto since 1966. His research and scholarly interests have been in the area of interaction between mathematics and computer science. His interest in the History of Indian Mathematics dates back to his undergraduate days but was revived by a chance encounter with a colleague, who challenged him to stop complaining about the Eurocentric reviews Indian Mathematics gets, and to do something about it. Since his retirement from teaching in 1996 he has spent part of his time relearning Sanskrit, and also done volunteer work for refugees.

Abdus Salam was Founder-Director of the International Centre for Theoretical Physics, established in 1964, and led the group of scientists who established the Third World Academy of Sciences in Trieste, Italy, in 1983. A Nobel Prize winning physicist, Professor Salam was appointed Professor of Theoretical Physics at Imperial College, University of London in 1957, and held this position for a long period of time. His publications include around 270 scientific papers in physics in addition to several reports on scientific and educational policies for developing countries. His untimely death in 1996 was a great loss to the world's scientific community.

Peter Swann was Director and Professor of East Asian Studies at the University of Waterloo, Waterloo, Canada, up until his retirement. Before this he held academic positions at the University of Toronto and York University, and was Director of the Royal Ontario Museum and the Seagram Museum. He was also Executive Director of The Samud and Saidge Bronfman Family Foundation's Donation Committee. His major research interest is in oriental art where he has published numerous books and articles.

Wang Fengxian is a Professor Emeritus in Education and Philosophy, also a doctoral supervisor at Northeast Normal University, Changchun, China. He is an executive member of the National Education Research Society, the National Education Science Committee on Moral Education, and the National Education Development Research Centre. Professor Wang has won numerous academic awards for his books and publications, and is known throughout China for his contribution to moral education.

Wang Yongquan is the former Director of the Institute of Higher Education, Peking University, Beijing, China. He is Senior Research Fellow at the National Research Centre for Educational Development and serves as Vice-Chairman in the Higher Education Section for National Educational Research Planning. He is also Vice-President of the Chinese Higher Education Society. Professor Wang's areas of expertise are in philosophy, comparative higher education and educational policy and administration.

Hans Weiler is an Emeritus Professor of Education and Political Science at Stanford University. He was a Professor of Comparative Politics and the founding Rektor (president) of Viadrina European University at Frankfurt (Oder)/Germany from 1993 to 1999 and a Visiting Professor at several universities around the World. In the 1970s he was the Director of the International Institute for Educational Planning (UNESCO) in Paris. Professor Weiler's expertise is in the area of comparative educational policy where he has published many articles and books. His most recent books include *Comparative Policy Research: Learning from Experience* (1987, with M. Dierkes and A. Antal) and *Educational Change and Social Transformation: Teachers, Schools, and Universities in Eastern Germany* (1996, with H. Mintrop and E. Fuhrmann).

Introduction

A Contribution to Dialogue among Civilizations

Ruth Hayhoe and Julia Pan[1]

The year 2001 was declared the Year of Dialogue among Civilizations by the United Nations. The purpose of this designation was to "emphasize that the present globalization process does not only encompass economic, financial and technological aspects but must also focus on human cultural, spiritual dimensions and on the interdependence of humankind and its rich diversity".[2] From the point of view of UNESCO, "Dialogue among Civilizations constitutes an essential stage in the process of human development that is both sustainable and equitable. It humanizes globalization and lays the bases of an enduring peace, by nurturing conscience and a common base for human existence rooted in history, heritage and tradition".[3]

This book had its genesis in a conference held in 1992, which had the purpose of drawing together scholars from three major civilizations on the Eastern side of the globe – Chinese, Indian and Arabic – to share with one another, and with scholars from North America and Europe, some of the contributions of their longstanding civilizations to scientific and social knowledge and to the patterns of modern higher education. The collapse of the Soviet Union in the autumn of 1991 had created space to think about modernity and human destiny in new ways, not bound to the categories of socialist and capitalist nations, developing and developed, which are based on the European Enlightenment heritage. It was finally possible to focus on the diversity of cultural inputs from countries and regions whose civilizational heritage was making possible diverse trajectories of modern development in the dialogue that emerged.

Almost all of the chapters in this volume were written originally in the early 1990s, a year or two before Samuel Huntington published his now famous thesis on the "Clash of Civilizations" which aroused heated debates throughout the 1990s. Huntington's focus was on warning the West of potential threats coming from civilizations whose influence has persisted outside of the European Enlightenment framework, and for this reason he called on universities in the West to develop "a more profound

---

[1] Julia Pan prepared information on the section entitled "The Genesis of the Project" in this introduction, and played a key role in liaising with Pinayur Rajagopal, Ursula M. Franklin, Renuka Narang, Lu Jie and Wang Yongquan, to facilitate the revisions and updating of their chapters.
[2] See the website http://www.unesco.org/dialogue2001/en/background.htm. Paragraph 2.
[3] *Ibid.* Paragraph 6.

1

understanding of the basic religious and philosophical assumptions underlying other civilizations and the ways in which people in those civilizations see their interests".[4]

The spirit of the writers contributing to this volume, however, whether they were from the West or the East, was one of mutual respect and an openness to the mutual enrichment that might come from understanding more deeply the treasures of knowledge and institutional patterning that each civilization had contributed to modern higher education. There was a sense that this kind of understanding would enable us to draw upon these treasures in a conscious and purposeful way as we worked together to envision how higher education could be re-shaped to serve our global future in the 21st century. We very much agreed with the principle recently expressed in the UN's call for a renewed commitment to international cooperation and understanding "on the basis of the recognition of the equal dignity of individuals and societies and the uniqueness of their contributions to human advancement".[5]

We realize that categories such as East and West are themselves conventions that reflect a somewhat distorted understanding of the globe and its dimensions. The restoration of concern about some of the deep economic inequities and imbalances between North and South in recent years, and calls for South-South solidarity, have provided an important counterbalancing to these categories. Nevertheless, the focus of our work had been on China, which we hoped would look sideways to some of the rich experiences and achievements of two other major Eastern civilizations, the Indian and the Arabic, even as it was energetically developing collaboration with Europe, North America and other parts of the Western world.

We have thus used these categories in a general or popular sense, while in no way excluding what might be called Southern contributions, such as those from ancient seats of learning in North Africa. Some of our contributors express their concerns in terms of North-South interrelations, but most use the framework of East-West interaction, respect and understanding. To be more precise, we might make the point that "the West" is seen by many as the tradition of Enlightenment Europe, which did so much to transform the globe in the 19th and 20th centuries under the aegis of modernization. While both Islam and Christianity were rooted in Judaism, a religion of the Middle East, there has been a tendency to associate Christianity with the West, and Islam with the East, due to their subsequent historical and geographical development. The way in which the term "Western" or the "West" is used by many in this volume largely reflects this popular assumption. The fact that it ignores the important contributions of Eastern civilizations to modernization is a core point of concern addressed by a number of the contributors. In the same spirit, we have kept the widely used convention of a calendar reflecting the influence of the Christian West, while adopting the terminology of the Common Era (CE) and Before the Common Era (BCE) to replace Anno Domini, in the Year of our Lord (AD) and Before Christ (BC).

The volume includes 25 chapters, and 29 scholars have contributed to its five parts. Eighteen might be regarded as Eastern in terms of their cultural heritage, while

[4] Samuel Huntington, "The Clash of Civilizations?", in *Foreign Affairs*, Vol. 72, No. 3, 1993, p. 49.
[5] http://www.unesco.org/dialogue2001/en/background.htm. Paragraph 2.

11 might be seen as Western. One of those 11, a scholar from the First Nations or indigenous peoples of Canada, sees the university in North America as a "Western" institution, in contradistinction to her own cultural heritage, and expresses a hope that it will open itself to respect for and reciprocity with this distinctive heritage. On another dimension, nine of the 29 scholars are women, and they have certain experiences in common across the East-West divide which may have shaped their approaches to scholarship.

Historically women had been largely excluded from participation in formal higher education up until the 19th century in all of the civilizations represented here, and the efforts they made to find a space to express their views have come to be recognized as important challenges to entrenched knowledge structures and institutional patterns. The nature of their roles within the family and local community may give them a stronger sense of local cultural context, and a greater facility for balancing the local with the global. The fact that they are relative newcomers to the world of higher education, in relation to long historical time, may also account for a certain freshness of insight and inclination to question established verities. We invite readers to make their own conclusions about the relative importance of gender differences across civilizations by keeping these points in mind while reading the chapters written by women, as well as by reflecting on the way gender is dealt with explicitly in a number of papers by both male and female contributors.

As is the case with many conference volumes, the style and approach of the various contributors differs considerably. Some presented thoroughly researched academic analyses, while others adopted a more informal dialogic approach, presenting ideas and questions intended to stimulate further discussion and research. To some extent these differences may reflect the different scholarly traditions represented. In inviting the updating and further development of chapters for this revised edition, we did not impose any requirements, but simply invited contributors to reconsider their work in the light of new developments over the decade, and new literature in the field. All of the reference literature they provided in footnotes, except for a few highly specialized items, has been integrated into a comprehensive bibliography at the end, which we hope will be useful for readers.

In this introductory chapter, we begin with a section that describes the genesis of the project and explains the practical concerns that stimulated efforts to nurture a dialogue among civilizations in the early 1990s. We then provide an overview of the major thematic parts of the volume, trying to show how one leads to the next, and what are the interconnections within and among the five parts. We conclude with some thoughts on how this volume may contribute to the field of comparative education as it takes on new tasks and new challenges in the 21st century.

THE GENESIS OF THE PROJECT

The decision to hold a conference in Toronto, Canada, in 1992, on the subject

"Knowledge across Cultures: Universities East and West", arose from the intellectual and practical demands of a major project of cooperation among seven normal universities in China and the Ontario Institute for Studies in Education (OISE), affiliated with the University of Toronto. Funded by the Canadian International Development Agency, the Canada-China Joint Doctoral Program in Education was designed to support the development of doctoral study in the field of education in China, after the disruption of the Cultural Revolution. Both sides were determined that it should not be simply a conventional effort to "upgrade" academic programs in China on the basis of Western expertise. Rather both sides sought a process of mutual enrichment, whereby Canadian students and scholars would learn from the wealth of educational knowledge and experience in China's rich civilization, while Chinese students and scholars had an extended exposure to a Western academic environment. Thus the project enabled 12 OISE doctoral students to spend periods of study in China, as well as making it possible for 22 Chinese doctoral students and young scholars to come to Canada for research related to their doctoral study, and the broadening of their academic experience.

The conference was an effort to create conditions for a genuine dialogue across civilizations, and we did not want to limit this to China and Canada. Thus in addition to inviting senior scholars and doctoral supervisors from the normal universities involved in the project, along with other outstanding Chinese scholars in scientific and historical fields, we sought out distinguished scholars from the Indian and Arabic world, along with Western scholars who were interested in participation in a dialogue of this kind. Our commitment to mutuality, together with the wider global develop-ments which followed the end of the Cold War, meant that this dialogue flourished, alongside the evolving practical developments of the project itself.

In 1994, our project supported a second major conference, this time in a classical Chinese academy, the Yuelu shuyuan, in Changsha, Hunan. It had been founded in 976 CE, more than a hundred years earlier than the first European university. The setting was beautiful, with low rise buildings on the side of the Yuelu mountain, in a complex facing south, with a series of courtyards, halls and side buildings unfolding from the imposing entry gate, back to the Library in the innermost part of the complex. To the west was a classical garden, attached to the former residence of the head of the academy, and to the east a Confucian temple, with a large ceremonial hall overlooking a series of Chinese-style cloisters. As one sat in the hall and looked out into the cloisters, the lovely low, curved roofs of the side and end buildings had decorative corners carrying one's eyes to the sky, trees and mountains above, and giving a sense of the inter-connectedness of humanity, earth and heaven.

To this enchanting location, we were able to draw scholars from India, the Arabic world, Europe and North America, as well as Hong Kong, Malaysia, Japan, and Korea. For the many Canadian graduate students and professors who had a role in the project, it was a culmination of the mutual learning experiences undergone in doctoral study and supervision, as they joined with Chinese professors and doctoral students in hosting this unique event in a classical Chinese setting. The theme of the conference,

"Indigenous Knowledge and Cultural Interchange: Challenges to the Idea of the University", directly addressed some of the ways in which Eastern approaches to knowledge and the institutional patterns of higher education in traditional Eastern societies might contribute to a rethinking of the university in the 21st century. The conference volume was entitled *East West Dialogue in Knowledge and Higher Education.*[6]

When the project reached its conclusion in 1995, the momentum of cross cultural exchange and understanding which had developed overflowed naturally into a second project, which ran from 1996 to 2001. Many of the same Chinese universities continued their involvement, and some new ones joined, while a second Canadian university, the University of British Columbia, also participated. The centre point for the second project moved from Beijing to Xi'an, reflecting a sense within China of the importance of the hinterland, where a wealth of traditional cultural resources compensates for lower levels of economic development. Two of the six Chinese universities taking part in the project were in this region, Shaanxi Normal University in Xi'an and Northwest Normal University in Lanzhou, while universities in Nanjing and Shanghai in East China, Wuhan in Central China, and Changchun in the Northeast were also partners. This time the focus was on collaborative research, and the themes were largely defined by the young Chinese scholars who had participated in the earlier project.

Women and minorities were identified as key agents of educational change and development at all levels of the education system in the new project. The first objective focused on women faculty and students in universities, offering them opportunities to participate in forms of study, teaching and research that would deepen their understanding of social change processes and enhance their leadership capacity. The second objective was to support both male and female secondary school teachers in their roles as moral educators and reflective practitioners during a time of rapid social change. Innovative research methodologies and pedagogical strategies were to provide a better understanding of the moral thinking of students and a more effective capacity for using dialogic forms of education. The third objective was to support minority primary and secondary school teachers in integrating indigenous knowledge into the curriculum through a genuinely bilingual education, which would bring minority values and cultures into the mainstream.

As the project reached its completion, in the summer of 2001,[7] it was possible to look back on the rich experiences of collaborative learning that had taken place in different parts of China and Canada, and to celebrate publications relating to all of the above themes. Many are being used in primary, secondary and tertiary classrooms in different parts of China, while some have been submitted for publication in the

---

[6] R. Hayhoe and J. Pan (eds.), *East West Dialogue in Knowledge and Higher Education* (New York: M.E. Sharpe, 1996).

[7] A final conference for the project was coordinated by Julia Pan, Wan Minggang, Wang Jiayi and Xu Jieying at Northwest Normal University, May 7-10, 2001. The Final Report of the project, *Women and Minorities as Educational Change Agents*, by Dwight Boyd and Julia Pan, was published by the Department of Theory and Policy Studies in Education, OISE/UT in July of 2001.

international literature. Perhaps the most remarkable of these publications is the first Tibetan/Chinese bilingual text for primary schools that brings Tibetan history, literature, and traditional scientific knowledge into the secular classroom. This indicates how the project's purpose of re-balancing Eastern and Western knowledge in the global community has also led to a re-balancing of knowledge and value among different groups within China itself.

We have taken a little time above in outlining the main contours of our longstanding and linked projects of collaboration, so that readers will understand that this volume has been part of a practical effort to engage in the experience of knowledge across cultures, and develop a genuine dialogue of civilizations, not only an exercise in theoretical reflection and scholarly exploration. As we look back over the years of project work, since this remarkable group of scholars gathered in Toronto in 1992 to share their wisdom and knowledge, we can see how much we learned from them.

We learned to respect the wealth of knowledge in the sciences and mathematics underpinning modern scientific development from India, the Arabic world and China. We learned about the need for openness to new paradigms of social and scientific thought. We noted the importance a high degree of awareness of cultural context, and the links which connect modern and traditional knowledge, and global and indigenous understandings. We were deeply aware of the inequities and imbalances likely to arise in the process of knowledge transfer, and we sought to mitigate these, while still recognizing the realities and constraints of different levels of economic development. We learned to listen to and respect the spiritual dimension of learning, realizing that it lies at the heart of all other forms of knowledge, and that traditional scientific and mathematical knowledge was often integrally linked to religious understanding.

We are thus delighted that our first conference volume is now appearing in an entirely new form, with the support and encouragement of the Comparative Education Research Centre of the University of Hong Kong. More than half of the original chapters have been revised and in some cases developed in new ways, with new collaborating authors.[8] One original chapter whose theme had little relevance has been left out, and one new chapter has been added as the final chapter in Part Five. There has been a complete reordering of all the chapters into a revised structure, under a new set of thematic headings. In this new introduction we attempt an overview which provides some background to the themes, the writers and their contributions, and also explores the inter-connections among them.[9]

---

[8] Chapters by the following authors have been revised: Hans Weiler, Verna Kirkness and Ray Barnhardt, Ali A. Mazrui (with Alamin M. Mazrui), Pinayur Rajagopal, Philip Altbach, Earl Drake, Samiha Sidhom Peterson, Ursula M. Franklin, Lu Jie, Renuka Narang, Li Bingde, Ralph Croizier, and Wang Yongquan (with Li Manli).

[9] The first edition of this volume was entitled *Knowledge Across Cultures: Universities East and West* (Wuhan: Hubei Education Press, and Toronto: OISE Press, 1993). It was edited by Ruth Hayhoe, with Hilda Briks, Andrew Gordon, Ray Kybartas, Jane Moes de München, Frank Moody, Julia Pan, Edward Synowski, Lorraine Wilson, Ian Winchester and Wenhui Zhong. It has been out of print since 1996. It had six sections, with a brief introduction to each written by the OISE doctoral students and professors listed above, who were co-editors. We are not able to republish these

CHALLENGES TO KNOWLEDGE

Part One includes five chapters which lay out some of the fundamental questions arising in the context of knowledge crossing cultures, particularly the questioning and rethinking of the patterns of the disciplines common to most modern universities. In the opening chapter Hans Weiler, distinguished German scholar of political science and comparative international education, also university rector, provides a broad overview of the ways in which knowledge is being transformed, and of the political dynamics that lie behind this transformation. In contradistinction to the notion of a unified science, Weiler identifies new domains of knowledge – normative, aesthetic and spiritual – which are challenging the existing order of knowledge. He draws attention to new discourses regarding indigenous knowledge, ways of knowing specific to gender, and pluralistic approaches to knowledge that arise from democratic practice. He shows how these have begun to break through the reciprocal legitimation between knowledge and power that has tended to link universities to established political power structures in both national and international contexts. His chapter opens up insights into the politics of knowledge which might be seen to constitute a kind of subtext to the volume as a whole.

In the second chapter, the noted Iranian scholar-diplomat, Majid Rahnema, launches a passionate attack on the "paradigmatic tyranny" of the natural sciences, which has often served to subjugate indigenous knowledge and subvert sustainable development practices rooted in this knowledge. He calls upon universities to "liberate themselves from the need to create unitary bodies of theory" and take pride in approaches to truth rooted in local knowledge. His main focus is on the natural sciences, with examples of the ways in which the orthodoxy they impose may suppress local creativity in areas such as agriculture and medicine. He also has some thoughts on the social sciences, suggesting that they should detach themselves from the models provided by the natural sciences and seek more artful modes of enquiry. He gives poignant expression to the hope that there be mutuality and even companionship in the journey of learning across cultural boundaries, rather than the approach whereby Western scholars are seen as providers of "advanced knowledge" to the Third World.

In the third chapter, Zahra Al Zeera, a scholar from Bahrain, takes up the issue of paradigms in the social sciences, providing a critical review of the conventional positivist paradigm of the social sciences in the West, followed by an overview of emergent paradigms of postpositivism, critical theory and constructivism. While Al Zeera finds that these emergent paradigms have provided some space for alternative ways of thinking and understanding, she suggests that they are nevertheless connected by an "invisible string" to the Aristotelian principle of "either or", which holds that every proposition must be either true or false. From this point she goes on to elaborate an Islamic paradigm of social knowledge which is rooted in the principle of *Tawhid* or

introductions, due to the changes in the structure of the volume, but we would like to acknowledge the valuable contribution they made to the first volume and to mention that we have drawn upon some of their insights in writing the introduction to this new edition.

"unity, harmony and oneness". This principle integrates the material, intellectual and spiritual dimensions of life, enabling individual and society to advance to higher stages of being, and avoid the kinds of fragmentation that have tended to characterize social thought in the West. This approach is not only valuable as an entry into understanding the social world of Islamic societies, but also sets a distinctive standard against which other approaches to the social sciences can be measured.

The fourth chapter in Part One is authored by Verna Kirkness, a senior scholar from the Canadian First Nations community, and Ray Barnhardt, an American colleague who has dedicated much of his scholarly career to issues of education among indigenous peoples. It was originally situated in a later section of the book, but we felt that it should be brought forward to Part One because of the powerful depiction it gives of how the North American university has excluded young people from First Nations communities at a fundamental level. This is done through the ways in which knowledge is organized, and through the tendencies to rigidity and triumphalism in the university's culture. The assumption has been that the adaptation of these young people to the culture of the university should be all one way, rather than a dialogue or a mutual accommodation whereby some of the wisdom and spiritual understanding of their indigenous cultures might come to enrich the university and broaden its perspectives.

The dilemma of First Nations youth in North America is a poignant expression of the wider global problem the book wishes to address, and highlights the urgency of a dialogue among civilizations replacing the kinds of accommodation to Western modernity, or indeed postmodernity, that have been expected of the "developing" world. We have described above the ways in which the work of our two projects led us to a similar set of concerns in China, where Tibetan and other minority young people are seeking respect, relations of reciprocity and opportunities for responsible action in the mainstream educational community in China. In this, they were supported by two Canadian scholars from First Nations communities who participated in the second project.

The final chapter in Part One is contributed by Ali A. Mazrui, renowned political scientist, scholar of global cultural studies, and Africanist. While North Africa is home to some of the oldest universities of the world, giving rise to some of the university's most revered symbols, this has not saved African universities from a position of marginality in the global community. Mazrui notes how Eurocentric, post-colonial universities have tended to marginalize indigenous cultures, through the nature of their curricula, the languages of instruction, and the focuses of research. Likewise, women have lost the centrality of their traditional role in food production in Africa, with greater personal rights and freedoms being associated with less influential roles in the service sector of modernizing societies. In the first part of this chapter, Mazrui lays out five strategies for change, which he suggests would open up the way to greater mutuality and reciprocity for African universities in the global community.

In addition to the African perspective, a substantial section has been added to this chapter, giving an Islamic perspective. Co-written with his nephew, Alamin M. Mazrui, it addresses new questions, which have arisen recently, around the digital revolution and its impact on global knowledge patterns. Possibilities for Islamic perspectives to be communicated through this network are posited, while the likelihood of these perspectives being revolutionized in the process is also explored. The historic transition of the Christian Reformation is put forward as a kind of parallel case which may help readers to anticipate possible future developments. The exploration into the transformation of gender relations in Islamic communities that could result from the use of these new technologies presages a possible breakthrough in this important arena.

Overall, these five chapters range from broad questions of the construction of knowledge, and competing paradigms of scientific and social knowledge in international, regional and national contexts, to very specific issues of access to knowledge and the university community by individuals marginalized by virtue of their birth within First Nations communities or their location in economically underdeveloped regions. In reflecting back on the conference itself, we have vivid memories of a moment when Verna Kirkness stood up to make her presentation following that of Hans Weiler. She began by saying that Weiler's paper dealt on a level of theoretical sophistication that was difficult to grasp, and then went on to say she nevertheless felt he was talking about the very same problem that was the central concern of her paper!

EASTERN CONTRIBUTIONS TO SCIENTIFIC KNOWLEDGE

Part Two of the volume moves to the consideration of history, and a set of chapters which provide detailed historical evidence of the important contribution of three major Eastern civilizations, Indian, Arabic and Chinese, to the development and achievements of modern science. While there can be little doubt about the benefits of modern science, especially in areas such as medicine, agriculture, engineering technology, and communications, there has been a tendency to see all of these achievements as a Western success story and to forget the important contributions of other major civilizations to the complex and delicate process of understanding that resulted in its emergence. Recognition of these historic contributions is important in fostering respect and in creating awareness of the reciprocity across cultures that has nurtured scientific development. The most recent century or two may have been dominated by the West, but no-one knows from where new impulses for major breakthroughs in scientific understanding may come.

In the first chapter, Pinayur Rajagopal, an Indian scholar educated in Madras and Cambridge, who taught mathematics and computer science for over three decades in Canada, elaborates on the rich contribution of Indian mathematics to the world heritage of science. He traces the development of Hindu-Arabic numerals from the earliest times, up till they were first introduced to Europe in 1202 CE, and subsequently integrated into Western mathematics in the 15th century. He points out how the roots of the science of geometry originated in Vedic religious rituals, which used numbers for daily useful applications, such as the construction of altars, as well as for cosmographic descriptions. He traces the development of several branches of mathematics in India, and their subsequent use in the development of Arabic science from the 9th century, which in turn made a significant contribution to the scientific development in Europe. Rajagopal's inspiration for this research arose from the challenge of a colleague who asked him to stop complaining about the Eurocentric reviews to which Indian mathematics are often subjected and do something about it!

The second chapter in Part Two, by J. Len Berggren, professor of mathematics at Simon Fraser University in Western Canada, traces the history of four major fields – geometry, astronomy, cartography and optics – from the period of Greek culture up till their introduction to medieval Europe. The Arabic contribution to world science has often been viewed as merely that of preserving Greek scientific knowledge until such a time as Europe took over the scientific enterprise. Berggren shows how utterly mistaken is this view, with his detailed overview of the critically important contributions made by Islamic scholars to these four major fields of science. He also points out how Islamic scholars had revived a long dead scientific tradition from Greece in the 8th and 9th centuries, while European scholars, who translated Arabic texts into Latin in the 12th and 13th centuries, were working with a scientific culture that was still active and dynamic. Into the thin layer of Greek learning imported through late Roman summaries, which provided a learning environment after the Dark Ages, these scholars were able to introduce the incomparably richer Arabic learning over subsequent centuries, and thus lay the foundation for the emergence of modern science.

The third chapter is contributed by Ji Shuli, a distinguished philosopher of science in China, known for his work in introducing Karl Popper's philosophy of science to Chinese readers in the 1980s. In a sense, Ji begins at the opposite end of the spectrum from Rajagopal and Berggren, in relating traditional views of science in China to the ideas of post-relativity physics in the West. After a brief summary of what he defines as dichotomic interpretations underlying Western science, he introduces some key concepts of traditional Chinese science. He shows the holism that ran through the understanding of an organic universe, embracing the unity of Heaven-humanity and a transcendental Way, that was nevertheless immanent in the universe. While Ji's focus is on the roots of natural science understanding in China, there are striking parallels with Al Zeera's social science paradigm in the second chapter of Part One.

Ji shows how Sinic interpretation prescribed specific aspects of Sinic science including astronomy, mathematics and medicine, giving them a unique trajectory of development. He then elaborates the shift in Western science, and in the philosophy of science, with the discoveries of Albert Einstein, Werner Heisenberg and Niels Bohr, and the subsequent reflection on these discoveries by Karl Popper, Thomas Kuhn and Larry Laudan. His conclusion bears repetition here, so fundamental is it to the dialogue of civilizations which this volume seeks to promote: "Every culture has or had, in principle, its own specific type of science as a mode of living in nature, though most have remained undeveloped. Only a few had matured into an integral system, worthy of the name 'science', among which Sinic science was the most salient model among the non-Occidental sciences. Occidental science, although the most complex system, has never been unique nor the manifestation of a unique truth. It will be, and is being, benefitted by other types of science, and Sinic science in particular". (p. 150)

Part Two concludes with a wonderfully reflective piece on the integration of inherited scientific traditions, which are linked to religious, social and artistic knowledge in most societies, into modern educational development intended to foster creativity and transform society. Abdul Rahman, founder-director of the National Institute of Science, Technology and Development Studies in India, and a member of the International Academy of the History of Science in Paris, and the Academy of Science in Berlin, counsels readers to reflect on the problem facing every society of how to balance inheritance with creativity, the old with the new, and develop a harmony between the two. He sees the role of universities as a dual one – providing a historical and critical perspective on inheritance, on the one side, and promoting an ongoing critique of novelty and invention and the technologies emerging from them on the other side. If education could play this role, he feels, it could promote harmony between inheritance and creativity, and allow for the fullest possible development of human capabilities without disrupting society and degrading the environment.

ISSUES OF KNOWLEDGE TRANSFER

Part Three of the volume moves to a core issue in the consideration of knowledge across cultures, that of knowledge transfer. There is a considerable literature in comparative education around this issue, with major concerns about the inequities and imbalances that arise in the process of knowledge transfer, reflecting different levels of political and economic power, and often analyzed in terms of patterns of domination and dependency, within both capitalist and socialist blocs. With the end of the Cold War, and the increasing pace of globalization throughout the 1990s, the pace of knowledge transfer has accelerated, becoming multi-directional, yet tending to draw even the most remote corners of the world into intense connectedness to diverse yet integrated centres of political and economic power.[10] Each of the five chapters in this section draws attention to specific national cases or aspects of knowledge transfer.

The first chapter, by Abdus Salam, begins with some reflections on the history of science, and then lays out some of the key issues that face developing countries in relation to the development of science and technology. A Nobel Prize winning physicist from Pakistan, Salam did much to promote Third World scientific cooperation through the International Centre for Theoretical Physics in Trieste, Italy, and the Third World Academy of Sciences, which he founded and to which he dedicated many years of his life. His purpose was to provide conditions for more equitable and fruitful knowledge transfers in the basic sciences. We thus begin Part Three with a view from the periphery by a scientist of great distinction who grew up in India and Pakistan.

Salam first noted that the science and technology gap between the West and the developing world is of relatively recent origin, and called attention to the historical

---

[10] Thomas L. Friedman, *The Lexus and the Olive Tree* (New York: Anchor Books, 2000).

contributions of Eastern societies to world scientific development. He then provided a classification of four types of science, including basic sciences, sciences in application, conventional low technology and science-based high technology, suggesting that developing societies have over-emphasized the second and fourth, not giving enough attention to curiosity oriented basic sciences and the transformation of conventional low technology. Salam gave detailed suggestions for steps that could be taken by developing countries to correct this balance, and also for ways in which international organizations could facilitate appropriate kinds of knowledge transfer to Third World countries. His untimely death in 1996 was a great loss to the world community, but the message he has left us here provides much food for thought in relation to issues of the transfer of knowledge across cultures.

The second chapter in Part Three focuses on the historical interaction between Chinese and Western medicine. It was written by Ma Kanwen, a research fellow at the Institute of Medicine and Medical Literature of the Chinese Academy of Traditional Medicine, and also senior research fellow in the Department of Sociology Applied to Medicine of the London Hospital Medical College. This chapter provides a striking historical example of knowledge transfer, with an important lesson relating to mutual understanding and the survival of indigenous knowledge systems. In Part Two, Ji Shuli noted how traditional Chinese medicine was a complete and highly developed sub-system of Chinese traditional science, premised on very different values and understandings of humanity and nature than Western medicine. The fact that it has been kept alive to the present time, and has recently experienced a revival of interest not only in China but also globally, is quite remarkable.

In this richly historical depiction of the meeting between Western and Chinese medical science in the 19th and early 20th centuries, Ma shows how near Chinese medicine came to extinction under the pressures of modernization and nation building. In the initial period, when Western medical science was introduced into China in the 19th century, there was a genuine attempt to integrate Western medical knowledge into the rich heritage of traditional Chinese medicine, allowing both kinds of medical knowledge to flourish and benefit from the stimulus of mutual interaction. Later, however, in the wake of the revolution of 1911, traditional Chinese medicine was rejected in favour of an all-out development of Western medicine. Traditional medical knowledge was given no further governmental support until the mid-1950s, when Mao Zedong revived it in the face of forms of Soviet educational imperialism that had become intolerable. Only because China had managed to "stand up" politically, after the Revolution of 1949, was it possible to maintain and develop an alternative knowledge heritage that is now being recognised globally for its contribution to human health and well-being. This could also be seen as an interesting case study in the politics of knowledge, and considered from the perspectives laid by Hans Weiler in the opening chapter of Part One.

The third chapter, by Philip Altbach, deals with the broad patterns of rela-tionship between universities and academies of science in India and China and the centres of scientific research in the United States and Europe which tend to define world standards of scientific advancement and to manage the international literature. In spite of the vast size of these two "gigantic peripheries" and the tremendous progress they have made in the development of modern science and technology, their scholars tend to remain on the periphery of major developments in world science. Altbach is known for his prolific research and publication around issues of domination and dependency in the worlds of scientific knowledge and publishing, and also for his extensive research on comparative higher education. In this paper he takes a rather pragmatic view, outlining similarities and differences in the higher education and scientific establishments of these two major Asian nations. He suggests how they may foster certain specialist areas of research at a world level, where the particular strengths they have may enable them to contribute actively to the global knowledge system. Altbach also notes the potential value of a much greater scientific and scholarly collaboration between these two Asian giants.

The fourth chapter continues the focus on India and China, comparing the ways in which they interacted with the World Bank in projects of knowledge and technology transfer from the 1950s up to the end of the century. Earl Drake had a distinguished career in the Canadian diplomatic service, culminating in his posting as Canadian Ambassador to China in the late 1980s, and including postings as Ambassador to Indonesia and as Canadian government representative in the World Bank. Since retirement he has been a professor at Simon Fraser University in Canada. He thus writes from the perspective of both diplomat and scholar, comparing the very different experiences of these two Asian nations in their relations with the World Bank. Differences in timing, in the approach of the Bank, and in the political systems of the two countries led to very different outcomes, levels of satisfaction with the processes of knowledge transfer, and contributions to national development.

The final chapter in Part Three provides a theoretical framework for reflecting on processes of knowledge transfer as an overall part of development initiatives. Written by Samiha Sidhom Peterson, a sociologist from Egypt who has had extensive experience in educational development projects, it proceeds from the macro context of international aid policies, down through the layers of national, organizational and individual filters, in terms of those engaged in the micro politics of the knowledge transfer process at each level. Through this multi-layered analysis, Peterson enables readers to focus on the people involved at each level in knowledge transfer, from policy maker to practitioner, each bringing a different set of life experiences, attitudes and cultural sensitivities to their work, and each having a impact on the ways in which knowledge transfer takes place. From the perspective of Egypt, and the real needs of rural schools and basic education, we can look up through the layers to such major international policy forums as the 1990 meeting of international organizations in Jomtien, Thailand, which led to the World Declaration on Education For All, and the 2000 summit in Dakar, Senegal, to review progress over the decade. Peterson provides a framework for reflecting on the many levels and layers at which people of differing backgrounds participate in knowledge transfer from the level of international policy-making, to the level of practical implementation in rural school settings.

INDIGENOUS KNOWLEDGE AND MODERN EDUCATION

The link between Peterson's chapter and the theme of Part Four of this volume is a natural one. From the nexus between the international community, and national or local participants in knowledge transfer, the book moves to concerns about the preservation and development of indigenous knowledge traditions, and the rooting of modern education, both formal and non-formal, in its local soil. It may be no coincidence that all four of the scholars whose papers have been included in this section are women, since women tend to be closer to their local communities than men. Women may also be more deeply aware of the need for modern institutions to have firm roots in their own cultural soil, and be better able to connect in interactive ways with diverse members of their communities.

The first chapter in Part Four is by Ursula M. Franklin, a distinguished scholar of metallurgy and materials science at the University of Toronto, Canada, who has lectured and published widely on the social impact of technology, women's issues, peace and human rights. Here she draws upon her rich knowledge of traditional metallurgy in societies such as ancient China, to illustrate how technology can be understood socially as the way in which things were done, and how people's way of working together is of fundamental social and cultural importance. In traditional Chinese bronze technology she discovered a division of labour around processes, and a consequent ordering of society, that did not exist anywhere else until the industrial revolution in Europe. This underlay the Confucian concept of *li* or the right way of doing something, both practical and moral. All technologies, Franklin suggests, are simply "ways of doing things", and decisions need to be made at the local level about how new technologies can be linked to traditional ones, and how it may be possible to maintain a diversity of ways of doing things in the face of an encroaching global techno-culture. The issues Franklin raises in this chapter pick up on themes found in Part One of alternative ways of knowing, as well as themes in Part Three on the conditions for knowledge transfer. They also lead into the following three chapters, which look at the rooting of modern ways of educating in the indigenous cultural soil of China, Iran and India.

The second chapter in Part Four focuses on China, and its rich heritage of educational thought and practice. A highly respected scholar in the area of moral education and the sociology of education, also the first woman to be appointed a doctoral supervisor in education in China, Lu Jie draws attention to two important value orientations in indigenous Chinese educational thought – the importance of fostering moral character, and a greater emphasis on collective rather than individual interests. She sees Chinese pedagogy as coming into its own in the 1980s, after experiences of Westernization and later Sovietization which had left little space for an appreciation and understanding of China's indigenous pedagogy, or its possibilities for supporting modern educational development. What can be seen here is a determination to build theories of education and teaching that are rooted in China's own cultural soil, and develop them into something that can be contributed from China to the global community. In the period since writing this paper, Lu has carried forward this vision, including the convening of a major international conference of Chinese educators from many parts of the world in 1997.[11]

The third chapter turns to Iran, a country with a rich civilizational heritage and an experience of cultural revolution having some parallels with that of China. The author, Fatemeh Bagherian, was a graduate student at Carleton University in Ottawa at the time of writing this paper. She reviews Iran's historical experience with importing Western educational patterns, which had no link to Iran's highly developed traditional schools for basic education and higher level scientific and social studies, the *maktab* and *madrassa*. From her overview of the traditional educational heritage, she draws out six points which could be introduced into modern Iranian education. Such a move would constitute a revival of progressive elements of its own traditions and make modern education relevant to local concerns and needs. There are interesting parallels between these points made by Bagherian for Iran and the dilemmas of modern educational development in China highlighted by Lu in the preceding paper. This chapter also has some resonance with Rahman's analysis of inheritance, creativity and society in Part Two.

The final chapter in this section focuses on non-formal higher education in the context of India. Renuka Narang is director of the Department of Adult and Continuing Education and Extension of the University of Mumbai (Bombay), and has devoted her career to issues of social justice and support for rural women's education and development. Here she describes in some detail the university's work in developing a full alternative system of education for rural women, from literacy up to secondary and higher education. One of the important off-shoots of the program is the opportunity it provides to urban youth in formal university programs to participate in this work and gain an appreciation of the richness and diversity of their indigenous local cultures. Through this program the University of Mumbai retains and develops rich interaction with indigenous knowledge and culture in its locality, while carrying out its other functions as a modern knowledge institution fully connected to the international community of higher education around the world.

CHINA'S INFLUENCES: PAST AND PRESENT

Part Five of this volume focuses on Chinese civilization, and on its past contributions to the global community, as well as potential future influences. The focus on China in this section reflects the projects of educational exchange and development which were the practical inspiration for the volume. Readers are reminded in several of the papers of the wealth of interaction between China and the West at different times in history, and of the fact that China was for a long period more of a donor than a recipient culture.

[11] Lu Jie (ed.), *Education of Chinese: The Global Prospect of National Cultural Tradition* (Huaren jiaoyu: minzu wenhua chuantong de quanqiu zhanwang) (Nanjing: Nanjing shifan daxue chubanshe, 1999).

Given the conflicts and difficulties surrounding China's interaction with the West over the past hundred years, when large-scale influences from both the capitalist and socialist West made a deep impact in the fields of education, science and the arts, it is important to remember that this was preceded by a much longer period in which Chinese scientific and artistic achievements were admired and sought after in the West.

In the first chapter of Part Five, Peter Swann details the admiration and appreciation with which Chinese silks, porcelains, lacquer works, cloisonné, enamels, wall papers and furniture were received in Europe, beginning with silk in the Roman period right up to the 17th and 18th centuries. The style of *Chinoiserie* has left its mark in many European palaces and gardens. At one time director of the Royal Ontario Museum and the Seagram Museum in Canada, university scholar and author of many books and articles on oriental art, Swann writes in a humorous and delicately ironic tone, suggesting that it is only most recently that the West has become aware of the deeper, spiritual springs of Chinese art which have flowed across this bridge. There is thus much more to be learned and absorbed, as the dialogue among civilizations unfolds in the coming years.

The second chapter focuses on another aspect of China's influence in Europe, specifically that of Chinese social thought and institutions, as introduced mainly by the Jesuits, on the Enlightenment movement in Europe of the late 17th and 18th centuries. Gregory Blue, professor of history at the University of Victoria in Canada, has contributed to Needham's great *History of Science and Civilization in China*, focusing on how traditional China was viewed from the West. While China's scientific contributions to agriculture, printing, silk technology, gunpowder, cast iron and the magnetic compass are well known, less has been written about the profound social, intellectual and cultural influences which China exerted on European Enlightenment thought. Blue explores in some depth the ways in which China's longstanding tradition of religious tolerance, and the coexistence of Confucianism, Daoism and Buddhism with little conflict, influenced European thinking. Given that secularization was one of the main characteristics of the Enlightenment, and was crucial to the subsequent development of modern science, and to the emergence of modern states, it is striking to note how this important transition in Western history was served by an Eastern example of calm secularism at a time of extreme religious strife in Europe.

While the first two chapters in Part Five were written by distinguished Western Sinologists, the third and fourth papers came from the pens of two of the senior Chinese professors and doctoral supervisors who were involved in our joint doctoral project. They provide analyses from the Chinese side of China's interaction with the West, and focus mainly on recent history.

An influential professor of education since the late 1930s, and the pillar of educational development in China's Northwest region since 1951, Li Bingde had a rich exposure to progressive pedagogy and educational experimentation in the heyday of American influence in the 1920s. He also gained a deep understanding of European educational thought through a study period in Switzerland, and visits to France and Germany, in the 1940s. At an earlier period he had worked with his professor, Li

Lianfang, to introduce ideas and methods of the Belgian educator, Ovide Decroly, into Chinese basic education. In this chapter he begins with an overview of classical Chinese history, showing the diversity of cultural and spiritual thought that always existed in spite of efforts at various times to make Confucianism the only defining ideology. This tolerant and widely embracing culture was fundamental to the strength of classical Chinese civilization in Li's view. Only in relatively recent times was a closed door policy adopted, under the Manchu or Qing dynasty, that was established in 1644 CE, leading to a disastrous weakening of the country just as Europe modernized, and culminating in the Opium Wars of the 1840s.

The whole subsequent period, up to 1979, Li defines as a "half-open door", seeing the period since Deng Xiaoping declared a commitment to modernization as the first full opening of the door again. In this new period of openness, it is crucial that Chinese people know themselves, and build upon their own rich cultural heritage while embracing all that is positive from the international community. Blind copying, such as happened with both Western and Soviet influences in the past, must be avoided, a point that echoes what was said by Lu Jie earlier. Here Li is challenging China's educators, in a period of globalization, to develop along the lines that have been suggested by Abdul Rahman in Part Two, transforming society through harmonizing the forces of inheritance and creativity, and calling for widespread collaboration with colleagues around the world to foster "cultural multiplicity" in an increasingly globalized world.

The fourth chapter in Part Five is contributed by Wang Fengxian, a senior professor and doctoral supervisor of Northeast Normal University in Changchun. His life experience has been somewhat different from that of Li Bingde, as he grew up in a region of China strongly influenced by both Japan and the Soviet Union, had no opportunity for study abroad, and came to be one of China's most respected scholars in the field of moral education. Like Li, he focuses on questions of China's interaction with the West, but his perspective is somewhat different from Li's. Over the lengthy period Li described as a "half-open door", he identifies four major transitions culminating in a set of reforms in the 1950s which he felt "provided new blood to the treasure house of human culture". Like Li, however, he emphasizes the importance of a deep awareness of China's own tradition and heritage, its native "genes", as the basis for the effective adaptation of desirable elements in foreign cultures and the "reconstruction of a new integrated culture". He concludes with a call for universities in China and abroad to function as "the bridge between cultures, as they have the necessary human and material infrastructures needed for the communication, transition, preservation and storage of knowledge". (p. 300)

The fifth chapter in Part Five addresses a particular aspect of cultural interaction between China and the West in the 1980s: that of artists and works of art. A highly respected historian and specialist in Chinese art history at the University of Victoria, Canada, Ralph Croizier depicts the dynamic and intense period of rejuvenation of modern art in China after the devastation of the Cultural Revolution decade. A new generation of young Chinese artists emerged, many of whom have made their mark internationally through the opportunities for exchange that opened up, and some have chosen to live in the West. Over the 20th century much of the flow of influence in the world of modern art was from the West to China, yet Croizier suggests that by the late 1980s this was beginning to change. Younger Chinese artists were exerting considerable international influence, in many cases developing new and creative ways of integrating Chinese and Western traditions and sensitivities. Because of the depth of understanding needed for genuine integration, Croizier saw the role of universities and institutes of art as an extremely important bridge for the ongoing dialogue in the arts between China and the West.

The last two chapters in Part Five bring the volume to its conclusion, with some reflections on the Chinese university and its experience of interaction with the West. Wang Yongquan, a distinguished scholar of higher education and former provost of Peking University, has devoted a whole lifetime to this premier institution of higher learning in China, as a lecturer in physics in the early 1950s, then as the young chair of a new department in radio electronics in 1958, subsequently as provost after the end of the Cultural Revolution, and finally as founding director of Peking University's Institute of Higher Education in 1985. In the penultimate chapter Wang outlines the historical development of modern higher education in China, showing how many features resulted from the fact that Chinese leaders and scholars were reacting to a deep sense of threat, with the encroaching influence of the imperialist powers of Europe and Japan, and thus were driven to copying those elements which they felt would strengthen China's capacity for economic, political and military independence.

Wang gives a sensitive portrayal of efforts to build upon some of the progressive elements in the Chinese heritage, through adapting a Western concept of general education in the 1920s, and then shows how this gave way to increasing specialization and emphasis on practical knowledge for national self-strengthening in the 1930s and in the 1950s. Only in the 1980s and 1990s, did it finally become possible for Chinese universities to create an ethos and a curriculum which represented a distillation of their own rich heritage, together with elements they had selectively introduced from international practice, due to China's position of strength and independence in the global community. In this revised version of Wang's chapter, his former doctoral student, Li Manli, now an associate professor at Tsinghua University, has introduced new elements drawn from her research on the concept of general education in Chinese universities in recent years.

The final chapter in Part Five, by one of the co-editors of this volume, is the only new piece to be added. Prepared first as a keynote lecture for an international conference in Europe, and subsequently presented also in Taiwan, Hong Kong and Mainland China, it has been adapted for this volume as a broad set of historical reflections which bring attention to some elements of the richness of China's intellectual traditions, and the institutions which supported their development over many centuries. Their core values are contrasted with those of the European university, which were first introduced to Chinese literati by an Italian Jesuit in the 17th century. The chapter outlines the development of the European tradition, along four distinct national trajectories – German, French, Soviet and American – and the ways in which these four "modern" traditions of the university subsequently affected the emergence of Chinese universities, and their development from the late 19th century up to the present.

The review of the Western university tradition in this chapter offers a background for reflection on the challenges to knowledge presented in Part One of this volume. In particular it may show how deeply rooted are some of the patterns of the Western university, epistemological and institutional, which are now subject to challenge. In addition, the identification of features from China's traditional scholarly heritage, which persisted and reinvented themselves at various points over the century, should add something to the many rich discussions of Eastern patterns of knowledge and institutional organization that appear in various parts of the volume. It allows the volume to end on a hopeful note, with a focus on lessons from the Chinese academy for higher education in the 21st century.

CONCLUSION: IMPLICATIONS FOR COMPARATIVE EDUCATION

We conclude this overview of the 25 chapters in five parts with the hope that this volume will contribute in valuable ways to an ongoing dialogue among civilizations. As noted at the beginning of this introduction, our starting point was a project of educational collaboration between China and Canada which drew us to explore deep issues of knowledge crossing cultures, and of the understanding of Eastern civilizations which have contributed so richly to the historical development of the sciences, social sciences, arts and higher education. The chapters prepared by the remarkable group of scholars who responded to our conference invitation in 1992 demonstrate the potential of a re-balancing of Western and Eastern patterns of knowledge after the end of the Cold War, and the possibilities this has for a genuine flourishing of human civilizations in the global era. Only a few of these scholars are part of the comparative education community, in terms of contributing to its many journals or participating in its conferences, yet we believe that this volume has much to contribute to that community.

Since the end of the Cold War, there have been significant efforts to re-frame comparative education, in light of the dramatic changes in the political and economic categories that had tended to form a matrix among capitalist and socialist, developing and developed countries. Much greater attention has been given to questions of culture and identity,[12] to an understanding of the multi-faceted and multi-dimensional pulls of globalization, and to responsive tendencies of localization, in what some scholars have seen as "a dialectic of the global and the local".[13] There is greater fluidity and flexibility in the concepts used, and contrasting positions of both greater optimism and greater

---

[12] See, for example, Glen Peterson, Ruth Hayhoe and Yongling Lu (eds.), *Education, Culture and Identity in Twentieth Century China* (Ann Arbor: University of Michigan Press, 2001).

[13] R. Arnove, "Introduction: Reframing Comparative Education: The Dialectic of the Global and the Local," in Robert Arnove and Carlos Alberto Torres, *Comparative Education: The Dialectic of the Global and the Local* (Lanham, Boulder, New York, Oxford: Rowman and Littlefield Publishers, 1999), pp. 1-23.

pessimism with regard to core concerns of equity, social and environmental sustainability, peace and justice in a global context.

One approach that has aroused considerable interest is that of postmodernism, an intellectual current arising first in the arts and other social science areas, and breaking into comparative education circles in the early 1990s. It would be foolish, if not impossible, for us to try to summarize its main tenets here, but it has been seen by some as a deconstruction of the foundations of modernity or by others simply as a historical period following upon and responding to that of modernity. Its determined efforts to contextualize and relativize many of the concepts underpinning modernity, which had been taken as universal and beyond rational question, have opened up new spaces of enquiry and privileged diverse sources of value and truth.[14] This aspect of its contribution is undoubtedly of great value for an emerging dialogue among civilizations.

Several of the contributors to this volume draw extensively on the postmodern literature, while others have preferred to communicate within the more widely used and understood discourses of modernity. From their perspective, modernity is not viewed simply as a Western construct, along lines depicted by Max Weber, Talcott Parsons and others. Rather it is seen as a phenomenon to which many civilizations have contributed in different ways and at different times.[15]

One of the purposes of the volume has been to trace some of the distinctive threads of these contributions, and to understand how they might be consciously drawn upon in shaping global patterns of development towards desired future directions for the human family. This might be seen as a process of redeeming modernity from a Judaeo-Christian perspective, of humanizing it from a Confucian perspective, of harmonizing it from a Buddhist perspective, or in yet other ways within other narratives.[16] Ali A. Mazrui, for example, has used the term "the Islamization of modernity" in his contribution to this volume. Of greatest importance is the readiness to listen to the narrative of the other, and to learn the lessons which can be discovered in distinctive threads of human cultural thought and experience.

Comparative education may have something to learn from comparative religion, as it joins actively in a dialogue among civilizations, particularly from the experience of inter-faith dialogue. What is needed is a deep commitment to mutual respect, mutual openness and a readiness to listen to the other, rather than the denigration or deconstruction of one's own faith tradition. Christians who listen intently and sincerely to the narratives of Islam, Buddhism or Confucianism are likely

---

[14] Rolland G. Paulson and Martin Liebman, "Social Cartography: A New Metaphor/Tool for Comparative Studies"; Val D. Rust, "From Modern to Postmodern Ways of Seeing Social and Educational Change", in Rolland G. Paulston (ed.), *Social Cartography: Mapping Ways of Seeing Social and Educational Change* (New York and London: Garland Publishing, 2000), pp. 7-28, 29-51.

[15] Gu Mingyuan, *Education in China and Abroad* (Hong Kong: Comparative Education Research Centre, University of Hong Kong, 2001), p. 110, makes the point that no general theory of modernization can find wide acceptance, until the East Asian experience has been taken into account.

[16] Ruth Hayhoe, "Redeeming Modernity", in *Comparative Education Review*, Vol. 44, No. 4, 2000, pp. 423-439.

to be rewarded with a rich and nuanced appreciation of their own faith, as well as an understanding of the common ground shared with these other faiths on which the future may be built. The same would be true for members of the other faiths. It is that spirit of respectful listening that we believe pervades the interactions presented within and among each of the parts of this volume, and that we hope will draw in members of the comparative education community. We hope these interactions come across as a true dialogue among ready listeners rather than as a struggle among contending interests such as Huntington portrayed in his "clash of civilizations".

Part I

Challenges to Knowledge

1

Knowledge, Politics, and the Future of Higher Education: Critical Observations on a Worldwide Transformation[1]

Hans N. Weiler

The second half of the 20th century has seen a major transformation of the prevailing order of knowledge production. Both the criteria by which we judge the validity and adequacy of knowledge (the philosophical or epistemological construction of knowledge) and the structural arrangements under which knowledge is being produced (the social and institutional construction of knowledge) have been and continue to be profoundly challenged in our time. These challenges originate in different parts of the world and from widely different premises; taken together, however, they represent an extraordinary moment of transition in our conceptions of what does and does not constitute "knowledge". The result is what Rajni Kothari has called "the deepening sense of crisis in the modern knowledge system"[2] – a remarkable mixture of uncertainty and liberation, of a loss of dependable standards and an openness towards new ways of knowing, of a profound doubt about established conventions in the production of knowledge and the exhilarating sense of a new beginning.

This chapter provides, in its first part, a brief account of the nature and scope of this transformation. It will then show that this transformation is a profoundly

---

[1] The origins of this chapter go back to work on the politics of international academic exchange (Hans N. Weiler, "The Political Dilemmas of Foreign Study", in *Comparative Education Review* 28, 2 (May 1984), pp. 168-179) and on the role of the World Bank in supporting educational research in countries of the Third World (Hans N. Weiler, "Technology and Politics in the Production of Knowledge: Some Notes on a New World Bank Initiative to Build Educational Research Capacity in Developing Countries", in *NORRAG News* 10 (July 1991), pp. 19-23). An earlier version was presented at a UNESCO/CRESALC conference on higher education in May of 1991 in Caracas/Venezuela (Hans N. Weiler, "The International Politics of Knowledge Production and the Future of Higher Education", in Gustavo López Ospina (ed.), *New Contexts and Perspectives* (Caracas: UNESCO/CRESALC, 1992), pp. 33-51) and became the basis for my chapter in the predecessor volume of this book (Ruth Hayhoe et al (eds.), *Knowledge Across Cultures: Universities East and West* (Wuhan and Toronto: Hubei Education Press and OISE Press, 1993), pp. 4-29). A presentation at an international congress of the Böll Foundation in Berlin in May of 2001 (Hans N. Weiler, Wissen und Macht in einer Welt der Konflikte: Zur Politik der Wissensproduktion (Berlin: Böll-Stiftung, in press)) provided an opportunity to review and update this work.

[2] Rajni Kothari, "On Humane Governance", in *Alternatives*, Vol. 12, No. 3, 1987, p. 283.

political process, the understanding of which has to rely heavily on recognizing the intimate relationship between knowledge and power. Against this background, I look in a third part at three domains where the changing order of knowledge manifests itself particularly clearly: the discourses of development, of gender, and of democracy. The chapter concludes by arguing that the nature and the results of this transformation have fundamental implications for the future international order of knowledge production, in general, and for the philosophical and structural orientation of higher education, in particular.

THE TRANSFORMATION OF THE EXISTING KNOWLEDGE ORDER

It would go well beyond the scope of this exercise to provide a comprehensive account of the many facets in the transformation of, and the ongoing challenge to, our existing knowledge order. The contributions to this process are legion, and reflect critical voices from many different cultural traditions: Claude Ake, Ali A. Mazrui and Paulin Hountondji from Africa; Syed Alatas, Homi Bhabha and Ashis Nandy from Asia; Brian Fay, Thomas Kuhn, Clifford Geertz, Nico Stehr and Paul Roth from North America; Pablo Gonzalez Casanova and Arturo Escobar from Latin America; and Michel Foucault, Zygmunt Bauman, Jean-François Lyotard, Paul Feyerabend, Steve Fuller, Helga Nowotny and the "Culturalism" project of the Reimers-Stiftung (Lackner and Werner 1999) from Europe – to name but a few, without any claim to being exhaustive.[3]

For purposes of this chapter, I will focus on just a few aspects of this transformation:

(a)   the disintegration of the epistemological tradition of a "unified science" and its consequences,

(b)   the attempts at a new synthesis of cognitive, normative, and aesthetic knowledge, and

(c)   the emergence of new ways of knowing.

In discussing these changes, I will look particularly at forms of knowledge that deal with social and human reality. While the transformation of the existing knowledge order encompasses *all* forms of knowledge, it has particularly serious and powerful implications for what we know about phenomena of *social* life, and for how we know it.

---

[3] The contributions of these and other authors are cited in the bibliography at the end of the volume.

Challenging the Tradition of a "Unified Science"

The Loss of Consensus

A key element in the erosion of the philosophical consensus on knowledge is the fundamental questioning of the epistemological tradition of a unified science, i.e., of a conception of knowledge that brought the same criteria and strategies to bear on any and all kinds of knowledge, regardless of its object. This postulate of homogeneity and consensus reflected the paramount position of the natural sciences in the hierarchy of knowledge, and their unquestioned claim to having their standards of validation accepted throughout the world of knowledge. This particular notion of scientific rationality has a special affinity to the positivist tradition in the social and behavioural sciences, which was historically shaped by an attempt to emulate the epistemology of the natural sciences; as Talcott Parsons put it so categorically in his (somewhat one-sided) discussion of Max Weber's work: "There is not 'natural' or 'cultural' science; there is only science or non-science and all empirical knowledge is scientific in so far as it is valid".[4]

In the wake of such major developments as the positivism debate in German sociology,[5] the emergence of phenomenological and hermeneutic forms of social inquiry,[6] the growing influence of non-Western[7] and feminist[8] epistemological thought, or the commotions of post-structuralist and post-modernist debates,[9] the supremacy of the paradigm of the natural sciences and its applicability to social inquiry has been thoroughly undermined. This process has led to a conception of knowledge that is at once more differentiated and more contingent, and in which the traditional tenets of scientific propriety have given way to more specific and less monolithic standards for the validation of knowledge.

Some of the more notable casualties in this transition have been the once

---

[4] Talcott Parsons, "Value-Freedom and Objectivity", in Fred R. Dallmayr and Thomas A. McCarthy, *Understanding and Social Inquiry* (Notre Dame: University of Notre Dame Press, 1977), p. 61.

[5] Theodor W. Adorno et al, *The Positivist Dispute in German Sociology* (London: Heinemann, 1976).

[6] Hans-Georg Gadamer, *Reason in the Age of Science* (Cambridge, MA: MIT Press, 1981); Jürgen Habermas, *Knowledge and Human Interests* (London: Heineman, 1978); John B. Thompson, *Critical Hermeneutics: A Study in the Thought of Paul Ricoeur and Jürgen Habermas* (Cambridge: Cambridge University Press, 1981).

[7] Kothari, "On Humane Governance," 1987; Ashis Nandy, "From Outside the Imperium: Gandhi's Cultural Critique of the West", in *Alternatives*, Vol. 7, 1981, pp. 171-194; Ashis Nandy, "Shamans, Savages and the Wilderness: On the Audibility of Dissent and the Future of Civilizations", in *Alternatives*, Vol. 14, No. 3, July, 1989, pp. 263-277.

[8] Mary Field Belenky et al, *Women's Ways of Knowing: The Development of Self, Voice, and Mind* (New York: Basic Books, 1986); Sondra Farganis, *Social Reconstruction of the Feminine Character* (Totowa, NJ: Rowman and Littlefield, 1986); Sandra Harding, *The Science Question in Feminism* (Ithaca: Cornell University Press, 1986).

[9] Gilles Deleuze and Félix Guattari, *A Thousand Plateaus: Capitalism and Schizophrenia* (Minneapolis: University of Minnesota Press, 1987); Michel Foucault, *The Order of Things: An Archeology of the Human Sciences* (New York: Pantheon, 1971); Michel Foucault, *The Archeology of Knowledge* (New York: Pantheon, 1972); Jean-François Lyotard, *The Postmodern Condition: A Report on Knowledge* (Minneapolis: University of Minnesota Press, 1984).

unquestioned tenure of such notions as *objectivity* (or the independence of the observed "subject" from the observer), *certainty* (or the elimination of doubt and equivocation), *prediction* (or the dependability of "if-then" statements), and *quantification* (or the special legitimacy of numerical representations of reality). While there is no easy replacement for any of these categories, challenging their universal reign over the world of knowledge has had major repercussions for social and educational inquiry. Two particularly consequential elements in this transformation have been the shifting debate on the relative "worth" of the general and the specific, or of nomothetic and idiographic knowledge, and the controversy over the difference between explanation and understanding.

Nomothetic vs. Idiographic Knowledge

It is particularly instructive to look for a moment at the debate about the relative importance of generality and singularity in the creation of knowledge, and about the priority to be given to the formulation and progressive validation of general "laws" or law-like statements about social reality. This debate appears under many labels: the "special" vs. the "general"; "theory" vs. "everyday life"; "nomothetic" vs. "idiographic"; "abstraction" vs. "contextualization"; "continuity" vs. "discontinuity"; "breadth" vs. "depth"; etc.[10] More concretely, the argument is about what is more "important" in generating knowledge about a given field of social activity:

–   To produce generalized statements about determinants of learning outcomes across a large number of cases and contexts, or to capture the full texture of how individual learning takes place in a particular setting?

–   To identify national or world-wide patterns in the financial returns to investments in education, or to reconstruct and understand the economic calculus that drives individual or group decisions about how much to invest in schooling and how?

–   To abstract from a wide variety of institutional settings to arrive at a general theory of organizational behaviour, or to understand how a specific organization's tasks interact with its environment and the social identity of its members to produce a particular "institutional culture"?

–   To develop and refine models of population growth and movement on a national or international scale, or to understand the cultural, social, and economic factors that affect people's decisions in matters of reproduction, health, resource allocation, and migration?

---

[10] Karl-Otto Apel, *Understanding and Explanation: A Transcendental-Pragmatic Perspective* (Cambridge, MA: The MIT Press, 1984); Peter Winch, *The Idea of a Social Science and its Relation to Philosophy* (London: Routledge and Kegan Paul, 1958); Traugott Schöfthaler and Dietrich Goldschmidt (eds.), *Soziale Struktur und Vernunft: Jean Piaget's Modell entwickelten Denkens in der Diskussion kulturvergleichender Forschung* (Frankfurt: Suhrkamp, 1985).

One could and should, of course, emphasize the complementarity of the different bodies of knowledge that each of these options would help create. However, the shift in emphasis between these options is unmistakable, and accounts for a significant change in the pattern of research strategies: in-depth case studies, historical analyses, ethnographic studies, biographical analyses, process, content, and critical incident analyses, and interpretive studies of both literary and social evidence are increasingly competing with the time-honoured approaches of hypothesis-testing on the basis of sampling strategies that permit generalization to a theoretically defined universe with identifiable sampling errors.

Explanation and Understanding

The debate over the relationship between explanation and understanding, the logic of which is closely related to the controversy just discussed, is another reflection of the progressive erosion of the scientific consensus. It recognizes how problematic it is to think of "explanations of behaviour which allow predictions concerning future behaviour",[11] and re-evaluates the relative significance of "understanding" the full context and dynamics of a given situation as compared to the "explanation" of events in the context of universal, law-like generalizations. Our most elaborate predictive models of voting, consumption behaviour, or warfare have provided little protection against surprises, serendipity, unexpected outcomes, and, indeed, banality. It is likely that this state of affairs is due not to faulty data, but to some more basic limitations in our ability to plot the future behaviour of entities that are by nature even more unpredictable than atoms, molecules and cells: "the central concepts which belong to our understanding of social life are incompatible with concepts central to the activity of scientific prediction. When we speak of the possibility of scientific prediction of social developments . . ., we literally do not understand what we are saying".[12] It is against the background of this kind of realization that the philosophical controversy about "Erklären und Verstehen", explanation and understanding, in which the work of Karl-Otto Apel has played such a critical role, becomes an important issue in re-thinking our ways of knowing.[13]

Cognitive, Normative, and Aesthetic Knowledge: Towards a New Synthesis

It was an integral part of scientific rationality that it defined knowledge primarily in cognitive terms, leaving the realm of both the normative and the aesthetic to ethical, literary, artistic, and other – strictly "non-scientific" – pursuits. The postulate of a

---

[11] Paul A. Roth, *Meaning and Method in the Social Sciences: A Case for Methodological Pluralism* (Ithaca NY: Cornell University Press, 1987), p. 3.

[12] Winch, *The Idea of a Social* Science, 1958, p. 94.

[13] Apel, *Understanding and Explanation*, 1984. Cf. Fred R. Dallmayr and Thomas A. McCarthy, *Understanding and Social Inquiry* (Notre Dame: University of Notre Dame Press, 1977).

"value-free" science and social science[14] is the logical correlate to such a conception.

It is not surprising that challenges to this separation of different realms of knowledge loom large in the struggle for a new conception of knowledge. Habermas deplores a kind of rationality that, by limiting itself to a purely "cognitivist-in-strumental" notion, has become incapable of interacting with the realms of the "moral-practical" and the "aesthetic-expressive"[15] – an observation echoed in the work of Putnam[16], Lepenies[17] and Lenk[18], and in Roth's diagnostic of the *Rationalitätsstreit* in the philosophy of the social sciences.[19] Ashis Nandy speaks along similar lines of the "mechanomorphic" bias in Western rationality, which he sees as closely related to "the masculinity principle in the Judeo-Christian cosmology".[20]

The answer to these kinds of criticism is a notion of knowledge that seeks to overcome the separation into cognitive, normative, and aesthetic domains. As part of this effort, the realization that "reality" is socially constructed[21] has led to a much more explicit recognition that the cultural location and, hence, the normative disposition, of the "observer" is a constitutive element in the process of knowledge creation, and that the results of that process unmistakably reflect these contingencies.[22] Here again, the contributions of both non-Western and feminist thought to a better understanding of the cultural determinants of knowledge production have been pivotal.[23]

Beyond Science: New Ways of Knowing

The tradition of scientific rationality had constructed specific criteria for determining what did and did not constitute legitimate knowledge, and had devised an elaborate system of institutional mechanisms for monitoring and enforcing adherence to those criteria in universities, academies, publications, and research funding. As the underlying claim to the sole authority of these criteria has begun to erode, other and formerly less legitimate forms of knowledge creation have moved into the mainstream

---

[14] "that a science need not be bound to the values of any particular historical culture", Parsons, "Value Freedom and Objectivity", 1977, p. 60.

[15] Jürgen Habermas, *Die neue Unübersichtlichkeit* (Frankfurt: Suhrkamp, 1985), pp. 134-137.

[16] Hilary Putnam, *The Many Faces of Realism: The Paul Carus Lectures* (La Salle, IL: Open Court, 1987), pp. 53-56.

[17] Wolf Lepenies, *Between Literature and Science: The Rise of Sociology* (Cambridge: Cambridge University Press, 1988).

[18] Hans Lenk (ed.), Zur Kritik der wissenschaftlichen Rationalität (Freiburg: Alber, 1986), pp. 349-463.

[19] Roth, *Meaning and Method*, 1987.

[20] Ashis Nandy, "The Traditions of Technology", in *Alternatives*, Vol. 4, No. 3, 1978-79, p. 373.

[21] Peter L. Berger and Thomas Luckmann, *The Social Construction of Reality: A Treatise in the Sociology of Knowledge* (Garden City, NJ: Anchor Books, 1967).

[22] Stephen Greenblatt, *Marvelous Possessions: The Wonder of the New World* (Oxford: Clarendon Press, 1991).

[23] Syed Hussein Alatas, "The Captive Mind and Creative Development", in *International Social Science Journal*, Vol. 26, No. 4, 1976, pp. 691-700; Pablo Gonzalez Casanova, *The Fallacy of Social Science Research: A Critical Examination and New Qualitative Model* (New York: Pergamon, 1981); Harding, *The Science Question in Feminism*, 1986.

of inquiry and into active competition with more established forms.

One result of this process is the recognition of "ordinary" or "folk" knowledge (as distinct from "scientific" or "official" knowledge) as an important source of insight into the nature of social reality.[24] Foucault speaks of "subjugated knowledges ... a whole set of knowledges that have been disqualified as inadequate to their task or insufficiently elaborated: naive knowledges, located low down on the hierarchy, beneath the required level of cognition or scientificity ... a popular knowledge (*le savoir des gens*)".[25] Such knowledge is seen not only as a useful complement to the knowledge generated by scientists, but sometimes as enjoying even greater legitimacy. In an article entitled "African Famine: Whose Knowledge Matters?" Gran makes a case for recognizing the African farmers' grassroots knowledge of what does and does not work in African agricultural development as a more legitimate source of knowledge than the top-down forms of knowledge production sponsored by national governments and international agencies.[26] And Ashis Nandy pleads in ever new variations for "the recovery of indigenous knowledge", for saving the kind of knowledge that, through the process of intellectual colonization, "has been cornered, marginalized, or even defeated".[27]

Following Habermas' appeal to reconstruct a more holistic notion of knowledge that includes both the normative and the aesthetic domain of knowing, the formerly rigid boundaries between scientific and non-scientific knowledge are increasingly questioned. We have learned to derive powerful insights into the nature of social reality from the literary testimony of writers such as Gabriel García Marquéz, Günter Grass, or Chinua Achebe, from painters and sculptors such as Pablo Picasso, Diego Rivera, Anselm Kiefer, or Joseph Beuys, or from film-makers like Rainer-Werner Fassbinder, Akira Kurosawa, Ousmane Sembene, or Andrzej Wajda.

Lepenies makes a particularly valuable contribution to our understanding of the "new" ambivalence in social inquiry by pointing out that it is not really new at all, at least when seen against the development of sociology as a discipline in Europe through the 19th and 20th centuries. He finds that, throughout its history, sociology "has oscillated between a scientific orientation which has led it to ape the natural sciences and a hermeneutic attitude which has shifted the discipline towards the realm of literature",[28] producing "sociology's precarious situation as a kind of 'third culture' between the natural sciences on the one hand and literature and the humanities on the other".[29] Approaching this same relationship between social and literary inquiry from

---

[24] Margaret Sutton, "Social Sciences and Ordinary Understanding: Coming to Terms with Tourism in Bali", [Unpublished Ph.D. dissertation], (Stanford, CA: Stanford University, 1991).

[25] Michel Foucault, *Power/Knowledge: Selected Interviews and Other Writings*, 1972-1977 (New York: Pantheon, 1980), p. 82.

[26] Guy Gran, "Beyond African Famines: Whose Knowledge Matters? ", in *Alternatives*, Vol. 11, No. 2, 1986, pp. 275-296.

[27] Ashis Nandy, "Recovery of Indigenous Knowledge and Dissenting Futures of the University", in Sohail Inayatullah and Jennifer Gidley (eds.), *The University in Transformation: Global Perspectives on the Futures of the University* (Westport, CT: Bergin & Garvey, 2000), pp. 115-123.

[28] Lepenies, *Between Literature and* Science, 1988, p. 1.

[29] *Ibid*, p. 7.

the other direction, as it were, Edward Said emphasizes the need to recognize the intimate linkage between literary criticism and the analysis of power – or between "the world, the text, and the critic".[30] This argument already evokes the theme of the "politics of interpretation" which is reflected in a variety of interesting ways in Said's newest book, *Reflections on Exile*.[31]

These are but a few of the developments that have made the transformation of our existing order of knowledge such a momentous phenomenon. Other and similarly consequential developments have to do with

–   the blurring of the time-honoured distinction between "observer" and "subject" in the pursuit of social inquiry, which has led to various forms of "action" or participatory research,[32]
–   a re-examination of our conventional assumptions about the linkage between knowledge production and technological change,[33]
–   the growing recognition of the role of language in the process and the politics of knowledge production.[34]

THE CHANGING POLITICS OF KNOWLEDGE

While all of these developments have profoundly affected our ways of thinking about knowledge and its production, perhaps the most important element in the transformation of our existing knowledge order has been the growing realization of the intimate linkage between knowledge and power – a realization that owes much to the seminal work of Michel Foucault[35] and his "highly wrought presentation of the order, stability, authority, and regulatory power of knowledge".[36] Among the many facets of

---

[30] Edward W. Said, *The World, the Text, and the Critic* (Cambridge: Harvard University Press, 1983).

[31] Edward W. Said, *Reflections on Exile and Other Essays* (Cambridge: Harvard University Press, 2000), pp. 118ff.

[32] Fals Borda, "The Challenge of Action Research", in *Development*, 1981, No. 1, pp. 55-61; Gran, 1986; Nelly P. Stromquist, *Action Research: A New Sociological Approach* (Ottawa: IDRC, 1982).

[33] Manuel Castells, "High Technology, World Development, and the Structural Transformation: The Trends and the Debate", in *Alternatives*, Vol. 11, 1986, pp. 297-343; Jacques Ellul, *The Technological Society* (New York: Knopf, 1967); Amilcar O. Herrera, "The Generation of Technologies in Rural Areas", in *World Development*, Vol. 9, (1981), pp. 21-35; Herbert Marcuse, *One-Dimensional Man: Studies in the Ideology of Advanced Industrial Society* (Boston: Beacon, 1964); Nandy, "The Traditions of Technology", 1978-79.

[34] Roland Barthes, *Writing Degree Zero* (Boston: Beacon 1970); Murray Edelman, *Political Language: Words That Succeed and Policies That Fail* (New York: Academic Press, 1977); Said, *The World, The Text and the Critic*, 1983.

[35] Foucault, *Power/Knowledge*, 1980; see also Arturo Escobar, "Discourse and Power in Development: Michel Foucault and the Relevance of his Work to the Third World", in *Alternatives*, Vol. 10, Winter 1984-85, pp. 377-400; Marc DuBois, "The Governance of the Third World: A Foucauldian Perspective on Power Relations in Development", in *Alternatives*, Vol. 16, No. 1, Winter 1991, pp. 1-30.

[36] Said, *Reflections on Exile*, 2000, p. 239.

this linkage between knowledge and power, I would like to emphasize (a) the prominence of *hierarchy* as a constituent characteristic in the existing knowledge order, (b) the relationship of *reciprocal legitimation* between knowledge and power, (c) the *transnational* nature of the contemporary knowledge order, and (d) a growing *commercialization* as a key ingredient in the political economy of knowledge production in the modern world.

Hierarchies in the Production of Knowledge

Hierarchies are the quintessential manifestation of power. They signify higher and lower ranks in a given order, domination and subordination, greater and lesser value, prestige, and influence. Wherever and in whatever form they occur, they represent structures of authority and power, and are thus a fundamentally political phenomenon. In the world of knowledge, hierarchies are a pervasive structural characteristic, in a number of different ways:

(a)   The different *domains of knowledge* are traditionally endowed with unequal status, representing a hierarchy in which the natural sciences reign as the epitome of scientific respectability, while other, "softer" or "less exact" forms of knowledge pursuits are ranked correspondingly lower.

(b)   In the realm of the *institutional* arrangements for the production of knowledge, some institutions, for a variety of reasons, enjoy greater status and prestige than others, as part of a hierarchy in which the institutional order of knowledge production is dominated by Max-Planck Institutes, Grandes Ecoles, selective private universities, exclusive think tanks, and expensive consulting empires like Rand or SRI International; this institutional hierarchy constitutes a form of politics of knowledge primarily at the national level, but has its international variant as well, as we shall show below.

(c)   Lastly, knowledge-related hierarchies operate as well in the *internal* politics of institutions – as between professor and student, senior and junior faculty, administrators and faculty, directors and staff.

Many of these hierarchical relationships, in all three of these categories, are based on widely or, at least, traditionally shared views of what constitutes appropriate grounds for status and authority in the world of knowledge. As these criteria are being challenged as a result of the transformations discussed earlier, the epistemological and institutional hierarchies that are based on them become increasingly contested. The resulting conflict is an important part of the new politics of knowledge.

Knowledge and Power: Reciprocal Legitimation

Among the many ways of looking at the relationship between knowledge and power, one that is particularly revealing focuses on how each contributes to the legitimacy of the other in what one might describe as a "symbiotic" relationship. In this relationship, power legitimates both knowledge and the existing modes of knowledge production while, on the other hand, knowledge is used to legitimate existing arrangements for the exercise of power. The former part of this mutual relationship – the role of political authority in legitimating knowledge – is amply illustrated by the role of the state in sanctioning what does and does not constitute proper knowledge. This is achieved through such devices as examination requirements in education, specifying entrance qualifications for the public service or professional certification, or the material and political support of certain kinds of research over others. Furthermore, one can argue that certain prominent characteristics of the modern state – notably its bureaucratic nature, its close affinity to, or even dependence on, technological developments, and its inherently competitive culture – determine the kinds of knowledge that the state is capable of, and interested in, legitimating.[37]

On the other side of this mutual relationship, knowledge has to be seen as a critical source of legitimacy for the modern state and its often precarious authority. There has always been a strong theoretical argument for the legitimating potential of knowledge, along the lines of Berger and Luckmann's notion of "symbolic universes" as, in their words, "sheltering canopies over the institutional order".[38] More specifically and concretely, however, the state tends to draw increasingly on the respectability and prestige of knowledge – especially scientific knowledge – in order to enhance its own legitimacy; expert commissions, research to prepare and accompany policy innovations, the systematic evaluation of social programs – these and other measures testify to the salience of knowledge in the modern state's quest for added legitimacy – and, by the same token, to the utility of knowledge as an instrument of both conflict management and social control.[39] Ashis Nandy goes one step further when he argues: "As more and more areas of life are 'scientized' and taken out of the reach of participatory politics to be handed over to experts, the universities as the final

---

[37] Hans N. Weiler, "Die Produktion von Wissen und die Legitimation der Macht: Zur politischen Ökonomie des internationalen Forschungssystems", in Walter Sülberg (ed.), *Demokratisierung und Partizipation im Entwicklungsprozess* (Frankfurt: IKO, 1988), pp. 17-38; Hans N. Weiler, "The International Politics of Knowledge Production and the Future of Higher Education", in Gustavo López Ospina (ed.), *New Contexts and Perspectives* (Caracas: UNESCO/CRESALC, 1992), pp. 33-51; Hans N. Weiler, "Wissen und Herrschaft in einer Welt der Konflikte: Die politische Ökonomie der internationalen Wissensproduktion und die Rolle der UNESCO", in Peter Haungs et al (eds.), *CIVITAS – Widmungen für Bernhard Vogel zum 60. Geburtstag* (Paderborn: Schöningh, 1992), pp. 649-659.

[38] Berger and Luckmann, *The Social Construction of Reality*, 1967, p. 102.

[39] Hans N. Weiler, "Legalization, Expertise, and Participation: Strategies of Compensatory Legitimation in Educational Policy", in *Comparative Education Review*, Vol. 27, No. 2, June 1983, pp. 259-277; Alvin W. Gouldner, *The Coming Crisis of Western Sociology* (New York: Basic Books, 1970), p. 50; Marcuse, *One-Dimensional Man*, 1964, pp. 158-159.

depository of expertise have become a major global political actor of our times. In addition to their other tasks, they legitimize the 'expertization' of public affairs and the reign of the professionals".[40]

The Transnational Knowledge System

The frame of reference for the production and the politics of knowledge is not merely institutional or national, but has an international dimension as well. Knowledge flows, through a variety of channels, around the world, and the media of modern communication assure the almost instant dissemination of new knowledge. This seeming openness of the international knowledge system, however, tends to obscure the fact that both the production and the consumption of knowledge are distributed quite unevenly in today's world. Indeed, one of the most significant characteristics of the international system of knowledge production is a division of labour in which key tasks, such as the setting of theoretical agendas and methodological standards, have long been the prerogative of a limited number of societies and institutions on which the remainder of the international system depends. This highly uneven distribution of roles in the production of knowledge, which parallels inequalities in economic influence and political power, has become the focus of a great deal of critical analysis in recent decades.[41] It has also led to challenges to the paradigmatic hegemony of Western social sciences, and to the assertion of "a new, plural, political ecology of knowledge".[42] Let me cast this analysis in terms of the argument about the reciprocal legitimation of power and knowledge. In many parts of today's world, the state operates to legitimate an essentially transnational system of knowledge production, while the system of research and knowledge production in turn serves to legitimate the status differential between centre and periphery and, thus, the transnational power structure of the international system itself.

What is really at issue here, of course, is not "just" the world of knowledge production and research, but a much more intricate web of relationships in which the production of knowledge is one of several interlocking elements for the consolidation and legitimation of the existing institutional order at the international level. The transnational system of knowledge production is inextricably linked to a transnational system of power, in which publishing interests, research funding, consulting firms, testing services, professional associations and development assistance agencies all

---

[40] Nandy, "Recovery of Indigenous Knowledge", 2000, p.116.
[41] John Brenkman, *Culture and Domination* (Ithaca NY: Cornell University Press, 1987); Carmen Garcia Guadilla, *Produccion y Transferencia de Paradigmas Teoricos en la Investigacion Socio-Educativa* (Caracas: Tropykos, 1987); see also her recent paper "Globalization, Regional Integration, and Higher Education in Latin America" (Keynote Paper at the conference on "Globalization and Higher Education. Views from the South", Cape Town, South Africa, March 27-29, 2001); Paulin J. Hountondji, *African Philosophy: Myth and Reality* (Bloomington: Indiana University Press, 1983); Kothari, *On Humane Governance*, 1987; A. Mattelart, *Transnationals and the Third World: The Struggle for Culture* (South Hadley, MA: Bergin and Garvey, 1983).
[42] Nandy, "Shamans, Savages and the Wilderness", 1989, p. 267.

form part of a powerful – if less than perfectly coordinated – source of domination. The fact that this coalition of knowledge and power is being increasingly challenged by researchers in Africa, Asia, and Latin America (with some support from agencies like the International Development Research Centre [IDRC] in Canada, the Swedish Agency for Research Cooperation with Developing Countries [SAREC], and the United Nations University [UNU]) has become one of the most significant aspects of the new international politics of knowledge.

Commercializing the Production of Knowledge

A final aspect of the contemporary political economy of knowledge production has to do with the growing commercialization of knowledge in the modern world. To be sure, certain kinds of knowledge have always had their economic utility, but it is an important part of modernity that the creation of knowledge has come to be regarded and treated so pervasively in economic and commercial terms. This has something to do with the increasing cost of knowledge production and, hence, the dependence of knowledge producers on external financial sponsorship; such sponsorship very often does have an economic and political agenda of its own under which the support and the production of new knowledge is being subsumed. More importantly, however, the very nature of modern economic activity has become so massively dependent on up-to-date knowledge of constantly increasing scope and complexity that the linkage between knowledge and both productivity and profitability has become inescapable. This is true not only for the "hard" sciences and their utility for industrial and other forms of engineering, but also for the knowledge of social and psychological processes and its significance for dealing with labour problems, enhancing productivity, and other forms of "social engineering".

As a result, a whole new set of power relationships has emerged around the world of knowledge. These relationships are dictated by both the interests and the resources of the commercial user of knowledge, and take a variety of forms – from outright research contracts between industry and universities to more subtle influences on research programs by philanthropic foundations, and from industry-sponsored research institutions inside universities (such as the Centre for Integrated Systems [CIS] at Stanford University) to the setting up of industry-owned research centres in more or less direct competition with other producers of knowledge in the academic realm. Whatever the specific institutional arrangements, however, the overall growth in the commercialization of knowledge production has added a further layer of politically constituted interests to the contemporary system of knowledge production: the politics of knowledge become less and less separable from the politics of production and profit, arguably the most powerful political dynamics in today's world.

NEW DISCOURSES: DEVELOPMENT, GENDER, AND DEMOCRACY

The impact of the transformation in the existing order of knowledge is being felt in many and varied domains of human knowledge – even in the hallowed quarters of the natural sciences.[43] It affects most prominently, however, that part of our knowledge that deals with human and social reality. Among the many manifestations of change, three domains of discourse reflect particularly well the impact of "new ways of knowing"; these three discourses have to do with the notion of development, the role of gender, and the meaning of democracy. A brief review of some of the major agendas in each of these three domains of knowledge will serve to make the point.

Development

It is not a coincidence that, in the extraordinarily rich debate about new conceptions of "development" that has emerged over the last two decades, the changing knowledge base of our thinking about development plays a particularly important role. Gran sees the development disaster in Africa primarily as a reflection of an externally imposed politics of knowledge that neglected the legitimacy of local, grassroots knowledge.[44] A new discourse on development looms large among the "counterdiscourses" that Escobar sees emerging in many countries of the Third World,[45] and it is instructive to note that this new discourse on development has moved much closer to the discourse on peace.[46] Jinadu emphasizes the linkage between the prevailing conception of development and the state of the social sciences in Africa; he speaks of "a view of development as incremental change in technological skills and efficiency and the consequent instrumentalist view of the social sciences that it encourages, [which] has tended to encourage the neglect of critical normative issues in development and in development theories".[47] In this regard, the point that Elise Boulding makes about the close relationship between the notion of development as economic growth and the scientific paradigm is noteworthy.[48]

Nandy carries this debate perhaps farthest in seeing "a subtle subversion of the

---

[43] Nancy Cartwright, *How the Laws of Physics Lie* (Oxford: Clarendon Press, 1983); James Gleick, *Chaos: Making a New Science* (New York: Viking, 1987).

[44] Gran, "Beyond African Famines", 1986.

[45] Escobar, "Discourse and Power in Development",1984-85.

[46] Björn Hettne, "Transcending the European Model of Peace and Development", in *Alternatives*, Vol. 10, No. 4, 1985, pp. 453-476; Hans Bosse, *Verwaltete Unterentwicklung: Funktionen und Verwertung der Bildungsforschung in der staatlichen Entwicklungspolitik* (Frankfurt: Suhrkamp, 1978), p.37ff.

[47] L. Adele Jinadu, *The social sciences and development in Africa: Ethiopia, Mozambique, Tanzania and Zimbabwe* (Stockholm: SAREC, 1985, SAREC Report R1: 1985), p. 19. See also Bosse, *Verwaltete Unterentwicklung*, 1978, p. 191; 198; R. Chambers, *Rural Development: Putting the Last First* (New York: Longman, 1983).

[48] Elise Boulding, "Cultural Perspectives on Development: The Relevance of Sociology and Anthropology", in *Alternatives*, Vol. 14, No. 1, January 1989, p. 107.

modern world's fondest – I almost said cleverest – charity, development".[49] He is suspicious even of the many alternative conceptions of development that have gained attention in recent years – "sustainable development", "ecodevelopment", "indigenous development", claiming that these, as well, are "products of the same worldview which has produced the mainstream concept of science, liberation, and development", and sees the real challenge in the construction of both "a post-modern science" and "a post-development world".[50]

The common denominator in all of this work, and in a great deal more like it,[51] is to see the discourse and debate about the notion of development very much in the context of a changing politics of knowledge. In Gran's words, "part of, indeed the heart of both generating and applying authentically developmental knowledge is the reduction of power differentials ... Power differentials both within a locale and between levels ... fundamentally determine how knowledge is perceived, whose knowledge matters, and the ensuing effectiveness of policies on which it is based".[52]

Gender

As in the case of the discourse on development, the discourse about gender is much more than an exercise in re-defining a concept; the content of the discourse – the importance of gender in the analysis of human and social affairs – is closely linked both with a fundamental epistemological claim – that women have a capacity for "new ways of knowing"[53] – and with the political agenda of the contemporary feminist movement.

Important contributions are being made by feminist scholars to a much better understanding of the role of gender in the construction of social and educational reality – including, incidentally, the discourse about development[54] and the many ways in which elements of patriarchy have pervaded our conception of such issues as performance, achievement, success, competition, and, indeed, knowledge.[55] Beyond that, however, lies an agenda that combines the fundamental re-thinking of gender roles in knowledge production – as in the five "research programs" that Sandra

---

[49] Nandy, "Shamans, Savages and the Wilderness", 1989, p. 269.

[50] *Ibid.*, p. 270.

[51] For example, the very useful collection of contributions to this debate in Majid Rahnema (ed., with Victoria Bawtree), *The Post-Development Reader* (London: ZED Books, 1997); Magnus Blomstrom and Björn Hettne (eds.), *Development Theory in Transition: The Dependency Debate and Beyond* (London: Zed Books, 1984); Hettne, "Transcending the European Model of Peace and Development", 1985; D.L. Sheth, "Alternative Development as Political Practice", in *Alternatives*, Vol. 12, 1987, pp. 155-171.

[52] Gran, "Beyond African Famines", 1986, p. 287.

[53] Belenky et al, *Women's Ways of Knowing*, 1986; Farganis, *Social Reconstruction of the Feminine Character*, 1986.

[54] Sue Ellen Charlton, *Women in Third World Development* (Boulder: Westview, 1984); Chandra Mohanty, "Under Western Eyes: Feminist Scholarship and Colonial Discourses", in *Boundary Two*, Vol. 12, No. 1, Spring/Fall 1984, pp. 333-357; Kathleen Staudt, *Women, Foreign Assistance, and Advocacy Administration* (New York: Praeger, 1985).

[55] Carole Pateman, *The Sexual Contract* (Stanford: Stanford University Press, 1988).

Harding describes[56] – with the political struggle for the presence and power of women in the institutions of knowledge production.[57]

Democracy

While the question of how those who govern can secure the consent and support of the governed – the question of how best to deal with the mandate of democracy – has been a perennial element in the history of political thought, it has in recent years re-emerged as the subject of a particularly lively and instructive debate. This is so for a number of reasons, including a renewed theoretical interest in the conception of democracy,[58] the growing concern over the viability and legitimacy of traditional Western systems of representative democracy,[59] and the striking pattern of transition from authoritarian to democratic forms of governance in many contemporary societies, most notably in Latin America, Eastern and Central Europe, and Africa.[60]

The discourse on democracy has the same kind of dual mode that we have already noted in the case of development and gender. On the one hand, it addresses some of the basic definitional questions about the nature of democracy in systems of political governance, notably the question of the relative importance of representative and participatory elements.[61] At the same time, however, it is also, once again, a discourse over the politics of knowledge and, more specifically, over the democratization of the process of knowledge production. This latter aspect of the discourse is reflected in a heightened recognition of the rights of the research "subject", in the kind of participatory research that Gran advocates for Africa,[62] or in Nandy's image of the "shaman" as "the ultimate symbol of non-cooptable dissent".[63]

Of particular significance is in this regard the debate over the structures of governance in the realm of knowledge production – "the governance of science"[64] – which deals, among other things, with the remarkable contradiction that scholarship has, over time, contributed significantly to the democratization of societies but has

---

[56] Harding, *The Science Question in Feminism*, 1986, pp. 20-24.

[57] Jill K. Conway et al (eds.), *Learning About Women: Gender, Politics, and Power* (Ann Arbor: University of Michigan Press, 1987).

[58] Carole Pateman, *Participation and Democratic Theory* (Cambridge: Cambridge University Press, 1970).

[59] Michel J. Crozier et al, *The Crisis of Democracy: Report on the Governability of Democracies to the Trilateral Commission* (New York: New York University Press, 1975); Jürgen Habermas, *Legitimation Crisis* (Boston: Beacon, 1975).

[60] Guillermo O'Donnell, Philippe C. Schmitter, and Laurence Whitehead (eds.), *Transitions from Authoritarian Rule: Prospects for Democracy* (Baltimore: Johns Hopkins Press, 1986).

[61] Pateman, *Participation and Democratic Theory*, 1970; Benjamin Barber, *Strong Democracy: Participatory Politics for a New Age* (Berkeley: University of California Press, 1984).

[62] Gran, "Beyond African Famines", 1986.

[63] Nandy, "Shamans, Savages and the Wilderness", 1989, p. 266.

[64] Steve Fuller, *The Governance of Science: Ideology and the Future of the Open Society* (Buckingham: Open University Press, 2000).

steadfastly refused to subject itself to democratic norms of procedure.[65]

THE NEW POLITICS OF KNOWLEDGE AND THE FUTURE OF HIGHER EDUCATION

The process of transformation that has been described thus far, and its profoundly political quality, have major implications for the organizational and institutional arrangements under which knowledge is produced and transmitted in today's world; it has particularly significant ramifications for the philosophical and structural orientation of higher education. These ramifications range from re-thinking the role of traditional disciplines in the organization of higher education to the criteria for the assessment of scholarship, and from issues of local and regional autonomy in the setting of research agendas to possible changes in the nature of professionalism. In order to illustrate the nature and scope of these changes, I will conclude this chapter by taking a brief look at some of the key issues that institutions of higher education face as a result.

Acknowledging and Analyzing the Politics of Knowledge

There is – in some parts of the world more than in others – a curious tendency on the part of academics and academic institutions to be oblivious to the complex web of political dynamics which surrounds and constrains the production of knowledge in a given field. The notion that higher education has its place outside "the hot and cold wind of politics" was wrong and naive when the Ashby Commission coined the phrase in its report on higher education in Nigeria in the early 1960s,[66] and it has not become any more correct since then. And yet it is striking how little intellectual energy is expended on better understanding the politics of knowledge in the various disciplines and fields of study that make up modern higher education; the important work of Nowottny[67] and Stehr[68] or the kinds of penetrating analyses that people like Lepenies have performed for sociology,[69] or Ricci for political science,[70] remain the exception. This is all the more remarkable in view of the fact that, as an earlier part of this chapter

---

[65] *Ibid.*, p. 135.

[66] *Investment in Education: The Report of the Commission on Post-School Certificate and Higher Education in Nigeria* (Lagos: Federal Ministry of Education, 1960), p. 31.

[67] Helga Nowottny et al, *The New Production of Knowledge: The Dynamics of Science and Research in Contemporary Societies* (London: Sage, 1994).

[68] Nico Stehr and Richard V. Ericson, *The Culture and Power of Knowledge: Inquiries into Contemporary Societies* (Berlin/New York: de Gruyter, 1992); Nico Stehr, *Wissen und Wirtschaften: Die gesellschaftlichen Grundlagen der modernen Ökonomie* (Frankfurt/Main: Suhrkamp, 2001).

[69] Lepenies, *Between Literature and Science*, 1988.

[70] David M. Ricci, *The Tragedy of Political Science: Politics, Scholarship, and Democracy* (New Haven: Yale University Press, 1984).

has shown, the role of knowledge in the legitimation of political authority continues to increase in importance across a wide range of policy fields – from nuclear energy policy to labour relations, and from education to foreign trade. Academic producers of knowledge will bring their own values to bear on how to assess these relationships between knowledge and power; the inescapable mandate, however, is for a much more self-conscious and systematic effort to reveal and analyze the many ways in which these relationships permeate the life of our academic institutions – from the agendas of external financial sponsors to the impact of foreign training, and from the real reasons for the competition between the humanities and the natural science to the obstacles to affirmative action for women and minority populations.

Disciplines and the Structures of Knowledge Production

There is something quite striking about the tenacity with which the traditional disciplines have retained their dominance over the structure of higher education – in spite of massive shifts and changes in the nature of knowledge and in our ways of producing it. Boundaries between disciplines have become blurred beyond recognition – between economics and political science, between sociology and psychology, and even between the social sciences and the humanities. Theoretical and methodological variation *within* disciplines is now often greater than that *between* disciplines. Just as importantly, vast new domains of knowledge have emerged that transcend disciplinary boundaries and become the source of important insights into such phenomena as biogenetics, symbolic systems, organizational behaviour, and social engineering.

All of this notwithstanding, the traditional disciplines continue to provide the principal matrix for the structural division of labour in our academic life – testimony to the extraordinary power of the established structures that buttress their existence: professional associations, complete with pension plans and medical insurance, journals, publishing interests, funding mechanisms, etc. While it is true that interdisciplinary centres and programs abound in universities around the world, it is the disciplines that continue to provide both the framework for the recruitment and promotion of personnel and the ultimate arbiter of the acceptability of methods for validating knowledge. The transformation in our ways of thinking about knowledge, in our recognition of the synergies to be achieved from breaking out of disciplinary identities, and in our challenges to the canons of knowledge production has not (yet) seriously subverted the role of the disciplines in the structure of our academic life. For the institutional politics of knowledge, the role and resilience of the disciplines remains one of the more intractable features.[71]

---

[71] Wolf Lepenies, *Benimm und Erkenntnis: Über die notwendige Rückkehr der Werte in die Wissenschaften. Die Sozialwissenschaften nach dem Ende der Geschichte* (Frankfurt/Main: Suhrkamp, 1997), pp. 93-94.

Evaluating Scholarship: Tradition and Diversity in the Assessment of Knowledge

It is not surprising that the evaluation of scholarship is one of the most contested domains in the politics of knowledge; after all, it is the evaluation of scholars, students, research proposals, manuscripts, and publications that determines the principal rewards of academic life: peer recognition, institutional standing and influence, research grants and, most importantly, publication. In higher education, much of this evaluation is done by "peer review", with variable degrees of intervention by state authorities, institutional administrators, and external sponsors. Unravelling the complex politics of this process and of the interests that are being brought to bear on it would be worth a chapter in itself. I am limiting my argument here to the inherently conservative nature of the existing evaluation process, and to its role as an obstacle in facilitating diversity and change in the production of knowledge. So as not to be misunderstood, I concede that in a matter as delicate and controversial as assessing the quality of knowledge, a certain degree of caution and conservatism may indeed be prudent. However, I would also argue that the institutional reality of evaluating the quality of scholarship has tended to become a force of retardation and hindrance in the quest for new and better forms of knowledge production.

It is here that the hierarchies of knowledge manifest their power most effectively; the "superior" epistemologies, research systems, institutions, and scholars, the ultimate arbiters over the "new growth" in knowledge vegetation, measure what is new against the established norm, and recognize and reward, not surprisingly, the familiar over the unfamiliar, the proven over the unproven. No wonder, then, that those judgments tend to go in favour of nomothetic rather than idiographic forms of knowledge, of explanation rather than interpretation, of cognitive representations of reality rather than more holistic efforts that include normative and aesthetic categories. New forms of social inquiry – hermeneutic work, participatory research, textual and interpretive analysis – and more generally the penetration of historical and ethnological perspectives into disciplines with a particular stake in generalization (such as sociology) are bound to encounter difficulties in this kind of a process. There is powerful and powerless knowledge in the established structures for the assessment of scholarship; one of the biggest challenges that the new knowledge order faces is to subvert and erode this distinction, and the processes of scholarly evaluation seem to be particularly in need of reform.

Pluralism and Decentralization in the World of Knowledge

Capturing many voices in today's world of knowledge, it was Rajni Kothari who had deplored what he saw as "the homogenizing monoculture of the mind", and who saw the answer in "the reaffirmation of a moral universe that respects the plurality of perspectives and paths to truth"[72] – a vision shared in Brenkman's appeal to "relativize

---

[72] Kothari, "On Human Governnance", 1987, p. 284.

and reinterpret the Western tradition, which has staked its claim to universality".[73] By and large, and again with important variations from one part of the world to another, our systems of higher education are far from responding to this momentous challenge.[74] Paradigmatic and institutional orthodoxies maintain a firm, if occasionally somewhat shaky, grip on the setting, encouraging, funding, and dissemination of research agendas. New and different conceptions of research and teaching – feminist studies, multi-cultural studies in undergraduate education, peace research, environmental studies – have a difficult time establishing their institutional identity and legitimacy. Notable exceptions (including many cited in this chapter) notwithstanding, much research in the non-Western world tends to emulate the strategies and standards of knowledge production in the West, and to aspire to its recognition and rewards in funding, acknowledgment, and publication. Powerful international organizations, notably the World Bank, establish specific and universal criteria for what is to be considered acceptable research, and assure conformity through their political and economic might, which makes deviance from the established knowledge norms a costly proposition.[75]

Against the background of this situation, the decentralization and democratization of the international knowledge order becomes one of the most pressing and noble tasks for our institutions of higher education. As always, change has to start in one's own backyard and requires a substantial enhancement of intellectual pluralism and democratic governance within the institution, and the aggressive pursuit of new and different quests for knowledge.[76] At the other end of the continuum, the United Nations system and its specialized institutions need to be reminded of their mandate to nurture an international knowledge order that reflects and supports the rich diversity in access to knowledge around the world, and that counteracts the tendency towards homogeneity and standardization fuelled by the interests of technology, communication, and commerce. As a guardian of the international democracy of knowledge, the United Nations system could become once again a critical partner of those forces in higher education that seek to break through the constraints of the "homogenizing monoculture" of the old, but very powerful knowledge order. The critical discourses of development, gender, and democracy might well serve as centres of gravity around which such a joint effort could be constructed.

---

[73] Brenkman, *Culture and Domination*, 1987, p. 230.

[74] Sohail Inayatullah and Jennifer Gidley (eds.), *The University in Transformation: Global Perspectives on the Futures of the University* (Westport, CT: Bergin & Garvey, 2000).

[75] Hans N. Weiler, "Technology and Politics in the Production of Knowledge: Some Notes on a New World Bank Initiative to Build Educational Research Capacity in Developing Countries", in *NORRAG News*, No. 10, July 1991, pp. 19-23.

[76] Hans N. Weiler, "Continuity and Change in U.S. Higher Education: Challenges to the Established Order of Knowledge Production", in *Zeitschrift für internationale erziehungs- und sozial-wissenschaftliche Forschung*, Vol. 7, No. 1, 1990, pp. 1-15.

2

Science, Universities and Subjugated Knowledges: A "Third World" Perspective

Majid Rahnema

Modern science, like development, has lost much of its lustre. Not only are some of its most cherished *"titres de noblesse"* now questioned by prominent insiders from within its imperium, but millions who once considered it as a hope and symbol of human liberation have also lost their illusions about it.

Larry Laudan is a well-known philosopher of science. As an insider, he offers the following thoughts:

> For a long time, many have taken the rationality and progressiveness of science as an obvious fact or a forgone conclusion... This confident attitude has been almost inescapable given the cultural biases in favour of science in modern culture. [Yet] attempts to show that the methods of science guarantee it is true, probable, progressive, or highly confirmed knowledge... have generally failed, raising a distinct presumption that scientific theories are neither true, nor probable, nor progressive, nor highly confirmed.[1]

> ...[On the other hand] some historians and philosophers of science (e.g., Kuhn and Feyerabend)... conclude that scientific decision-making is basically a political and propagandistic affair, in which prestige, power, age, and polemic decisively determine the outcome of the struggle between competing theories and theorists.[2]

These are harsh words, indeed, for a science which can still take pride in some of its literally spectacular feats and achievements. In fulfilling the Baconian dream of

---

[1] As "philosophers of science have generally found that their models of rationality find few, if any, exemplifications in the actual process of scientific activity", Laudan proposes that rationality consist "in making the most progressive theory choices". Larry Laudan, *Progress and Its Problems: Towards a Theory of Scientific Growth* (Berkeley: University of California Press, 1977), p. 6

[2] *Ibid.*, pp. 2-4.

"dissecting", "penetrating", and eventually torturing nature to make it yield its secrets[3], it has, no doubt, led to discoveries and inventions of significant importance to some aspects of human life. In many a well-defined area of human activity, science has extended human knowledge and power to frontiers never reached before. Similarly, it has helped a relatively small portion of the world's inhabitants reach higher material comfort, widen the scope of their needs and resources, develop their capacities and opened them up to a growing variety of goods and services.

Yet, these achievements have hardly served to improve the lot of the overwhelming number of human beings. Quite the contrary. Scientific rationality has served, more than often, to impose on them sufferings and indignities of an unprecedented nature. Particularly in the so-called Third World, imperatives based on economics, agronomy, medicine, social and political sciences, and now development and management sciences, have used their life spaces as huge laboratories. The science-development nexus has transformed entire segments of population into disposable or dispensable people, targeted for different "planning" objectives. Everywhere, human beings are realizing that "science has no place for the defeated except as objects of an experiment".[4]

On another plane, vernacular societies are discovering that science and its prodigious child, technology, threaten an even more vital dimension of their life: their cultural memory and their age-old capacity to regenerate ways of doing and self-expression. A whole set of actual and symbolic tools are used to subjugate those deep-rooted knowledges which have enabled them, throughout ages, to preserve their culture and identity.

Recently, a generation of new scientists, fully aware of these threats, and acting as "genealogists"[5], have set out to contain these processes. On the one hand, they make these subjugated knowledges known to others. On the other hand, they seek to help threatened communities to develop new modes of resistance. Their attempts have resulted not only in shedding light on such knowledges and bringing them to the attention of the communities concerned, but also in helping everyone to understand the very processes through which vernacular knowledges have been subjugated and "phagocytosed", as it were, by modern science.

In many ways, this new breed of scientists, is giving audibility to the silenced

---

[3] See Francis Bacon, "Advancement of Learning", in Joseph Devey (eds.), *The Physical and Metaphysical Works of Lord Bacon* (London: Bell and Sons, 1911), Bk II, Ch.II, p. 82: "For as a man's temper is never well-known until he is crossed; in like manner the turns and changes of nature cannot appear so fully, when she is left at liberty, as in the trials and tortures of art".

[4] See the incisive comments of Shiv Visvanathan on this question in his essay "On the Annals of the Laboratory State", in Ashis Nandy (ed.), *Science, Hegemony and Violence: A Requiem for Modernity* (Delhi, Oxford University Press, 1988). This book contains many other remarkable essays on the actual impacts of the scientific discourse and practices on people's lives. I consider all of them as "required reading" for all persons concerned with the question.

[5] As an example of these groups, I could mention, for India alone, the thinkers and activists associated with such centres and movements as the Indian Centre for the Study of Developing Societies and Lokayan; amongst them, Ashis Nandy, Dharampal, Shiv Visvanathan, Vandana Shiva, Seshadri, Bajaj, Manu Kothari, Lopa Mehta and many others who, I know, are working with their people, seldom coming to international seminars or meetings.

voices of threatened communities. The fact that most of them have indeed been trained in reputable modern institutions of "scientific excellence" has not prevented them from representing what Foucault has called the "insurrection of subjected knowledges", or the "return of knowledge" through processes of "local criticism".[6]

To elaborate briefly on this concept of "subjugated knowledges", they represent, for Foucault, two sets of knowledges. On the one hand, they are constituted by "those blocs of historical knowledge which were present but disguised within the body of functionalist and systematizing theory and which criticism – which obviously draws upon scholarship – has been able to reveal".[7]

On the other hand, they belong to an altogether different "set of knowledges that have been disqualified as inadequate to their task or insufficiently elaborated; naïve knowledges located low down on the hierarchy, beneath the required level of cognition or scientificity".[8] Considered as low-ranking or unqualified, even directly disqualified knowledges (that of the diseased or the mentally ill person, or the delinquent, or the nurse, or the doctor – parallel and marginal as they are to the mainstream knowledge of medicine), they belong to what Foucault calls *le savoir des gens*. It is not commonsense knowledge, but "a particular, local, regional knowledge, a differential knowledge incapable of unanimity and which owes its force only to the harshness with which it is opposed by everything surrounding it".[9]

These two types of subjugated knowledges, that is, the "buried knowledges of erudition" and those disqualified from the hierarchy of knowledges and sciences differ from each other in many ways. Yet if one proceeds to their genealogy, or rather to a multiplicity of genealogical researches, Foucault's hypothesis is that both could lead to a historical knowledge of the struggles associated with them. The proposed *genealogy* represents "the union of erudite knowledge and local memories which allows us to establish a historical knowledge of struggles and to make use of this knowledge tactically to-day".[10] However, Foucault adds that such genealogies are possible only if the "tyranny of globalizing discourses with their hierarchy and all their privileges of a theoretical *avant-garde*" is eliminated.

Modern science continues to look at subjugated knowledges with nothing but contempt. Now is not this attitude "unscientific"? Does it not close the door to new possibilities of knowledge and discovery? Does it not, more than anything else, cripple science in areas of great importance to its own growth, as for instance, in medicine, agriculture, and environmental studies, as well as in economics, political and other

---

[6] See Michel Foucault, *Power/Knowledge* (New York: Pantheon Books, 1980), p. 81. "What I mean by that phrase", explains Foucault, "is this: it is a fact that we have repeatedly encountered, at least at a superficial level, in the course of most recent times, an entire thematic to the effect that it is not theory but life that matters, not knowledge but reality, not books but money etc.; but it also seems that over and above, and arising out of this thematic, there is something else to which we are witness, and which we might describe as *an insurrection of subjugated knowledges*".

[7] *Ibid.*, p. 82.

[8] *Ibid.*

[9] *Ibid.*

[10] *Ibid.*, p. 83.

social sciences?[11]

The question is not indeed to opt for "the virtues of direct cognition" and experience as against "the abstract unity of theory". Neither is it "to vindicate a lyrical right to ignorance or non-knowledge", with a view to disparaging the contents, methods or concepts of a science. What is at stake is the refusal to accept the centralizing and hegemonistic power of that science, a power which is linked to the institution and the functioning of its discourse, a power which, in the name of the only recognized truth or rationality, dismisses any other claim to truth or rationality.

The "paradigmatic" tyranny[12] has not, however, prevented creative minds in the scientific community from entertaining the claims to attention of local, discontinuous and delegitimized knowledges. Nor has it discouraged dissidents from opposing the claims of a unitary body of theory which would filter, hierarchize and order these knowledges, in the name of science. On the contrary, this new breed of scientist-genealogists seems united in their resolution not to be impressed by the paradigmatic rule. Fully realizing the importance of all forms of insight and experience, they consider it their duty to help them blossom. They are convinced that even the wildest or the "oddest" plants and flowers should be fully protected, particularly if they belong to unknown or undiscovered sceneries. It may make sense that "scientific truth is defined as that which scientists say or think to be true",[13] but there is a truth in all flowers that no self-proclaimed universal "régime of truth" should be allowed to destroy with impunity.

For different reasons (some of them dubious), the last decades have witnessed

---

[11] An observation related by Carl Rogers is worth mentioning here. Talking about intuitive thinking, he says that "it may be clearly wrong, and yet fundamentally right. For example, I have chuckled at the natives in the Caribbean who would not think of planting their crops except at the time of the new moon, when 'the moon is right'. All of us 'know' that the moon cannot possibly affect this seed that is placed in the ground; the native is acting on a ridiculous hypothesis. Now, however, centuries after the natives formulated their adages, scientists find to their puzzlement that rainfall during the week following the new moon is significantly greater all over the world than rainfall during the other portions of the moon's cycle. In other words, the hypothesis that the moon affected the seed is as wrong as we in our superior knowledge thought that it was. But the sensing of the pattern, by natives immersed for a lifetime in the growing of crops, was correct! This accords very deeply with my belief that the human organism, when operating freely and non-defensively, is perhaps the best scientific tool in existence, and is able to sense a pattern long before it can consciously formulate one". Carl Rogers, "Some Thoughts Regarding the Current Presuppositions of the Behavioral Sciences", in William R. Coulson & Carl R. Rogers (eds.), *Man and the Science of Man* (Columbus, Ohio: Charles E. Merrill, 1968), p. 63.

[12] For Thomas Kuhn, what he calls "normal science" is based on an uncritical attitude toward the fundamental theories and concepts which are accepted by a scientific community in its field or discipline. These are embodied in a "paradigm", or a set of theoretical doctrines constituting a worldview. The paradigm prescribes some beliefs as essential and proscribes others. If a scientist fails to reconcile theory and evidence, it represents a failure of the scientist, not the theory. In short, a paradigm is a set of inviolable theoretical doctrines accepted by members of a scientific community. Those who do not fully accept the key elements of the paradigm are read out of the community. Their work is not taken seriously, and their criticisms are listened to only politely, if at all. A summary of Kuhn's views on this question can be found in Joseph Rouse, *Knowledge and Power* (Ithaca, N.Y.: Cornell University Press, 1987), pp. 26-40.

[13] The quotation is from Michael Polanyi, "The Growth of Science in Society", in W. Coulson & C. Rogers (eds.), *Man and the Science of Man* (1968), p. 12.

greater interest in the re-discovery of subjugated knowledges.[14] The interest has sometimes been too affected by a syndrome proper to the pharmaceutical industries that living plants or minerals are only worth their "active ingredients" or "principles". As such, many of these knowledges have been studied and sometimes condescendingly acknowledged, but with a view to only utilizing their useful active ingredients for higher "scientific" purposes.

In what follows, I would like to show, through a couple of examples, what the "active principle" of modern science has actually done to the other knowledges; how it has disqualified, "dis-valued", and ultimately de-vitalized and destroyed them, together with entire cultures and *epistemes* living on the latter. My first example is borrowed from the works of the Indian scientist C.V. Seshadri. It concerns the role played by the Second Law of Thermodynamics in dis-valuing a whole constellation of local knowledges. Seshadri argues that the law in question, dramatically supported by the technologies it helped produce, ended up by replacing a sustainable and culturally adapted concept of efficiency with one which made its future consumers increasingly dependent on sources of energy and capital which are both uncontrollable and out of their reach.

Seshadri bases his argument on the following facts: the Law in question stipulates that high temperatures are of a superior value, as are resources such as petroleum, coal, etc., with which we can achieve such temperatures. In this sense, the law of entropy provides a guideline for the extraction of resources and their utilization.[15] In effect, it is fused with a particular kind of resource utilization, requiring a total rupture with the modes of knowledge, based on the sustenance of the local culture and environment.

S.N. Nagarajan, another Indian scientist, supports this argument. He adds that tropical agricultural practices were all built on principles of efficiency which followed "nature's way", a way which

> is slow, peaceful, non-harmful, non-explosive, non-destructive, both for others and for itself. Take for example, the production of fibre by plants and animals compared to machines. The machine... produces a large quantity in a short time. But at what cost? The costs are borne by the weaker sections and by nature. The people who are chained to the machine (workers) are also consumed by it.[16]

---

[14] David Brokensha et al, *Indigenous Knowledge Systems and Development* (Lanham, MD: University Press of America, 1980), is a useful book, amongst many others published recently, which contains both selected descriptions and reviews of some of these knowledges. The book contains a good number of "case studies", on subjects going from "potato taxonomies in Andean Agriculture" to "the animal of friendship in Niger", "the Mbeere knowledge of their vegetation", "a three-culture – Massai, Kikuyu and USA – study of body parts", etc. It also includes a 45-page bibliography which could be quite helpful to a student of such knowledges.

[15] C.V. Seshadri and V. Balaji, *Towards a New Science of Agriculture* (Madras, MCRC, undated), p. 4, quoted by Claude Alvares in Wolfgang Sachs (ed.), *The Development Dictionary* (London: Zed Books, 1992), p. 222.

[16] S.N. Nagarajan, in a personal communication to Claude Alvares dated 7 May 1990. See Wolfgang Sachs, *The Development Dictionary*, 1992, p. 223.

Claude Alvares, whose works on the effects of modern science and technology on the cultures of the South are quite well known, concludes: "All processes of work effected at ambient temperatures are [thus] discounted in the suzerainty of modern science", including those of tribals, bamboo workers, honey bees and silkworms, who all process the resources of the forest at ambient temperatures and without the polluting side-effects of waste heat and effluent associated with big industrial processes.

Alvares provides us with another example, this time linked to medicine. Charaka, a physician of ancient India, expressing a view held in many vernacular medical knowledges, defined disease as imbalance or inequilibrium. In that context, staphylococci, for instance, are normal inhabitants of our body. Most of the time, their relationship to us is symbiotic; only sometimes does the balance break down. For Ayurvedic medicine, the problem is therefore to restore the balance, not to make the germ disappear altogether.

The discovery of antibiotics was, per se, a great achievement of modern science. Yet, each type of antibiotic destroys a wide spectrum of germs, and this has produced two sets of negative results. The first has been the appearance of increasingly greater numbers of organisms which are resistant to antibiotics and are therefore more virulent in their parasitic relationships with humans. The second, of greater epistemic and cultural importance, has been the dis-valuing of a vernacular knowledge system. Thus:

> Ayurveda, which began once as the science of nutrition and health, has increasingly focused on the treatment of disease under the pressure of modern medicine. The patient in India is now forced to choose between an anti-life allopathic system or a perverted indigenous system.[17]

As time is running out, I will confine my remaining comments to the social sciences and universities.

ON THE SOCIAL SCIENCES

As long as social sciences (or *sciences humaines*) try to copy the model of the natural or even the so-called "mature" sciences (in the Kuhn-Lakatos sense), particularly if they continue their flirt with biology, they will never become the artful mode of knowledge and enquiry they are meant to be. My guess is that if social scientists perceive themselves as both genealogists and archaeologists (in the sense Foucault has meant)[18], and thus liberate themselves from the need to create unitary bodies of theory

---

[17] Claude Alvares, "Science, Colonialism and Violence: A Luddite View", in Ashis Nandy (ed.), *Science, Hegemony and Violence*, 1988, p. 101.

[18] In Foucault's terms, if "a genealogy should be seen as a kind of attempt to emancipate historical knowledges from subjection, to render them capable of opposition and of struggle against the coercion of a theoretical, unitary, formal and scientific discourse,... 'archaeology' would be the appropriate methodology of this analysis of local discursivities, and 'genealogy' would be the

based primarily on quantitative data, they could then even take pride in being called a "doubtful" science.

What we need today is that a new breed of creative and sensitive researchers applies their insight and their idea of truth, together with their critical erudition, to the understanding and re-discovery of other human beings engaged in their localized struggles for their own truth. We are in need of listening minds able to vibrate with those subjugated knowledges, from within, as it were. People of concern to us should not be perceived as needy strangers in desperate need of our knowledge and assistance, but rather as newly found fellow travellers who, because of their familiar knowledge of the road, could also help us from going astray.

Social sciences can play a role in that type of companionship and dialogue, but only if they see in the present insurrection of subjugated knowledges a unique opportunity for their own self-transformation. Communities trying to regenerate their life spaces do not want to see their old familiar roads replaced by a super-highway of our design, even if it is "enlightened" by the powerful megalamps of a new *Aufklärung*. To this date, such megalamps have only served their producers. For the millions who have learned to find their way under the archaic stars, using nothing but their own inner or locally produced lights, the imported ones have but blinded them to things they used to see and discover before.

Social sciences, as they have developed, and are actually taught and practised, particularly in Third World universities, are often insensitive to, and suspicious of local lights. Busy working on "populations", rather than humans who refuse to be labelled, busy computing dead statistics and data of a general character on the same "populations", what they do is also often manipulative and harmful.

CAN UNIVERSITIES PLAY A ROLE IN REDRESSING THE SITUATION?

To the extent that they seek to be a nursery garden for the growth of modern science, universities breed the same kinds of problems. In addition, they are called upon to perform a series of functions, e.g., to play an instrumental role in the reproduction of the society; to make it possible for the most "qualified" graduates to succeed in society, and to preserve and improve the hierarchical bases of success in different fields of activity; to be the seedbed for the definition of the "régime of truth" for the coming generations; to promote the types of knowledge and power aimed at creating productive and "docile bodies", and to help create the instruments and the disciplinary power required for various processes of "normalization". Universities are bound by a series of constraints related to their funding sources, the social and economic claims on them, and often to the politics of their survival.

Yet, universities are, at the same time, privileged spaces for critical dissent and

tactics whereby, on the basis of the descriptions of these local discursivities, the subjected knowledges which were thus released would be brought into play". Foucault, *Power/Knowledge*, 1980, p. 85.

subversion, in their noblest senses. No doubt, they have lost much of what originally made a Medieval university, or *universitas*, which meant gathering, union, community. These were associations which started by bringing together craftsmen and other "workers of their hands" (*ouvriers de leurs mains*, to use Rutebeuf's formulation); later, in bigger cities like Bologna and Paris, masters and students came there to share or acquire knowledge. As such, they remained, for long, true bastions of resistance toward an expanding royal power.[19]

Although modern universities, as institutions, have now little in common with their earlier ancestors, many of them surprisingly maintain within them refreshing spaces of freedom, where similar types of resistance are formed against organized knowledge and power. Many students and teachers, all over the world, actively participate in the process.

In most Third World countries, while open resistance sometimes takes the shape of dramatic encounters on campuses, a host of structural reasons seriously reduces their possibility on a lasting basis. As universities constitute the crowning stage of the school system, both their students and parents perceive them primarily as factories for the production of the diplomas required for further escalation on the ladders of socio-economic success. The state, for its part, wants them to be the main producers of its badly needed "human resources". At the same time, because governments are fully aware of the repercussions of possible student unrest on their own survival, they tend to keep universities under tight political control.

For all these reasons, Third World universities are increasingly becoming cheap or distorted copies of their Western originals. Nowhere, has there been any serious attempt to replace them by alternatives capable of meeting the needs of more serious learners or of regenerating deep-rooted local traditions of education and scholarship. Even in countries where such traditions had existed even before Europe (Think of the Jondi Shahpoor university in the 7th century, and the impressive higher education complex of *Rub 'i Rashidi* in Tabriz, in the late 13th century), the image and the status-giving functions of Western universities seem so internalized by the élites that reforms are generally limited to technical face-lifting operations. The explosion of the student population at the secondary level, together with the permanent priorities of governments in terms of their so-called security and development purposes, are further reasons to block serious change.

Under such circumstances, is it possible not to end without a note of despair? Perhaps, however, new hopes are to be found in the very fact that the macrostrategies of power are all crumbling. To quote the great Marx who should now be turning in his grave, "all that's solid melts into air". No doubt, we live in a turbulent and

---

[19] Many a historian has wondered how, for instance, in the early 13th century, masters and students in the University of Paris, and later, of Orleans, of Oxford and of Toulouse, used the weapons of strike and dispersion against the violence of power. Thus, "a group of intellectuals without status, without organized power, and receiving no backing from any economic force" could, for instance, maintain their autonomy both toward the powerful bishop of Paris and the royal power. See Paul Benoit, "*La Théologie au XIII° siècle: une science pas comme les autres*", in Michel Serres, *Eléments d'histoire des sciences* (Paris: Bordas, 1989), pp. 179-180.

unpredictable world. But such times are perhaps also ideal for localized struggles to create new forms of knowledge and power, free from the tyranny of massive and totalizing ideologies. Who knows where such struggles could take us all?

3

Paradigm Shifts in the Social Sciences in the East and West

Zahra Al Zeera

INTRODUCTION

We are nationally and internationally engaged in a major debate about issues related to (a) knowledge creation, and (b) knowledge transfer (rather than knowledge distribution) among cultures. Since the major theme of this book is "Knowledge Across Cultures", then we should be engaged in a dialogue about issues related to knowledge at two levels: (a) at the paradigm level, to discuss issues related to knowledge creation, and (b) at the cultural level, to discuss issues related to knowledge transfer among cultures and the problems associated with this.

In this chapter I try to address four major issues regarding knowledge creation and knowledge transfer. First, the conventional paradigm, positivism, and such emergent paradigms as postpositivism, critical theory, and constructivism will be reviewed and presented to show the ontological, epistemological, and methodological foundations of each paradigm. Second, knowledge generated and accumulated on the basis of conventional and emergent paradigms will be analyzed to reveal the structure of knowledge produced under each paradigm and to examine if contemporary paradigms are able to encompass the complexity and wholeness of other cultures. Third, an Islamic world view and an Islamic epistemology will be presented to support an argument for the need of alternative paradigms for Islamic social sciences if they are to develop and maintain the sense of identity of Islamic universities. Finally, an alternative paradigm is proposed, not to replace other paradigms but to add to them, since the aim of this book is to acknowledge other voices and carry on an intelligent and just dialogue among universities of the East and the West.

A REVIEW OF CONVENTIONAL AND EMERGENT PARADIGMS

In this section, E. Guba's book entitled, *The Paradigm Dialogue*[1] is used as a base from

---

[1] E. Guba (ed.), *The Paradigm Dialogue* (Newbury Park: Sage Publications, 1990).

which to review both conventional and emergent paradigms. According to Guba, all paradigms can be characterized by the way their proponents respond to three basic questions:

(1)   Ontological: What is the nature of the "knowable"? or, what is the nature of "reality"?

(2)   Epistemological: What is the nature of the relationship between the knower (the enquirer) and the known (or knowable)?

(3)   Methodological: How should the inquirer go about finding out knowledge?

The answers to these questions define the basic belief system or paradigm that is adopted and thus provide a useful basis on which to analyze conventional and emergent paradigms. It is important to note that the discussion below is not at the method level but rather at the paradigm level as a wholly different way of viewing the world.

The Positivist Paradigm

The positivist paradigm can be defined as "a family of philosophies characterized by an extremely positive evaluation of science and the scientific method".[2] Positivism began in Europe in the 19th and early 20th centuries. According to the conventional positivist paradigm, reality is single, tangible, and fragmentable. Knower and known are independent and constitute a discrete dualism. The aim of positivist inquiry is to develop a nomothetic body of knowledge in the form of generalizations that are truth statements free from time and context. In addition, positivists believe that every action can be explained as the result of a real cause that precedes the effect temporally. Inquiry is value-free by virtue of the objective methodology employed. The basic belief system (paradigm) of conventional positivist inquiry is summarized by Guba[3] as follows:

Ontology: Realist – reality exists "out there" and is driven by immutable natural laws and mechanisms and is conventionally summarized in the form of time- and context-free generalizations. Some of these generalizations take the form of cause-effect laws.

Epistemology: Dualist/objective – it is both possible and essential for the

---

[2] J. Greene, "Three Views on the Nature and Role of Knowledge in Social Science", in E. Guba (ed.), *The Paradigm Dialogue*, 1990.

[3] E. Guba, "The Alternative Paradigm Dialogue", in E. Guba (ed.), *The Paradigm Dialogue*, 1990, p. 20.

inquirer to adopt a distant, non interactive posture. Values and other biasing and confounding factors are thereby automatically excluded from influencing the outcomes.

Methodology: Experimental/manipulative – questions and/or hypotheses are stated in advance in propositional form and subjected to empirical tests (falsification) under carefully controlled conditions.

The Postpositivist Paradigm

Postpositivism is best characterized as a modified version of positivism. Prediction and control continue to be the aim. However, postpositivism differs from positivism in that "Where positivism is concerned with surface events or appearances, the new paradigm takes a deeper look. Where positivism establishes meaning operationally, the new paradigm (post positivism) establishes meaning inferentially. Where positivism sees its central purpose to be prediction, the new paradigm is concerned with understanding. Finally, where positivism is deterministic and bent on certainty, the new paradigm is probablistic and speculative".[4] Guba also states that postpositivism acknowledges that many imbalances have been allowed to emerge in the zeal for achieving realistic, objective inquiry; postpositivists believe that, if these imbalances can be addressed, positivism can be useful again.[5]

The basic belief system (paradigm) of postpositivism is summarized by Guba as follows:

Ontology: Critical realist – reality exists but can never be fully apprehended. It is driven by natural laws that can be only incompletely understood.

Epistemology: Modified objectives – objectivity remains a regulatory ideal, but it can only be approximated, with special emphasis placed on external guardians such as the critical tradition and the critical community.

Methodology: Modified experimental/manipulative, emphasizing critical multiplism. Redress imbalances by doing inquiry in more natural settings, using more qualitative methods, depending more on grounded theory and reintroducing discovery into the inquiry process.

---

[4] Y. Lincoln and E. Guba, *Effective Evaluation* (San Francisco: Jossey-Bass, 1985), p. 30.
[5] E. Guba, "The Alternative Paradigm Dialogue", 1990, p. 21.

The Critical Theory Paradigm

Critical theory, or "ideologically oriented inquiry" as Guba calls it,[6] also includes neo-Marxism, materialism, feminism, and participatory inquiry. These perspectives reject the claim of value-freedom made by positivists and postpositivists. According to Habermas, claims to value-free knowledge obscure the human interest inherent in all knowledge.[7]

Popkewitz argues that what counts as truth, adequacy, and procedure is tied to institutional history and social struggles.[8] He believes that values exist at all layers of science. However, the focus on rules and procedures in science dulls us to the pervasiveness of values and creates "methodological individualism". Critical social science views methodology as inherently political, as inescapably tied to issues of power and legitimacy.

Methods, then, are politically charged "as they define, control, manipulate and report".[9] An important issue in critical inquiry is how to bring together scholarship and advocacy in order to generate new ways of knowing that interrupt power imbalances:

> If values do enter into every inquiry, then the question immediately arises as to what values and whose values shall govern. If the findings of studies can vary depending on the values chosen, the choice of a particular value system tends to empower and enfranchise certain persons while disempowering and disenfranchising others. Inquiry thereby becomes a political act.[10]

The task of inquiry in the critical theory paradigm is, by definition, to raise people to the level of "true consciousness" so that they are energized and facilitated toward transforming the real world. Thus, it is argued, something other than a manipulative, interventionist methodology is required to raise the consciousness of participants.[11] Critical theorists take a dialogic approach that seeks to eliminate false consciousness which, in turn, will lead to transformation of the world.

Guba summarizes the basic belief system of the critical theory paradigm as follows:[12]

Ontology: Critical realist, as in the case of postpositivism.

Epistemology: Subjectivist, in the sense that values mediate inquiry.

---

[6] *Ibid.*

[7] J. Habermas, *Knowledge and Human Interests* (Boston: Beacon, 1971).

[8] T. Popkewitz, "Whose Future? Whose Past? Notes on Critical Theory and Methodology", in E. Guba (ed.), *The Paradigm Dialogue*, 1990.

[9] A. Gouldner, *The Coming Crisis in Western Sociology* (New York: Basic Books, 1970), p. 50.

[10] E. Guba, "The Alternative Paradigm Dialogue", 1990, p. 24.

[11] *Ibid.*

[12] *Ibid.*

Methodology: Dialogic, transformative, eliminating false consciousness and energizing and facilitating transformation.

The Constructivist Paradigm

A naturalistic or constructivist[13] paradigm emerged and developed gradually in the social sciences as a result of disenchantment with positivist and postpositivist modes of inquiry. Constructivists believe that positivist and postpositivist paradigms are "badly flawed and must be entirely replaced".[14] According to constructivists, realities are multiple, inquirer and inquired should interact actively and constructions are compared and constructed dialectically. Based on these assumptions, Guba and Lincoln believe that "there is no alternative but to take a position of relativism. Relativism is the key to openness and the continuing search for even more informed and sophisticated constructions. Realities are multiple and they exist in peoples' minds". Epistemologically, the constructivists choose to take a subjective position. It is argued that if realities exist only in respondents' minds, then subjective interaction seem to be the only way to access them.[15] Methodologically, the constructivist proceeds in ways that aim to identify the variety of constructions that exist and bring them into as much consensus as possible. This process has two aspects: hermeneutics and dialectics. The hermeneutic aspect consists of depicting individual constructions as accurately as possible, while the dialectic aspect consists of comparing and contrasting these existing individual constructions so that each respondent must confront the constructions of others and come to terms with them. The hermeneutic/dialectic methodology aims to produce as many informed and sophisticated constructions as possible. Constructivism thus intends neither to predict and control the "real" world (as positivists and postpositivists do) nor to transform it (as critical theorists/ideologists intend to). Rather, they aim to reconstruct the "world" at the only point at which it exists: in the minds of the constructors. It is the mind that is to be transformed, not the world.[16]

The constructivist belief system is summarized by Guba as follows:

Ontology: Relativist – realities exist in the form of multiple mental constructions, socially and experientially based, local and specific, dependent for their form and control on the persons who hold them.

Epistemology: Subjectivist – inquirer and inquired are fused into a single (monastic) entity. Findings are literally the creation of the process of interaction between the two.

---

[13] Re-named at the 1989 Alternative Paradigm Conference in San Francisco.

[14] E. Guba, "The Alternative Paradigm Dialogue", 1990, p. 25.

[15] Y. Lincoln and E. Guba, *Effective Evaluation*, (San Francisco: Jossey-Bass), 1985.

[16] E. Guba, "The Alternative Paradigm Dialogue", 1990, p. 26.

Methodology: Hermeneutic, dialectic – individual constructions are elicited and refined hermeneutically, and compared and contrasted dialectically, with the aim of generating one (or a few) constructions on which there is substantial consensus.

WESTERN PARADIGMS AND FRAGMENTED KNOWLEDGE

Analysis of the three emergent social science paradigms from the ontological, epistemological, and methodological point of view reveals an invisible string that connects all these paradigms despite apparent contradictions in their stance or premises. That string is the Aristotelian principle of "either or" which has formed the Western way of thinking for centuries. This principle is rooted deeply in the Aristotelian Law of the Excluded Middle, which holds that every proposition must either be true or false. The three emergent paradigms, postpositivism, critical theory, and constructivism, move from one extreme to another, from pure realism to pure relativism. Each paradigm accepts one way or another, either realism or relativism. Even constructivism, despite the claim of multiple realities, rejects strongly realities based on positivism because they cannot accept at the same time realist and relativist stances. They have to be either this or that.

The "either or" way of thinking has been reinforced by the industrial revolution and the move towards a secular scientific world. Gradually, a wall has been built differentiating clearly and strongly between the secular and the spiritual, the cognitive and the affective, the propositional and the tacit, the subjective and the objective, the soul and the mind, the individual and the society. This wall has fragmented the consciousness of Western secular society as well as the knowledge that has been produced in and for this society.

If one analyzes the three emergent paradigms in the social sciences, it is seen that each paradigm focuses on one aspect of "reality" and rejects or denies other aspects. Positivism, under the legitimacy of scientific method, reinforces objectivity, value-freedom, manipulation, intervention, and control. Constructivists push the pendulum to the other extreme and move away from objectivity to subjectivity, from control and manipulation of subjects to dialogue and active participation with participants, from verification of grand theories to discovering grounded theories. On the middle ground between positivism and constructivism stand critical ideologists who focus on the transformation of the world through political engagement and through the elimination of false consciousness by means of critical theory.

It is obvious that none of the conventional or emergent paradigms encompasses the complexity of life and of human beings. Each paradigm focuses on one side of the "reality". It is either realist, critical realist, or relativist. Despite the merits that both critical ideologists and constructivists/interpretivists have in understanding, reconstructing, interpreting, and transforming human action, and hence catching a glimpse of the "truth", they remain handicapped in understanding reality as a "whole". Reality, according to all mentioned paradigms, starts and ends on this earth, in this temporary world. From an ontological point of view, "reality" for religious, spiritual people differs from "reality" for secular people in the East and the West. A quick look at the emergent paradigms shows that there is no consideration for people who believe in God and believe that this life is only temporary and a passage that leads them to another life – to eternity.

Fragmentation in the West has happened at two concurrent levels: ontological and epistemological. At the epistemological level, social sciences are separated from natural sciences. At the ontological level, the spiritual world is separated from the material world. As a result, knowledge created under conventional wisdom and emergent secular paradigms is fragmented. In particular, it does not encompass the complexity of both spiritual and material life. Thus, conventional scientific paradigms have fragmented knowledge by separating science from art, literature, and philosophy, and creating two separate conflicting worlds that fight each other for survival. Science, of course, usually prevails in these battles.

By analyzing contemporary social problems and their causes, we realize that these paradigms are unable to encompass the sophistication and complexity of human beings, and the world around them. Therefore, an alternative paradigm is needed to answer certain questions that cannot be answered by secular, scientific paradigms or secular, emergent paradigms. A holistic Islamic paradigm will be proposed as an alternative paradigm for social studies in Islamic countries.

WESTERN EDUCATION IN THE ISLAMIC CONTEXT

The impact of Western education in Islamic countries reveals conflicts between (a) the East and the West, and (b) the religious and the secular.

Muslim countries, for many years, have suffered a degeneration and a disintegration between knowledge and action. Lack of harmony, inconsistency and distortion has characterized Muslim societies. In most Muslim countries, one can notice the split and disharmony between the political, the economic, and the social spheres of society. However, despite modernization and Westernization, Muslim societies are still religious, traditional societies. The majority of Muslim nations still do believe in God, the Prophets, the Sacred Text, Angels, the Day of Judgement, and the Hereafter. Thus, while most educational, social, and economic systems, on the one hand have adopted a Western secular worldview, with Western education, technology, and all the culture which comes with it, on the other hand, the remainder of society still resembles early Muslim societies. Communities and family life, based on legal marriages, are still the foundations of Muslim societies. Respect for the elderly, parents, and teachers is still the prevailing spirit. Spirituality, piety, temperance, and self-sacrifice have not vanished completely. The mismatch between the Islamic, religious foundation of society, and the secular, modern Westernized education system (especially the higher education system which is a complete transplantation of the

Western education system with all of its materialistic and secular characteristics) has and will continue to cause fractures and possibly severe damage, to the point of the possible collapse of Islamic societies.

Scientific, quantitative, and secular approaches to research have led to a colonizing knowledge, not only in the West and in Western institutions but also in developing countries through the various international agencies.   Knowledge developed in the West under specific social, cultural, economic, and political conditions has been generalized and transferred to developing countries.[17]   King remarks on this intellectual colonialism:

> It became a mark of modernity that the economically privileged nations have an obligation to foster the economic and cultural development of the Third World. Unilateral and multilateral national assistance through the United Nations was accepted as an obligation by the formerly colonial powers . . . The successes of this innovation in global scale and political experimentation have been less than spectacular . . . They assumed for the most part that the body of knowledge about social science learned in the universities of the West was pertinent to societies in general . . . It has been a shock to accept that the social processes we know to operate in the West are often absent or very subordinate to other social forces in the Third World.[18]

Knowledge created and developed in Western societies is not necessarily suitable for Eastern societies.   In the following section, an Islamic world view, an Islamic epistemology, and an Islamic paradigm will be presented to lay the foundation of knowledge that should be created and accumulated for and in Islamic universities.

THE RECONSTRUCTION OF ISLAMIC STUDIES

In reconstructing knowledge that facilitates and creates an Islamic epistemology, methods of social study should be reconstructed first.   Disenchantment about scientific research methods has been expressed by Islamic scholars as well as Western scholars. Al Faruqi highlights three major shortcomings that render scientific approaches to research as being inappropriate to Islamic knowledge: (a) the denial of relevance to a priori data, (b) a false sense of objectivity, and (c) a personalist versus an *ummatic* axiology.[19] He states that:

> The Western student of human nature and society was not in the mood to realize that not all pertinent data of human behaviour are observable by the senses and hence

---

[17] Z. Al Zeera, "Evaluation of the Orientation Program at the University of Bahrain: A Sociocultural Perspective" (unpublished Ph.D. thesis, University of Toronto, 1990), p. 92.

[18] K. King, "Two Key Fragmentations", paper presented at the Capri conference, 1989, p. 3.

[19] I. Al Faruqi and A. Nasseef (eds.), *Social and Natural Sciences: The Islamic Perspective* (Jeddah: King Abdul Aziz University, 1981).

subject to quantification and measurement . . . Being spiritual, these elements are not isolable, separate from their natural carriers. Nor are they ever subject to the only measurement science knows, the quantitative. Science treated them as inexistent or irrelevant.[20]

In addition, Al Faruqi explains how empathy and perception of values itself creates subjectivity in any intellectual inquiry:

The perception of value is impossible unless the human behaviour is able to move the observer. Similarly, the observer cannot be moved unless he is trained to be affected, and unless he has empathy with the object of his experience. The subject's attitude toward the data studied determines the outcome of the study. This is why the humanistic studies of the Western scientist are necessarily "Western" and cannot serve as models for the study of Muslims or their society.[21]

Finally, Al Faruqi discusses an important feature of scientific, Western methodology that violates a crucial requirement of Islamic methodology, namely, unity of truth:

Perhaps the most distinctive characteristic of Islamic methodology is the principle of the unity of truth. This principle holds that the modality of God is inseparable from him, that truth is one just as God is one . . . It is hence invalid to seek to establish a knowledge of human reality without acknowledging what that reality ought to be. Any investigation of a human "is" must therefore include its standing as an "ought to be" within the realm of possibility.

This principle of Islamic methodology is not identical to the principle of relevance of the spiritual. It adds to it something peculiarly Islamic, namely, the principle of *ummatism* [the concept of Islamic community and nations]. This principle holds that no value, hence, no imperative, is merely personal, pertinent to the individual alone.[22]

An important feature of Islamic methodology and knowledge is its wholeness. A holistic, phenomenological or naturalistic methodology creates an integrated and a unified knowledge that leads to the realization of the unity of truth. By realizing and accepting the dialectical concept of *tawhid*, Muslim scholars are challenged to search for truth in contradictory and opposing ideas and situations. Studying any problem naturalistically allows the researcher to examine the situation as it reveals itself naturally without *a priori* conditioning. It also allows the researcher to observe the relationship between various elements as they interact in a natural setting. By doing so, the researcher is in a position to see and experience a "whole" picture, or at least as

---

[20] *Ibid*, p. 20.
[21] *Ibid*, p. 12.
[22] *Ibid*, pp. 13-14.

whole as human limitations permit.[23]

This section was intended to assist the reader to conceptualize the notion of the wholeness and unity of knowledge which is suggested as an alternative theory of knowledge for Islamic universities. It was shown that neither the prevailing scientific methodology in social sciences nor secular theories of knowledge are appropriate for Islamic universities.[24]

THE ISLAMIC WORLDVIEW OF *TAWHID*

As the affirmation of the absolute unity of God, *tawhid* is the affirmation of the unity of truth. For God, in Islam, is the truth, His unity is the unity of the sources of truth. God is the creator of nature whence man derives his knowledge. The objects of knowledge are the patterns of nature which are the work of God. Certainly God knows them since He is the author, and equally certainly He is the source of revelation. He gives man of His knowledge, and His knowledge is absolute and universal. God is perfect and omniscient. He makes no mistakes. Otherwise, He would not be the transcendental God of Islam.[25]

The Islamic worldview as stated by Mutahhari is religious, philosophical and rational. It is a worldview of *tawhid* or monism. This worldview regards God as the absolute reality and the source of being. *Tawhid* is the essence of Islam, it is the act of affirming God as the One, absolute, eternal and transcendental creator. Since *tawhid* is the essence of Islam, it will be discussed in detail.

Tawhid is discussed by Muslim scholars on two levels: theoretical and practical. From a theoretical point of view, Muslim scholars believe in God as the One and Absolute being and the only source of truth and knowledge. According to Ibn Sina, because an actual infinite is deemed impossible,

> this chain [of being] as a whole must terminate in a being that is holy, simple and one, whose essence is its very existence, and therefore, is self-sufficient and not in need of something else to give it existence. Because its existence is not contingent on or necessitated by something else but is necessary and eternal in itself, it satisfies the condition of being the necessitating cause of the entire chain that constitutes the eternal world of contingent existing things.[26]

From a practical point of view however, Muslims are obliged to follow the

---

[23] I. Al-Faruqi, in *The Cultural Atlas of Islam* (New York: MacMillan, 1986), p. xii, regards the phenomenological method, which requires that the observer let the phenomena speak for themselves rather than force them into any predetermined ideational framework, as an alternative to scientific methods of inquiry for studying problems holistically.

[24] It should be noted that some western scholars share the same worldview as Muslim scholars.

[25] Al Faruqi, *The Cultural Atlas of Islam*, 1986, p. 79.

[26] M. Mahdi, "The New Wisdom: Synthesis of Philosophy and Mysticism", in *Encyclopedia Britannica* (1987), p. 27.

dialectical path of *tawhid* not only as the essence of their belief, but also to bring unity and harmony to their life and thoughts through *tawhid*. Since reality according to Islam is of two generic kinds: absolute and relative, spiritual and material, worldly and other worldly, stable and mutable, eternal and temporary – Muslims use the concept of the dialectic of *tawhid* to unify these apparently contradictory concepts. From an Islamic standpoint, these concepts are complementary. Thus, Muslims do not believe in either-or schools of thought. Realities are two-fold of which a simple and self-evident example is humankind. Human beings have body, mind, and soul. To be able to function properly, one aspect should not be developed at the expense of the other. The duty of humankind is to maintain the balance so that each part complements the other instead of each part being in conflict and fighting against the other.

By adopting and practicing *tawhid* as a worldview, Muslims are trained to be one whole integrated self, with the ultimate aim of reaching the highest level of perfection through the struggle for ideal knowledge and action. *Tawhid* and the concept of unity saves humankind from a continuous struggle against ideals and from having a split society and a split personality that thinks, speaks, and acts in a contradictory way.

The concept of unity should not stop at the individual level but also be extended to society. Community life and family structures are the foundations of Islamic societies. If the dialectic of *tawhid* and unity underlies the relationships in these communities, people with different philosophies in life learn, not necessarily how to bring their differences together and homogenize the society, but rather, how to be tolerant and accept each other's differences. It is a "dialectic of love", the thesis and anti-thesis struggle not against each other but for the "other", leading individuals, masses, classes, nations, and civilizations to higher levels of achievement. [27] Ultimately, the dialectic which is embedded in *tawhid* elevates human beings from the material to the spiritual life through knowledge and action.

Tawhid is a divine policy for free thinking which gives the opportunity for everyone to express their opinions. However, this expression of opinion must be based on investigation into truth and knowledge. Free speech and free choice of philosophy is rooted in knowledge and actual realization of facts, not in public opinion nor in the distorted images purveyed by a politically motivated media.

The challenge for Muslims is, on the one hand, to believe in the oneness of God, the Active Intellect. Among all contradictory phenomena, He is the only source of being and His knowledge is all encompassing. On the other hand, Muslims are challenged to live in a unifying and harmonious way amongst all controversies and contradictory phenomena, and to be able to realize the ideal and the truth, and to strive for that truth and knowledge of the self and the universe which is manifested in doing good deeds to serve society and humankind in general. It is by adopting the Islamic worldview of *tawhid* that Muslims can attain this level of perfection.

---

[27] M. Sharif, *A History of Muslim Philosophy* (Wiesbaden, Germany: Otto Harrassowitz, 1963), p. 11.

AN ISLAMIC PARADIGM

An Islamic paradigm that is holistic, comprehensive and integrated and that can encompass the wholeness of Islamic thought is necessary for Islamic universities and for the production of Islamic knowledge. One of the objectives of this chapter is to establish the foundation for grounded theories in the Islamic university. Thus, defining and establishing the underlying principles of an Islamic paradigm provides the cornerstone for developing Islamic theories.

Grounded theories at universities in Islamic countries should be based on an Islamic paradigm and an Islamic methodology to produce theories related to Muslim societies. In turn, theories based on the Islamic paradigm will have the capacity to encompass the wholeness of human beings as well as the wholeness of society and life in general. This will help to overcome the fragmentation and polarization of individuals and society, which is the task of holistic, integrated knowledge. Therefore, an Islamic paradigm includes Islamic spiritual psychology, epistemology, ontology, eschatology, methodology, and sociology. The common theme in all these areas is the dialectic of *tawhid* or the concept of oneness. The Islamic paradigm can be defined as a holistic, integrated paradigm. On the one hand, it is divine, spiritual, religious, eternal, constant, absolute and ideal. On the other hand, it is human, material, rational, temporary, mutable, and relative. These two opposites are intimately interwoven by the dialectic of *tawhid*.

ISLAMIC ONTOLOGY AND METAPHYSICS: UNITY OF COSMOS AND NATURAL ORDER

The first principle in the Islamic paradigm is the realization of the unity of the universe and metaphysics, and its connection with Islamic epistemology and Islamic psychology. Reflection on the cosmos and the natural order illuminates the spiritual facets of the relationship between people and the world around them. The Qur'an invites people to reflect on the signs in nature as well as on the signs within themselves, to realize the underlying unity between these interrelated orders of reality. The emphasis, in terms of spiritual development, is on the illumination of the inward signs:

> Islamic spirituality is therefore based not only upon the reading of the written Qur'an (*all-Qur'an al-tadwini*) but also upon deciphering the text of the cosmic Qur'an (*al-Qur'an al-takwini*) which is its complement. Nature in Islamic spirituality is, consequently, not the adversary but the friend of the traveller upon the spiritual path and an aid to the person of spiritual vision in his journey through his forms to the world of the Spirit, which is the origin of both man and Cosmos. [28]

---

[28] S. H. Nasr (ed.), *Islamic Spirituality* (New York: Crossroad, 1987), p. 345.

This conception of nature finds its appropriate place in the overall context of Islamic cosmology, which acts as a bridge connecting pure metaphysics with the branches of science that deal with the physical world. The study of nature therefore can reveal an aspect of Divine wisdom provided that such study does not divorce the world from its Divine principle. Thus, an Islamic holistic curriculum built on this conception of nature is able to plant, in the learner's mind, the seeds of the oneness and unity of the Divine Principle. Relating the secrets of the soul to the unity of God's knowledge and the signs in the cosmic order, connects students to the concept of *tawhid* and hence to realizing the Divine wisdom and the significance of life and death. Realization of the relationship between the microcosm (human being) and macrocosm (universe) is developed as a major principle in the Islamic paradigm.

ISLAMIC ESCHATOLOGY: UNITY OF LIFE

A major principle in the Islamic paradigm is realization of the final destination. The concept of the Hereafter is one of the most fundamental and basic themes of the Qur'an, and one of the pillars of Islam. The Hereafter is important in Islamic holistic education because it enhances the spirituality of learners by directing their attention to the other-world. In addition, by presenting the themes of the Hereafter and the Here-and-Now at the same time, students will be able to see the importance of both this world and the other world. This will help students to develop their dialectical thinking and to keep the balance between the two opposing ideas.

The theme of the Hereafter provides Muslims with the concept of the last destination in the journey of life. It presents the totality and the vision in the journey of perfection and search for unity. The theme of the Hereafter inculcates spirituality in Muslims' actions throughout their life, if they follow the words of God. More importantly, the difference of this world and the other world develops in students dialectical thinking and the dialectic of *tawhid*. Ultimately, the soul and the mind of Muslim students reach a state of equilibrium and contentment which is considered a stage of perfection:

> In the Islamic view, the human perfection realized when the soul attains to the stage of peace with God means that the will of the individual is totally integrated into the Divine will. Every command and prohibition of God becomes the natural tendency of the soul. Through the full actualization of the intellect, the human being is able to see all things in their proper places and act accordingly. Duality and dispersion, the result of following the soul's descending tendency, are left behind.[29]

---

[29] S. Murata, "Masculine-Feminine Complementary in the Spiritual Psychology of Islam", in *The Islamic Quarterly*, Vol. 33 No. 3, 1989, p. 182.

ISLAMIC SOCIOLOGY: UNITY OF THE COMMUNITY

Another principle in an Islamic paradigm is related to the community and society in general. The development of human beings in Islam is not only emphasized because it leads to the perfection of individuals, but also because it leads to the perfection of society, so as to fulfil collectively the Divine Will for perfection. Islam realizes the importance of collective action for fulfilment of any task. It is not only a religion that teaches about spirituality and purification of the soul, it is also a complete social system whose laws are stated in the Sacred Text. Thus, the intimate relationship between the individual and society is another level of the wholeness of Islam and of the mutual effect the society and the individual can have on each other:

> The social order is the heart of the society, and stands prior to the personal. Indeed, Islam views the personal as a necessary prerequisite for the societal, and regards human character as warped if it rested with the personal and did not transcend it to the societal.[30]

ISLAMIC EPISTEMOLOGY: UNITY OF KNOWLEDGE

The main concern of epistemology is with theories of knowledge. Theories of knowledge in the golden ages of Islamic civilization were derived from the Qur'an. Since the main concern of this study is to establish the foundation for grounded theories for universities in Islamic societies, this section sheds some light on the source of Islamic epistemology.

It is important at this stage for the reader to realize that the Islamic worldview is not a purely religious one. The uniqueness of Islam is in the profound and challenging belief in both the secular world and the religious world. The knowledge and action that Muslims spend their entire life cultivating is to take them higher up the ladder of humanity and perfection and to bring them closer to God and therefore to eternal life.

Islamic epistemology is deeply rooted in religion. Therefore, any attempt to introduce a theory of knowledge for Islamic societies which does not take into account religion and spirituality side by side with the scientific and rational will be one dimensional and will not fulfil the needs of Muslim students. However, Islam is not strictly a religion, it is a complete way of life. Human beings, from an Islamic point of view, possess body, mind, and soul. Islamic epistemology therefore, takes into account this fact and builds its theories on it. A purely materialistic and rationalistic epistemology which takes only mind and matter into account and which draws its experience through the senses is not suitable for Muslims because it does not address an important part of their beings – their soul – and does not teach them to know how

---

[30] Al Faruqi, *Tawhid: Its Relevance for Thought and Life* (Malaysia: Polygraphic Press, 1983), p. 99.

to deal with it. An idealistic epistemology, which considers only a person's soul and inner being and the person's relation to her or himself, will not suit Muslims either, because it will neglect their body and the materialistic aspect of life. Thus, neither the pure materialistic nor the pure idealistic epistemology is appropriate for the Muslim world. An Islamic epistemology is required to fulfil the needs of both the religious and secular aspect of life.

Besides the real world we live in, there is an ideal or "unseen world" which, according to Islam, is the world that we strive for. The belief in the unseen is essential to Islamic faith. God, His Angels, the Day of Judgement, and the Hereafter are all "unseen". It is the duty of Muslims to believe in them, not blindly, but through search and reflection on God's creation, and through being guided by the Sacred Text. It is a "commonplace" methodology, starting from the concrete reaching to the abstract; starting from the known to discovering the unknown. The unseen world is considered to be a challenge for Muslims to move from the concrete to the abstract – the highest stage of adult development. The goal of Muslims is to try to reach that ideal through knowledge of self, the universe, and God, and through good deeds.

Ibn Sina (Avicenna), the 10th century Muslim philosopher, in his theory of knowledge "distinguishes between a 'potential intellect' in man and an 'active intellect' outside man, through the influence and guidance of which the former develops and matures".[31] Thus, the 'potential intellect' in human beings tries to understand, analyze and rationalize, while the 'active intellect', God, sheds some light on human beings' intellect to help them to understand and to find answers to their questions.

Sharif explained Ibn Sina's epistemology as follows: ". . . the universal cannot emerge from the images of sense because it does not lie there . . . the essence is not really a universal; it only behaves as such when it is in our minds.[32] Besides, no amount of particular instances would suffice to produce the universal essence which is applicable to infinite instances. Ibn Sina, therefore, declares that the task of our minds is to consider and reflect upon the particulars of sense experience. This activity prepares the mind for the reception of the (universal) essence from the active intellect by an act of direct intuition. The perception of the universal form, then, is a unique movement of "the intellective soul", not reducible to our perceiving the particulars either singly or totally and finding the common essence among them; if this were so, it would be only a spurious kind of universal.[33]

Moreover, the origin of knowledge is mysterious and involves intuition at every stage. Of all intellectual knowledge, more or less, it is not so much true to say "I know it" as to admit "It occurs to me". All seeking for knowledge, according to Ibn Sina, has this prayer-like quality: the effort is necessary on the part of man; the response is the act of God as the active intellect. We are, indeed, often not aware as to what it is we want to know, let alone go ahead and "know it". A theory of knowledge

---

[31] M. Sharif, *A History of Muslim Philosophy*, 1963, p. 495.
[32] *Ibid.*
[33] *Ibid.*, p. 496.

which fails to notice this fundamental truth is not only wrong but blasphemous.[34]

During the period when Islamic civilization flourished and produced great scholars, knowledge flowed in all disciplines due to consistency between the Islamic worldview, philosophy, and epistemology. This consistency, the source of which was the Qur'an, was reflected in Islamic education by its ability to accommodate both the religious and secular needs of people. Not surprisingly, a review of the Islamic worldview and epistemology shows clearly the inconsistency and lack of harmony and disconnectedness in Islamic societies with the importation of the Western, secular higher education system.

The second principle in an Islamic paradigm deals with the unity of knowledge. Unity of the self and awareness of the self leads to the realization of the unity of God's knowledge. A holistic education should lead its followers through observation and reflection on nature to apprehend the unity that connects God's creation. A holistic education integrates and unites the spiritual and the physical. Spirituality in Islam never opposes the use of matter,

> Rather, it always makes use of the formal, which it interiorizes. Also, the spiritual cannot be simply equated with the esoteric as opposed to the exoteric. Although the spiritual is more closely related to the esoteric dimension (al-batin) of Islam than to any other aspect of the religion, it is also very much concerned with the exoteric acts and the Divine Law as well as theology, philosophy, the arts and sciences created by Islam and its civilization. But its concern with the exoteric is always a journey from the outward to the abode of inwards.[35]

Thus, a holistic curricula should be established on the Quranic foundation that integrates physical, scientific, and religious or spiritual knowledge. The theory of knowledge of Ibn Sina and Al Ghazali is built on a Quranic foundation. Both scholars recognize knowledge as both temporal and perennial but acknowledge that perennial knowledge is the goal Muslims should strive for. Ibn Sina defined the aims of theoretical philosophy as the perfecting of the soul through knowledge, such as "the occurrence of positive belief of things", whereas the aims of practical philosophy are defined not only as the perfecting of the soul through knowledge, but also in accordance with requirements of that knowledge. Therefore, the aim of theoretical philosophy is truth, whereas the aim of practical philosophy is goodness.

Ibn Sina divided theoretical philosophy into three kinds of sciences according to the degree of their involvement with matter and motion and their independence of them. These sciences are (1) natural sciences, which he called the lowest sciences, (2) mathematical sciences, which he called the middle sciences, and (3) theological or metaphysical sciences, which he called the highest sciences, that is according to their abstraction and independence from matter. Ibn Sina also divided practical philosophy into three branches of knowledge: (1) ethics (akhlaq) which is concerned with the

---

[34] Ibid.

[35] S.H. Nasr (ed.), Islamic Spirituality, 1987, p. xviii.

management of human behaviour as an individual or the purity of oneself, (2) household management (*'ilm tadbir al-manzil*) or the pragmatics of man as a member of a family, which is concerned with the relation of a man to his wife, his children and his maids, as well as the management of livelihood and family income, and (3) public management (*ilm tadbir al madinah*) or the pragmatics of man as a member of a community, which is concerned with the politics of a city, a state as well as a community of states. After having made this division Ibn Sina remarked that "All these can only be implemented as a whole with critical thinking and the guidance of the *Shari'ah* [Islamic Law] and, in details, with the guidance of God's *Shari'ah*".[36]

What characterizes classic Muslim philosophers is their diverse knowledge in various disciplines and, at the same time, their ability to unify this diversity and to realize the unity of God's knowledge. It is spirituality and the dialectical concept of *tawhid* – the essence of Islam – that creates wholeness and unity in self and in knowledge. Therefore, Islamic epistemology, as outlined above, should be the guideline for holistic curricula in schools and universities.

ISLAMIC SPIRITUAL PSYCHOLOGY: UNITY OF THE SELF

A stable holistic system is possible only when built on the firm psychological nature of the human being. According to the Islamic school of thought, individuals are God's representatives on earth and have the potential for existing on a higher plane than that of "angels":

> Islam sees man as the viceregency of God on earth and the projection, as it were, of the vertical dimension and the horizontal plane. Gifted with intelligence in the true sense of the term, he alone of all creatures is capable of knowing the reality of which he himself is manifestation and, in the light of this knowledge, of rising above his own earthly and contingent self-hood.
>
> Gifted with the power of speech, he alone stands before God as His valid interlocutor. Through Revelation as also through inspiration God speaks to His creation, through prayer as also through an awareness which is a silent form of communication man speaks to God and does so on behalf of the inarticulate creation that surrounds him. He is, potentially if not actually, higher than the angels, for his nature reflects totality and can be satisfied with nothing less than the total. It is a synthesis from which no element, from the highest to the lowest, is excluded, and it is a mirror in which are reflected the Names and Attributes of the God before whom he stands upright, now and forever.[37]

Therefore, because of the position granted to the human being in Islam, any

---

[36] H. Langgulung, "Ibn Sina as an Educationist", in *The Islamic Quarterly*, Vol. 32, No. 2, 1988, p. 120.
[37] C. Eaton, "Man", in S. H. Nasr (ed.), *Islamic Spirituality*, 1987, p. 358.

education system in Islamic countries should first acknowledge and develop an integrated human being. The education system should address its Muslim learner as a whole person who possesses body, mind, and soul. The purpose of developing an integrated and whole person is to prepare one's faculties to realize the wholeness of life and hence the unity of the Divine Principle.

THE ISLAMIC METHODOLOGY OF *TAWHID*: THE ULTIMATE UNITY

The fourth principle in the Islamic paradigm is the fostering of the concept of *tawhid*. According to Islamic thought, an eternal Divine Principle of Unity pervades and rules all things. It is expressed in the metaphysical world of the Hereafter and the Day of Judgement, in the external world of the cosmos and nature, and in the inner world of mind and spirit. Underlying this universal order of things is a living unity which is all-pervading and everlasting. Everything has a purpose, which is the realization of the essence of the Divine nature developing within so as to prepare the soul for receiving the Divine Truth. To be able to realize and reveal the essence of one's being and of existence in general, Islam points its follower to the path for realizing the essence of life. *Tawhid* is the path that reveals the unity of God. It is through the dialectic of *tawhid* that Muslims accept contradictions in their being, in nature, and in the universe around them. It is the concept of *tawhid* that keeps the balance among diverse multiplicities and contradictions. Ultimately, it is *tawhid* that gives Islam its spirituality by reminding its followers of the ultimate goal of this life:

> The spirit manifests itself in every religion where the echoes of the Divine world are still available, but the manner in which the manifestations of the spirit take place differs from one religion to another. In Islam, the spirit breathes through all that reveals the One and leads to the One, for Islam's ultimate purpose is to reveal the Unity of the Divine Principle and to integrate the world of multiplicity in the light of that Unity. Spirituality in Islam is inseparable from the awareness of the One, of Allah, and a life lived according to His Will.

> The Principle of Unity (*al-tawhid*) lies at the heart of the Islamic messages and determines Islamic spirituality in all its multifarious dimensions and forms. Spirituality is *tawhid* and the degree of spiritual attainment achieved by any human being is none other than the degree of his or her realization of *tawhid*. For the Word manifested Itself in what came to be the Islamic universe in order to declare the glory of the One and to lead human beings to the realization of the One.[38]

Therefore, rooting the holistic curricula in the concept of *tawhid* and using it as a method of inquiry will develop students' dialectical thinking. From an educational

---

[38] S.H. Nasr (ed.), *Islamic Spirituality*, 1987, p. xv.

point of view this mode of inquiry enhances students' critical thinking.

In brief, the Islamic paradigm proposed here is all-encompassing, developmental, purposeful, and integrated. It is based on the Quranic school of thought and derives its principles from the Sacred Text. Thus, all the principles of the Islamic paradigm lead to the realization of the Unity of the Divine Principle. Islamic ontology and metaphysics address the wholeness of the cosmos and the natural order. It deals with nature and universal laws, scientifically and spiritually. Moreover, Islamic eschatology deals with issues of the Hereafter and the Here-and-Now. This leads individuals to think of both worlds, but also to remember that this world is the means to be cultivated for the end, which is the Hereafter. In addition, Islamic sociology deals with social and community issues in which it is considered the duty of each individual to participate in, to develop and to improve societal life. More importantly, individuals are responsible for maintaining the unity of the society. Because Islamic epistemology is holistic, it addresses both the secular and the scientific as well as the religious and spiritual aspects of knowledge. Spiritual psychology integrates body, mind, and soul as one unified whole. Furthermore, the Islamic methodology of *tawhid* helps Muslims to understand the controversial issues involved in life and in education and enhances dialectical and critical thinking which is considered to be the highest stage of adult development. Therefore, through an Islamic holistic education, it is hoped that Muslims can reunite inwardly and outwardly.

CONCLUSION

This study was stimulated by concerns for the appropriateness of knowledge created through conventional and emergent paradigms in Western universities and transferred to other cultures and other universities under the name of modernization and development. The mismatch between Eastern, Islamic traditional society and Western, secular knowledge transferred through educational programs creates conflict between the two.

It is suggested that knowledge transferred from the West through university programs be re-evaluated and reconstructed in the light of the principles of an Islamic paradigm. This paradigm aims at a holistic integrated development of the individual – body, mind, and soul. It aims at a comprehensive development of society as a whole. Both the individual and society should evolve and rise above the material level to higher spheres of spirituality.

4

First Nations and Higher Education:
The Four R's – Respect, Relevance,
Reciprocity, Responsibility[1]

Verna J. Kirkness
Ray Barnhardt

INTRODUCTION

American Indian/ First Nations/ Native people [2] have been historically under-represented in the ranks of college and university graduates in Canada and the United States. From an institutional perspective, the problem has been typically defined in terms of low achievement, high attrition, poor retention, weak persistence, etc., thus placing the onus for adjustment on the student. From the perspective of the Indian student, however, the problem is often cast in more human terms, with an emphasis on the need for a higher educational system that *respects* them for who they are, that is *relevant* to their view of the world, that offers *reciprocity* in their relationships with others, and that helps them exercise *responsibility* over their own lives. This paper examines the implications of these differences in perspective and identifies ways in which initiatives within and outside of existing institutions are transforming the landscape of higher education for First Nations/American Indian people in both Canada and the United States.

There is a story of a tribe of people in Indonesia that has an ingenious method for capturing monkeys alive. They cut a hole in a hollowed out coconut shell, just large enough for a monkey to stick its hand through. They then place a peanut inside and attach the shell to a tree. The monkey reaches through the hole in the shell to grab the peanut, but then is unable to withdraw its fist without letting go, and in this state of

[1] This article first appeared in *Journal of American Indian Education*, Vol. 30, No. 3, May 1991, pp. 1-15. We would like to thank Dr. Karen Swisher, Editor of the journal, for giving us permission to re-publish it. We also note that it has been revised and updated for this 2001 version of the volume.

[2] There have been a number of generic terms adopted in Canada to refer to the indigenous people of this land. The article uses Indian, First Nations, Native or Aboriginal depending on the period in which the term was popular. In the United States, the terms American Indian, Alaska Native and Native American are used to distinguish between Indian populations in the contiguous states and the Eskimo, Indian and Aleut people of Alaska, or all people of Native descent.

single-minded obsession with the peanut is readily captured and sold to the zoo trade.

At first glance, we as human beings may identify ourselves with the tribal people in this story and view it as just another example of the successful application of human ingenuity to the solution of an everyday problem. However, if we take a closer look, we may also see a reflection of ourselves in the predicament of the monkey. We needn't look far to find examples of situations in which we as humans, individually and collectively, have become so captivated by habitual behaviour as to be unable or unwilling to make timely adaptations in the interest of our future well-being. Consider, for example, the efforts to entrench English-only (or French-only) language policies in an attempt to impose unilingualism on an increasingly multicultural society, or the various resource extraction policies and practices that we adhere to while depleting limited resources with little consideration for the needs of future generations. These are but two examples of where we, like the monkey, attempt to ignore the consequences of our infatuation with the status quo. In this paper we will examine the extent to which similar head-in-the-sand, hand-in-the-coconut myopia is evident in the policies and practices of universities in Canada and the United States with regard to the educational opportunities for First Nations (Native/Indian/Indigenous/ Aboriginal) students. While universities generally have adopted the political rhetoric of "equal educational opportunity for all", many of the institutional efforts to convert such rhetoric into reality for First Nations people continue to fall short of expectations. Why is this so?

If we are to address this perennial issue in a serious manner, we have to ask ourselves some hard questions:

*   Why do universities continue to perpetuate policies and practices that historically have produced abysmal results for First Nations students, when we have ample research and documentary evidence to indicate the availability of more appropriate and effective alternatives?

*   Why are universities so impervious to the existence of *de facto* forms of institutionalized discrimination that they are unable to recognize the threat that some of their accustomed practices pose to their own existence?

*   What are some of the obstacles that must be overcome if universities are to improve the levels of participation and completion of First Nations students?

There are no simple or single answers to these very complex questions, but those of us who are associated with universities in one form or another must continue to seek effective solutions, and along the way we must be prepared to set aside some of our most cherished beliefs and free ourselves to consider appropriate alternatives. Let us take a look as some of the issues we are likely to encounter in this quest, and some of the policy and practice options we may need to consider along the way.

COMING TO THE UNIVERSITY VS. GOING TO THE UNIVERSITY

First, let us take a look at what attending the university can mean from a couple of different perspectives, one coming (the institution's perspective of the student) and the other going (the student's perspective of the institution). From the vantage point of the university, students are generally viewed as "coming" to partake of what the university has to offer. From this perspective, it is presumed that the university is an established institution with its own long-standing, deeply-rooted policies, practices, programs and standards intended to serve the needs of the society in which it is imbedded. Students who come to the university are expected to adapt to its *modus operandi* if they wish to obtain the benefits (usually translated to mean better, higher paying jobs) of the knowledge and skills it has to offer, the desirability and value of which are presumed to be self-evident. From this point of view, when particular clusters of students, such as those from First Nations backgrounds, do not readily adapt to conventional institutional norms and expectations and do not achieve levels of "success" comparable to other students, the typical response is to focus on the aberrant students and to intensify efforts at socializing them into the institutional milieu. The lack-of-performance issues in such circumstances tend to be defined by the university in terms such as "low achievement", "high attrition", "poor retention", "weak persistence", etc., thus placing the onus for accommodation on the students and fortifying the entrenched nature of the university as an institution.

The institutional response, when faced with these internally-constructed and externally reinforced problems of inadequate achievement and retention, is usually to intensify the pressure on First Nations students to adapt and become integrated into the institution's social fabric, with the ultimate goal that they will be "retained" until they graduate. Typical solutions that emanate from this "blame-the-victim" perspective are special counselling and advising centres, "bridging" and "developmental" programs, tutorials, and an array of additional student support services, all of which are intended to help problem students successfully partake of what the university has to offer. To the extent that students are willing and able to check their own cultural predispositions at the university's gate, these kinds of initiatives can and do assist them in making the transition to the culture of the institution, but such intensification efforts alone do not appear to produce the desired results of full and equal participation of First Nations people in higher education. Even with the many well-intentioned support services that have been proliferating for two decades in institutions across Canada and the U.S., the overall "attrition" and "retention" rates of First Nations students remain near the bottom of all university students in both countries. The statistics speak for themselves:

- In Canada in 1986, only 1.3% of the First Nations population had completed a university degree, compared to 9.6% of the general population. In other words, non-Indians were 7.4 times more likely to have successfully completed a degree program than First Nations people.[3] While initial enrolment of First Nations, American Indian and Alaska Native students increased significantly in the 1990s, their graduation rate has lagged behind that of the general population by up to fifty percent.[4]

• In the U.S. in 1984, less than 60% of the American Indian students completed high school, and approximately one-third of these went on to college, but only 15% of those who went on to college completed a four-year degree, for an overall average college graduation rate of 3%, compared to 16% for the general population.[5] Of the American Indian students entering university in the mid-1990s, only 24% had completed a pre-college curriculum compared with 56% of all college-bound graduates.[6]

• In 1986, only 25% of the First Nations population in Canada completed high school compared to half of the non-Indian population, and of those, only 23% went on to the university, compared to 33% of the rest of the population. Of those First Nations students who commenced university studies, 25% earned a degree, compared to 55% of non-Indians.[7]

• In 1986, only seven four-year institutions in the U.S. had 500 or more American Indian students enrolled, and most of these were tribally-controlled colleges located on reservations.[8]

• The largest increases in funding, enrolments and college completion for First Nations, American Indians and Alaska Native students are occurring in Tribal Colleges in the U.S.[9], and Aboriginal-run institutions in Canada.[10]

• Only 5% of American Indian and Alaska Native college students maintained a 3.5 grade point average, compared to 19% for the general population.[11]

• Native American students are more likely to drop out of college for non-academic reasons than for academic deficiencies.[12]

---

[3] R. Armstrong, J. Kennedy & P.R. Oberle, *University Education and Economic Well-Being: Indian Achievement and Prospectus* (Ottawa: Indian and Northern Affairs Canada, 1990).

[4] D.M. Pavel, R.R. Skinner, E. Farris, M. Calahan, J. Tippiconnic and W. Stein, *American Indians and Alaska Natives in Postsecondary Education* (Washington D.C.: National Center for Education Statistics, 1998). D.J. Carter and R. Wilson, *Minorities in Higher Education 1996-97: Fifteenth Annual Status Report* (Washington D.C.: American Council on Education, 1997).

[5] W. Tierney, *Official Encouragement, Institutional Discouragement: Minorities in Academy – The Native American Experience* (Norwood, N.J.: Ablex Publishing Corp., 1992). J. Fries, *The American Indian in Higher Education, 1975-76 to 1984-85* (Washington D.C.: Office of Educational Research and Improvement, U.S. Department of Education, 1987).

[6] D.M. Pavel et al, *American Indians and Alaska Natives in Postsecondary Education*, 1998.

[7] R. Armstrong et al, *University Education and Economic Well-Being: Indian Achievement and Prospectus*, 1990.

[8] W. Tierney, *Official Encouragement, Institutional Discouragement: Minorities in Academy – The Native American Experience*, 1992.

[9] American Indian Higher Education Consortium, *Tribal Colleges: An Introduction* (Washington D.C.: Institute for Higher Education Policy, 2000).

[10] *Postsecondary Education for Status Indians and Inuit* (Ottawa, Ontario: Indian and Northern Affairs Canada, 2000).

[11] D.M. Pavel et als, *American Indians and Alaska Natives in Postsecondary Education*, 1998.

[12] W. Tierney, *Official Encouragement, Institutional Discouragement: Minorities in Academy – The*

It is clear that despite the many efforts to improve First Nations' participation in higher education, U.S. and Canadian mainstream universities, by and large, do not yet provide a hospitable environment that attracts and holds First nations students at a satisfactory rate. University policies and programs aimed at decreasing First Nations student attrition are typically oriented toward helping the students make the transition from their home culture to the culture of the university.[13] In a study of the college experiences of American Indian students in the U.S.: Tierney identified five implicit "axioms" or assumptions held by universities, that serve as the basis for most of their efforts to integrate the students into the ways of the institution:

* Post-secondary institutions are ritualized situations that symbolize movement from one stage of life to another.
* The movement from one stage of life to another necessitates leaving a previous state and moving into another.
* Success in post-secondary education demands that the individual becomes successfully integrated into the new society's mores.
* A post-secondary institution serves to synthesize, reproduce, and integrate its members toward similar goals.
* A post-secondary institution must develop effective and efficient policies to ensure that the initiates will become academically and socially integrated.

However, from the perspective of the American Indian students Tierney interviewed, who had their own distinctive reasons for "going to the university", social integration into the culture of the university was not what they had in mind, at least not if it was going to be at the expense of the culture they brought with them. He quotes one student who had dropped out in his first attempt at college after two semesters, and then returned to the local community college ten years later with a different cultural perspective:

> I think white people think education is good, but Indian people often have a different view. I know what you're going to say – that education provides jobs and skills. It's true. That's why I'm here. But a lot of these kids, their parents, they see education as something that draws students away from who they are... I would like to tell them (at the university) that education shouldn't try and make me into something I'm not. That's what I learned when I wasn't here – who I am. And when I learned that, then I could come back here. I sort of walked away for a while and then came back. It's one

Native American Experience, 1992. J. Reyhner and J. Dodd, "Factors affecting the Retention of American Indian and Alaska Native Students in Higher Education" (paper presented at the Expanding Minority Opportunities: First Annual National Conference) (Tempe, Arizona: Arizona State University, 1995).

[13] J. Beaty & K.B. Chiste, "University Preparation for Native American Students: Theory and Application", in *Journal of American Indian Education*, Vol. 26, No. 1, 1986, pp. 6-13. R. Pottinger, "Disjunction to Higher Education: American Indian Students in the Southwest", in *Anthropology and Education Quarterly*, Vol. 20, No. 4, 1989, pp. 326-344.

of the best gifts I've ever had. But a lot of us just walk away. [14]

In these comments, we see the university from a perspective in which what it has to offer is useful only to the extent that it respects and builds upon the cultural integrity of the student. The university must be able to present itself in ways that have instrumental value to First Nations students; that is, the programs and services that are offered must connect with the students' own aspirations and cultural predispositions sufficiently to achieve a comfort level that will make the experience worth enduring. If we cannot create an environment in which First Nations students began to "feel at home" at the university, all the special programs and support services we can dream up will be of little value in attracting and holding them in significant numbers. We must recognize that attending the university is not an all-or-nothing proposition, and many students, such as the one quoted above, will move in and out of the university over a period of many years, depending on how well it suits their purposes.

While improved job opportunities alone may provide sufficient motivation to keep some students interested, in the case of many First Nations students, these "jobs" are often linked to aspirations with much broader collective/tribal considerations, such as exercising self-government, or bringing First Nations perspectives to bear in professional and policy-making arenas. The inadequacy of our understanding of, and attention to, these kinds of considerations was pointed out in a recent government report on "university education and economic well-being" for First Nations people in Canada, which concluded: "A greater understanding is needed about motivating factors if policy and programs are to be successful in their intent to increase participation and success at university". [15] Wendy Hull, chair of the Aboriginal Students' Association at Dalhousie University in Halifax, illustrates the point in her observation: "(University) education is not important to me in my life. But it is important when we start dealing with the government". [16] We need to recognize that there can be many reasons for pursuing a university education, reasons which often transcend the interest and well-being of the individual student. For First Nations communities and students, a university education can be seen as important for any of the following reasons:

*   It can be seen as a means of realizing equality and sharing in the opportunities of the larger society in which we live.
*   It can be seen as a means for collective social and economic mobility.
*   It can be seen as a means of overcoming dependency and "neo-colonialism".
*   It can be seen as a means of engaging in research to advance the knowledge

---

[14] W.G. Tierney, "The College Experience of Native Americans: A Critical Analysis," in L. Weis & M. Fine (eds.), *Silenced Voices: Class, Race and Gender in United States Schools* (Albany, NY: State University of New York Press, 1993), p. 311.

[15] R. Armstrong et al, *University Education and Economic Well-Being: Indian Achievement and Prospectus*, 1990, p. 19.

[16] J. Harrington, "Education System Forces Alien Values on Natives", in *The Ubyssey*, Vol. 73, No. 36, 1991, p. 4.

of First Nations.
* It can be seen as a means of providing the expertise and leadership needed by First Nations communities.
* It can be seen as a means to demystify mainstream culture and learn the politics and history of racial discrimination.

From the extra-institutional point of view of a First Nations student who is "going" to the university for any of these reasons, the problems they encounter along the way are not constructed as matters of attrition and retention, which make sense only from an internal institutional perspective. Rather, the issues are likely to be framed in more humanistic, culturally-sensitive terms, such as a desire for "respect", "relevance", "reciprocity", and "responsibility", and as such, reflect a larger purpose than simply obtaining a university degree to get a better job. First Nations students and communities are seeking an education that will also address their communal need for "capacity-building" to advance themselves as a distinct and self-determining society, not just as individuals. In this context, a "job" may be important, but more as a means to an end, than an end in itself.

In the effort to sustain their own cultural integrity, there is an urgent need for First Nations people to assume roles as teachers, doctors, lawyers, administrators, comptrollers, architects, historians, etc. This need is reflected in an observation by Chief Simon Baker, an elder from the Squamish Nation in British Columbia who has often pointed out that, "Having White lawyers running your band government is not First Nations self-government". These sentiments are echoed by Patricia Monture, a Mohawk and professor of law at Dalhousie Law School, who has pointed out that getting a university education is an indispensable, if often unpleasant step to attaining self-determination. She goes on to state, however, that "Canada is not making an effort to talk to us. We're the ones who have to do double-time and learn how to talk to them".[17] How then can the monolithic/ethnocentric institution of the university be reoriented to foster a more productive two-way exchange that increases its capacity to respond effectively to the higher education and human resource needs of First Nations students and communities? To begin to respond to that question, let us examine more closely the implications of the "Four R's" of respect, relevance, reciprocity and responsibility.

RESPECT OF FIRST NATIONS CULTURAL INTEGRITY

The most compelling problem that First Nations students face when they go to the university is a lack of respect, not just as individuals, but more fundamentally as a people. To them, the university represents an impersonal, intimidating and often hostile environment, in which little of what they bring in the way of cultural knowledge,

---

[17] J. Harrington, "Education System Forces Alien Values on Natives", in *The Ubyssey*, Vol. 73, No. 36, 1991, p. 4.

traditions and core values is recognized, much less respected. They are expected to leave the cultural predispositions from their world at the door and assume the trappings of a new form of reality, a reality which is often substantially different from their own.

The physical and social environment of a typical university campus is intended to protect faculty and students from "the real world", or put another way, it is a reality unto itself. It is a literate world in which only decontextualized literate knowledge counts, and that knowledge must be displayed in highly specialized literate forms. As an institution for perpetuating literate knowledge, the university has served us well. But there are other kinds of knowledge in the world and there are other ways of conveying knowledge than those embodied in the "Ivory Tower".

One variation of another kind of knowledge is that which has typically been associated with First Nations people, usually referred to in terms such as traditional knowledge, oral knowledge, indigenous knowledge, etc., depending on which literate tradition you draw upon.[18] While the manifestations can vary considerably from one group of people to another, some of the salient features of such knowledge are that its meaning, value and use are bound to the cultural context in which it is situated, it is thoroughly integrated into everyday life, and it is generally acquired through direct experience and participation in real-world activities. If considered in its totality, such knowledge can be seen to constitute a particular world view, a form of consciousness, or a reality set.

In an examination of contemporary values and lifestyle in the context of a northern Athabaskan community, Ron and Suzy Scollon[19] identified four aspects of what they described as a "Native reality set" (patterns of behaviour and ways of thinking) which they felt distinguished it from "modern consciousness", as articulated by Berger and others.[20] Native people who live in isolated northern communities, in Scollons' view, tend to favour a lifestyle that exhibits a high respect for individual self-reliance, non-intervention in other people's affairs, the integration of useful knowledge into a holistic and internally consistent world view, and a disdain for complex organizational structures. The Scollons go on to point out that these aspects of local consciousness create considerable interactional tension and conflict when Native people encounter the componentiality, specialization, systematicity, bureaucracy and literate forms characteristic of Western institutions and modern consciousness. The holistic integration and internal consistency of the Native world view is not easily reconciled with the compartmentalized world of bureaucratic institutions.

For the First Nations student coming to the university (an institution that is a virtual embodiment of modern consciousness), survival often requires the acquisition

---

[18] J. Goody, "Alternative Paths to Knowledge in Oral and Literate Cultures", in D. Tannen, (ed.), *Spoken and Written Language: Exploring Orality and Literacy* (Norwood, NJ: Ablex Publishing Corporation, 1982), p. 201.

[19] R. Scollon & S. Scollon, *Narrative Literacy and Face in Interethnic Communication* (Norwood, NJ: Ablex Publishing Corporation, 1981), p. 100.

[20] P. Berger, B. Berger & H. Kneller, *The Homeless Mind: Modernization and Consciousness* (New York: Random House, 1973).

and acceptance of a new form of consciousness that not only displaces, but often devalues their indigenous consciousness, and for many, this is a greater sacrifice than they are willing to make. If they enter and then withdraw before "completion", however, they are branded by the university as a "dropout" – a failure. Those who persevere and make the sacrifice can find themselves in the end, torn between two worlds, leading to a further struggle within themselves to reconcile the cultural and psychic conflicts arising from competing values and aspirations.

Some of the institutional implications of this struggle for recognition of competing realities were summarized by Scollon in a study of communication patterns and Native student retention at the University of Alaska Fairbanks:

> The problem of retention in an institution of higher education lies as much in the definition of the problem as in any other factor. Previous research has indicated that the problem of communication between modern bureaucratic institutions and members of non-Western cultural groups can be understood to a considerable extent as a problem in conflict of world view or reality set. More recent research has argued that this difference in reality set is associated with the predominant modes of communication, with the modern bureaucratic institutions showing a strong association with literacy. While the extent and power of Western bureaucratic institutions is well known, it is also well known that these institutions are highly unresponsive to their environments. Some researchers have referred to this unresponsiveness as an institutional incapacity to learn.[21]

Scollon went on to characterize the problem of high Native student attrition at the University as a conflict between "the institution's knowledge" and "human knowledge".

> The institution's knowledge characterizes the relationships between individual members or clients which are governed by institutional considerations. 'Human knowledge' characterizes the relationships between members or clients which are governed by human interpersonal considerations. By framing the problem as a problem of 'retention' the institution was incapable of perceiving the issue from the point of view of the affected population, Alaska Native students. It is recommended that what is required is not increasing the involvement of students in the institution, but on the contrary, increasing the domain of human knowledge of institutional members.[22]

Increasing the university's domain of human knowledge to include and respect First Nations cultural values and traditions is a formidable task, but it is a task

---

[21] R. Scollon, *Human Knowledge and the Institution's Knowledge: Communication Patterns and Retention in a Public University* (Center for Cross-Cultural Studies, University of Alaska Fairbanks, 1981), p. i.

[22] *Ibid.*

that we must begin if we are to make the institution more "user friendly" for First Nations students. What then can be done to begin to reduce the cultural distance and the role dichotomy between the producers and the consumers of knowledge in university settings?

RELEVANCE TO FIRST NATIONS PERSPECTIVES AND EXPERIENCE

If universities are to respect the cultural integrity of First Nations students and communities, they must adopt a posture that goes beyond the usual generation and conveyance of literate knowledge, to include the institutional legitimation of indigenous knowledge and skills, or as Goody has put it, to foster "a re-valuation of forms of knowledge that are not derived from books". [23] Such a responsibility requires an institutional respect for indigenous knowledge, as well as an ability to help students to appreciate and build upon their customary forms of consciousness and representation as they expand their understanding of the world in which they live.

The complexity of the task of incorporating a First Nations (oral) perspective in the everyday functioning of the (literate) university is exacerbated by the inherent problem of speaking of two reality sets in the idiom of only one of them. [24] Nevertheless, with the help of an emerging group of First Nations scholars, we are beginning to see the outlines of a more culturally accommodating view of how knowledge is constructed and passed on to others. One example of an attempt to reconcile differences in the ways knowledge is understood and conveyed is a contrastive study of orality and literacy by Jo-ann Archibald, a member of the Sto:lo Nation in British Columbia, in which she points to the need "to define and create new ways of thinking and writing about literacy and its relationship to orality".

> With the technological advances of video, television and film, our world has become a combined oral/literate/visual one. This combination has exciting possibilities for First Nations because it is nearing the traditional holistic approach to teaching and learning which is needed to heal our people who have been adversely affected by history. [25]

Eber Hampton, a Chickasaw originally from Oklahoma and now in Alaska, has made an effort to identify some of the qualities that he considers important in the move to construct an "Indian theory of education". [26] He lists the following as twelve "standards"on which to judge any such effort:

---

[23] J. Goody, "Alternative Paths to Knowledge in Oral and Literate Cultures", in D. Tannen, (ed.), *Spoken and Written Language: Exploring Orality and Literacy*, 1982, p. 201.

[24] R. Scollon, *Human Knowledge and the Institution's Knowledge*, 1981, p. 24.

[25] J. Archibald, "Coyote's Story About Orality and Literacy", in *Canadian Journal of Native Education*, Vol. 17, No. 2, 1990, p. 66.

[26] E. Hampton, "Toward a Redefinition of American Indian/Alaska Native Education" (Doctoral Dissertation. Harvard University, 1988), p. 19.

* Spirituality – an appreciation for spiritual relationships.
* Service – the purpose of education is to contribute to the people.
* Diversity – Indian education must meet the standards of diverse tribes and communities.
* Culture – the importance of culturally determined ways of thinking, communicating and living.
* Tradition – continuity with tradition.
* Respect – the relationship between the individual and the group recognized as mutually empowering.
* History – appreciation of the facts of Indian history, including the loss of the continent and continuing racial and political oppression.
* Relentlessness – commitment to the struggle for good schools for Indian children.
* Vitality – recognition of the strength of Indian people and culture.
* Conflict – understanding the dynamics and consequences of oppression.
* Place – the importance of sense of place, land and territory.
* Transformation – commitment to personal and societal change.

Such a list of qualities begins to offer universities (and schools) a set of standards against which to examine their policies and practices to see how respectful and relevant they really are to First Nations considerations. While Hampton's set of standards may differ from those against which the university is accustomed to being judged, it is in fact a more inclusive list of criteria whereby all students can find something with which to identify. To the extent universities are able to reconstruct themselves to be more relevant to, and accepting of First Nations students' perspectives and experiences, they will be that much more relevant and responsive to the needs of all students.

RECIPROCAL RELATIONSHIPS

One of the most frustrating aspects of the university experience for First Nation students is the role dichotomy between the producers and the consumers of knowledge in university settings. The conventional institutionalized roles of a university faculty member as the creator and dispenser of knowledge and expertise and the student as the passive recipient of that knowledge and expertise have a tendency to interfere with the establishment of the kinds of personalized "human" relationships to which First Nations students are most likely to respond. Scollon described the problem in Alaska as follows:

> Our research leads us to believe that the only way that modern institutions such as the University of Alaska can become responsive to their environments is to acknowledge and exploit the institutional/human interface that each member negotiates in each

institutional act. In the phrasing of the students, we must constantly "expose" ourselves to the human and non-institutional. In the phrasing of the faculty we must allow ourselves to become vulnerable. Institutional invulnerability is the mark of institutional unresponsiveness.[27]

In an effort to help Native students understand the nature of the institution in which they were situated and to learn how to successfully negotiate their way through it, Scollon developed an entry level course titled "Cultural Differences in Institutional Settings". The course, which continues to be one of the more popular for beginning Native students, is described in the 1990 University of Alaska Fairbanks catalog as follows:

> Introduction to the phenomena of culturally organized thought processes, with emphasis on the communication patterns resulting from the interaction of peoples from different linguistic/cultural traditions in modern institutional settings. Special attention is paid to Alaskan Native and non-Native communication patterns.

Another example of a course with a similar purpose but a different focus, is a course offered at the University of British Columbia titled, "Cross-Cultural Education (Native Indians)", described in the 1990-91 Calendar as follows:

> Instructional techniques for adapting teaching to the needs of Indian students; methods of enriching the curriculum by including the cultural background of all students; the course will include some examination of the anthropological, sociological and historical backgrounds of Native Indians with an emphasis on contemporary situations as these relate to teaching.

In both of these courses, the emphasis is on making teaching and learning two-way processes, in which the give-and-take between faculty and students opens up new levels of understanding for everyone. Such reciprocity is achieved when the faculty member makes an effort to understand and build upon the cultural background of the students, and the students are able to gain access to the inner-workings of the culture (and the institution) to which they are being introduced.

One of the few examples of situations in which university faculty members make a deliberate effort to be more accessible and "vulnerable" to accommodate First Nations students is in field-based programs in which faculty are physically located in outlying communities. The out-stationing of faculty has been an inherent feature of many of the Native/First Nations teacher education programs that have been established across Canada and the U.S. over the past twenty years. The effect of such a move on the role of faculty and students is reflected in the following account of the "field-coordinator" faculty position in the Cross-Cultural Education Development

---

[27] R. Scollon, *Human Knowledge and the Institution's Knowledge*, 1981, p. 18.

(X-CED) teacher education program situated in rural Alaska:

> The most effective faculty members in our field programs have been those who have been able to engage themselves and their students in a process of sense-making and skill-building through active participation in the world around them. They use books and pencil and paper as a means to add breadth and depth to the students' understanding, but not as the sole source of knowledge. They measure their students' achievement through the students' ability to effectively perform meaningful and contextually appropriate tasks. They engage the students in tasks that allow for the integration of various forms of knowledge and the application and display of that knowledge in a variety of ways. They jointly build knowledge from the ground up with their students through an inductive process that allows the students to develop their own emic perspective, at the same time using literate forms of knowledge to acquaint them with other perspectives. They experience with students, the ambiguity, unpredictability and complexity of the real world, and in the process, prepare students who are better equipped to find solutions to problems for which we may not yet even have a theory.[28]

Faculty members and students in such a reciprocal relationship are in a position to create a new kind of education, to formulate new paradigms or explanatory frameworks that help us establish a greater equilibrium and congruence between the literate view of the world and the reality we encounter when we step outside the walls of the "Ivory Tower". It is not necessary that all faculty leave the security of the university campus with its protective structure of academic disciplines and venture into the uncertainty of the world outside, but it is important that enough do so to provide a reality-check for the institution as a whole. Even those who do venture out, however, sometimes hesitate to make themselves vulnerable to any challenging of the efficacy of their authority and beliefs, and find ways to protect themselves behind a veneer of academic aloofness and obfuscation. For First Nations students and communities, such a posture is no longer acceptable.

RESPONSIBILITY THROUGH PARTICIPATION

In the context of a First Nations perspective of the university, higher education is not a neutral enterprise. Gaining access to the university means more than gaining an education – it also means gaining access to power, authority, and an opportunity to exercise control over the affairs of everyday life, affairs that are usually taken for granted by most non-Native people. For First Nations students, this is a matter of necessity, for in order to survive the formal curriculum, they must also learn to navigate through the alien power structure of the institution. In effect, they must engage in an

---

[28] R. Barnhardt, *Domestication of the Ivory Tower: Institutional Adaptation to Cultural Distance* (Fairbanks, AK: University of Alaska Fairbanks, 1986), p. 6.

educational strategy comparable to what Henry Giroux refers to as "border pedagogy":

> Students must engage knowledge as a border-crosser, as a person moving in and out of borders constructed around coordinates of difference and power. These are not only physical borders, they are cultural borders historically constructed and socially organized within maps of rules and regulations that limit and enable particular identities, individual capacities, and social forms. In this case, students cross over into borders of meaning, maps of knowledge, social relations, and values that are increasingly being negotiated and rewritten as the codes and regulations which organize them become destabilized and reshaped. [29]

For universities that are seriously committed to finding ways to create a more hospitable climate for First Nations students, the institutional implications of such border negotiations can be far-reaching. Tierney, building on Giroux's form of critical analysis, outlines what he sees as some of the steps that need to be considered:

> I am suggesting that organizations need to be constructed where minority students' lives are celebrated and affirmed throughout the culture of the institution. The point is not simply to have a Native American Studies Center or a course or two devoted to Native peoples. Minority students need institutions that create the conditions where the students not only celebrate their own histories but also are helped to examine critically how their lives are shaped and molded by society's forces. Such a theoretical suggestion has implications for virtually all areas of the organization – from how we organize student affairs, to the manner in which we construct knowledge, from the role of assessment, to the role of the college president.[30]

Clearly, such "theoretical suggestions" for comprehensive reform are not likely to spread like wildfire through college campuses, but that does not mean that systemic changes are not possible; in fact, they are already happening. The most promising sign on the horizon of First Nations people exercising responsibility and increasing participation in the arena of higher education is the burgeoning number of First Nations post-secondary/adult education initiatives, both within and outside existing institutions across the U.S. and Canada. Examples range from the 24 Tribal Colleges in the U.S. to the Saskatchewan Indian Federated College, the Nicola Valley Institute of Technology, the Secwepemc Cultural Education Society, the James Bay Education Centre, the Gabriel Dumont Institute, the First Nations House of Learning, and many other similar First Nations institutions across Canada, all of which are having a marked effect on the level of participation and success of First Nations students.[31]

---

[29] H. Giroux, "Border Pedagogy in the Age of Postmodernism", in *Journal of Education*, Vol. 170, No. 3, 1988, p. 169.

[30] W.G. Tierney, "The College Experience of Native Americans: A Critical Analysis", 1993, p. 322

[31] P. Boyer, *Tribal Colleges: Shaping the Future of Native America* (Princeton, NJ: The Carnegie

The structure and focus of each of these institutions vary greatly, with services aimed at clientele ranging from the local community to national levels, and with program emphases ranging from adult and vocational education to graduate level programs. Typical program offerings are in the areas of band/tribal/municipal self-government, rural/community/economic development, Native/ Indian/ Aboriginal law, land claims and natural resources management, Native teacher education, First Nations health and social services, Native language revitalization, First Nations performing and creative arts, and adult education/literacy development. Underlying all of these programs and institutions, is an explicit commitment to culturally appropriate, readily accessible, quality post-secondary education for First Nations people. Typical of the mission statements associated with such institutions is that of the Nicola Valley Institute of Technology (NVIT) in Merritt, British Columbia:

> To provide First Nations people with access to a system of the highest quality post-secondary, academic and career/technical education in a culturally reinforced environment. [32]

While NVIT functions as a more or less independent First Nations institution, similar purposes can be achieved within the structural framework of existing public institutions. At the University of British Columbia (UBC), for example, the First Nations House of Learning draws on the following mission to broaden the cultural attributes of all UBC programs by helping them better serve the needs of First Nations people:

> The mandate of the First Nations House of Learning is to make the University's vast resources more accessible to British Columbia's First People, and to improve the University's ability to meet the needs of First Nations. The House of Learning is continuously seeking direction from the First Nations community in determining priorities and approaches. This is achieved through consultation meetings and workshops held throughout the province. The First Nations House of Learning is dedicated to quality preparation in all fields of post-secondary study. We believe that quality education is determined by its relevance to the philosophy and values of First Nations. [33]

Similar missions, goals and programs can be found in most of the other higher education initiatives coming from First Nations people across Canada and the U.S. It is the exercise of First Nations leadership and responsibility through institutions such as these that offers the best long-term promise for improving First Nations participation

Foundation for the Advancement of Teaching, Princeton University Press, 1989); R.D. Chrisjohn & M.L. Mrochuk, *First Nations House of Learning Program Evaluation Report* (Vancouver, BC: First Nations House of Learning, University of British Columbia, 1990).

[32] *Nicola Valley Institute of Technology, 1990-91 Calendar* (Merritt, B.C.: NVIT, 1990), p. 1.

[33] V. Kirkness, *First Nations House of Learning, 1990-91 Calendar* (Vancouver, BC: University of British Columbia, 1990), p. 4.

in higher education.[34] Through institutions of their own making and/or under their own control, First Nations people are creating a more comprehensive definition of "education" and reaffirming their right to respect and self-determination. The significance of this undertaking was summarized by the Carnegie Foundation in its report on U.S. Tribal Colleges:

> At the heart of the tribal college movement is a commitment by Native Americans to reclaim their cultural heritage. The commitment to reaffirm traditions is a driving force fed by a spirit based on shared history passed down through generations, and on common goals. Some tribes have lost much of their tradition, and feel, with a sense of urgency, that they must reclaim all they can from the past even as they confront problems of the present. The obstacles in this endeavour are enormous but, again, Indians are determined to reaffirm their heritage, and tribal colleges, through their curriculum and campus climate, are places of great promise.[35]

The need for such a shift in cultural emphasis such as that sought by the Tribal Colleges is no less important in existing Western-oriented institutions of higher education serving First Nations students, but the structures and processes for engaging with First Nations people through these institutions are necessarily different. The nature of some of those differences are spelled out by Tierney in his use of critical analysis to examine the role of colleges with regard to Native American students:

> The emphasis of a critical analysis shifts away from what strategies those in power can develop to help those not in power, to analyzing how power exists in the organization, and given how power operates, to developing strategies that seek to transform those relations. All organizational participants will be encouraged to come to terms with how they may reconstruct and transform the organization's culture. As opposed to a rhetoric of what mainstream organizations will do *for* Native Americans – a top-down managerial approach – the struggle is to develop strategies and policies that emerge from a vision of working *with* Native Americans toward a participatory goal of emancipation and empowerment.[36]

Tierney's call for the reconstruction and transformation of the university's culture to better serve First Nations ends may seem at first to be a daunting task, but it really is no more than a matter of shifting to a policy, posture and practice of actually working with First Nations people, and in doing so, attending to the "Four R's" of respect, relevance, reciprocity and responsibility. We have ample evidence that this can be, and is being done, within existing institutions, as well as through institutions of First Nations peoples own making.

---

[34] R. Barnhardt, "Higher Education in the Fourth World: Indigenous People Take Control", in *Tribal College: Journal of American Indian Higher Education*, 1991, Autumn.

[35] P. Boyer, *Tribal Colleges: Shaping the Future of Native America*, 1989, p. xiii.

[36] W.G. Tierney, "The College Experience of Native Americans: A Critical Analysis", 1993, p. 323.

CONCLUSION

It is the notion of empowerment that is at the heart of First Nations participation in higher education – not just empowerment as individuals, but empowerment as bands, as tribes, as nations, and as a people. For the institutions to which they must turn to obtain that education, the challenge is clear. What First Nations people are seeking is not a lesser education, and not even an equal education, but rather a better education – an education that respects them for who they are, that is relevant to their view of the world, that offers reciprocity in their relationships with others, and that helps them exercise responsibility over their own lives. It is not enough for universities to focus their attention on "attrition" and "retention" as an excuse to intensify efforts at cultural assimilation. Such approaches in themselves have not made a significant difference, and often have resulted in further alienation. Instead, the very nature and purpose of higher education for First Nations people must be reconsidered, and when we do, we will find that the entire institution, as well as society as a whole, will be strengthened and everyone will benefit. The only question remaining is, can those who are in a position to make a difference seize the opportunity and overcome institutional inertia soon enough to avoid the alienation of another generation of First Nations people, as well as the further erosion of the university's ability to serve the needs of society as a whole? Can we make the necessary adaptations and escape the misfortune of the monkeys in Indonesia? Let us hope so, because the university is too vital an institution to end up in the zoo.

5

The Challenge of Cultural Dependency:
An African and Islamic Perspective

Ali A. Mazrui
with Alamin M. Mazrui

This chapter consists of two parts. Part one was written ten years ago and presented at the conference in Toronto on "Knowledge Across Cultures" in 1992. It looks at issues of knowledge in the university, gender and culture largely from an African perspective, outlining some of the debates underway at the time, and suggesting five strategies for change in universities. Part two was written recently in collaboration with Alamin M. Mazrui, my nephew, and emphasizes an Islamic perspective in relation to rapidly changing issues of knowledge and gender in the contemporary era of the digital revolution. It suggests some solutions to the dilemmas of dependency and gender inequity arising from the new possibilities of digital technology and the internet. At a deeper level it explores the possibility of an Islamic Reformation that may have some parallels with the historical precedent of the Protestant Reformation in Christianity.[1]

PART ONE: AN AFRICAN PERSPECTIVE

There are three major struggles affecting university life, both East and West, in different degrees as we approach the end of the 20th century: (1) the struggle between contending cultures, (2) the struggle between genders, and (3) the struggle between state and society. The struggle between contending cultures takes the form of a raging policy debate in North America on multiculturalism, Afrocentricity, and issues of that kind. But it takes other forms elsewhere.

In the United States, I served on a Syllabus Reform and Development Committee of the State of New York on which we examined precisely the issue of whether American children in high school were in fact receiving a style of education, a content of education, that was excessively Eurocentric. In Eastern Europe and sub-Saharan Africa, contending cultures sometimes produce ethnic conflicts and

---

[1] Part two of the paper is indebted to previous work by Ali A. and Alamin M. Mazrui on Islamic culture and intellectual history, including "The Digital Revolution and the New Reformation: Doctrine and Gender in Islam", in *Harvard International Review*, Vol. xxxii, No. 1, Spring, 2001, pp. 52-55.

ethnocultural rivalries. In the Muslim world, the debate is often between the claims of classical Islamic traditions and the claims of a more secular culture. Universities in all these parts of the world have been deeply affected by the cultural struggles in the wider societies.

The struggle between genders is not simply a matter of how many women are admitted into colleges and universities, it is also a debate about feminist perspectives in the syllabus and about policies of hiring women as teachers, professors, administrators. The debate is also about research into the role of women in the history of knowledge and the role of women in the history of society. This gender struggle is at its most complex in the Western world but, allowing for cultural variation, it has also begun in other parts of the globe. In the Muslim world, are there special attributes to the gender struggle? And how have these affected Muslim universities?

In addition to the battle between cultures in search of multiculturalism, and the battle between genders in search of androgyny, higher education in East and West, has probably felt the impact of the even more pervasive tension between state and society. Budgets and academic freedom have sometimes been at stake, conditioning relations between the state and students, the state and academic staff, the state and university administrators. In Eastern Europe, Latin America, and Africa, pro-democracy movements in the wider society have had repercussions on academic campuses.

There have been occasions when the state has felt so threatened by pro-democracy movements that it has clamped down on campuses. Academic freedom has been a martyr to the struggle for wider democracy in places like Zaire (now the Democratic Republic of Congo-Kinshasa), and the Republic of Korea. Algeria has been in an intermediate position as the nation has agonized between the claims of democracy as majority rule which is in favour of Islamic principles, and the demands of democracy as the protection of minorities which is against the possible suppression of minorities by any future Islamic state. Academics in Algeria have been caught up in the enfolding dialectic of violence.

In Africa, there are some of the oldest universities including Al Azhar University in Cairo and Fez University in Morocco, which are over 1000 years old each. Some of the youngest institutions of higher learning are also in Africa. In between has been the experience of colonialism, from Cape to Cairo, from Dar-es-Salam to Dakar. The impact of Europe has created new forms of cultural tensions which themselves have fed into this contest between contending cultures. Universities in Africa and much of the Arab world, have become instruments for the creation of a Westernized or semi-Westernized elite. In the case of Muslim Africa and the Arab world, Islam has sometimes served as a counterforce.

The most pressing academic need is how to transform post-colonial universities from their role as factories of cultural dependency into a new role as fortresses of cultural self-defence. It is sometimes ironic because the West learned things from other cultures before the West became hegemonic and transformed, also sometimes undermined, other cultures. For example, the academic gown of Oxford had its origins in the Arabian robes in the Middle East. Also, the notion of a "chair" as a position in universities came from a tradition in medieval Egypt for the *alim* or the "learned one" to sit in a chair and the *talibul ilm* or those who are the "seekers of knowledge" to sit on mats around the chair. This in turn originated when the Muslim preachers stood on the *mimbar* or the pulpit, and the congregation sat on mats in the Mosque facing it. The literal professorial chair at Al Azhar University in medieval times became the academic title of my present Albert Schweitzer chair in the Humanities at the State University of New York at Binghamton from the second half of the 20th century.

But the impact of Arab and Muslim universities was not limited to the organizational and ritual traditions of Western universities. For example, the following English words: "algebra", "chemistry", "cipher", "tariff", and so on, are of Arabic derivation. Also, the term "Arabic numerals" is a fusion of Arab and Indian legacies. But while the longest surviving universities may indeed be in Cairo and Morocco, Timbuktu in Mali, West Africa, did have a vigorous academic tradition for a while in medieval times.

However, in much of the rest of Africa and the Arab world, universities are much more recent and are often the direct result of contact with European colonialism and imperial occupation. Because so many of the universities are colonial creations, they suffer from fundamental neo-colonial flaws; this is particularly so with universities in sub-Saharan Africa.

But while the neo-colonialism is particularly acute, the debate about changes is relatively weaker than it is in Canada or the United States. There appear to be far more debates on Afrocentricity in North America than in Africa. There appears to be far more rebellion against Eurocentrism in North America than in Africa. And yet African universities were sometimes literally born out of the metropole where degrees from African universities were granted by, for example, the University of London in the case of Makerere University, and where the curriculum was also under colonial control. Those origins in the metropole, though now not directly institutional, are part of the reality of most African universities. They continue to be a kind of subsidiary of what elsewhere has been called a cultural multinational corporation, where they are involved in academic "goods" manufactured in the metropole, that is in the Western world. There is not much of a rebellion against this development.

Africa is sentenced further to a problem that is barely scrutinized in Africa, that is the fact that much of teaching has to be in European languages. Taking a degree in an African language is still relatively rare on many campuses. Taking a Ph.D in an African language, or studying in an African language after the Ph.D level, is almost totally unknown. Learning history, or economics, or political science in an African language is never done. Thus academic discussion in these areas is strictly in the languages of the imperial powers – without any apparent resentment!

This must be contrasted with the State of New York's study on whether its students were receiving an overwhelmingly Eurocentric curriculum. The report recommended a reduction in Eurocentrism and an expansion of cultural perspectives. In fact, the committee proceeded on the premise that while the United States was perhaps the most ethnically diverse nation in the world, by comparison, its culture was not, and thus a balance needed to be restored. Having become somewhat a national issue, and given New York State's political constraints, a committee was considering ways to implement the recommendations in the early 1990s.

The struggle between the two genders in the educational domain in Africa has had its paradoxes. Although Great Britain has had a woman as head of government before Africa, Africa has had women as heads of universities (or vice-chancellors) earlier than Great Britain. The United States is behind Britain in providing a head of government, but ahead of Britain and Africa in terms of women as presidents of universities. A more fundamental paradox of Western education in Africa is that it has tended to marginalize women functionally, removing women from the productive sector of the economy and moving them to the service sector of the economy.

According to African legend, God had originally intended woman to be custodian of fire (symbol of light and heat), custodian of water (symbol of survival and cleanliness), and custodian of earth (tied to the doctrine of dual fertility – the fertility of the womb, woman as mother, and the fertility of the soil, woman as cultivator). In real life, the role of custodian of fire made woman in the African countryside disproportionately involved in obtaining and managing the main source of rural energy, firewood. The role of custodian of water meant trekking long distances in search of water. As custodians of earth, or farmers, women became the main cultivators of food, though men are sometimes the cultivators of cash crops such as coffee and tea.

With Western education, including that of the universities, the impact has been such that the functions of the woman, which were very central to society, are changed. Women acquire more freedom as a result of Western education but they lose some of the functional importance they had as custodians of fire, water, and earth. Western education has tended to have the effect of expanding a woman's freedom and reducing her significance to society, except in her role as mother. Most Western educated African women move from the farm to the office, from production to service. Many middle range Western educated women become secretaries and clerks. From custodians of fire, water, and earth, to typists and junior administrators.

Western education improves the rights of women but often shrinks the roles of women in Africa. The balance is still not right. The previous situation overburdened women with too large a role, the new situation, while giving women more freedom, marginalizes them functionally. Better rights for women but narrower roles for women. Thus the question for educators in Africa is: can we restore the balance?

Some African countries have begun the debate. For example, in Nigeria, the most hotly debated book is a male chauvinist one entitled, *The Anatomy of Female Power*. Other male chauvinists have re-titled it the "Power of Female Anatomy". That it is being debated so vigorously is a sign that gender issues have begun to be taken seriously. In 1991, when I was invited by one of the leading newspapers in Nigeria to give their annual birthday lecture on "The Black Woman", they agreed with my request that the chair be a woman and that the distinguished guest also be a woman. In response to the first request, the paper had already invited a distinguished jurist who is a woman and for the second request, they invited the First Lady of the country. This immediately gave the occasion tremendous publicity, making the gender issue one of widespread discussion and considerable examination.

While chauvinism still exists, Nigeria is beginning to examine the gender issue. However, it won't be adequately addressed until it is realized that the impact of Western culture up to the present has been marginalizing, and that the contending cultures have been detrimental to women. In fact, it is the indigenous cultures which permit women to be priestesses, sometimes even military leaders, while the imported cultures of the Arabs and of Islam as well as of the West, sometimes rule out women in major religious or military roles.

The latest illustration has been in Uganda. There, Alice Lakwena approached the battle-hardened and martial tribe, the Acholi, saying that she could show them salvation from their oppressors and proceeded to invoke indigenous religion combined with Christianity, allowing her a leadership role for battle. The warriors followed her into battle even though the protection of indigenous religion proved tragic in the face of gunfire. However, the wider significance is that the decision to follow a woman was a function not of the imported culture but of the indigenous culture of Uganda. Thus, the contending cultures at play have a bearing on the gender issue and this should be examined with closer scrutiny than has been attempted before.

In conclusion, in education and in the wider society, Africans should formulate the following strategies for change: (1) the strategy of indigenization, that is including more indigenous material in courses, using indigenous languages in education, making them part of the package of self-education and enhancement; (2) the strategy of domestication, that is making the colonial university more pertinent and relevant to the local scene; (3) the strategy of diversification, that is developing a trilateral dialogue among Arabs, Africans, and Westerners, as well as exposing themselves to Chinese, Indian, and other civilizations; (4) the strategy of horizontal interpenetration, that is wider South-South cooperation among universities, encouraging the movement of scholars, researchers, students across different parts of the Third World and finally (5) the strategy of counterpenetration with the South counterpenetrating the North and seeking influence in the corridors of power, making northern education systems respond to Afrocentricity and multiculturalism, as was the case for the State of New York study described above. This can also be an opportunity for individuals of African ancestry, Indian ancestry, and Chinese ancestry who are resident in the West, to become bridges between their ancestral cultures and the West, enhancing understanding between the northern hemisphere and the South.

PART TWO: AN ISLAMIC PERSPECTIVE

In the United States there is increasing evidence that immigrants from South Asia (especially India and Pakistan) have responded faster to the computer culture than most other Americans. Indeed, India is already emerging as one of the great digital powers

of the 21st century.   On American campuses there is indeed evidence that Ko-
rean-American students seem to be more calculus-friendly than Italian-American
students.   And Jewish-American students seem to be more at ease with the digital
revolution than African-American students.

The question arises whether such differences also occur between religious
traditions. Do some religions respond faster to science and technology than others?
Will this difference affect their comparative performance in the computer revolution?
Is a digital divide likely to aggravate relations between the West and the Muslim world?

Mathematical prowess differs by individuals as well as by cultures. Calculus-friendly cultures produce a larger proportion of people who are comfortable with
mathematics. This does not mean that calculus-challenged cultures produce no
brilliant mathematicians at all. It only means that they produce far fewer.

Nor should we forget economic factors. Sometimes what may appear like
cultural reasons for the digital divide may in fact be due to economic differences and
financial access. If white Americans are economically richer per capita than Black
Americans then the digital divide between White and Black is likely to have economic
as well as cultural reasons. Indeed, at this stage of this kind of research, we cannot be
sure which reasons are weightier than which – economic or cultural.

At the general level this second part of the chapter is about the perennial
interplay between technology and religion, but we will focus more specially on doctrine
and gender in Islam, and the chances of a dual reformation.

From Information to Reformation

The impact of the first industrial revolution on Western Christianity probably included
no less momentous a movement than the Christian Reformation itself and its survival
and spread. Will the impact of the new revolution of information include a momentous
movement of Islamic Reformation?

In the 20th century Westerners have debated whether the Protestant Reformation was the mother of capitalism in Europe or whether the Christian Reformation
was itself a child of earlier phases of the capitalist revolution. Max Weber's book, *The
Protestant Ethic and the Spirit of Capitalism*, puts forward a powerful case for the
Reformation as the mother of capitalism rather than a child of economic change. On the
other hand, other thinkers have identified pre-Reformation technological inventions as
part of the preparation for both Protestantism and capitalism. Francis Bacon identified
the compass, the printing press and gun powder as three forces which have transformed
"the appearance and state of the whole world".[2]

In our own day Francis Robinson, Professor of History at the University of
London, has placed the printing press centrally in the Protestant movement and within
the Catholic counter-offensive. Professor Robinson has argued:

---

[2] Francis Bacon, "Novun Organum, Aphorism 129" in Francis Bacon, *Advancement of Learning and
Novun Organum* (New York: The Colonial Press, 1899), p. 366.

Print lay at the heart of that great challenge to religious authority, the Protestant Reformation; Lutheranism was the child of the printed book. Print lay at the heart of the Catholic counter-offensive, whether it meant harnessing the press for the work of Jesuits and the office of Propaganda, or controlling the press through the machinery of the Papal Index and the Papal Imprimatur.[3]

The question which has now arisen is whether what printing and the first Industrial Revolution did to Christianity, the Internet and cyberspace and the third industrial revolution will do to Islam. The printing press shook the foundations of Christian tradition. Will the Internet and World Wide Web shake the foundations of Islamic tradition?

Christianity, under the shock of earlier socio-technological changes, produced its own Protestant movement. Will Islam in the course of the 21st century give birth to its own Martin Luther and its own John Calvin, if not its own King Henry VIII? It is arguable that in Sunni Islam there has not been a major shake up in theology since the death of Abu Abd Allah Malik, the Muslim jurist and founder of the Maliki *madh'hab*,[4] in 795 CE. Will the new technology of information re-open more widely the doors of *ijtihad*?[5] Will the technology of World Wide Web allow for the emergence of new *madhahib*? Are the gates of Islamic creative synthesis being reopened?

In some respects the Christian Reformation was a return to the basics of Christianity. Likewise the information revolution may help Islam realize some of its earliest aims more effectively. The first casualty may be national sovereignty – the shrinkage of sovereignty in the wake of the Internet and cyberspace. The printed word may have been playing a major role in the construction of nationhood and in reinforcing national consciousness. Computer communication, on the other hand, is contributing to the breakdown of nationhood and may be playing a role in the construction of other trans-ethnic communities.

While the first industrial revolution of capitalist production and the Christian reformation became allied to the new forces of nationalism in the new Western world, the third industrial revolution and any Islamic reformation will be increasingly hostile to the insularity of the nationalism of the state. Islam and the information revolution will be allies in breaking down the barriers of competing national sovereignties. The new technology will give Islam a chance to realize its original aim of transnational universalism. The Internet and the World Wide Web could in part become the Islamic super-highway.

Linked to the shrinkage of sovereignty is indeed the death of distance. In some

---

[3] Francis Robinson, "Technology and Religious Change: Islam and the Impact of Print", inaugural lecture given on March 4, 1992, at Royal Holloway and Bedford New College as Professor of the History of South Asia, University of London. See *Modern Asian Studies*, Vol. 27, No. 1, 1993, pp. 229-251.

[4] The term *madh'hab* means a religious denomination or sect in Islam. The plural form of the term is *madhabib*. The main denominations are Sunni and Shia, though each has sub-denominations.

[5] The term *ijtihad* means the principle of judicial review of Islamic law by the most learned, subject to strict rules and strict limits.

ways this also takes Islam back to its roots. Islam has tried to kill distance. This is a religion which has always wanted to celebrate both movement and direction. The Islamic era or calendar does not begin when the Prophet Muhammad was born in 570 CE. It does not begin when he became a prophet forty years later. It does not begin when the Prophet died in June 632 CE. The Islamic era or calendar begins when the Prophet Muhammad moved in 622 CE. The *Hijjra*[6] is, in a sense, a celebration of purposeful movement. The Prophet not only changed and synthesized religious paradigms, from pre-Islamic to Islamic. The Prophet also physically changed cities from Mecca to Medina. Islamic time began with physical movement.

Islam is a religion which has three holiest cities, each of which signifies different levels of the death of distance. We have already mentioned Medina as the destination of Muhammad's momentous decision to turn nascent Islam initially into a tale of two cities – from intolerant Mecca to receptive Medina. Islam has also sought to kill distance through faith. Mecca signified other aspects of the primordial death of distance. Five times each day millions of Muslims turn to Mecca, communicating with God through a city thousands of miles away. Mecca is a constant point of religious convergence for those in communication with the Ultimate. Distance is threatened by faith. And, as intimated earlier, Islam did not hesitate to enlist scientific and technological know-how in this quest to overcome the barriers of distance. Mecca is also the city of the annual pilgrimage, receiving millions every decade from diverse corners of the world. They come by jet and camel, on foot and by boat. Distance has been threatened by the Internet. Will the pilgrims one day perform the *umra*[7] by Internet? How far will the new creative synthesis go?

The third most sacred city for Islam is, of course, Jerusalem over which Israelis and Palestinians are today in a stalemate. Especially sacred to Muslims is Al-Quds, focused on the Dome of the Rock. Muslims believe that on the night of *Mi'raj,*[8] distance truly died at three different levels – the Prophet Muhammad moved from Mecca to Jerusalem in a single night in the age of the camel; and he moved from earth to the Heavens during the same night, ascending from Jerusalem; and while in the Heavens the present age communicated with the ages of the past, for the Prophet was able to talk to Jesus, Moses and all the way back to Adam during the same night. The Prophet was back in Mecca before morning – breaking at least three sound barriers of cosmic experience:

- killing distance between Mecca and Jerusalem;
- killing distance between the earth and the heavens;

---

[6] The term *Hijjra* means, literally, migration, and refers to the flight of the Prophet from Mecca to Medina in search of religious asylum. The Islamic calendar begins from that event in 622 CE.

[7] The *umra* is referred to as the "junior pilgrimage". It involves going to Mecca for the same rituals but on days of the year other than the prescribed dates. Throughout the year in Mecca there are Muslims performing the *umra*.

[8] The term *Mi'raj* means "ladder" and later "ascent". It refers to the night when, according to Muslim tradition, the Prophet Muhammad was transported first from Mecca to Jerusalem, then from Jerusalem to the Heavens, and then back to Mecca before daybreak.

killing distance between the past and the present.

And it is in this sense that Islam prepared believers for the age of the end of distance and the age of globalized digital simultaneity. This was a prophecy of digital philoscience.

Many Muslims have already risen to this challenge of the new information age with Islamic Resource Guides on the Internet, Cyber Muslim Guides, Islamic Information and News Network, and Web Servers with Islamic material. What all this means is that in the area of shrinkage of sovereignty and in the area of death of distance Islam and the new information revolution are, on the whole, historical allies. And contrary to some assumptions that "modern communications would engender a new and generally Western-oriented cosmopolitanism, they are predominantly spreading the idea of a freedom that is translated by the receivers as endogenous freedom – including freedom to rejoin one's real kinship (whether larger or smaller) and to re-examine the validity of one's own ancient social values".[9] Civilization is pushing towards new frontiers of creative synthesis.

From Private Harem to Private Ballot

There may be one fundamental area where Islam and the new information revolution need to find accommodation. This could also be at the heart of any Islamic Reformation movement if it occurs. This area of tension concerns the relations between men and women. Will the new technology of information fundamentally alter the gender playing field forever? If the first two issues were about shrinkage of sovereignty and the death of distance, this third issue is about privacy unveiled.

On the gender question the Muslim world has alternated between two doctrines. One doctrine has been to treat genders as separate but equal. The United States once attempted to implement the constitutional doctrine of treating Whites and Blacks as separate but equal. However, by 1954 the Supreme Court was ready to conclude that separation of the races resulted in or perpetuated inequality. In the momentous decision of Brown versus the Board of Education in 1954, the U.S. Supreme Court at last rejected the doctrine of "separate but equal" for the races. Racial segregation became unconstitutional.

If "separate but equal" was untenable for races, why should the doctrine work for genders? Because genders live together in homes in a way in which races never used to do in the United States. Every man's mother is a woman. So are men's wives, daughters and granddaughters, aunts and other female relatives. So separation of genders is inevitably moderated by family ties. This is a qualitative difference from the separation of races. The gender doctrine of "separate but equal" could survive the new

---

[9] Erskine B. Childers, "Amnesia and Antagonism", in Farish A. Noor (ed.), *Terrorising the Truth: The Shaping of Contemporary Images of Islam and Muslims in Media, Politics and Culture* (Penang, Malaysia: Just World Trust, 1997), pp. 140-141.

information revolution.

Under the new technology the computerized *hijab*[10] is at hand: Women can more easily stay at home and still be equal computer workers. This possibility is amply demonstrated by a woman from the British Asian community in her response to a BBC radio presenter who expressed concern that the computer can, in fact, enhance the isolation of women of that community. In the words of the woman interviewee:

> Well, if they're just stuck at home then why not use the Internet to get connectivity with people across the world…the Internet can also provide an access for women to possibly start up providing their own services – maybe hobbies that they're interested in or business that they have a keen eye on. For example, if they have a hobby in maybe cooking, or, you know, they have collected a series of recipes over the years – they could then use those recipes – publish them on the Net and start some sort of business. There have been a number of cases in the past where women actually started a business up using the Internet.[11]

The Internet, in other words, is gradually abolishing the distinction between home and the work-place. This is a whole new depth of creative synthesis.

But many Muslim societies treat women as "separate and unequal". Aspects of it are rooted in a view of the *Shari'a*[12] which made women inherit half of what men inherited; and made the testimony of women in court be worth less than that of men in certain circumstances. Such Muslim societies have assumed that there were two different doors of knowledge – one for men and one for women. Many Muslim societies had assumed that there were branches of knowledge which were not fit for women and children under 16. Partly for reasons of modesty women were spared certain areas of know-how. Today the Taliban in Afghanistan have carried this theory of two tiers of gender knowledge to the extreme. This not synthesis but segregation.

The new information technology is going to blow that discrimination totally out of social existence. More and more information may refuse to be susceptible to gender differentiation. The digital divide may give way to digital democracy. What men know about sex, pornography, politics and corruption may also be accessible to women through the World Wide Web, Internet and the emerging information super-highway.

In time the veil as the modesty of the face is bound to be destroyed by the new technology. Women may cover other aspects of their personality, but increasingly they will be totally available facially to the viewer through the Internet and the approaching image telephone system. The new technology will pass a death sentence on the old

---

[10] The term *hijab* originally means a partition or veil of modesty. It has come to mean the Islamic dress code for women.

[11] Sharon Goodman and Denise Graddol, *Redesigning English: New Texts, New Identification* (London, New York: Routledge, 1996), pp. 109-110.

[12] The term *Shari'a* means Islamic law, based mainly on principles derived from the Holy Book, the Qur'an, and from the sayings and precedents set by the Prophet Muhammad, as interpreted by later generations of learned Muslim jurists.

tradition of the harem which has been in existence since the Abbasid dynasty in many Muslim societies.

The traditional forms of seclusion of women will no longer survive a technology in which women can declare their presence and in time assert their rights. Women will also be able to introduce themselves to others more easily than ever before. Our daughters visually telephoning their boy friends can become the order of the day before very long.

The hurried nature of the Internet may endanger the quality of literature. But does the computer promise to narrow the gender divide in publishing? Does the digital divide widen or narrow the gender divide? These are questions which affect much more than the Muslim world. There is evidence that where the information technology captures children in the Northern hemisphere, before long the mothers follow their children into the mysteries of computer games. Is there evidence in the Northern hemisphere that women are keeping pace with men in the new Information Revolution much faster than they ever did in the old Industrial Revolution? Is the digital divide between Northern women and Southern women much wider than between Northern men and Southern men? Indeed, is it conceivable that the information super highway has the makings of not only a Protestant Reformation but also of a sexual reformation? Will the impact of the new revolution of information include a momentous movement of gender reformation?

In parts of the Muslim world women entered the computer culture because of the previously sexist specialization of women as secretaries. The marginalizing status of secretarial typing became a key to the technologically upward mobile culture of the computer and the Internet.

The Internet is potentially a threat to the quality of literature. But does it have more positive potential with regard to the future of women in publishing? Will the closing of the digital divide help to close the gender divide in publishing and book-selling, as well as in literary output? Figure 5.1 provides a set of questions for reflection around this issue.

Figure 5.1: Books and the Gender of Technology

Technology of Research and Writing	Technology of Printing and Publishing	Technology of Promotion and Distribution
Shakespeare created with the pen and ink Milton dictated Paradise Lost because Milton was blind In the course of the 20th century most writers turned to the typewriter rather than the pen. Female participation increased. By the year 2000 the writer was into the word processor and the computer Are women catching up faster in the computer age than they ever did in the age of the pen?	Charles Dickens serialized some of his novels in magazines in the 19th century Stephen King in the year 2000 tried to serialize his latest book on the Internet – charging a dollar per chapter. Was his experiment premature? Writers are beginning to close the gender gap as writers. But are publishers closing the gap as publishers? Is the percentage of women who are publishers far smaller than the percentage of women who are writers?	Distributing books through Amazon.com. Is book distribution more male dominated than book production? Downloading book orders from the Internet. Is the process still sexist? The technology of advertizing: Here again is the commercial side of the book business – as distinct from the creative side – still too male dominated? Is this almost as true in the West as it is in the Muslim world?

The sexual reformation may be under way, but for the time being the male of the species is still more digitized. Even among writers, scholars and publishers we must not forget the trends of life.

The frantic look without seeing;
The patient see without looking.
Deign on the passing world to turn thine eyes
And pause a while from books to be wise.[13]

And yet a chapter a day, may keep innocence at bay!

If the new information technology affects (a) the shrinkage of sovereignty (b) the death of distance and (c) privacy unveiled, what is the fourth arena for our concern in this analysis? If there is an Islamic Reformation, its fourth component is likely to be the prospect of democratizing theocracy.

---

[13] A free paraphrase from Samuel Johnson, *The Vanity of Human Wishes*, first published in 1749.

Democracy is a people-focused system. Theocracy is a God-focused system. Are the two totally mutually exclusive? Or is it conceivable that a God-focused system could become at the same time people-focused? Will the digital divide not only give way to digital democracy but move on to further humaneness? By marrying the Islamic Reformation to a sexual reformation, the digital revolution could indeed be a democratizing force.

Towards Islamizing the Internet

In spite of the new freedoms and new possibilities afforded by the Internet, the technology is not necessarily free of existing systems of inequality – economic, political and social. The new computer technology and the Internet may be inaugurating new kinds of stratification and new types of reform. Muslim countries are bound to be affected. For quite a while now distribution of real power in the world has been based not on "who owns what" but on "who knows what". It has not been the power of property but the power of skill which has been the ultimate international arbiter. Oil-rich Muslim countries like Saudi Arabia or Kuwait have not been able to exploit their own petroleum resources without the skills of Western companies and their engineers.

The latest area of skill concerns computer communication and the Internet. Is there uneven distribution of these skills in the world in a manner which is potentially divisive? One major university in the United States may have more computer literate people than several states of the Nigerian Federation. We are back to the digital divide on the world scene – the divide between the computer-skilled and computer-challenged. Literacy as a source of empowerment has shifted from the print to the computer medium. There is the lingering danger that cyberspace will consolidate the gap between the haves and the have-nots, and the forces of global apartheid between the West and the Rest.

One additional anxiety is whether the digital divide will coincide with the racial and class divide even within societies. This issue is beginning to rear its head in the United States. While access to the technology is tied to socio-economic background, there is evidence to suggest that even within the same income brackets, African Americans are being left behind in computer skills at least temporarily. Part of the problem is attitudinal: many young African Americans at school regard proficiency in computers as a form of "imitation of white kids" – and therefore distasteful. Peer pressure continues to discourage many bright African American young men (more so than young women) that mathematical skills are a white man's lifestyle and therefore to be shunned. It is partly such pressures which run the risk of making the digital divide coincide with the racial divide. It is already estimated that African Americans constitute less than five percent of computer programmers in the USA.

If African Americans lag behind whites in computer skills, are Asian Americans ahead of whites in such skills? Is culture an important variable in the cultivation of certain skills? There is evidence of considerable mathematical and computer prowess among South Asians and East Asians, especially Indians and Koreans. The number of South Asian Muslims qualifying for immigration to the United States on the basis of skills has risen dramatically in recent years. These come from India and Pakistan. The digital divide is affecting comparative migrations of people.

But it is not just class, ethnicity and race, both locally and globally, which are affected by the new technology of communication. The computer, the Internet and the World Wide Web may also carry the seeds of moral, ideological and gender reform. Jon Snow has commented:

> The Internet is a male world, a lone male world. It is self-seeking, self-serving and self-fulfilling. Surfing shuts out all other physical and environmental contact and takes the user deeper into a world of 'me', 'my choice', and 'f... you'. Not for nothing is the Net peppered with porn; not for nothing do statistics show that most surfers are men and that the Internet holds less attraction for women.[14]

Thus the Internet continues to raise anxieties and issues about both individual personal lives and relationships and more collective social and cultural experiences. But when women get interested, they can catch up speedily.

How is the Muslim *ummah*[15] to relate to these "negative" consequences of the Internet and computer communication? How can we ensure that synthesis is creative and not self-destructive? There is now a growing movement among Muslims that seeks to Islamize scientific (and other forms of) knowledge – perhaps as part of a bigger project, the Islamization of modernity itself. The Islamization of computer communication is seen as a core component of this quest. As Nasim Butt explains:

> As information technologies are becoming the basic tools of manipulation and control, access to them will become the decisive factor between control and power or manipulation and subservience. In this powerful dilemma, the way forward, surely, is to modify the technology at the point of use to meet the needs and requirements – the goals – of Muslim society. All such modifications must, of course, be done in accordance with the ethical dictates of Islam.[16]

Butt devotes a full chapter to elucidating an alternative scientific paradigm that is supposedly more in keeping with the values of Islam and to providing some broad guidelines for the Islamization of science and technology.

As indicated earlier, science in the more isolationist Muslim discourse has often been seen to be separate from religion. More recent Islamic revival initiatives, however, insist on a greater convergence between the two. There is a new nostalgia for

[14] Jon Snow, "All the News that Fits on Screen", in *Guardian* (London), Sept 19, 1995.
[15] The term *ummah* refers to the communil of believers in Islam worldwide.
[16] Nasim Butt, *Science and Muslim Societies* (London: Grey Seal, 1991), p. 62.

ancient sacred science. The advocates seek to apply Islamic ethical parameters both to scientific research and, more importantly, to applied science. Some Islamicist interpretations would now regard as un-Islamic any scientific venture that carries the potential of harmful and/or unnatural consequences. Under this paradigm research in the germ warfare would probably be disallowed outright. But how about areas of mixed blessings, like genetic engineering, which may be put to beneficial as well as unnatural and harmful uses? The verdict here may depend on the particular application. For example, nuclear weapons have been seen as defensive against Zionist, Hindu or Western enemies. Pakistan is now a nuclear power (since 1999).

The Islamization of science may also refer to attempts to accord science, greater Islamic identity and Muslim representation. At some point this quest may entail both indigenization and domestication. Indigenization involves increasing the use of indigenous resources, ranging from native personnel to aspects of traditional local knowledge, in the process making them more relevant to the modern age. Domestication, on the other hand, involves making imported versions of science and technology more relevant to local needs. Domestication is a form of cultural synthesis.

In the realm of computer technology, domestication would begin with a substantial indigenization of personnel. This would require, first, greater commitment by Muslim governments and institutions to promote relevant training at different levels for Muslims, both men and women; second, readiness on the part of both governments and employers to create a structure of incentives which would attract Muslim men and women of the right calibre; third, greater political pressure on computer suppliers to facilitate training and co-operate in related tasks; and fourth, stricter control by Muslim governments of the foreign exchange allowed for the importation of computers.

The indigenization of high-level personnel in the local computer industry should in time help indigenize the uses to which the computer is put and tasks that are assigned to it. When the most skilled roles in the computer industry in a Muslim country are in the hands of Muslims themselves, new types of problems will in turn be put to computers. The cultural and political milieu of the Muslim personnel could greatly affect and perhaps modify problem-definition. This Islamization and androgynization of computer personnel should also facilitate in time further Islamization of the users of computer services. What should be borne in mind is that efficient indigenization and domestication of the computer requires a gradualist and planned approach. Creative synthesis of cultures is sometimes achieved in stages.

The difficulty of this task is compounded by the technological dependence engendered by transnational corporations and their respective governments. As technology levels increase in Muslim countries, so too may these countries' dependence on transnational corporations in order to maintain it. Additional strategies for decolonization of computer technology, therefore, are required. And these may include diversification (of the sources on which a country is dependent), horizontal interpenetration (to promote greater exchange between Muslim countries themselves), and vertical counterpenetration (increasingly enabling Muslim countries to counterpenetrate the citadels of power in the West).

Conclusion: Civilization and Gender

The possibility that the Internet may stimulate an Islamic Reformation is based on the assumption, of course, that Muslim men and women are real actors in the information revolution and not merely objects; that they are producers of knowledge and not merely consumers of knowledge. The power of skill is still more vital than the power of income. Are Muslims of both genders making progress in narrowing the technological gap between Islam and the West? The religion of the *Hijjra*, the religion of the *Hajj*,[17] and the religion of *Mi'raj* needs to be ready for its next *Hijjra* – the information super-highway.

But what would be the implications of an Islamic Reformation for world peace? Will not a reinvigorated Muslim *ummah* lead to the predicted clash of civilizations? If history is anything to go by, then it can be argued that Islamic renewal will not only galvanize the Muslim *ummah* from within but also, by rekindling the spirit of *ijtihad*, it will reopen the doors of constructive engagement with other civilizations. Ancient Islamic philobiblia and philoscience could extend creative synthesis. Perhaps above all an Islamic Reformation has to be accompanied by a sexual reformation.

It must be remembered that at the height of its glory Islam tried hard to protect religious minorities even if Muslims did not always protect women's rights. Jews and Christians had special status as People of the Book – a fraternity of monotheists. Other religious minorities were later to be accorded the status of protected minorities (*dhimmis*). Under the system Jewish scholars rose to high positions in Muslim Spain. During the Ottoman Empire, Christians sometimes attained high political office: Sulaiman I (1520-1566) had Christian ministers in his government, as did Salim III (1789-1807). The Moghul Empire integrated Hindus and Muslims into a consolidated Indian state; Emperor Akbar (1556-1605) carried furthest the Moghul policy of bringing Hindus into the government.[18] All this may be an indication that Islam is most inclusive and most open to dialogue precisely at its hour of greatest strength. And it is this historical precedent that is likely to undergo a resurgence under an Islamic Reformation. A self-confident and self-assured Islam is a better partner for peace than a threatened Islam. Tareq Aziz is a Christian Vice-Premier in Iraq; Boutros-Boutros Ghali was Minister of State. There has been hardly any Western equivalent of Muslims in power until the new millennium.

Part of the dialogic thrust of Islam across religious faith and human civiliza-tions is, of course, rooted in the Qur'an itself. Calling on Jews and Christians to join hands with Muslims in pursuit of common goals, the Qur'an enjoins:

> Say O people of the Book!
> Come to common ground
> As between us and you (Qur'an, 3:64).

---

[17] This refers to the annual pilgrimage to Mecca which is obligatory for every Muslim at least once in a lifetime. Every year at least two million Muslims perform the *Hajj* in Mecca.

[18] Ali A. Mazrui, "Islam and Western Values", in *Foreign Affairs*, Vol. 76, No. 5, 1997, p. 126.

And even though, like other universalistic religions, Islam has been less ecumenical than some more indigenous religions of Africa and elsewhere in the world, Islam has tended to be far more accommodating of indigenous traditions than Christianity. Edward W. Blyden was among the first to capture this cultural dialectic of Islam in his monumental work, *Christianity, Islam and the Negro Race.*[19] There are thus both doctrinal premises and historical precedents that can inspire the Muslim *ummah* to play a leading role in fostering inter-faith and inter-civilizational dialogue and collaboration towards a more just and peaceful world order.

      Synthesizing monotheistic religions
      Synthesizing Faith with reason (Ibn Rushd)
      Synthesizing Religion with sacred science (ancient Islamic science)
      Synthesizing Religion with secular science in the new frontier

The toughest synthesis of all is yet to come – synthesizing the rights of women with the rights of men into a more balanced moral equilibrium. It would be particularly fitting if the Martin Luther of the Islamic Reformation turned out to be a woman, posting her ninety-five theses of reform not on the door of a Wittenberg mosque but universally on the Internet.

---

[19] Edward W. Blyden, *Christianity, Islam and the Negro Race* (London: W.B. Whittingham & Co., 1888, reprinted by Edinburgh University Press, 1967).

Part II

Eastern Contributions
To Scientific Knowledge

6

Indian Mathematics and the West

Pinayur Rajagopal

INTRODUCTION

A Sanskrit work by Brahmagupta, written in India in 628 CE was translated in Baghdad in about the year 770 CE. About half a century later al-Khwarizmi wrote a book "concerning the numbering of the Indians". Several Latin translations of this Arabic work seem to have existed at various times. A popular and influential version was the book *Liber Abaci* of Leonardo of Pisa, written in 1202 CE. The contents of this subject included the decimal numerals, the place value principle, arithmetic operations, and their use in solving practical problems. This arithmetic was found to be more efficient for commercial uses than the traditional Roman methods, and began to be used by merchants. Commercial arithmetic schools were set up to teach this arithmetic as well as methods of bookkeeping. In the three centuries following the publication of *Liber Abaci* the Hindu-Arabic system spread slowly, and became part of the knowledge of the West by the 15th century.

THE GEOMETRY OF THE VEDIC RITUALS AND THE JAINA USE OF NUMBERS (FROM ABOUT 800 BCE TO ABOUT 300 CE)

The Vedic religious rituals through their elaborate details in measurement and geometrical shape gave rise to the science of geometry. The Jainas were interested in numbers and revelled in using them, not only for their cosmographic descriptions, but also for other useful applications. These two great traditions – the geometric or constructive and the algebraic or computational – together provided the basis and the inspiration for Indian Mathematics.

Geometrical constructions are part of the *Sulvasutras*. They contain methods for the construction of altars (or "*agnis*") of various shapes, the shapes depending on the particular ritual. Often a requirement was that the shapes be of the same area; when one has to construct a shape whose area is the same as that of another, geometry is born. Thus there are square altars, circular altars, and altars of many other shapes. They include methods for the construction of a shape equal in area to another: for example a square equal to a circle (and vice versa), a square equal to a rectangle, a square equal to the sum (or difference) of two squares. Mensurational formulae for the areas of standard shapes, such as square, rectangle, right triangle formed from them, and trapezium are given. One of the more complicated ones is that of a flying falcon. Such a complicated figure is made up from the basic shapes listed earlier, whose areas are known, and hence the area of the required shape is obtained by addition. The altars were, for the most part, composed of five layers of bricks that together reached to the height of the knee; for some cases ten or fifteen layers and a corresponding increased height of the altar were prescribed. Most of the altars had a level surface and these were referred to in accordance with the shape and area of the top of the surface. The basic falcon-shaped altar had an area of 7 1/2 square *purushas*: a *purusha* is the height of a man from toe to tip of his arm stretched upwards, that is about 7 1/2 feet. A square *purusha* is about 56 1/4 square feet. The area of the altar surface is thus about 422 square feet.

If mathematics played an important part in the religious observances of the ancient Vedic rituals, on account of the precision it gave in the construction of their sacrificial altars, besides providing the means for an accurate determination and measurement of time, equally did mathematics play an important role in the Jaina religion. The Jainas went to the extent of regarding mathematics as an integral part of their religion. A section of their religious literature was named *ganita-anuyoga* (literally the system of calculation). Mahavira, the founder of the Jaina religion (c. 540 to 468 BCE) was well-versed in that mathematics.

The original mathematical works of the Jainas have not come to light, but our present knowledge about them is almost entirely based on the available commentaries of the original works. The Jainas required very large numbers for their descriptions of the magnitudes of the earth, the various seas surrounding the earth, the mountains on the earth and so on. But our planet constitutes only an infinitesimal portion of the universe. That perception, shared by all three of the major religions of India, gave rise to a number of conceptions of the universe, some of remarkable complexity. And all these cosmographic entities required quantitative estimates; numbers like 10^{27} and 10^{62}. But 10^{140} they labelled "uncountable". They were also interested in counting the number of ways in which items can be combined, and or arranged – a branch of mathematics which we now call 'combinatorics'.

To conclude this brief prelude to the antecedents of Indian Mathematics it is instructive to look at a verse from a Jaina classic of about 300 BCE. According to the *sthananga sutra* the topics for discussion in mathematics are ten in number: (1) the four fundamental operations of arithmetic; (2) the applications of arithmetic to concrete problems; (3) plane geometry calculations; (4) mensuration of plane figures and solids; (5) fractions; (6) the study of "that which is unknown"; (7) squares and square-roots; (8) cubes and cube-roots; (9) higher powers and higher roots; and (10) permutations and combinations. These ten topics can be put into four groups:

(a) fundamental operations and fractions (1, 5, 7, 8, and 9);

(b) applications of a) to practical problems (2, 3, and 4);

(c) means of solution or problem-solving techniques (6)

(d) combinatorics (10).

Such a grouping points to the way in which succeeding authors added to and expanded this conception of mathematics.   This definition or "program" of mathematics includes both geometrical, and computational traditions.[1]

During the next few centuries no named mathematical work or manuscript belonging to that period has been discovered.   The structural and grammatical development of Sanskrit was actively pursued; Indian Mathematics carries the stamp of the linguistic precision and concern for metre of Sanskrit.   Grammar and prosody form part of the branches of learning that India respected; the grammarian, Panini, was the author of a definitive work on structural linguistics of Sanskrit that was written about 350 BCE.   The terse style in which texts were written is an outgrowth of this background.   The knowledge of mathematics and its applications was probably part of the heritage and the culture of the people, and was in their practices.   The amount of geometrical knowledge, as well as the knowledge of complicated mathematical series which went into the derivation of the easy-to-handle rules of computation found in astronomical manuals, was probably hardly appreciated by the astronomer and astrologer.   Relatively few new developments in astronomy seem to have taken place, except for updating of the calendar.   The use of mathematics in astronomical calculations however continued to show much ingenuity.   Another indication is the geometrical and mensurational aspects of mathematical usage in the development of the science of temple building, whose flowering is seen in a later period.[2]

FROM RITUALS AND COSMOGRAPHY TO ARYABHATA (499 CE) AND BHASKARA I (628 CE)

In the Vedic literature certain synonyms for zero are suggested; these arise in part from having to describe Nothing (*sunya*).   There is thus a need to have a symbol for the absence of all qualities.   Mixed in this argument is an attempt to express the presence of the Universal God (*Brahma*) in "the minutest of the minute", and so the Nothing needs a representation: a dot was used.   It must have taken some time to recognize the necessity for a symbol to represent this Nothing.   From this recognition, its acceptance

[1] See P. Rajagopal, "The Sthananga Sutra Programme in Indian Mathematics", in *Arhat Vachana*, 1991, No. 3, pp. 1-8.

[2] The Vedic ritual is a live and continuing tradition; for a description of the performance of the *Agnichayana* ritual in 1975, please see Frits Staal, *Agni: The Vedic Ritual of the Fire Altar*, 2 vols. (Berkeley: Asian Humanities Press, 1983).   The design and construction of temples is another continuing tradition.   Please see Stella Kramrisch, *The Hindu Temple*, 2 vols. (Delhi: Motilal Banarsidass, 1946); Alice Boner, Sadasiva Rath Sarma and Bettina Baumer, *Vastusutra Upanisad* (Delhi: Motilal Banarsidass, 1982); and P. Rajagopal, "Meaning through Geometry: Temple Design in Medieval India", paper presented to the Canadian Society for the History and Philosophy of Mathematics, at the University of Prince Edward Island, Charlottetown, May 1992.

and eventual use and appearance in common language had occurred by about the 5th century in the common era. Very early indications of this interest are shown in the numerals found in the Nanaghat caves (2nd century BCE), and copper plates from Samkhela (from about 4th century CE). It appears in inscriptions and in literature by the 7th century.

In addition to such a dot for zero in Shahpur (stone image inscription from Behar from 672 CE), and Sambor (Khmer inscription from 682 CE), there is the following verse from *Vasavadatta* by Subandhu (late 6th century or early 7th century):

> And at the time of the rising Moon with its blackness of night, bowing low, as it were, with folded hands under the guise of closing blue lotuses, immediately the stars shone forth ... like zero dots ...[3]

From the earliest times numbers seem to have been represented on a purely decimal scale. Each succeeding power of ten had a separate name, not connected to the preceding. The learning of this series was considered to be an achievement of merit. The epics *Ramayana* and *Mahabharata* have verses that use such numbers to describe the sizes of the various armies involved in the battles. In addition to the introduction of a symbol for zero, another development over that same period of time was the development and acceptance of the decimal system. There are two parts to this system. First is the use of numerals – ten symbols (or ciphers) for the digits to represent the numbers from one to nine and the symbol for zero. The other is that the value of a number depends on the place it is in. The 2 in 124 has a value different from the 2 in 2786: in 124 2 stands for 2 times 10, but the 2 in 2786 stands for 2 times 1000. This is the place value principle. The ten numerals, and the place value principle together are called the decimal number system.[4]

In the early centuries of the common era the representation of large numbers by various mnemonics is widely found in India. The consonants were used to represent the nine digits and zero and vowels were inserted at pleasure in such a way as to make words to be remembered. With Roman letters *b, c, d, f, g, h, j, k, l, m* would represent 1, 2, ..., 8, 9, 0; *n, p, q, r, s, t, v, w, x, z*, again 1, 2, 3, ... ,8, 9, 0. Then "Toronto" could represent the number 6416; "poem" 20; 512 *gbc* or *snp* and hence the word "sonic". Also some digits could be described by words typical of the digits: "Sun" represented one, "eyes" two, "shiva" three, "Vedas" four, "point" zero and so on. Since mathematical and scientific rules were put in verse the latitude in choice of representative words suited the exigencies of verse.

---

[3] See A. A. Macdonell, *A History of Sanskrit Literature* (New York: Haskell House, [1968 reprint of a 1900 book]), and R. N. Mukherjee, "Background to the Discovery of the Symbol for Zero", in *Indian Journal for the History of Science*, Vol. 12, 1977, pp. 225-231.

[4] I have summarized developments in India from the times of the *Sulba sutra* until after the epic period and the Jaina writings, leading up to Aryabhara. There are some similarities between the decimal system described here and calculations with counting rods done by the Chinese; there is a vertical form, and there is a horizontal form and both are described in Li Yan and Du Shiran, *Chinese Mathematics, A Concise History* (Oxford: Clarendon Press, 1987).

In terms of mathematical work the use of this system can be seen in the writing of Aryabhata (b. 476 CE). Indications are that he lived near Pataliputra and may have taught in Nalanda. The *Aryabhatiya* of Aryabhata is primarily a work on astronomy and was written in 499 CE. It has four chapters containing 118 verses. In verse 2 of chapter 1 he describes the word system. The mathematics needed for his book is all in chapter 3, titled *ganitapada*, which has 33 verses. Included in these 33 verses is a succinct treatment of all but one of the topics of the program in the last section; the exception was combinatorics. Also, there is a definition of, and a table for the trigonometric sine function. In compiling the table he used the ratio of the half-chord to the radius as a fundamental definition of the trigonometric sine, and used the value 62832/20000 for the ratio of the circumference to the diameter of a circle. Another new subject in the *Aryabhatiya* is "indeterminate equations": finding solutions to one equation in two unknowns. Both these subjects have been contributed to by many mathematicians since the times of Aryabhata. Aryabhata thus extended the *sthananga sutra* program to include new mathematics needed for the problems of astronomy and the reckoning of time, which are the main topics of his book. The brevity and the terseness of the verses must have caused difficulty to pupils; in the following centuries a large number of commentaries, and glosses, and "aids" were written to supplement the meagre and sparse text. Many of these were in languages other than Sanskrit.

Mathematics is useful to a number of sciences or *sastras* in India as elsewhere – the *sulbasutras*, astronomy, and prosody as well as alchemy, medicine and philosophy (particularly Jaina). But there also exists a literature directly concerned with mathematics, in particular with arithmetic (especially its commercial and other applications), algebra, and geometry (both constructive and mensurational versions). While there was never a class of people who did mathematics, most practitioners of mathematics were astronomers, astrologers, or calculators of intervals or moments of time appropriate for performance of rituals. The subject, *ganita*, already contained in the Jaina term *ganita anuyoga*, was first used as the title of chapter 2 in Aryabhata's work. Many useful illustrations to Aryabhata's rules were given by his early commentator, Bhaskara I, in his *Aryabhatiya bhasya* written in 629 CE. It also includes about 125 exercises; he observes that only by solving a large number of exercises one understands the rules. The same Bhaskara gave the name *kuttaca* ("pulverizer") to the method Aryabhata used to solve indeterminate equations. Many of the exercises in his commentary are on the application of the "pulverizer" to problems of planets' mean motions. Bhaskara I provides a further expansion of the contents of mathematics; in addition to arithmetical operations and applications, Bhaskara adds four *bijas*. These are problem solving methods. They are all methods which say to the reader: "to solve a problem, let x be the unknown; use the given information to set up an equation involving the unknown; solve it using the methods described in the rules, and then, look! you have the answer". If it is a problem involving more than one unknown the corresponding equation would be an indeterminate equation. These *bijas* are an expansion of the *yawat tawat* (number 6) in the *sthananga sutra* list.

THE *BRAHMASPHUTA SIDDHANTA* OF *BRAHMAGUPTA* (628 CE); TRANSMISSION TO BAGHDAD (C. 770 CE)

Bhaskara's contemporary, Brahmagupta, wrote the book *Brahmasphuta siddhanta* in his thirtieth year (according to his own statement).[5] It is a corrected and up-dated version of the old astronomical work, the *Brahma siddhanta*, and he devotes two chapters of this work to mathematics – chapter 12, of 66 verses to arithmetic, and chapter 13 of 98 verses to the pulverizer. This chapter 12 is the earliest extant formal treatise on arithmetic in Sanskrit. (Compared to the *very brief* treatment of these topics given by Aryabhata, Brahmagupta's presentation is a formal treatise!) In it he gives succinct rules for twenty arithmetical operations (*parikarma*), and eight applications (*vyavaharas*). Chapter 18 is devoted to algebra (*kuttaca* or the pulverizer). Among the topics discussed, in addition to the pulverizer itself, are the mathematics of zero and of surds, quadratic equations, equations with several unknowns, and indeterminate equations of the second degree.[6]

The arithmetic chapter includes sections on arithmetic operations, on interest calculations and the use of progressions, mensuration formulae for plane geometry, calculations of both approximate and accurate values for volumes of pyramidal (pile of wood and lumber) and conical volumes (pile of grains, or sand), formulae for number of bricks and logs in a pile, heights of towers and trees using both similar triangles and trigonometry, and simple formulae for calculating time elapsed since sunrise using the shadow of a stick. All this becomes *patiganita*, or practical mathematics in later Indian writings. The first book of that title was written by Sridhara in the 8th century.[7] In the writing of history of mathematics practical mathematics gets little attention, probably because one is much more attracted to the more glamorous aspects of 'higher' mathematics.

The algebra chapter of Brahmagupta's book includes sections on the pulverizer, methods for solving simple, quadratic, and indeterminate equations, and more complicated problems as well as methods. He admits negative solutions and devises symbolic representation of negative quantities. All these have been extensively commented on in both Indian and Western mathematical treatments – given that it is all higher mathematics! It may be worth mentioning in passing that the phrase *bija ganita* for algebra (literally the "science of calculation with unknown elements") was used by Prthudaka, who flourished about the year 850 CE, and wrote a commentary on Brahmagupta's work, which included many examples.[8]

It was through the *Brahmasphuta siddhanta* of Brahmagupta that the Muslims

---

[5] See H. T. Colebrooke, *Algebra, with Arithmetic and Mensuration, from the Sanscrit of Brahmegupta and Bhascara* (London: John Murray, 1817).

[6] There is no convincing evidence to support the theory that Brahmagupta had a Greek source. See B. J. Van Der Waerden, "Pell's Equation in Greek and Hindu Mathematics", in *Russian Mathematical Surveys*, Vol. 31, 1976, pp. 210-225.

[7] See K. S. Shukla, *The Patiganita of Sridharacarya* (Lucknow: Department of Mathematics and Astronomy, Lucknow University, 1959).

[8] See G. G. Joseph, *The Crest of the Peacock* (London: Tauris and Co., 1991).

came to know and became conversant with Indian Astronomy and Mathematics. They learned early in their history of the Hindu achievements in algebra, for Brahmagupta's astronomical work was one of those that Indian scholars brought to the Caliph al-Mansur around 770 CE, and it was translated by al-Fazari into Arabic. The translation must have been no easy task for al-Fazari, especially given the terse and the poetic style of the Sanskrit books. Another commentator mentions that it was not uncommon for the early translators of Indian material to leave certain words untranslated, simply spelling them out in Arabic.[9]

THE WORK OF AL-KHWARIZMI (825 CE) AND ITS LATIN TRANSLATIONS

In tracing how the Hindu-Arabic numerals came to Europe all of our references point in the direction of al-Khwarizmi. It is known that he was working in the early 9th century in the "House of Wisdom" (*Bayt al-Hikma*) of Caliph al-Mamun in Baghdad. The House of Wisdom was the centre for the translation of texts, and in the 9th century Arabic science and learning became dominant around the Mediterranean. In the course of Muslim conquests the Hindu-Arabic numerals and their arithmetic were carried by the Moors through North Africa and into Spain. Nevertheless they do not seem to have been used outside the Moorish lands before the middle of the 11th century. Now Arabic numerals were known in the 10th century. The mathematical revival of the 970s has been linked with Gerbert of Aurillac, later Pope Sylvester II; Gerbert may have heard of the numerals but since he left Northern Spain by 972 it is doubtful that he had become familiar with al-Khwarizmi's arithmetic. He came to write a booklet of about four pages but he found the "toil so hard to be almost impossible". After that he returned to the study of logic which he found "easy". Legend has played a part in keeping Gerbert as pointing to the future: namely the gradual conquest by arithmetic of the educated Western mind. But that conquest was to be by the Hindu-Arabic numerals and its arithmetic based on ten numerals including zero. An excellent general account of this period is found in Murray.[10]

The processes involved in using Hindu-Arabic numerals, as opposed to Roman numerals, acquired the name "algorism" in the West. It is generally agreed that the word "algorithm" comes from the name of the scholar Abu Jafar Muhammad ibn Musa al-Khwarizmi, who lived about 800-847 CE and used the Arabic language. His arithmetical work, referred to earlier, *The Book of Addition and Subtraction According to the Hindu Calculation* introduced the decimal system and the place value principle that the Hindus had developed by the 6th century. Al-Khwarizmi also wrote another book, *The Book of Restoration and Balancing*, a book on algebra. The Arabic title of the book, *Kitab al-jabr wal-muqabala* contains the word from which "algebra" is

---

[9] See J. L. Berggren, *Episodes in the Mathematics of Medieval Islam* (New York: Springer-Verlag, 1986).

[10] A. Murray, *Reason and Society in the Middle Ages* (Oxford: Clarendon Press, 1978).

derived. Al-Khwarizmi's writings included works on astronomy, geography, arithmetic, and algebra. The word "algorithm" was originally spelled "algorism" in its English version from about the 12th century on; only in this century, after the advent of digital computers did the spelling "algorithm" come to be used in English. The subject to which al-Khwarizmi gave his name, algorism, seems to derive from a lost Arabic original.[11] Crossley and Henry[12] point out that there are sufficient differences between the four types of Latin texts on algorisms (identified by Vogel) to assert that some are not direct translations from a single original text. They give a careful narration of the different versions. A copy of a Latin translation made from an earlier Arabic version (or versions) of an original *Arithmetic* by al-Khwarizmi is in a Cambridge Manuscript and they give a complete translation of that Manuscript. They conclude that it could be from the 13th (but no later than the 14th) century.

There are a number of other algorisms. Halliwell published in 1841 the *Carmen de algorismo (Poems on algorism)* of Alexander de Villa Dei (originally published in 1220 CE). The other popular algorism text was written by John of Sacrobosco, who died in 1256 CE. It is called *Algorismus vulgaris (Common algorism)* or *De arte numerandi (On the art of numeration)*. English translations of the two texts were published by Steele.[13] The *Carmen de algorismo* became *The Crafte of Nombrynge* and *De arte numerandi* became *The Art of Nombryng*.

The Muslim mathematicians were ready to appreciate the effectiveness of numerical procedures for solving quadratic equations or indeterminate equations. They had inherited both the Babylonian sexagecimal system and the decimal system of the Hindus, and these systems provided a good basis for numerical techniques in mathematics. Combined with their desire to do astronomical calculations associated with their ecclesiastical needs they combined the Hindu arithmetic and algebra, with the astronomical results to devise many methods which extended the application of trigonometry, and algebra.[14] On the other hand the Greek geometrical approach had behind it the authority of men whom the Muslims admired and respected. These two approaches were combined – the numerical and the geometric – to create the new science of algebra. In arithmetic and astronomy he introduced Hindu methods to the Islamic world, while his exposition of algebra was of seminal importance in the development of that science in the Islamic world.

Decimal arithmetic was an important system of calculation in the Islamic

---

[11] See K. Vogel, *Mohammed ibn Musa Alchwarizmi's Algorismus, Das fruehste Lehrbuch zum Rechnen mit Indischen Ziffern* (Aalen Osnabrueck: Zeller, 1963).

[12] J. N. Crossley and A. S.Henry, "Thus Spake al-Khwarizmi: A Translation of the Text of Cambridge University Library Ms. Ii.Vi.5", in *Historia Mathematica*, Vol. 17, 1990, pp. 103-131.

[13] See R. Steele, *The Earliest Arithmetics in English* (Published for The Early English Society by the Oxford University Press, 1922).

[14] "Hindu" is a word coined by the Muslim writers and used by al-Khwarizmi and al-Uqlidisi in phrases like "mathematics according to the Indi" or "mathematics written in the style of the Hindi". Since the phrase "Hindu mathematics" occurs in many later European writings in this sense it is easier to use it that way. Thus the phrase "Hindu mathematics" refers to "mathematics of the Hindi people" rather than "mathematics done by the people following the Hindu religion". See A. S. Saidan, *The Arithmetic of Al-Uqlidisi* (Boston: D. Reidel Publishing Co., 1978).

world. By about the middle of the 10th century al-Uqlidisi solved some problems by the use of decimal fractions in his book on Hindu arithmetic (called *Kitab al-Fusul fi al-Hisab al-Hindi*). That book was written in Damascus in the years 952/3 CE. Thus in about two centuries, from the al-Fazari translation of the *Brahmasphuta siddhanta* to the work of al-Uqlidisi, the Hindu arithmetic (using decimal system and place value principle) was adapted and extended to include decimal fractions. So it is appropriate that the system used since that time is called the Hindu-Arabic system.

LEONARDO OF PISA AND THE *LIBER ABACI* (1202 CE)

Leonardo of Pisa, also called Fibonacci (1170-1250 CE) introduced scientific calculating methods into business practice. At the time of his birth Pisa ranked with Venice and Genoa as one of the great commercial centres of Italy. These towns had large warehouses where goods could be stored and duty paid, and the heads of such establishments were men of considerable prominence. It was such a position that the father of Leonardo held in the port of Bugia, on the north coast of Africa. Leonardo received his early education from a Moorish schoolmaster. As a young man he travelled about the Mediterranean, meeting with scholars and becoming acquainted with the various arithmetic systems in use among merchants of different lands. All the systems of computation he counted as poor, however, compared with that which used the Hindu-Arabic numerals. He therefore wrote a work in 1202 CE, the *Liber Abaci*, a popular encyclopedia of medieval mathematics widely quoted by later writers. It is not known why Leonardo selected this title since the book has nothing to do whatever with the ordinary abacus but instead deals entirely with the Hindu-Arabic numerals and methods of reckoning. In fact it was the chief means by which this system was introduced into the West. In that book he gave a treatment of arithmetic and elementary algebra.

In the title *Liber Abaci*, abaci has the more general meaning of mathematics and calculation (or applied mathematics) rather than merely of a counting machine. The word is derived from the name of an ancient counting and reckoning device which employs counters or beads placed on a series of lines, slits, or wires to represent numbers. In medieval and Renaissance times, however, the word *abaco* lost its specific connection with the reckoning board and came to be used in a more general sense in the title of *Liber Abaci* in the book of Leonardo. The book was not a product of the academic schools of his day but was based on his observation and practice during his extensive travels. The work is divided into fifteen chapters. Seven are on different arithmetic techniques. Five are on different applications of those techniques to practical problems. The next two chapters are about the setting up of problems for solutions. The last chapter was also on practical problems, but included many mensuration formulae. A comparison of the contents of the *Liber Abaci* with the *ganita* chapter of *Brahmasphuta siddhanta* is very informative. They are quite similar in that they both are about arithmetic and practical problem solving. But the *kuttaca* chapter of Brahmagupta's work includes more methods and problems in algebra. Leonardo was writing for an audience to which he was presenting the case for using Hindu-Arabic arithmetic methods and so remained very much the practical mathematician.[15]

THE ARITHMETIC SCHOOLS OF FLORENCE (C. 1300 CE); THE *TREVISO ARITHMETIC* (1478 CE)

By the beginning of the 14th century we find schools of mathematics called *scuole* or *botteghe d'abaco* when there is no evidence that an abacus was ever used in them, while the teachers who taught in these schools were called *maestri d'abaco* when they may have never handled a reckoning board. The older abacus itself became known as a *tavola d'abaco*.

The *libri d'abaco* or "books of the abacus" then should not be confused with any kind of physical or mechanical reckoning device, nor are they, as their name might suggest, instruction manuals in the use of such devices. They assist in reckoning, but operate entirely with the Hindu-Arabic numerals and methods of reckoning associated with them. They did not rely on material objects to perform calculations but they were part of a movement towards the adoption of pen-and-paper reckoning methods. It was this method that spread in the West.

The abaci are in one sense an introduction to the use of the Hindu-Arabic numerals and methods of reckoning. What seems to be really distinctive about them is that they seek to put this knowledge to use. Their emphasis is not on how to reckon but on how to use it in the solution of mathematical problems. This unification of knowledge and action is reminiscent of early Indian mathematics books. It is by their large collection of problems that we are able to distinguish the abaci from other forms of mathematics prevalent in the period; it is this that identifies them as a distinct genre of mathematical literature. The abaci are primarily collections of mathematical problems. Several writers have called them "commercial" or "merchant arithmetics". This does not quite describe their content, because their material was not confined to only arithmetic. Many manuscripts included extensive treatments of geometry, again with a practical bent. Volume of grain in a pyramidal pile, calculating the height of a tree or tower by means of similar triangles, or determining the number of bricks needed to build a wall, and so on. Chapter IV of Van Egmond's Doctoral Dissertation on *The Commercial Revolution and the Beginnings of Western Mathematics* contains a detailed summary of the contents of an abacus manuscript.[16] Clearly Italy was the place to learn computational mathematics.[17] The *Liber Abaci* of Leonardo may have

---

[15] See P. Rajagopal, "Practical and Commercial Problems in Indian Mathematics", in *Arhat Vachana*, No. 4, 1992, pp. 55-70.

[16] See Warren Van Egmond, *The Commercial Revolution and the Beginnings of Western Mathematics in Renaissance Florence, 1300-1500* (Bloomington: Indiana University, 1976).

[17] Tobias Dantzig, in his book *Number: the Language of Science* (New York: Macmillan and Co., 1954) quotes an anecdote about a German merchant of the 15th century who sought advice on where to

put Italy in the forefront of that movement; the arithmetic schools and books of Florence and Pisa gave them the momentum.

The final manuscript in this category is a mathematics textbook known simply as the *Treviso Arithmetic*. It provides us with a glimpse of the mathematical transition taking place, and hints at some of the forces shaping it. The book bears no formal title, and its author remains anonymous; therefore it has been named after its place of origin. Treviso is a northern Italian city, about 30 miles north of Venice. Frank Swetz gives not only a translation of the book but also gives a perspective of the climate and the context in which the book arose.[18]

Two concluding comments are in order. The first is that we see a transition from the Arithmetic of the Learned to an Arithmetic of the People; that is, from a theoretical treatment to a practical one. The advent of printing enables the changeover from counters on boards to numbers written on a surface, and propels that transition. The other comment is that universities appear to have played a relatively minor role in this dissemination.

THE *ALGEBRA* OF RAFAEL BOMBELLI (1572 CE)

By the end of the 16th century more than two hundred such arithmetics had been published; among them the works of Borghi, Calandri, Sfortunati and Ghaligai, which were published in more than one edition. The first to break away from the tradition of writing an arithmetic for a particular section of the community was Pacioli, who instead addressed a wider public. His *Summa de arithmetica, geometria, proportioni et proportionalita*, published in Venice in 1494 CE, was an encyclopedia which contained the mathematical knowledge of his time. However his treatment of equations did not go beyond the solution of the quadratic. During the first half of the 16th century the cubic and the biquadratic equations were solved, the first by Del Ferro and Tartaglia (independently), and the second by Ferrari. Their methods of solution were given by Girolamo Cardano in his treatise on algebraic equations.

It is in such a background that Rafael Bombelli conceived the idea of writing a treatise on algebra, which he did in 1572. It was the first textbook of algebra to be published in Italy and was titled *L'algebra parte maggiore dell' arithmetica divisa in tre libri*.[19] Its publication marked the end of a movement which began in Italy at the beginning of the 13th century when Leonardo introduced the rules of arithmetic and

---

send his son for advanced commercial education. He appealed to a prominent professor of a university as to where he should send his son. The reply was that if the mathematical curriculum of the young man was to be confined to adding and subtracting, he perhaps could obtain the instruction in a German university; but the art of multiplying and dividing, he continued, had been greatly developed in Italy which, in his opinion was the only country where such advanced instruction could be obtained.

[18] See Frank J. Swetz, *Capitalism and Arithmetic* (La Salle: Open Court, 1987).

[19] See S. A. Jayawardene, "The influence of Practical Arithmetics on the *Algebra* of Rafael Bombelli", in *Isis*, Vol. 64, 1973, pp. 510-523.

algebra in his *Liber Abaci.*

CONCLUSION

The Hindu-Arabic numerals were introduced into Europe through Latin translations of Al-Khwarizmi's book in the 12th century. They were popularized by the book *Liber Abaci*. It took four hundred years before the new numeral system finally asserted its supremacy in Europe. The spread of the system was aided by the use of paper which had become easily available and by the introduction of printing. It was actually printing which brought about the standardization of the shapes of the ten signs. The entry of the new numerals into Europe was timely – at the end of the Dark Ages and at the beginning of a revival of learning. The exploration of the scope and potential of the system coincided with a period of a new upsurge in scholastic activities. Eventually, the new system not only prepared the way for the development of natural sciences but also laid the foundation of modern mathematics, and brought about the universalization of the subject.

While much of this knowledge is available it does not appear to be widely known. The traditional approaches in history have been to evaluate Arabic or Indian knowledge against a Western yardstick of technical innovation. This perception of the relative importance of *our* history and *their* history[20] put Asian contributions on the periphery of European science and mathematics.

A CHRONOLOGY

800 to 300 BCE	*Sulva sutras*	Pythagoras
500 to 300 BCE	Jaina sutras	Euclid
499 CE	Aryabhata	
628 CE	Bhaskara I, Brahmagupta	
750 CE	Sridhara	
770 CE	al-Fazari (in the court of Caliph al-Mansur)	
825 CE	al-Khwarizmi (in the court of Caliph al-Mamun)	
(850 CE:	Mahavira, *Ganita sara sangraha*)	
952/953 CE	Al-Uqlidisi, *Kitab al-Fusul fi al-Hisab al-Hindi*	
(1150 CE:	Bhaskara II, *Lilavathi, Bijaganita*)	
1202 CE	Leonardo of Pisa	
(1258 CE:	Baghdad destroyed by the Mongols)	
c. 1300	Arithmetic schools of Florence	
(1348:	The Black Death)	
(c. 1400	Madhava)	

---

[20] See Bernard Lewis, "Other People's History", in *American Scholar*, Vol. 59, no. 3, 1990, pp. 397-405, esp. p. 397.

1478	Anonymous, *Treviso Arithmetic*
(1484:	Nicholas Chuquet, *Triparty en la science des nombres*)
(1522:	Adam Riese)
(1542:	Robert Recorde)
1572	Rafael Bombelli

7

Historical Reflections on Scientific Knowledge:
The Case of Medieval Islam

J. Len Berggren

INTRODUCTION

In this chapter I shall confine my discussion to the exact sciences in medieval Islam, namely mathematics itself and three sciences, astronomy, cartography and optics, where mathematics played a fundamental role. However, since the theme of this volume is "Knowledge Across Cultures", I also want to treat briefly the transmission of these sciences, both to medieval Islam and to the Latin West. As regards the transmission of ancient science to medieval Islam I shall focus almost entirely on the transmission from Greek culture, simply because it was Islam's source for most of the science I shall discuss.[1]

CONDITIONS OF THE TRANSMISSION OF ANCIENT SCIENCE

The first point to note about the transmission of ancient sciences to medieval Islam late in the 8th century and throughout the ninth is that it took place in a learned environment. When the armies of Islam overran the world from the borders of France to the borders of China they occupied areas that were the homes of communities, Christian, Jewish and pagan, with a long tradition of learning and scholarship. The great Christian translators, Hunayn b. Isḥāq and his son Isḥāq b. Hunayn, the great translator, astronomer and mathematician Thābit b. Qurra from the pagan centre of Harran, and the Jewish court astronomer and astrologer Māshā'allāh did not acquire their expertise after they got their posts in Baghdad. Rather, they knew languages, the techniques of

---

[1] It is worth noting, however, that the decimal positional system of arithmetic, together with many of its computational algorithms, the Sine function in trigonometry and many geometric methods in astronomy originated in India. On the first two some details may be found in J. L. Berggren, *Episodes in the Mathematics of Medieval Islam* (New York and Heidelberg: Springer Verlag, 1986). For astronomy see E. S. Kennedy, *A Commentary on al-Bīrūnī's Kitāb Tadīd Nihāyāt al-Amākin. An 11th Century Treatise on Mathematical Geography* (Beirut: American University of Beirut Press, 1973).

scholarship and the sciences when they began their work.

My second point, however, is that one should not infer from the above that the transmission of ancient science to medieval Islam was all the doing of non-Muslims. Indeed it was only Muslim interest, support and participation that enabled these ancient cultures to make their contributions to a culture that soon surpassed them all in science.

Having made these preliminary remarks I now turn to the four areas where Greek influence was paramount: geometry, astronomy, cartography and optics.

ISLAMIC GEOMETRY, I – TRADITION OF EUCLID'S *ELEMENTS*

In geometry it was Greek mathematical texts that set the stage for the development of Islamic traditions in geometry. The greatest work of Euclid, the *Elements*, was translated twice by Hajjāj b. Matar (for Hārūn al-Rashīd and for al-Ma'mūn). It was again translated by Ishāq b. Hunayn. And one sign of the care with which these things were done is that when Thābit b. Qurra came to revise this translation he again went back to Greek manuscripts.

Of course translation of a work of this size, scope and complexity is only the beginning of the process of its assimilation into the intellectual life of a culture. So in addition to the translations there was an astounding amount of work aimed at a wide variety of audiences: the beginning students, the professional researchers and the philosophers. Thus two commentaries were done on the whole of the *Elements*, an immense task, as well as numerous commentaries on individual books or groups of them. In addition to these there were numerous summaries, like that of the philosopher Ibn Sīnā (the Latin *Avicenna*), recensions and emendations. These included critiques of the famous parallel postulate which, translated into Latin in the 17th century, had an influence on the European developments that were to lead to non-Euclidean geometry.

The Latin Transmission of the Arabic *Elements*

As regards the transmission of the Arabic *Elements* to the West, this occurred in the context of a Greek-to-Latin tradition stemming from the late Roman empire. However, the material in this tradition faded quickly into the background when the Latin translations from the Arabic Euclid began to appear. The most widely used of these were versions done by the English philosopher and mathematician Adelard of Bath in the first half of the 12th century.

Perhaps it is not surprising to learn that the briefest of Adelard's three versions was the most popular. In it he gives not the actual proofs of Euclid but remarks about how one would go about proving the theorems if one wished to! What is happening here, of course, is what happened in the Arabic world. First a translation from another language and then an (more or less) independent recasting of the material into a form suited for study. And it is in the same spirit that Campanus of Novara took over

Adelard's formulations of the theorems, again recast the proofs, and fashioned what is, mathematically, the most adequate Arabic-Latin Euclid of all.[2] The Arabs would have been proud of their Latin pupils, who obviously caught the spirit of the whole enterprise!

ISLAMIC GEOMETRY, II – ADVANCED GEOMETRY

To return now to Islam, with the base of the *Elements* secured, geometers were able to go on to the study of higher geometry, for example Archimedes' works on the measurement of areas and volumes and those of Apollonius on the geometry of the conic sections (the parabola, ellipse and hyperbola).

In the case of Archimedes, medieval Islam got two works – just enough to show what was possible and to provide some tantalizing clues about what other things could be done. The first was the *Measurement of the Circle*, translated by Thābit. The second, the much deeper *On the Sphere and Cylinder*, was, like the *Elements,* translated by Ishāq b. Hunayn and revised by Thābit. And it was the latter work that furnished one of the first great tasks undertaken by medieval Islamic mathematics: the problem of finding the area of a segment of a parabola. In his preface to the *Sphere and Cylinder* Archimedes had said what the area of the segment was, but he had not said how he proved it. Thābit took this as a challenge and by a long series of propositions discovered a proof of the result. Moreover he derived and proved a similar result for the volumes of nine solids derived from the parabola by rotating it around various lines.

However, those who read Thābit's treatise on the parabola found it too long, and difficult to follow. These criticisms evidently wounded the family pride, so his grandson, Ibrāhīm ibn Sīnā ibn Thābit, found another, simpler derivation of the result. This he did, in a short, elegant series of propositions that certainly bear comparison with Archimedes' own approach. And following on the work of Thābit on the solid figures later writers of the 10th century, Abū Sahl al-Kūhī and Ibn al-Haytham (the Latin "Alhazen"), found new ways of deriving the volume of the paraboloid.

Taste for such abstruse geometrical work is a rare quality, and nothing shows this better than the fate of the work of Archimedes' younger contemporary, Apollonius of Perga. Of his great work on the conic sections, called simply the *Conics*, only four of the eight chapters survive in Greek and evidently the work was not much studied in late antiquity. However, three more of the books survived in Arabic translation. And this is why the Maronite scholar, Abraham Ecchellensis, was able to make available to scholars of the 17th century a paraphrase of seven of the eight books, together with other advanced geometrical material which he had gathered from Arabic treatises. In addition, the scientist Ibn al-Haytham (whose name we have already met with in

---

[2] J. Murdoch, "Euclid: Transmission of the *Elements*", in C. C. Gillespie (ed.), *Dictionary of Scientific Biography*, Vol. 4 (New York: Charles Scribner's Sons, 1971), pp. 437-459. The material quoted is on p. 446, but I have drawn freely from the whole article for my account of the Arabic and Latin traditions of Euclid.

connection with the paraboloid and shall meet several times again) attempted a reconstruction of the eighth book.

I have dwelt on this material at some length because of, not in spite of, its technicality, for it is too often emphasized that the primary interest of medieval Islamic society in mathematics was due to the subject's utility. And to the extent that Muslims were interested in mathematics useful to the Muslim community this is true. But the continuing Muslim study of highly abstruse works of Archimedes and Apollonius (to mention only two), extending over a period of several centuries, suggests that the love of learning and research must also be counted among the motivations for Islamic science.

ISLAMIC GEOMETRY, III – CRITIQUES OF GREEK GEOMETRY

Another feature of mathematics in medieval Islam is the controversy about mathematical methods that intruded into mathematical discussions. The scientists of medieval Islam were not content simply to take over and to develop methods inherited from the ancients. They also felt free to criticize them and to debate their validity.

Of the many examples that could be given I take two. The first is Abū Sahl al-Kūhī's criticism of Archimedes' approach to finding the circumference of the circle in his treatise *On the Measurement of the Circle*, and the reason for his criticism is that instead of using exact methods Archimedes uses a technique of approximation. In Abū Sahl's view any such method is fundamentally flawed. As he puts it, "...it is clear that the method [of approximation] does not lead to the truth at all..." But his respect for Archimedes, whom he calls "the imām" of mathematics, is so great that later he writes: "Archimedes is above seeking the measurement of the circumference of the circle by this method, and...this is because of the greatness of Archimedes and the abasement of that method of calculation".

And he repeatedly says that truth comes from exact arguments built on sound premises, not from approximations. In the course of discussing values of π al-Kūhī speaks scornfully of "the natural philosophers", such as Aristotle and Galen, whose "knowledge is through opinion, dogma and likelihood", and it seems that his rejection of approximation as a valid mathematical technique stems from his desire to put as much intellectual distance between such thinkers and himself as possible.

My other example is that of 'Umar al-Khayyāmī late in the 11th century, who criticized the theory of proportion found in Euclid's *Elements*, a cornerstone theory of a key work in ancient mathematics. Yet despite this status 'Umar criticized its inability to convey the intuitive meaning of the proposition "A is related to B as C is related to D". He also suggested an alternative theory based on the idea that ratios too were a certain kind of quantity which could be compared with numbers. And in working out the details 'Umar led mathematicians as close to the idea of a real number as they were to get before the Renaissance.

That Abū Sahl was a great mathematician who was mistaken in his view of the authenticity of Archimedes' treatise and the value of approximation for mathematics and that 'Umar was a great mathematician who was on to a potentially fruitful idea is not the point here. The point is that both felt themselves quite competent to evaluate ancient ideas and to point out weaknesses where they existed.

ISLAMIC GEOMETRY, IV – APPLIED GEOMETRY

Having earlier mentioned mathematics as a subject of practical utility in Islam, I should mention that the Greeks too were interested in the utility of the subject, even of such a subject as geometry. And there are three particularly apt examples, all from the work of the Alexandrian scientist Ptolemy (2nd century CE), where the Greek traditions went over to the Islamic world.

The Tradition of the Astrolabe

The first is Ptolemy's treatise, the *Planisphærium,* which treated the theory of the design of astrolabes. Its Greek original has been lost, but its surviving Arabic translation gave rise to a rich literature on the topic, both on the use and the theory of such an instrument.

      One of the earliest Arabic treatises on the use of the astrolabe was that of 'Alī b. ʿĪsā in the 9th century, who explained both how to use the instrument for finding the time of day or night and how to use it to find the direction of prayer, i.e., of Mecca. (This latter is obviously a response to the needs of Islamic society.[3]) But in order to use the astrolabe to find the direction of Mecca certain lines had to be added to it to indicate directions (i.e., azimuths) on the horizon, for finding the direction of Mecca is just the problem of finding Mecca's azimuth. The introduction of such lines was just one of the innovations that Muslim scientists introduced into that instrument. But it turns out that the azimuth lines are exactly those curves that it is not easy to draw on the instrument. Hence their introduction led to a problem of some geometrical complexity. And Muslim efforts to solve this problem led to a series of solutions, until what was obviously "the" elegant and simple construction was discovered some time during the late 10th century.[4]

      Ptolemy's treatise on the subject was translated from Arabic into Latin by Hermann of Carinthia in the 12th century in a compendium which included additional material by the Maslama al-Majrītī (i.e., "from Madrid") on the astrolabe. Such material would have been very necessary since, by the 12th century, the practice of the craft of making astrolabes had gone well beyond the material in Ptolemy's treatise.

---

[3] Although it should be noted that few medieval mosques were aligned by astronomical methods.
[4] See J. L. Berggren, "Medieval Islamic Methods for Drawing Azimuth Circles on the Astrolabe", in *Centaurus*, Vol. 34, 1991, pp. 309-344.

The Islamic Transformation of Trigonometry

The second Ptolemaic work I shall discuss here is the *Almagest,* in which Ptolemy explains both how to derive models for the motion of the planets from observations and how to construct the tables that astronomers use to find out where the planet will be at a given time. And in the first part of this work Ptolemy gives the basic tool of Greek trigonometry, a table of lengths of chords in a circle of fixed radius.

However, Islamic astronomers completely transformed this Greek material with the aid of an idea from Indian mathematics, namely the Sine function. At first sight replacing the chord by the Sine, which is half the length of the chord of twice the angle, seems to be a strange idea. But it turned out to be just what was needed to make trigonometry easier to use.   In addition Islamic astronomers used the five other trigonometric functions that are known today, and discovered some basic theorems, such as the Law of Sines, commonly used in modern trigonometry, which allowed many problems to be attacked more directly. And the net effect of all these innovations was to create out of a subject which had been very much the handmaiden of astronomy an autonomous mathematical discipline. Nasīr al-Dīn al-Tūsī's perception of this fact in the 13th century enabled him to write a book that is the first systematic text on trigonometry as a mathematical discipline.

The Cartographic Tradition

My final example of useful Greek geometrical methods that were transmitted to medieval Islam is found in the *Geography* of Ptolemy. In the early part of the work Ptolemy explains methods for mapping the curved surface of the Earth on a plane, methods which are not particularly easy. And since Ptolemy admits that such maps are needed only for representing large areas of the Earth's surface (as opposed to separate kingdoms), the tradition of cartography seems to have been a frail one both in the ancient world and in medieval Islam. In fact the first major advance on Ptolemy's cartography we know of is that of the Central Asian polymath al-Bīrūnī (10th – 11th centuries CE) who described two new projections of the sphere. One of these is the polar azimuthal projection and the other is Nicolsi's projection, wrongly credited to the Renaissance cartographer of that name. It has acquired a certain degree of familiarity today by virtue of its use until recently as the National Geographic Society's logo.

That other cartographic ideas were "in the air" in the Muslim world is certain, since the Muslim geographer al-Idrīsī, working at the court of Roger II in Norman Sicily, constructed a world map which appears to be based on some mathematical system, but which is certainly not Ptolemaic.

Bīrūnī's projections were not transmitted to the Latin West, and what the influence of Idrīsī and other geographers was we cannot yet say. The Muslim influence on the Latin West in geography appears to have been rather in the field of locations of important localities, for lists of latitudes and longitudes of these – including numerous places which would have been at best "names" to the Latin West – were transmitted in the astronomical handbooks referred to above.

ISLAMIC ASTRONOMY, I – THE TRADITION OF THE *ALMAGEST*

As Euclid's *Elements* was the basis for Islamic geometry so was Ptolemy's *Almagest* the basis for its astronomy. We have already given details of the many types of works that were necessary for the complete integration of this book into Islamic intellectual life. So we shall say of the *Almagest* only that in its case there had already developed in the Greek world a preparatory curriculum which followed on the mastery of the *Elements* and which included works like Euclid's *Phænomena,* Theodosius's *Sphærica* and a work of the same title by Menelaus of Alexandria.

All of these were also translated into Arabic and formed part of a curriculum, known as "The Middle Books". As such they played the same role in the professional training of the Islamic astronomer that their Greek versions had played in the training of the Hellenistic astronomer. And, just as the tradition of study of the *Elements* bore abundant fruit, so the Islamic tradition of the *Almagest* produced a flood of *zījes* (astronomical handbooks) which continued and developed the tradition of their Greek prototype.

And even very early works of this type were transmitted, as witnessed by Adelard of Bath's translation of the tables of Muhammad ibn Mūsā al-Khwārizmī as revised by Maslama al-Majrītī. This work, composed originally in the early 9th century, incorporated a certain amount of Indian material,[5] so its Latin translation was responsible for the spread of Indian methods as far as England in the 13th century CE.

To survey this extensive literature here would be impossible. So let me take only one further example, the *Sabean zīj* of the astronomer al-Battānī. Like Thābit, al-Battānī came from the ancient intellectual centre of Harran, where his father made astronomical instruments. And so good an observer was al-Battānī that he was able to show that at least three astronomical parameters that Ptolemy had thought were constant in fact changed over time.

Such was the quality of al-Battānī's observations, and so extensive were his tables, that his *zīj* became a standard work not only in Islam but in the Latin West following Plato of Tivoli's translation of it in the early 12th century CE. Indeed, so successful was it that it was printed twice (once in Nuremberg in 1537 and over a century later in Bologna in 1645) and was studied carefully by many astronomers – among them Copernicus.

Taken together, the Islamic astronomical handbooks that became known to the Europeans represent these improvements over that of Ptolemy:

    (1)   Understanding of the variable nature of some fundamental

---

[5] Indeed the work is of a very different character than that of the *Almagest*, and is cited here only as an example of an early astronomical handbook.

astronomical parameters, such as the angle between the zodiac and the celestial equator, and consequently better values for these.

(2)   Better star catalogues, which not only located known stars more accurately but listed stars unknown to the Greeks.

(3)   Better mathematical methods, both the improved trigonometry mentioned earlier and improved methods of interpolation in astronomical tables.

ISLAMIC ASTRONOMY, II – CRITIQUES OF GREEK ASTRONOMY

As with geometry so with astronomy. Here too the Islamic astronomers pointed out flaws in the Ptolemaic system. I have already mentioned al-Battānī as one astronomer (in fact one of several) who exposed Ptolemy's erroneous assumptions that certain astronomical values[6] were constant for all time. But a more fundamental problem concerned Ptolemy's statement[7] that it is the mathematician's task to explain the motion of the Sun, Moon and planets by uniform motions, that is, as he puts it in Book III 3,

> ...if we imagine the bodies or their circles being carried around by straight lines, in absolutely every case the straight line in question describes equal angles at the centre of its revolution in equal times.[8]

Although this was the ideal, several Islamic astronomers pointed out that it was one Ptolemy fell noticeably short of, for in certain cases the motion was not uniform with respect to the centre of the circle, but with respect to an eccentric point located elsewhere in space. Quite apart from the computational complexity which this introduced, and the philosophical strictures which it violated, it also violated, as we have just seen, Ptolemy's own stated criteria for his system.

A prominent critic of this feature of the Ptolemaic models was the astronomer Ibn al-Haytham, in his work *Puzzles in Ptolemy*. Written around the year 1000 CE this criticism resulted in no immediate reform, but beginning in the 13th century a series of astronomers, including the already-mentioned Nasīr al-Dīn al-Tūsī, discovered mathematical methods which allowed them to eliminate this objectionable feature of the Ptolemaic system. The most famous result of this work is a mathematical device known as the Tusi couple, which produces a point moving in a straight line by subjecting it to two circular motions.

In a sense, of course, this work was deeply conservative, since its aim was to

---

[6] The values in question included the obliquity of the ecliptic, the solar eccentricity and the solar apogee. Details may be found in W. Hartner, "Al-Battānī", in C. C. Gillespie (ed.), *Dictionary of Scientific Biography*, Vol. I (New York: Charles Scribner's Sons, 1970), pp. 507-516.

[7] See G. Toomer, *Ptolemy's Almagest* (New York: Springer-Verlag, 1984), pp. 140, 141 and 420.

[8] *Ibid.*, p. 141.

repair a fault in a system which was soon to be shown to have outlived its usefulness. But the mathematical methods in it were very important, and one finds them again in Copernicus's *De revolutionibus*. Indeed, for the Moon, where both the Ptolemaic and Copernican systems recognize the same centre of motion, the Copernican model is identical with one developed by the astronomer Ibn al-Shātir. Most historians of astronomy suppose there was some transmission of these ideas to the West, although as yet there is no completely convincing evidence of this.

ISLAMIC OPTICS, I – THE TRADITION OF GREEK OPTICS

I have already mentioned the name of Ibn al-Haytham, a scientist who was active in the late 10th century CE and the first half of the eleventh in Basra and Cairo. He made important contributions both to geometry and to astronomy, but it is to the field of optics where he made his greatest contribution, for he completely transformed this subject from what it had been in antiquity.

The Optics of Euclid and al-Kindī

In the ancient world the task of optics was to provide a theory of vision, and the Arab writers learned of optics through a variety of Greek sources, for example from the physical writings of Aristotle and Euclid's *Optics*. This treatise was studied throughout the medieval period in Islam, and one of the earliest Arabic treatises that it inspired was al-Kindī's *De aspectibus* (as it is known from the title of its Latin translation by Gerard of Cremona). The theory of Aristotle was physical and non-mathematical, and accounted for vision by images of objects arriving as a whole at the eye. In contrast, Euclid explained vision as resulting from a cone of visual rays emitted by the eyes. Al-Kindī accepted this but added the important idea of punctiform emission of light, i.e., the idea that light is emitted from every point of an illuminated object and proceeds outward in straight lines in all possible directions. However, al-Kindī did not apply this to vision, and all of the ancient theories left major questions unanswered.

Ptolemy's *Optics*

An important development of the Euclidean theory was that of Ptolemy. His *Optics* was a much larger work than that of Euclid's and also more ambitious, in the sense that it attempted to provide a theory of refraction and appealed not only to common experience but to a variety of experiments to demonstrate the principal features of the theory. Although Ptolemy attempted to explain certain features of vision by reference to Aristotelian physics these were *a priori* explanations, imported into the theory which, on the whole, suffered from the same defects as that of Euclid.

Ptolemy's work could have aided in an understanding of refraction in the early years of Islamic science, but it seems not to have been nearly so well-known as his *Almagest*. For example in his early writings even Ibn al-Haytham shows a naive view of refraction that could not have been written by anyone who knew Ptolemy's work.

ISLAMIC OPTICS, II – DEVELOPMENT OF GREEK TRADITION

However, it is fairly clear that we do not yet have all the pieces of this historical puzzle. A recently-published Arabic text shows that Abū Sa'd, a contemporary of Ibn al-Haytham, was aware of the mathematical content of what we now know as the Law of Refraction. This law is known as Snell's Law, after the 17th century scientist Willebrord Snell, who was until recently thought to be the discoverer of the law. It says that although a refracted ray makes a different angle with the perpendicular to the surface at the point of incidence than does the incoming ray, the ratio of the sines of these two angles is always the same for a given substance, whatever the incoming angle might be.

Such a fact is not likely to have been discovered by speculation, nor can it be derived mathematically from other laws known at the time. Eight centuries before Abū Sa'd, Ptolemy had tried to discover the relationship between the angle of the incoming ray and that of the refracted ray. In his *Optics* he even describes an apparatus he designed for the purpose and gives results of experiments he conducted with the apparatus. However the true relationship between the two angles eluded him. It appears, then, that sometime between that of al-Kindī and Abū Sa'd some clever experimenter found the correct relationship. (The extant text of Abū Sa'd's work does not suggest that he was the one to make the discovery, since he treats it in such an offhand way.)

And, whoever made it, the result surely marks one of the first great successes of the experimental method, since it would seem to have been arrived at by an experiment aimed not simply at confirming a predicted result but at discovering a new result. Yet this major discovery was so little known that Ibn al-Haytham was evidently unaware of it when he came to write his *Optics*, despite the fact that he knew of Abū Sa'd and other work of his related to refraction.

ISLAMIC OPTICS, III – TRANSFORMATION OF GREEK TRADITION

Thus it was against the background of Aristotle, Euclid and Ptolemy that Ibn al-Haytham commenced his optical studies, and by the early part of 1027 CE he had made summaries both of Euclid's and Ptolemy's *Optics*. After a false start (which he warned people not to read in case they should ever find a copy!), he wrote his great

Optics,[9] which completely transformed the field and provided the basis for all important work done in optics until the time of Kepler.

Part of Ibn al-Haytham's achievement lay in his transformation of the Aristotelian theory of vision. Ibn al-Haytham taught that what arrives at the eye is not the whole image that Aristotle posited but rays of light and colour emitted from every point of an illuminated object, which we have met in al-Kindī, although in his work they were not directly responsible for vision. Of these incoming rays the eye is sensitive only to those that are perpendicular to its surface, so that because each point on the object corresponds in this way to a unique point on the eye the object may be clearly seen. It was thus that Ibn al-Haytham gained the benefits both of the physically correct intuition of Aristotle and Euclid's geometrically useful idea of a cone.

Another innovation of Ibn al-Haytham was the introduction of the mind of the observer into the process of vision. Ibn al-Haytham argued that, apart from the immediate perception of light and colour, vision involves psychological aspects, such as memory and judgement. And only when these act on the entering pattern of light and color do we recognize objects for what they are. Thus a psychology of vision, combined with the geometry of the visual field and that of the visual apparatus,[10] provides a theory that accounts not only for correct vision but for mistakes and optical illusions.

It is an irony of history that Ibn al-Haytham's Optics made an impression on Western science[11] before it had any important effect on Islamic science,[12] and during the 13th century it furnished abundant material for writers like Roger Bacon, John Pecham and Witelo. In the Muslim East it attained importance only in the 14th century, following Kamāl al-Dīn al-Fārisī's paraphrase of it. On the basis of Ibn al-Haytham's work Kamāl al-Dīn was able to give a satisfactory explanation of the rainbow. And, in just one of many examples of simultaneous discovery in science, the same thing happened at about the same time in the West in the work of Theodoric of Freiburg.

CONCLUSION

I would like to conclude with some comparisons of the acquisition and development of the exact sciences in medieval Islam and the Latin West. First of all, in both cases the traditions of the various exact sciences are ones that the cultures acquired from outside. In the case of medieval Islam it was from the ancient source cultures mentioned early in this chapter, and in the case of the Latin West it was initially a thin layer of Greek learning imported through late Roman summaries and encyclopedias which provided

---

[9] In Arabic the *Kitāb al-Manāzir.* The first three books of this work are now available in the splendid edition and translation of A. I. Sabra, *The Optics of Ibn al-Haytham,* Parts I and II (London: The Warburg Institute,1989), where a reference to the published Arabic text will be found. The remaining books, done by the same author, will appear in due course.

[10] Including that of a second part of the eye, namely the vitreous humour.

[11] The name of the Latin translator is not known.

[12] For details see Sabra, *The Optics of Ibn al-Haytham,* 1989, Part II, pp. lxiv-lxvii.

the "learned environment" for the reception of the incomparably richer Arabic learning in the 11th – 13th centuries.

The second conclusion is that in both cases the acquisition of the exact sciences from earlier cultures led not simply to the preservation of these materials but to their active development and, in certain cases, even to their transformation. In the case of the Latin West this is well known and led to the scientific revolution of the 17th century. In the case of medieval Islam, however, it needs to be stressed since one still reads books treating medieval Islamic culture as one whose principal contribution was that of preserving ancient learning until such time as a culture that could really make use of it took over the scientific enterprise. Quite apart from the absurdity of the notion that a culture would occupy itself for five hundred years in copying highly technical books for which it had no important use, such a view of the Islamic contribution hardly squares with even the brief account presented here.

And such a view is particularly unfortunate in light of a major difference between the transmission of Greek science to the Islamic world and that of Islamic science to the Latin West. The difference, namely, is that although the Greek scientific tradition was dead when the great period of Arabic translation began in the 9th century CE, the Islamic tradition was still active when the majority of the Latin translations from the Arabic were done during the 12th and 13th centuries CE. To cite only one, though admittedly spectacular, example, the astonishingly fine mathematical work of Jamshīd al-Kāshī in Samarqand in the early 15th century CE was completely unknown in the Latin West. Thus, even though as a matter of principle it is historically misleading to look at *any* culture simply in terms of what it bequeathed a later one, this is particularly unfortunate in the case of that of medieval Islam, since it leaves out some of its finest scientific achievements.

8

A Modern Interpretation of Sinic Science

Ji Shuli

There has been a controversy as to whether Sinic knowledge of nature is a "science", or merely a primitive technology or necromancy. However, the advent of modern quantum physics has revealed the essence of science as just a human interpretation of the world. The new challenge is whether natural science is merely a description and explanation of the world as classical Occidental science asserted, or essentially a human interpretation of that world as ancient Sinic science had long held. This has shed new light upon old science and upon the controversy.

DICHOTOMIC INTERPRETATION IN OCCIDENTAL SCIENCE

Interpretation in Occidental science from its very origins might be traced back to primitive Hebraic Christianity and early Greek thought. As a culture it associated the paramount value of human beings with God, and thus bifurcated the world into two, the transcendental entity and the mortal earth, or God and man.

In this cultural light, Plato interpreted the world as a dichotomy between the real and the phenomenal worlds. All visible figures in the latter are merely images or shadows of their originals, the invisible Ideas or Forms in the former. True knowledge of the world or *episteme*, the absolute truth, could only be obtained by imitating these real ideas through rational thought, not on the basis of what man sees with the naked eye. All particular knowledge was thus gained by means of deductive logic, the only reliable method of *episteme*, and from this could be constituted a pure axiomatic system as the only form of science. Abstract geometry was naturally the exemplary ancient Greek science. All other sciences, mainly statics and astronomy, were merely extensions of it. Thus the dichotomic interpretation of the world, based on religious faith, opened the way for the development of Occidental science in later periods.

There had been an embryo of another construct, which was reflected in Aristotelian biology, a certain organismic and holistic way, which was somewhat closer to the Sinic way of thinking. But the idea of the transcendental entity, God as the Creator, finally distinguished theistic Occidentalism from non-theistic Sinicism.

From the Renaissance onwards, Occidental science proposed to understand the

139

universe by direct observation. The term "interpretation", to which science is related, first appeared in Francis Bacon's *Novum Organum* as *interpretatio naturae*. This was a continuation of Galileo Galilei's earlier call, to "read the great book – I mean the universe – before our eyes".[1] For both of them, this term "interpretation" meant a specific way of reading or understanding by means of experience, instead of through mental anticipation or *anticipatio mentis*, to use Bacon's terms. Hence, the only correct way to knowledge was through inductive logic, moving from experience to theory, from the particular to the general, in direct contrast to deductive logic. In fact, by the term "interpretation", Bacon meant merely natural forms of observation and description, rejecting its more profound implication of the reading and understanding of Nature. It was somewhat a misuse of the term, especially in its modern sense.

Following Bacon, Isaac Newton constituted a world other than the Platonic one, a world of discrete atoms, moved by external force and moving in absolute space and time. It was conceived, for about two hundred years, as an absolutely objective description of reality based on observed phenomena. Yet in spite of his promise that there would be "no hypothesis", Newton in fact integrated a series of hypotheses based on idealized notions, not only the "atom" unobserved at that time, but also the absolutely unobservable "force", also "space and time", to constitute an axiomatic system after Greek geometry. Distinct from ancient science, Newtonian mechanics now linked axiom with experience, deduction with induction, and offered the observational foundation and empirical verification for the rational structure.

At first sight, the Newtonian world appealed only to human experience and did not refer to religion. In fact, however, the new world was still a result of the dichotomic interpretation derived from religion. Instead of abolishing the real world in heaven, Newton had only drawn it from heaven to earth, from the supernatural to the natural, and from God *per se* to His Creation. It was indeed a giant stride in secularizing Occidental religious culture. Yet dichotomy still persisted. The dichotomy of God-man was replaced by that of Nature-man, or object-subject. Human beings were now permitted to admire and view Creation, yet still as spectators from a detached perspective. While the Newtonian world had been generally accepted as an absolute object, the creator of this world, Newton himself, had never attempted to conceal his religious desire to reveal the glory of God.[2]

HOLISTIC INTERPRETATION IN SINIC SCIENCE

Sinic interpretation has gone through a necromantic line as the antipode to the religious line. Ancient necromancy originated from the perspective of primitives who regarded nature as an undifferentiated whole. All things were viewed as interpenetrating and of One Body. Hence human persons were capable of actively

---

[1] See Karl Popper, *Conjectures and Refutations* (New York: Harper & Row, 1963), p. 13.

[2] W. H. Newton-Smith, "The Rationality of Science: Why Bother?" in W. H. Newton-Smith and Jiang Tianji (eds.), *Popper in China* (London: Routledge, 1992), p. 73.

affecting all natural processes in a mysterious and irrational correspondence, in accordance with the "law of participation". This does not imply, however, that interpretation in Sinic science is still a pre-scientific naiveté, unable to distinguish between the object and the subject. Instead, as a form of scientific interpretation it had been elaborated, far beyond its original background, as a highly mature organismic and holistic philosophy. Its approach to interpretation might be boiled down to the following fundamental ideas in science:

(1)   *Ziran* or Nature means "self-so" literally in Chinese. It is derived from the analogy of the human body, interpreting the cosmos as an organic whole and a spontaneously self-generating and self-regulating life process. In the *Mo-Jing* (The Classic of the philosopher Mozi), the cosmos was called *yuzhou* in Chinese, which means space (*yu*) defined as "covering different places of the East and West, South and North", and time (*zhou*) as "covering different durations of the past and present, and the morning and evening".[3] Both forms were synthesized into a specific space-time continuum. In this connection, the cosmos neither leaves space for One above, nor needs a Creator to make and manipulate it.

(2)   There is in the organic universe the unity of Heaven-man (*tianren heyi*).[4] And there is indeed something transcendental called *Dao* (*Tao*), which refers to the Way, the Order, or the Reason of Heaven, and is the fundamental value and ultimate concern of man. It is not estranged or separate from, but immanent within, this world, by being incarnate in an omnipresent way in everything and in everyday life. It would be rather an internal transcendence than an external one. As consanguineous with Nature, human persons are capable of knowing Nature, through knowing their own Nature.

Man, the subject, participates in the world, the object, and they are related to each other through "affection-response" (*tianren ganying*).[5] The cosmos, constituted as a unity between human beings and Heaven, might be then viewed as a system of communication, in which human beings resonate internally with Heaven, or understand Nature sympathetically. That is, human beings bring themselves into conformity with Nature, rather than controlling or conquering it.

(3)   *Qi* is the realization of the metaphysical *Dao*. They are conjugate, closely connected with each other, and not so distinctly separated as are essence and phenomena in Occidental philosophy. *Qi* is the basic stuff of the world, drifting erratically throughout all existence. As a physical force it is capable of "converging

---

[3] *Jingshuo Mojing* (*Contemporary Explanations of the Moist Classics*), Part One.

[4] The theory was advocated by Mencius, developed by Dong Zhongshu in the Former Han, and elaborated by Neo-Confucianists in the Song-Ming Dynasties. Cheng Hao, for example, said: "Heaven and man are not two things originally, and there is no need to speak of their unity". See *Quotations from Cheng Hao*.

[5] The theory of *Tianren ganying* was posed by Dong Zhongshu, and elaborated by Neo-Confucianism. Cheng Yi culminated it by saying: "What is there anything else between heaven and earth but *gan* (affection) and *ying* (response)?" See *ErCheng yishu* (*Posthumous Works of Both Chengs*).

into being and diverging to restore the *status quo ante*",[6] something similar to "ether" in classical physics or "mass-energy" in modern physics. As a vital force it is capable of "converging to life and diverging to death"[7] among both animate and inanimate worlds.

As the embodiment of the internal resonance, *Qi* comes to a sympathetic understanding of nature which could only be the merging of the subject into an expansive object through human participation. It is neither an appropriation of the naked object by the subject, as in Occidental naive realism on the one hand, nor an imposition of the subject upon the object, as in subjective idealism on the other hand. In the context, *Qi* is not merely a vital force; it entails a conceptualization of the communication between Nature and human beings, and thus approaches the concept of "information" in modern science. Furthermore, it implies also the texture of the attributes and degree of order and organization of all that is in the process of becoming. Coincidentally, the ancient Chinese term *xiaoxi* (used as the word information today), when it appeared in the *Yi Jing* (Classic of Change), also meant both a message from outside and the ups and downs of the world itself, exactly the meaning of "information" in cybernetics.[8]

Qi is polarized as opposite aspects, tendencies, or properties, most essentially *yang* and *yin*, signalizing such antitheses as heaven and earth, male and female, dynamic and static, real and void, rigid and soft, and the like. Nevertheless, unlike diametrical confrontation in Occidental dichotomies, they interpenetrate in mutual balance, any severance or antagonism being a pathological disorder. "To say *yin-yang* in general means only two ends", said Zhu Xi, "while there is *yin* in *yang* and *yang* in *yin*".[9] Thus both can be dividing continuously from one into two, constituting a system of the Eight Diagrams (*bagua*), to symbolize the being and becoming of the natural world. The Qi of *yang* and *yin* further shape physically the Five Agents (*wuxing*): water, fire, wood, gold, and earth.[10] In contrast to the Four Elements in ancient Occidental philosophy, they are, by and large, not isolate basic elements but five forces, qualities, functions, and/or potentialities. They generate and supersede each other in the "great transformation" (*Da Hua*), jointly constituting a dynamic system to signal the becoming of everything in the whole world.

(4)   *Xiang* or physiognomy shows the limitation of human knowledge, caused by the transcendence of the *Dao*. "The Heavenly Dao is remote", as Confucius admitted,[11] and the *Dao* is unspeakable, as Lao Zi held.[12] Therefore human participation is restrained by sensory organs, and the explicability of language. "Do

---

[6] Zhang Zai, "The Great Harmony" in *Taihe zhengmeng (Correcting Youthful Ignorance)*, in *Zhang Hengju ji (Collected Works of Zhang Zai)*.

[7] Zhuang Zi, "The Chapter of *Zhi beiyou*", in *Waipian (Additional Chapters)* of Zhuang Zi.

[8] *Jingshuo Yijing (Contemporary Explanations of the Classic of Change)*.

[9] *Zhu Zi yulei (Classified Conversations of Zhu Zi)*.

[10] The theory of the Five Agents originated from remote antiquity and was systematically explicated in "The Chapter of *Hongfan*" in *Shang Shu*.

[11] Confucius, *Analects*.

[12] At the beginning of *Dao De Jing* (The Classic of the Way), "The *Dao* that can be said", wrote Lao Zi, "is not the eternal *Dao*".

not speak of ice to the worm living in summer", Zhuang Zi cautioned mortal human beings, "because of the restraint of time; nor about the ocean to the frog living in a well, because of the localization of place".[13] The fable of a few blind persons feeling the elephant in a Buddhist classic, which was widespread in China, offered an even more vivid metaphor for such limitations. A pillar was perceived by one of them who felt the elephant's leg, a wall by another who felt its stomach, a big fan by the third on feeling its ear, etc. There seem to be many-worlds, depending upon one's visual perspectives.[14]

Nevertheless, through the "metaphysical glance" (*xuanlan*)[15] of Lao Zi, or the "intuitive apprehension" (*liangzhi*)[16] of Mencius, the essence within these physiognomies can still be grasped, because of the *Dao*'s immanence. Chinese sages were thus never entrapped into the Buddhist fantasy of "the flowers in the mirror or the moon in the water". Nor were they ensnared by the well-known Occidental thesis, "to be is to be perceived".[17] In general, they stressed the interaction between mind and matter rather than the detachment of mind from the external world. The correlative or double-edged way of thinking is used, precisely, to grasp *Dao* from its different dimensions, first of all to unify the essential opposites, *yang* and *yin* into one, and to see them as complementary to each other. Lao Zi made the point that "to have and to have not follow each other, difficulty and easiness complement each other, the long and the short are mutually shaped, the high and the low are comparative".[18] Human beings have always to consider both sides of everything. "The gentleman will be prepared for danger in tranquillity", states the *Yi Jing*, "for national defeat in victory, and for turbulent days in times of peace, so that your body will be safe and your nation will survive".[19] Instead of logical thinking, the Chinese prefer a flexible, ambiguous but also creative way of thinking about the changing and complex world, using a synthesis of *yang-yin*.

(5) The unity of knowing-acting (*zhixing heyi*) results from human participation in Nature.[20] Despite differences among Chinese sages in the priority and importance given to knowing and acting, they generally preferred immediate contact with the world – moral, social and natural worlds – to knowledge completely detached from human practice. There has never been a systematic epistemology in China, in

---

[13] "The Chapter of *Qiu Shui*", in *Additional Chapters of Zhuang Zi*.

[14] The fable is found in *Bai Yu Jing* (*The Scripture of Hundred Analogies*), a collection of popular stories from Buddhist Classics.

[15] Lao Zi, *Dao De Jing*, Chapter 10.

[16] The idea was first posed by Mencius, (see "The first Part of *Jinxin*," in *The Book of Mencius*,) and greatly developed by Wang Yangming's theory of "extension of intuitive apprehension" The term has been variously rendered as "innate knowledge" or "primordial awareness" also.

[17] Bishop George Berkeley, *Three Dialogues between Hylas and Philonous*.

[18] Lao Zi, *Dao De Jing*, Chapter 2.

[19] "*Xici xiazhuan*" of the *Yi Jing* (*Classic of Change*).

[20] The theory was systematically expounded in Neo-Confucianism, especially by Wang Yangming, who wrote in his *Chuanxi Lu* (*Instructions for Practical Living*): "I have said that knowledge is the direction for action and action the effort of knowledge, and that knowledge is the beginning of action and action the completion of knowledge". The translation is quoted from Wing-tsit Chan (trans., with notes), *Instructions for Practical Living and Other Neo-Confucian Writings* (New York: Columbia University Press, 1963), p. 11.

which human beings play the role of disinterested observers in an estranged world. Human persons are rather participants and actors in the world, not merely observers or spectators. Wang Yangming held that "genuine knowledge" (*zhen zhi*) is necessarily incarnated in human actions,[21] though he stressed moral cultivation more than practice in Nature. In the final analysis, both human knowing and acting are nothing but the internal resonance of *qi*, running through Nature-man (*tianren*), or human sympathetic mutuality and immediacy in relation to Nature.

SINIC SCIENCE AS INTERPRETATION

Sinic interpretation prescribes the specific aspects of Sinic science. Priority was given to the disciplines most adapted to this kind of interpretation, namely astronomy, mathematics, and particularly medicine, which deals directly with the human body, the prototype of the whole of Sinic interpretation. Sinic medicine thus serves as the exemplar of this approach to science, as did geometry in ancient Greece.

Sinic astronomy was an immediate expression of the affection-response between human beings and Heaven; ancient Chinese believed that Heaven would be affected by earthly affairs, and would respond to them through monstrous celestial phenomena, to warn or punish the dynastic rulers. Somewhat different from astrology, it aimed mainly at predicting the fate of nations and societies rather than that of individuals. And it could utilize national resources for systematic observations and calculations of all changes in the sky and occurrences, carried out by established institutions and formally appointed officials. Hence very early records of comets, sunspots, novae, and the first supernova ever observed, which was noted in 1054 CE and is still under observation at present. Careful observation was needed for the establishment and revision of the calendar, in order to provide celestial legitimacy for the emperor. However absurd and incredible it seems, Sinic astronomy as a preliminary attempt to predict the future might be regarded as an ancient "futurology". It also functioned as a benevolent political strategy to moderate the relationship between the emperor and his subjects, under the aegis of Heaven.

Sinic mathematics considers numbers as inherent connections within the holistic organ of man-Heaven. Number-counting was an approach to solving practical problems in addressing the *Dao*. When the Pythagorean theorem was independently discovered, it was called the *gouguxian* theorem. The purpose was to discover the *Dao* within the numerical relationship by means of the operation of square-counting and paper-folding. In this context, mathematics is application-oriented. In its earliest systematic classic, *The Nine Chapters on the Mathematical Art* (written in the 1st century BCE), such an advanced question as the cubic root of number 1,860,867, was solved by a method similar to that developed in the 19th century in Europe. *Nine Chapters* refers to the nine categories of practical mathematical problems without

---

[21] See the First Part of Wang Yangming, *Chuanxi Lu* (*Instructions for Practical Living*).

logical connection. There was also a predisposition towards algebra over geometry. As early as in the 3rd century, the *Sea Island Mathematical Manual*, a series of geometrical propositions were expressed in algebraic form, and geometrical figures were described by algebraic equations. This highly developed algebra is exemplified by Zhu Shijie who, in the 14th century, solved mathematical problems of fifth degree equations for the first time in world history.

Sinic medicine as a categorization of human-body sciences, namely physiology, pathology, therapeutics, pharmacology, and even athletics and martial arts (*gongfu*), features prominently in Sinic science by reflecting an organismic and holistic style of interpretation.

As a physiology, the human body is viewed as an integral and functional system, instead of an accumulation of parts and organs. Viscera (*zangfu*) are vested with corresponding tract-channels in the body (*jingluo*), through which vital energy circulates. A diseased organ is therefore not necessarily obvious, as the symptoms may appear elsewhere in the body through the tract-channels. Many, if not all, diseases are caused by the blocking-up of these passages, and can thus be relieved by taking herbs, or by doing acupuncture, moxibuxtion, or massage on the related acupoints, the places where the *jingluo* intersect and where vital energy flows together. The basic stuff of the system is breath and blood (*qixue*), while *qi*, the sublimation of *xue*, serves as vital information to regulate and control the body. Viscera and channels pertain respectively to Five Agents and their physiological states, transformed constantly according to the law of their generation-supersession.

As a pathology, Sinic medicine attributes all diseases to an imbalance between *yin* and *yang* within and outside of the body. The internal dislocation is caused by inappropriate diet, sex, housing and other forms of excess, while external imbalance is caused by the invasion of the six evil *qi*: wind, cold, dampness, heat, aridity, and fire. "As *yin* remains tranquil and *yang* stable, the spirit is in order; as they break away from each other, the vital energy is done for".[22]

As diagnostics and therapeutics, Sinic medicine aims mainly at finding the symptoms of maladjustment and recovering the normal homeostasis. Hence its basic principles, the four methods of diagnosis (observation, auscultation and olfaction, interrogation, and pulse palpitation), and the eight principal syndromes (*yin-yang*, exterior-interior, cold-heat, hypofunction-hyperfunction), called *si-zhen ba-gang*. As an organic whole, any appearance of imbalance in complexion, smell, and the rhythm and strength of pulse are all direct expressions of internal states. In particular, the physiognomy of the pulse, its rhythm, strength and other subtle differences, were carefully discriminated into twenty-eight types indicated, as the significant signs of health. For Sino-physicians medical treatments do not depend exclusively upon medical herbs, but also upon the deployment of patients' inner vitality through such means as acupuncture, massage, and Sinic meditation (*qigong*).

---

[22] "The Chapter of *Su Wen*", in *Huangdi Neijing* (*The Yellow Emperor's Manual of Corporeal Medicine*), the most important medical document among all the Sinic medical works, written in the 1st century BCE.

Sinic science as a whole has already declined. The goal of Sinic astronomy has proven to be an ancient fantasy. The methodology of Sinic mathematics has been completely superseded since the 18th century. Nevertheless, Sinic medicine, with its derivatives, has survived and remains as an antipodean type to modern Occidental medicine. It is backward indeed in technology; for example, the four diagnoses are evidently insufficient today. But the problem lies in the interpretation behind the practical level, an interpretation which has preserved its integrity as rational and plausible throughout history.

THE INTERPRETATION SHIFT IN OCCIDENTAL SCIENCE

Since the latter half of the 19th century a re-interpretation of the world has been occurring as a revolt against the hegemony of empiricism and scientism. History is concerned with human persons and the human mind, with values rather than with physical phenomena. It is not so much a "nomothetic" study in search of general laws as in natural science, as an "idiographic" study, dealing with the individual. Thus, history can only be comprehended by empathetic understanding of historical texts, not merely by the records of "historical facts".[23] At the same time, some philosophers put forward hermeneutics, that is an approach that sees all human knowledge as interpretations of texts, no matter whether they be old Classics or historical records.

There arose also the parallel trend within science itself. The Newtonian motion of particles was menaced by undulation in electromagnetic fields, moved by the "curvature" of space, in lieu of atom, force and absolute space. Albert Einstein dealt the fatal blow to Newton's interpretation with his special relativity, in which space and time are observed with different density and rate from different frames of reference taken by the observer. The subjective "observer" was thus for the first time squeezed into science *per se* and seen to participate in scientific formulation. Reflecting this trend, Friedrich Nietzsche dared to write, "that physics, too, is only an interpretation of the world and an arrangement of it (to suit ourselves, if I may say so!) – and not an explanation of it".[24]

Yet Einstein had not surmounted the Occidental separation of man-nature. His failure in physics aside, he completed a new world of the "unified field" where there are neither dispersed particles nor external force, nor absolute space and time, but only the four-dimensional space-time continuum, whose curvature dominates all celestial and earthly motions. At this point, the classical three-dimensional world turned out to

[23] These works were coincidentally published within a ten year period: Dilthey's *Introduction to Human Studies (Einletung in die Geistwissenschaften,* 1883), Croce's *History Subsumed Under the Concept of Art (La Storia Ridotta Sotto il Concetto Generale dell'Arte,* 1893), and Windelband's *History and Science* (Geschichte und Naturwissenschaft, 1894). See Franklin L. Baumer, *Modern European Thought: Continuity and Change in Ideas, 1600-1950* (New York: Macmillan Publishing Company, 1977), pp. 272-273.
[24] Friedrich Nietzsche, *Beyond Good and Evil,* trans. A.C. Danto, *Nietzsche as Philosopher* (New York: Macmillan, 1968) p. 87.

be merely a section of the new four-dimensional one. Einstein created a non-Euclidian world beyond human daily experience to supersede the Newtonian giant machine, which had been inferred by induction from those observations within the zone between microcosm and macrocosm. Is that really the ultimate reality? Einstein claimed so, but once again he created, as Newton had done, a world on behalf of God. It is a world now run by a "God of the Universe", playing no dice,[25] but still entirely estranged from human beings, who remain disinterested spectators. The Einsteinian revolution did not move beyond dichotomic forms of interpretation. It is a kind of interpretation that stems from the secularization of Christian culture, in which God has shifted his role from Platonic geometrician, to Newtonian mechanician, and then to the present non-Euclidean geometrician.

Either Einstein or Newton might be questioned as to whether they or anyone else has the capacity to stand for God, to proclaim His ultimate arcana of Creation, and to prescribe how He should run the world. Recalling the development of quantum physics in the past few decades, it looks as if we might be better to modestly restrain ourselves in our wish to exhaustively explain His great work, trying our best rather to choose the most significant world among the many-worlds of possibilities.

THE FUNDAMENTAL SHIFT OF QUANTUM PHYSICS

Controversy was provoked by the recent advance of quantum physics which was dubbed "medieval necromancy".[26] Perhaps this was less a slur than an expression of surprise at the drastic interpretation-shift from the dichotomic to the holistic, or, one might say, from the religious to the necromantic, in view of its cultural origin. The whole course of the great shift might be summarized as follows.

(1) The discovery of "quanta", the rhythmical motion in jerks, showed motion to be as discontinuous as matter itself. The general discontinuity in nature caused a serious challenge to the causality principle in classical physics which claims every effect is preceded by a unique cause without fissure on the chain of cause-effect in the uninterrupted flow of motion. Hence the impotence and imprecision of our knowledge of the fissure of the chain.

(2) The new interpretation began with the wave-particle duality of microscopic objects, which enabled Erwin Schrodinger to develop a "quantum wave equation", supposing all matter in motion as a wave. He used the idea to make a case for "matter waves" that set up harmonic modes of vibration inside atoms, so as to make discontinuous quantum leaps as continuous transitions from one state to another. Max Born further interpreted the "wave function" in the equation as an undulating wave of possibilities, or a collection of potentialities, of a particle to emerge in a given time at

---

[25] Quoted in P.A. Schlipp (ed.), *Albert Einstein: Philosopher Scientist* (Evanston: Library of Living Philosophers, 1949), p. 176.

[26] John Horgan, "Quantum Philosophy", in *Scientific American*, July 1992, p. 98.

a given position. Thus arose a paradox that the particle would "smear" as a "wave pocket" in space, entailing a superposition of different states of matter, such as a cat being alive and being dead at the same time. The problem is to find a way for the reduction of the wave packet, that is, the transition from potentiality to actuality.

(3)   The Uncertainty Principle raised by Werner Heisenberg simply justified the "coexistent state". "What we observe is not nature in itself, but nature exposed to our method of questioning".[27] The latter is in turn only a limited vision, either of the state of matter in certain positions or the motion of matter with certain momentum. Our knowledge of nature is necessarily limited – as soon as we grasp one part, another part slips through our fingers. Therefore Heisenberg extracted the novel implication of "the word 'state' as describing some potentiality rather than a reality – one may replace the term 'state' by the term 'potentiality'".[28] He introduced the observer as the agent of the reduction of wave packets: "...we may say that the transition from the 'possible' to the 'actual' takes place as soon as the interaction of the object with the measuring device, and thereby with the rest of the world, has come into play".[29]

(4)   Only through Niels Bohr's theory of complementarity however, could the philosophical implication of modern quantum physics be established. To Bohr, matter acts sometimes like waves, sometimes like particles, but really has no definite form until it is measured. Hence the two pictures, wave and particle, are complementary to each other and can only be described complementarily as including "...all relevant elements of the experimental apparatus", within which is human observation.[30] Reality would, therefore, no longer be a lethargically estranged alienation from man, but must be involved in the mobility of the separation between the subject and the object.[31] Naturally he identified the harmony of *yin-yang* with his complementarity, and invoked once and again the Oriental idea that "in the great drama of being, we are both spectators and actors". (Lao Zi) This implies the unification of the observer and the observed, or in Sinic terms, the great unity of human beings and Heaven.

(5)   The development of quantum physics after Bohr, seemed to have still followed his clues. Some new technologies have enabled quantum physicists to carry out experiments which Einstein and Bohr could only imagine. The wave-particle duality of microscopic objects seems now to show any property the observer desires. A so-called delayed-choice experiment devised by John A. Wheeler demonstrates, that even having travelled both routes to fashion an interference wave, the object can still behave as a particle. And another experiment demonstrates that even after the particle-like property has emerged, or the collapse of the "wave packet" has taken place, the observer can still "erase" it, to restore its wave-like property. Some circumstantial evidence now shows strongly that the object does exist in a superstition of two or more states. All of this seems to prove the question of what an object really is when we are

---

[27] W. Heisenberg, *Physics and Philosophy* (New York: Harper Torchbooks, 1962), p. 58.
[28] *Ibid.*, p. 185.
[29] *Ibid.*, p. 60.
[30] N. Bohr, *Atomic Physics and Human Knowledge* (New York: Wiley, 1958), p. 4.
[31] *Ibid.*, p. 91.

not looking at it, is nothing more than speculation. The many-worlds interpretation of the 1950's thus enjoys new attention. It holds that when we observe a phenomenon, we can only see one outcome of the many allowed by probabilities. That is to say, when we force a particle to make a choice between going left and going right, the world splits into two separate worlds, the particle-go-left one and the particle-go-right one.[32] Modern scientists seem to be going back to blind persons feeling the elephant, who split the world into the pillar-like, the wall-like, the fan-like and other worlds.

In comparison with the holistic interpretation in Sinic science as simply a deduction from metaphysical speculation to physical reality, the Occidental interpretation-shift seems much more a natural evolution from scientific experiments to a new holistic speculation in favour of its antipode. Here lies precisely the meeting of the Oriental and the Occidental, the ancient and the modern. Among all of the contemporary thinkers, Bohr was most clearly conscious of the necessity of the meeting. He so much appreciated Sinic wisdom as to engrave on his family badge a Chinese *yin-yang* chart, annotated with "*Contraria sunt Complementa*".

Let us go back now to our first section, where modern science was linked to "medieval necromancy", and a "law of participation" was seen to dictate interaction between human beings and nature. To be sure, modern science could never return to primitive necromancy, but it could and should benefit from its insights, just as it has done from primitive religion.

THE SHIFT IN THE PHILOSOPHY OF SCIENCE

Corresponding to the development of modern science, the modern philosophy of science has also gone through three phases.

(1)   As early as the very beginnings of modern science, Bacon and Newton held that man could only know the world through observation, and rejected any knowledge beyond human experience. It seemed to them that the only way to interpret the world was to describe it as it "really was", and natural science could only be a description of the world derived from human experience. They confined their view of science to an empirical level.

(2)   Since the end of the 19th century it has become evident that every scientific theory, Newtonian mechanics in particular, is a hypothetico-deductive system, which deduces from hypothesis to empirical propositions. From this point of view, nature could only be explained with a pre-established cosmic model and pre-theory which are to be verified or falsified by empirical data, instead of being simply described through observation. Einstein believed scientific theory to be a product of "free creation", or "wild thinking". It is theory that features prominently in science as the basis of natural interpretation, and thus elevates science from empirical description to

---

[32] John Horgan, "Quantum Philosophy", 1992, pp. 101 & 104.

theoretical explanation. Thereafter science was to be viewed at a theoretical level.

This level, however, had in no way gotten rid of entanglement with experience in this context. Having recognized theory as starting point, modern positivism still asked for pure and neutral observations without any subjective pollution as the solid ground of science. Even while Karl Popper insisted as firmly as ever that every theory was merely a temporal conjecture to be falsified sooner or later,[33] it still seemed to him that through constantly falsifying established theories, science could increase continuously the degree of corroboration with empirical data. The theoretical level, similar to the empirical one, still confines the knowledge subject to an outsider in relation to reality, though an explainer in place of a describer. A thoroughgoing philosophy of science could not remain at that level either.

(3) Partly illumined by the findings of contemporary science, some philosophers of science began to raise the issue to a higher level. Thomas Kuhn, for example, designated a significant theoretical system by the term "paradigm".[34] For him, a paradigm is directly bound to the support of the scientific community and the identification of the psychology of scientists, which is usually conditioned by certain cultural values rather than by value-neutral empirical data or mere theoretical assumptions. Others, like Larry Laudan, define the goal of science as "problem-solving"[35] instead of verification or falsification, with problems being posed within research traditions and entrenched in their metaphorical or theological framework. Now the world in science is evidently understood by human preference in certain historical phases and cultural milieux, and science is in turn disposed to be interpreted at the level of culture. The way science is viewed has then reached a higher cultural level.

At this level, science is open to various interpretations of the world, and thus to many varieties of approach. Every culture has or had, in principle, its own specific type of science as a mode of living in nature, though most have remained undeveloped. Only a few had matured into an integral system worthy of the name "science", among which Sinic science was the most salient model among non-Occidental sciences. Occidental science, although the most complex system, has never been unique nor the manifestation of a unique truth. It will be, and is being, benefitted by other types of science, and Sinic science in particular.

Perhaps there is great promise in the fact that different sciences are being unified through their very nature of complementarity, the complementarity of Occidental and Sinic sciences in particular, as Neils Bohr so ardently longed for. Perhaps various civilizations are being interfused, in spite of the disputes and chaos that exist, and Humankind is heading for the Great Harmony of the whole world (*shijie*

---

[33] Karl R. Popper, *The Logic of Scientific Discovery* (London: Hutchinson, 1959).

[34] Thomas S. Kuhn, *The Structure of Scientific Revolutions*, 2nd ed. (Chicago: The University of Chicago Press, 1970).

[35] Larry Laudan, *Progress and Its Problems* (Berkeley: University of California Press, 1977).

datong),[36] or the one family within the Four Seas (*sihai yijia*), as Chinese sages had dreamt long ago.

---

[36] The idea of *Datong* (Great Harmony) first occurred in the *Book of Rites*, an ancient document of, perhaps, the early years of the Zhou Dynasty (from the 11th century BCE), and systemized as one of the Six Classics by Confucius (551-479 BCE). The idea became a legendary and idealized human society in Sinic culture in later ages and made notable impact on a series of reformists through Chinese history, up to Sun Yat-sen at the beginning of the 20th century.

9

Inheritance, Creativity and Society

Abdul Rahman

Analytical method, and the specialized approach to knowledge have led to the creation of techniques and methods which have made possible a vast storehouse of knowledge. They have provided us with insights and generated capabilities that are almost unlimited. They have also imposed certain limitations on our approach to and understanding of problems. The contemporary approach is involving us so much in present, immediate problems and their projection into the future, that we are losing the sense of history. The latter is so vital for creating an understanding of our inheritance, our problems and institutions in the context of their historical evolution, and for bringing about a harmony between our past and our present, so as to make them a part of our future. If we look at ourselves dispassionately and historically, we may come to realize that not only our knowledge, but also our institutions, customs and practices, have evolved as a result of interaction, over different periods of history, with those of Egypt, Phoenecia, Babylonia, India, China, Greece and Arabia, as well as the West, the latter particularly after the Renaissance. This is part of our unrecognized, or implicity recognized inheritance, to which we often do not give much thought.

Before the British introduced Western education systems, India had multiple educational systems, each one of which was linked to a religion and a different language. Brahmanical with Sanskrit, Buddhist with Pali, Islamic with Arabic and Persian.

The word for education in the Islamic system was *talim*, which meant seeking knowledge. *I'lm* means knowledge, *talib-e-i'lm*, seeker of knowledge or student, *Mua'llim*, giver of knowledge or teacher. *Aa'lim* means one who has attained a degree of knowledge. *Aa'lim* was rated highly as it would be evident from the Arabic saying "the death of a scientific scholar is the end of an epoch" (*Mautal Aa'lim maut-al-Aa'lam*).

The second part of this education was *Tarbiat* or training in the art of living. The third part was apprenticeship. It included knowledge as well as practical training and covered such areas as music, medicine, architecture, astrology, astronomy and military arts, or purely professional training as in textiles, dyeing, printing, building, construction and so on.

This system of education, though imparted in Arabic, Persian and Urdu in

India, was not isolated from the knowledge imparted by different religious systems in different languages. It incorporated both knowledge and various practices. These different systems were overlaid by the European educational system and knowledge, though there was an early reaction against them, even a boycott. Slowly and gradually, many dimensions of knowledge, institutional frameworks, as well as practices, were incorporated into the indigenous systems.

Today, all this is a part of our inheritance in an independent India, and there is considerable effort to look at the content and practices of the medieval systems, as well as the contemporary, to work out the one which suits the cultural traditions and contemporary needs and requirements as well.

The questions which naturally arise are: what is the nature of this inheritance? What are the areas it covers? The inheritance covers the cultural as well as the natural environment. The cultural environment covers various systems and their institutions and the philosophies and values which provide their framework. They are religious, social, economic, political and educational systems. In addition, there is the stored knowledge, methods of acquiring knowledge covering science and technology, on the one hand, and arts, literature and performing art on the other hand. Further, there are artifacts, technologies and the productive systems, which meet the needs of providing the basic necessities of everyday life.

The differences in attitude toward the natural environment and our knowledge of it, which one generation inherits from the previous one, covers the eco-system with its bio-diversity, as well as attitudes and knowledge changes. This is evident if one compares the pre-industrial and post-industrial attitude to the material environment. Earlier, human beings were part of nature and its custodian, responsible to keep it as it was or to improve it. There is a dialogue between man and God by the great poet Iqbal, which goes like this:

Man says to God: "You created the night, I created the lamp (to dispel darkness); You created barren rocks and deserts, I created gardens, parks and beautiful plantations".

However, after the industrial revolution, the attitude toward and the knowledge of the natural environment underwent a complete change. The environment became a source of vast quantities of raw material and had to absorb the resulting waste. If we set a person educated in contemporary Europe beside a comparable Indian, African, Arab or Chinese, we can see differences in attitude towards the environment. The same applies to the people inhabiting tropical, desert or temperate climates or cold climates.

What applies to the area of natural environment also applies to cultural environment. In this sphere, one may also notice a diversity of views despite the claims for unity, which may be in the name of religion, nationality or political ideology. For instance, one may realize this when one notices ethnic differences even in a country like England among South England, the Midlands, Scotland and Wales. This has also become most evident in the states of the former Soviet Union, which tried to eliminate cultural diversity by substituting political ideology. The impact of cultural inheritance would also be evident in the Islamic world, and its impact even on religious practices, if one compared the culture and practices of people from Algeria to Indonesia and China.

The point which I want to emphasize is that inheritance, covering cultural and natural environment, which I term as the sphere of inheritance, is a vital base for any development which may take place. Further, in this base knowledge plays a decisive role, both knowledge that has been stored over the years and that which is newly acquired. The role of the educational system, including the content of education and the values, philosophy and institutions which the system promotes, is critical. The sphere of inheritance can be compared to a mother's womb, from which a child draws nourishment and grows till a time comes when it should come out of the womb, into a new sphere.

From the sphere of inheritance every individual of a generation passes on to the sphere of the self and society, but carries along his or her own cultural and genetic inheritance. The genetic inheritance can now be plotted, though the cultural and natural inheritance cannot be clearly defined. Its nature, character and degree may vary from person to person. The inheritance may show itself as it emerges in different cultural environments. The Africans who were brought to America centuries ago, carry with them their inheritance even to this day and it emerges, for example, in their music, or other art forms or performing arts. The same is true for Indians who went from India to other parts of the world. The same applies to Europeans who colonized the Americas, Australia, New Zealand and other parts of the world. The interaction of different cultures, of the original inhabitants and the new entrants, creates both tensions as well as new cultural forms, and lays the basis for new developments.

Every individual has a two dimensional approach to life. One is directed to the self – the inner probing – who is the person? What is the goal and objective of his or her life? The second dimension arises out of the interaction with society, to find a niche for oneself. The inheritance of cultural ethics on the one hand and education on the other play a critical role in both dimensions.

In the past pre-industrial society, the dominant cultural ethic was dictated by religion, and education was centred around religion, the promotion of religious values and the maintenance of a dual society – of noble men and kings on the one hand and of the rest of the people, on the other. The latter were the actual producers of goods and wealth but were oppressed. Gautama Buddha in his search of the self and for a purpose and goal, gave up his princely life of luxury and went out to find an answer. He developed a way of life devoid of all rituals, which advocated the abolition of caste. Christ took upon himself the suffering of humanity, and promoted love and compassion. Mohammad was appalled by the prevailing inter-tribal wars (*jihalat*) and promoted the concepts of peace and knowledge – *salam* or peace upon you and *i'lm* or knowledge to enlighten yourself, and find a purpose in life.

All three of these great religious personalities promoted the concept of self-discipline, a code of conduct for oneself and for dealing with others, as well as in relation to the material world. Educational systems promoted these values and directed people to find a place for themselves. Some of the people found it in religions studies, in trying to understand the meaning and content of religion, or reforming it when they thought it had moved away from the original purposes. Others expressed it in literature and poetry. Their longings gave a meaning to their lives and suggested meaning for the lives of others. The artisans and craftspersons expressed themselves in their arts and crafts, and took pride in their products, wishing to fulfil the purpose of their lives, and to pass on their art to the coming generations. They sought a continuity in the purpose of their lives and the flourishing of their arts.

The Renaissance in Europe changed the context of seeking for the self and the character of societal interaction. As the ethics of society changed, people looked at the self in terms of what they could do to society, to modify it according to their desires. They tried to develop a new production system, through inventing new machines and processes to meet the needs of people. People directed their energies to understanding nature as it was, its functioning and the way its resources could be used. People started travelling and exploring the world. Artists and litterateurs began providing a new perspective and a new vision. The education system came to be institutionalized and made to suit the new needs and requirements, in contrast to earlier times, when it was built around individual scholars.

The industrial revolution further changed ethics and the search for the self, as well as the interaction of the self with society. While some found their goal in life in promoting the objectives of the industrial revolution – in inventions and their uses, others bothered about the impact of these developments on humans and society. In the later context some took to social reform, others to organizing workers and trying to redress their working conditions, still others to political activities. All this came to be reflected in art, literature, poetry and other activities. There is a long list of those who thus sought to fulfil the purpose which they had given to their lives in the fields of religion, social life, political activities, reform movements, science and technology, industrial development, art and literature. In our own period, one can find parallel concerns in professional life, in the ecology movement, the movement to liberate women, anti-nuclear and peace movements, in environmental protection dealing with the use of natural resources, checking pollution and environmental degradation. Criticism or concern is also expressed in movements for peace and justice, for promoting equality for all people.

The following question was posed in the medieval Islamic tradition. A teacher had three students; one became a grand vizier, a good administrator and patron of art and learning; a second became a poet, mathematician and astronomer; the third one organized a band and carried out political assassinations. What had the teacher taught the disciples? The point was that each had picked from the teachings what he had wanted for his life.

As one searches one's innermost self to find a purpose for one's life, goals are set through the educational system and through interaction with society. The goal may become an ambition for money and power. The story is told that a queen of France, making a confession to Saint Vincent, confided that as young girl she had wanted to be the most beautiful woman in the world; when she achieved that, she wanted to be the richest; when she succeeded in that, she wanted to be the most powerful. So she became the queen of France. And now, she said, she found a void which she could not fill. Queens of France can be found everywhere, seeking to realize their ambitions through conquest, through industry and trade, or through politics.

In others ambition is transformed into a commitment to seek knowledge, to enlighten people, to liberate them from ignorance, and provide them new opportunities. The same ambition may be used as an instrument of control by keeping the knowledge limited to a small elite which forms around the knowledgeable. Knowledge may also be utilized to find shortcomings in society, the inequality and injustice people suffer, or damage done to society and the environment. This was the situation of the 19th century critics of the industrial revolution, later of socialists, and now in our day of various movements such as the Greens, the peace movement and so on. The critics may organize themselves to produce reforms or revolutionary movements. Or they may produce engineers and technologists, who may endeavour to change society through their inventions.

Finally, self-searching through education and interaction with society may produce visionaries who provide an alternative to existing society through new models. Some may remain contented with their working routine, while others may become activists endeavouring to translate their vision into a working reality. In the 19th century the Utopian writers put forward such models, and persons like William Morris and Robert Owen tried to put them into practice. The same applies to a large number of socialist writers and workers. If we examine literature, poetry, inventions, the establishment of industries and their production, as well as the religious, political, social, economic, and cultural activities of people and the nature and character of the movements in which they have become involved, we find personal ambition, commitment and vision.

For example, Henry Ford's ambition was a vision as well as a desire to have wealth and power. It was expressed in Ford's motor car and was neatly summed up in one sentence: what is good for Ford Motor Company is good for America. Marx's vision of a socially equitable and just society was converted into an instrument of power. This in turn became an ambition to have absolute power over people and an instrument of domination under Stalin. The commitment of Gandhi and Nehru to India's freedom led to two different visions of India's future. For Gandhi it was to reform society, to raise up the down trodden, to respect artisans and craftspersons and promote their products. He wanted to see the promotion of a low energy, decentralized production system built around human labour and using traditional skills. This was totally different from Nehru's vision of an equitable and just society built around a highly centralized large scale production system, the promotion of education, the development of scientific technological capacities and the fostering of a kind of democracy intended to follow the lines of European Socialist thinking. Nehru's model was based on a vision of the future as a part of a projection of present knowledge and capabilities; Gandhi's was based on the interpretation of the past and its projection into the future. However, in the context of the present situation, new visions of a future society are being projected totally on the basis of the past and on the basis of different religions. This revitalization of religion and its use as an instrument of power, represents the ambitions of those who have not gained by present day developments.

The ambitions, commitments and visions which people nurture as a part of their interaction with society and through the guidance of knowledge provided to them by education and experience, motivate them to change their inheritance as well as the society in which they find themselves. The desire to change is the sphere of creativity. In earlier societies such creativity was expressed in art and literature, arts and crafts, in religious systems which aimed to change social conditions and bring about reforms. It is now by and large expressed in science and technology. While scientific knowledge provides new visions and perspectives, technology provides new capabilities. Consequently, the ambitions, commitments and visions of people drive them to promote science and technology, to develop ever new industries, organizations, institutions and codes. The sphere of creativity can roughly be divided into two categories: (a) those which tend to promote science and technology and (b) those providing a critique and warning of the possible disadvantages and dangers. Those who do either of these can be roughly divided into three types: (1) those who possess the necessary knowledge and know the potential and possibilities as well as the disadvantages and dangers; (2) those who benefit or are likely to benefit from new developments, and (3) those who are likely to be adversely affected by them.

Having discussed the ambitions, commitments and visions which drive people, on the basis of knowledge acquired by them through education and interaction with society, it may be worthwhile to emphasize the multi-dimensionality of people's commitments and affiliations. For instance, in contemporary society, a person may be part of an ethnic, linguistic or regional group which may represent his or her cultural inheritance and which may also determine or condition his or her attitude to the natural environment. One may also profess a religion which may give one another perspective and view on culture or the environment shared with another ethnic group. Further, as a member of a professional, academic, literary and artistic community one may develop new ideas and another perspective. Or as a member of a trade union, social, political or environmental movement, one may have yet another understanding of culture and the natural environment. As a result of these affiliations, every individual builds linkages which are vital for creativity and social action. The role of education could be to promote this multi-dimensionality, and the integration of these into a new perspective to promote creativity or otherwise. Figure 9.1 illustrates the interaction among the three spheres, of inheritance, self and society, and creativity.

The problem which is faced by every society is one of balancing the inheritance with creativity, the old with the new, and developing a harmony between the two, since each new creative development tends to replace some aspect of inheritance. Earlier societies of Asia, which had a high level of civilization, stifled creativity or allowed it only in a limited way, so as not to upset their cultural inheritance and social order, also their ideas and views of nature and the environment. In contrast, contemporary society

Figure 9.1: Inheritance, Self and Society, and Creativity in Interaction

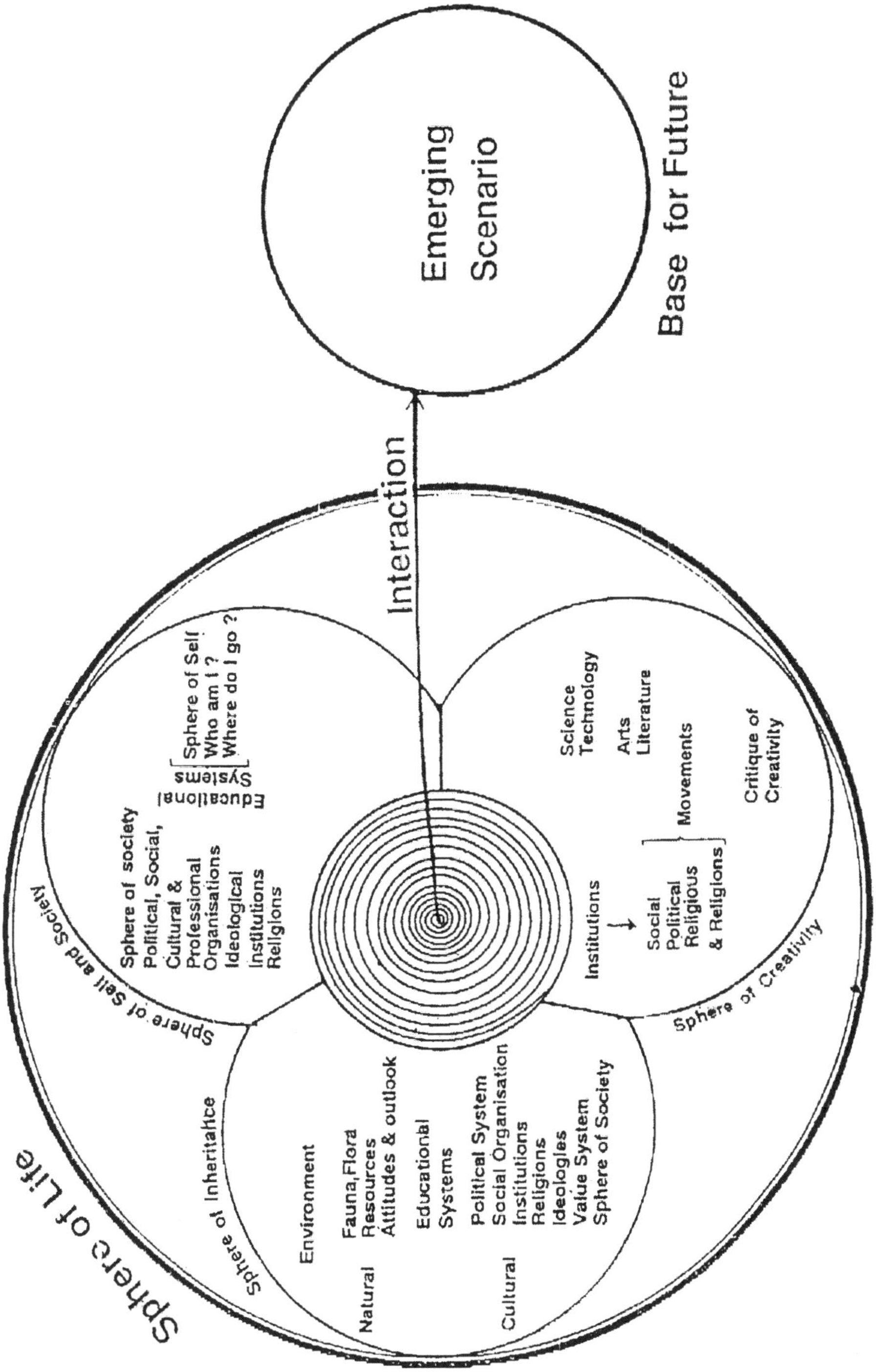

lays emphasis only on creativity and on perpetual change, ignoring or marginalizing the inheritance. In promoting creativity, it is also minimizing the multi-dimensionality of human beings and converting the future into a technological future. The result of this has been adverse for humanity, society and the environment. The conflict or disharmony, which has emerged between inheritance and creativity, is centred around values. The values of cultural inheritance are centred around the promotion of self-discipline, of a code of conduct among human beings and in the use of the material world. Inherited values are also usually aimed at the promotion of love, compassion, a desire to help one another in difficulties and distresses, to share grief and happiness. Some also promote the desire to establish a just and egalitarian society or to live in harmony with nature.

The unilateral promotion of creativity through science and technology leads to the creation of laws and codes which meet the demands of creativity, that is efficiency, productivity and decisions based on the demands of the latter, as well as scenarios developed by non-human systems. These ignore the values of inheritance and human needs. This has led to the paradox of a society which has plenty of everything while even the basic needs of the vast majority remain unmet. Considerations of efficiency and productivity have led increasingly to promoting a limited role for education, namely that of producing specialized workers for research, for operating industry and for promoting efficiency. Universities, which at one time used to act as centres of independent opinion, with their members providing a critique of creativity and its impact, are sucked into the system to promote technical values.

The role of education, if one is to learn from one's inheritance, is really to provide a balance between inheritance and creativity. This can be done by providing a historical and critical perspective on inheritance and a critique of novelty and invention and its development and utilization in society. If education could play this role, then it could promote harmony between inheritance and creativity and allow for the fullest possible development of human capabilities without disrupting society and degrading the environment. That is the challenge which education faces today.

Part III

Knowledge Across Cultures: Issues of Knowledge Transfer

10

Science, Technology and Science Education
in the Development of the South

Muhammad Abdus Salam

SCIENCE AND TECHNOLOGY, A SHARED HERITAGE OF MANKIND

The first thing to realize about the Science and Technology gap between the South and the North is that it is of relatively recent origin. In his monumental *History of Science*, George Sarton chose to divide his story of achievement into ages, each age lasting half a century. With each half-century he associated one central figure. Thus 450-400 BCE Sarton calls the Age of Plato; this is followed by the half century of Aristotle, of Euclid, of Archimedes and so on. There were scientists from the Greek Commonwealth consisting of Egyptians, Southern Italians and ancestors of modern Syrians and Turks, in addition to the Greeks.[1]

From 600 CE to 650 CE in Sarton's account is the Chinese half-century of Hsiian Tsang. From 650 to 700 CE is the age of I-Ching and of the Indian mathematician, Brahmagupta, followed by the Ages of Jabir, Khwarizmi, Razi, Masudi, Wafa, Biruni, and then Omar Khayam – Chinese, Hindus, Arabs, Persians, Turks and Afghans – an unbroken Third World succession for 500 years. After the year 1100 CE the first Western names begin to appear: Gerard of Cremona, Roger Bacon and others – but the honours are shared for another 250 years with the Third World men of science like Ibn-Rushd, Naseer-ud-dinTusi, Musa bin Maimoun and Sultan Ulugh Beg.

The same story repeats itself for technology in China (the Chinese invented the technology of printing on paper, gunpowder and the magnetic compass) and in the Middle East (at least till around 1450 CE when the Turks captured Constantinople because of their mastery of superior cannonade). No Sarton has yet chronicled the history of medical and technological creativity in Africa – for example of early iron-smelting in Central Africa 2500 years ago.[2] This is also the case for the pre-Spanish Mayas and Aztecs – with their independent invention of the zero and of calendars, their discovery of the moon and Venus, as well as their diverse

---

[1] George Sarton, *A History of Science* (New York: Norton, 1970).
[2] *Scientific American*, June, 1988.

pharmacological discoveries, including quinine. But one may be sure, it is a story of considerable achievement in manufacturing technologies and applied sciences.

From around 1450 CE, however, the Third World begins to lose out, except for the occasional flash of individual brilliant scientific and technological work – principally because of the lack of tolerant attitudes to the creation of sciences and technology. And that brings us to the present times when the cycle begun by Michael the Scot, who went from his native glens in Scotland around the year 1220 CE, south to Toledo and then to Sicily, in order to acquire knowledge of the works of Razi and Avicenna, and even of Aristotle (the only available translations being in Arabic), turns full circle. Now it is we in the developing world who must look Northwards for sciences.

It is good to recall that three centuries ago, around the year 1660 CE, two of the greatest monuments of modern history were erected, one in the North and one in the South: St. Paul's Cathedral in London and the Taj Mahal in Agra. Between them, the two symbolize, perhaps better than words can describe, the comparative level of architectural technology, the comparative level of craftsmanship and the comparative level of affluence and sophistication the two cultures had attained at that epoch of history. But about the same time, there was also created – and this time only in the North – a third monument, a monument still greater in its eventual import for humanity. This was Newton's *Principia*, published in 1687. Newton's work had no counterpart in the India of the Mughuls.[3]

Science and technology are cyclical. They are a shared heritage of all mankind. East and West, South and North have all equally participated in their creation in the past as we hope they will in the future, a joint endeavour in sciences becoming one of the unifying forces among the diverse peoples on this globe.

THE FOUR AREAS OF SCIENCE AND TECHNOLOGY

Civilian science and technology may perhaps be divided into the four categories of (1) Basic Sciences; (2) Sciences in Application; (3) Conventional Low Technology; and (4) Science-based Higher Technology. Let us consider each of these areas in turn.

Basic (curiosity-oriented) Sciences

There are at present five sub-disciplines comprising Basic Sciences which have been defined as "man's systematic effort to understand natural phenomena". These are: (1) Physics (including Geophysics and Astrophysics); (2) Chemistry; (3) Mathematics; (4) Biology; plus (5) Basic Medical Science.

Research and training for Basic Sciences is conducted in universities or in the

[3] Abdus Salam, *Ideals and Realities* (third edition, Singapore: World Scientific Publishing Co. Ltd., 1989), pp. 5-6.

research centres specifically created for this purpose in the North. As a rule, these are funded by National Science Foundations or by Academies of Sciences which are also responsible for international contacts among scientists.

So far as developing countries are concerned, by and large we have tended to neglect this area of science assuming for some reason that we could live off the scientific results obtained by others. This has been an unmitigated disaster in that it has also deprived us – in the Third World – of men and women who know about the basics of their disciplines, and who could act as a reference to whom one could turn, when we need to discuss the inevitable scientific problems which arise when applications of science are made and soluble applied problems are defined.

Professor Jean-Patrick Connerade of Imperial College, London, has remarked on this birthright of every good young scientist: "In our culture, the enthusiasm (for science and technology) is fired by supporting basic research. Successful university laboratories are essential to attract the best young brains into a scientific career. Whether they remain in research or opt for development is up to them to decide. ... This is one of the hidden benefits of fundamental research. Its glamour has inspired many scientific careers which did not end up in the (basic) research laboratory".

Sciences in Application

One may list five areas of Sciences in Application: (1) Agriculture (including Livestock, Fisheries and Forests); (2) Medicine, Health and Population; (3) Energy Policies; (4) Environment and Pollution; (5) Earth Sciences (including Irrigation and Soils, Meteorology and Oceanography, as well as Seismology).

As a general rule, Research and Development in Applied Sciences are carried out in the North under the auspices of research councils or by private industry. This includes Research, Development (Adaptation and Modification) and the Application of Scientific Methodology to developmental problems. In spite of the large technological content of some of these areas, it is important to realize, particularly for the economist, that these are not areas of Manufacturing Technology, but of Applied Science. The loose use of the word technology to designate what should more precisely be called science, had unfortunate consequences for the development of Applied Sciences in the Third World.

The Research and Development effort, in order to be effective, must be supplemented by first-class extension services. In this respect, let me mention with approval the South African Industrial Research Council's use of the initials R D & I – Research, Development and Implementation. In accordance with this usage, R & D is meant to read as R D & I in this chapter.

It is important to realize that the distinction between Basic and Applied Sciences on the one hand and Applied Sciences and Technology on the other is not absolute. There are inevitably gradations which change with time!

Technology may be looked upon differently depending on what one wishes to emphasize. One possible way to subdivide Technology is into classical low technology and science-based high technology.

Classical Low Technology

The five sub-areas of this are: (1) Bulk Chemicals; (2) Iron, Steel and Other Metals Fabrication; (3) Design and Fabrication in (indigenous) Industries (like Cotton and Leather); (4) Petroleum Technologies; (5) Power Generation and Transmission including Heavy Electrical Industry.

Here no new scientific principles remain to be discovered. However, developmental work relating to design, adaptation and modification, is important. This is the traditional area of craftsmanship and skills – the science employed is of yesteryears. Thoroughness (in all aspects of manufacture and after-services), beauty of design, quality of workmanship, cost, and manufacturing-competitiveness are all important. These are just the areas where developing countries should *not* be deficient, though, unfortunately, they often are.

This is also the classical area of "negotiated technology transfer" and the area on which centrally-planned economies of the Second World as well as some developing countries such as India in the beginning placed their strongest emphasis. Any country which wishes to industrialize will have to develop one or more of the technologies listed above as, for example, Japan, USSR and South Korea initially had to do. For these countries, imported Low Technology played a big role in building up their technological base.

We have used the generic word Technology whenever we wish to refer to the whole area of Manufacturing Technology. The words "Low Technology" are not used in any pejorative sense. This nomenclature is meant to differentiate this type of technology from Science-based High Technology. Perhaps "Classical" Technology gives a better flavour of what is meant.

One should state clearly and emphatically that Classical Low Technology is like Basic Sciences – it must be developed by any nation wishing to industrialize – particularly the "design" and fabrication part of it. A nation may develop engineering expertise and a skilled and disciplined work-force in the first instance – i.e. undertake only development and no research. Such an attitude towards research will, of course, eventually prove short-sighted – particularly in the areas of modern Higher Technologies, which developed countries will not easily part with.

Science-based High Technology

Finally, there are five areas of Science-based High Technology which, in the conditions of today, may comprise: (1) Communications, Information and other Sciences which consist of two types of sub-disciplines – (a) Microelectronics (including development of Software; Microprocessors, Computer-aided Design; Eventual Fabrication of Microchips and their applications to other industries, for example, the automotive); and (b) Microphotonics (including Lasers and Fibre Optics); (2) Space Technologies; (3) New Materials (including composite materials and High Temperature Superconductors); (4) Pharmaceutical and Fine Chemicals; (5) and finally, for the 21st century, Biotechnology and Gene-splicing, so full of promise for a true revolution in the future methods of Agriculture, Energy and Medicine.

As Giles Merritt, writing in the *International Herald Tribune* in the early 1990s, said: "During the past year or so the bio-revolution has begun to spin off significant new developments in areas of agriculture that are far apart. These include the following: (1) A gene-splicing breakthrough that could shortly revolutionize the economics of dairy farming with the first bovine somatotropin (BST), a genetic growth hormone that offers increases in milk yields of 15 to 20 per cent without raising feed costs; (2) Calves can now be 'harvested' from cows at a greatly increased rhythm thanks to embryo duplication techniques that enable a single cow to produce twin calves five times a year (see the report of the Bank of Credit and Commerce International's [BCCI] NEST [4] Foundation set up in London); (3) Industrial tissue-culture techniques may soon eliminate the need to grow whole plants ... biotechnology specialists, notably the UK company Plant Science, are already producing digitalis, opium, ginseng and pyrethrum by culturing root cells in a fermentation vessel.

Big chemical companies like Monsanto and Sandoz have bet ... on strategies of switching emphasis away from industrial chemicals into biotechnology. Their sights are firmly set on an industry that is forecast to grow from its present turnover of around $25 billion a year to an annual $100 billion by the year 2000".

High Technology differs from Classical Low Technologies in that high expertise in the relevant Basic Sciences (like Physics or Chemistry, or Biology, or Mathematics) is crucial. The materials used are minimal in their bulk and size.

Very few of the developing countries, with the exception of the "Confucian belt" countries – like Singapore, South Korea, China, Malaysia, or Brazil or India – are conscious of the need for or have made progress in High Technologies, the general feeling being that this whole area is beyond them. It is this feeling of lack of faith in their own scientists and technologists that one must fight against, since the future undoubtedly lies here. This is on account of the enormous value-added potential of the industries based on High Technology and the possibilities of exporting its products. There can be little "High technology Transfer" from the North, unless this is of yesteryear's technology.

Of the four aspects of Sciences and Technology which have been mentioned above, the first to be developed so far as our Southern countries are concerned, is Classical Low Technology. The next may be Sciences in Application. (This is assuming that expertise in Basic Sciences is already available). The last to develop, as a general

---

[4] NEST stands for the International Foundation for the Promotion of New and Emerging Sciences and Technologies.

rule, is Science-based High Technology.

To conclude this section, for a moderate sized developing country, there is no option to developing all the four areas of Science and Technology enumerated above. The two failures in the Science and Technology situation in the Third World are: (1) the confusion between Applied Science and Manufacturing Technology which has kept Applied Scientists from receiving their proper share of State help; and (2) the emphasis on importation of foreign Manufacturing Technologies by most of the developing countries.

Regarding the first point, it is to be noted that the words "Science" or "Science Transfer" do not occur in the Brandt Commission Report[5] so that Science and, in particular, Applied Science, even as contrasted with Manufacturing Technology, has been treated as a marginal activity by the South.

Regarding the second point, what has been wrong with importing technology has been a lack of emphasis on training and on development of indigenous technologies and the requisite sciences. Very few within the developing world appear to appreciate that the science of today is the technology of tomorrow.

THE SUB-CRITICAL SIZE OF SCIENCE AND TECHNOLOGY IN THE SOUTH AND SOME REMEDIES

As indicators of the sub-critical size of Science and Technology in the developing world, we could use two criteria: (a) the funds which the South provides for R&D and (b) the numbers of scientists and engineers actively engaged in these activities.

Funds for Science and Technology

One of the revealing indices of the size of Third World Science and Technology is the funding which the South provides for Research, Development and the Utilization of Science and Technology. Industrialized countries spend 4.35% of their GNP on defence, while developing countries spend 5.3%. Educational expenditures are also at a similar level – 5.2% of GNP in industrialized countries versus 3.8% in developing countries. For health, it is 4.7% in industrialized countries versus 1.6% in developing countries, admittedly about three times as low, yet still not as striking as the gap in spending on Science and Technology. The ratio of GNP expenditures on Science and Technology between the industrialized North and the South lies between a factor of five and nine. While industrialized countries spend relative average figures of 2.46% of GNP, the average for developing countries is 0.46%. As a result, the absolute total expenditures on Science and Technology in the South come to no more than 3.1% of

---

[5] Willy Brandt, *Common Crisis: North-South: Cooperation for World Recovery/The Brandt Commission* (Cambridge, Mass.: MIT Press, 1983).

the world total.[6]

Industrialized countries generally spend 2.5% of their GNP on Research, Development and Modification, Adaptation plus the Utilization of Science and Technology. No country in the South approaches this, except for South Korea, which was spending 2% of its GNP on R&D in Science and Technology in the early 1990s. The other "high spenders" among the developing countries at that time were Chile, Cuba, India, Kuwait and Mexico which spent between 0.5% and 0.9% of their GNP on Science and Technology. Though one may argue that increased spending is only a necessary condition for the developmental aspects of Science and Technology, not a sufficient one, it remains a fact that industrialized countries are expending (in GNP terms) at least five times more every year on Science and Technology than the Third World. We in the Third World are just not serious about Science and Technology.

The profession of Science and Science-based Technology is hardly a respectable or even valid profession in the South. Some responsibility for this may rest on our former colonial masters. For example, in the British Colonial Empire, Britain did not leave us the concept of a Scientific Civil Service, which, incidentally, has been part of the United Kingdom's own administrative and professional structure for a long time.

Total Numbers of Scientists and Engineers

The total number of scientists and engineers in the industrialized countries is around 1,400 per million of population, in contrast with 195 engineers and scientists per million in the case of developing countries. The ratio between the North and South is highly unfavourable with the South between 14 and 24 times lower than the North.

SCIENCE AND TECHNOLOGY EDUCATION POLICIES IN DEVELOPING COUNTRIES, PARTICULARLY POLICIES TOWARDS SECONDARY AND TERTIARY SCIENCE EDUCATION

> "Unless it has its own scientists and technicians, no country can call itself free. This involves the whole problem of scientific and technical training from secondary education to fundamental research..." – Rene Maheu, UNESCO Director General (1965).

> "If I could do it all again, I would start with education". – Jean Monnet, founder of modern Europe.

Science and technology education lies at the heart of all these developments. It is imperative that we should take note of what is going on in this field. The World

---

[6] These figures refer to the early 1990s when this chapter was written.

Bank figures for educational enrolments for developing countries[7] showed in the early 1990s the wide variations among different countries, as well as between industrialized and developing countries. The starkest variations, however, are in the average numbers we educate in the South between the ages of 12 to 19 (secondary education) and 20 to 24 (tertiary education). The averages in low income developing country were particularly small compared with those of developed countries, 22% to 37% in the South, versus 93% in the North for secondary education, and 5% in the South versus 39% in the North for tertiary education. This means that a student in most of our Southern countries is ill-equipped for the modern world, when he or she has reached the earning stage.

If we consider the balance between professional and liberal education, after a period of compulsory lower-secondary education up to about the age of 15 or 16, most modern societies provide for two parallel educational systems. Using the terminology of the United Kingdom in the 1970s these two systems may be called the system of professional education, which comprises technical, vocational, agricultural and commercial courses, and the system of liberal education, which consists of courses leading on to university level studies in the sciences, engineering, medicine and the arts.

A major structural failing of the Third World educational system has been that, in general, no credible professional system has developed. It is true that a half-hearted system has had scant prestige attached to it. As a general rule, such systems have been run by ministries of labour and employment, rather than ministries of education.

To see how inadequate such a system has been, one may recall that in industrialized countries the proportion of those enrolled in the two streams is about 50:50. In the Third World, however, the proportion of professional versus liberal enrolments at the secondary level is normally around 10:90. This makes for a preponderance of technologically illiterate young people, which is a major cause of unemployment in the Third World and of technological backwardness.

Thus one of the main educational tasks facing the Third World is to change this ratio of 10:90 to 50:50. In the conditions of the contemporary period, the professional education system should be accorded equal status with the better appreciated liberal educational system. Our first concern should be to bring a measure of prestige to the professional system of education. That could be done through the institution of national certificates, which might be closely identified with the prevailing certificates given for liberal studies at the same level. What I have in mind is this. Parallel to the present liberal system of education, we should create a second professional system of education. Each certificate – the secondary school leaving certificate, the matriculation, or the Bachelor's Degree – may be obtained either after the present liberal courses in arts or sciences, as is presently the case, or after technical, agricultural, or commercial courses from a polytechnic, an agricultural, or a

---

[7] These figures unfortunately do not distinguish between Science and non-Science studies. I have tentatively assumed that a quarter to one third of the total number of students are pursuing science studies.

commercial college.   So far as job opportunities in administrative services are concerned, all matriculates or degree holders, whether from liberal, technical, or commercial streams, would count as equivalent, provided the intellectual level of the courses provided were the same. This will mean that exclusive hold on the public mind of the present prestigious university-led liberal education system in our status-conscious countries will be broken.

At the secondary level, all science subjects are compulsory in countries such as Japan and the former USSR. Even future musicians or footballers or seamstresses must study physics, chemistry, mathematics and biology till they are sixteen. However, there is no such compulsion in the educational systems of most of our Southern countries. We are too soft on our students! We should consider the possibility of making science compulsory for all students up to a certain level, as is done in Japan, the former USSR and South Korea.

INTERNATIONAL MODALITIES FOR THE GROWTH AND UTILIZATION OF SCIENCE AND TECHNOLOGY

In the end, the growth of science and its utilization by the South is a Southern problem, though outside help can make a crucial difference, if it is effectively organized. The modalities for growth and utilization of science and technology entail two types of actions: those needing to be adopted in and by the South and those that need to be carried out in concert with the North. In this section some modalities are suggested through which the North could help the South to build up its scientific and technological base.

Firstly, 10-15% of aid given by developed countries should be specifically earmarked in the next twenty years to enhance science and technology in the South. This would mean the linking of aid for science and technology with the total bilateral aid provided by the North, as an important political modality. At the present time only 5% of aid from the USA appears to be spent in this way.

Secondly, it should be considered as part of the birthright of scientific communities in a developing country that the country has at least one complete Central Science Library containing most scientific and technological journals and all scientific books. Arrangements by aid organizations and/or the World Bank should make these materials available at a fraction of their present price, with at least one copy for each country to be sent to a designated Central Library in those developing countries which can immediately make use of this literature. We estimate there are at least fifty such countries.

Thirdly, various United Nations agencies, including the United Nations University, should play a prominent role in building up scientific infrastructure in their areas of competence. This should be part of their charters. Developing countries need international research institutions on the applied side like the Wheat and Rice Research Institutes in Mexico and the Philippines and the International Centre for Insect

Physiology and Ecology in Kenya. There is also the experience on the basic side of the International Atomic Energy Agency (IAEA) and UNESCO, combined with generous Italian support, in relation to the International Centre for Theoretical Physics (ICTP) in Trieste, or, of UNIDO for the International Centres for Biotechnology and Genetic Engineering, at Delhi and Trieste. The ICTP hosted visits of 4,901 physicists during 1989, 3,141 of them coming from developing countries and 1,760 from industrialized countries. Both centres are run by the scientists for the scientists. At the very least, the South should ensure proper utilization of those trained at these centres and urge other United Nations Organizations to set up international centres of training for research in relevant disciplines.

Fourthly, there is the question of the acquisition of Ph.D. degrees by nationals of developing countries. While a Ph.D. degree may be important, the experience of the International Centre for Theoretical Physics demonstrates that a full-fledged doctorate is not essential for subsequent research work. A diploma from a United Nations Centre, of a similar standard to the Diploma of the Imperial College, London University (DIC), in Science, Technology or Medicine, may be what is needed by those who are already teaching in developing countries. Further thought should be given to the institution of such diplomas and the value accorded to these by universities in developing countries.

In this context, there is the proposal to create in Trieste an International Centre for Science which will have five components: (1) the existing International Centre for Theoretical Physics; (2) the existing local branch of the International Centre for Genetic Engineering and Biotechnology; (3) a new International Centre for High Technology and New Materials; (4) a new International Centre for Chemistry, Pure and Applied; and (5) a new International Centre for Earth Science and the Environment. This International Centre for Science has been planned by the Government of Italy, with United Nations sponsorship.[8]

It has been further proposed that twenty world class Centres for Science, High Technology and Environment, with training and research equally emphasized, should be started with the World Bank cooperation – on lines similar to the agricultural institutions of the Consultative Group in International Agricultural Research (CGIAR). Their suggestion was endorsed by the Non-aligned Movement during its meeting in Belgrade in September 1989. The Heads of State or Governments concluded that "there is a need to support the establishment in developing countries of a world class Network of Research and Training Institutes dedicated to the development and application of High Technology" (and the environment) "and we appeal to the international community, particularly the developed countries and the multilateral financial and developmental institutions, especially the World Bank, to support this network within the framework of international cooperation".

[8] This is now known as the Third World Academy of Sciences, advertized on its website (http://ww.ictp.trieste.it/TWAS) as having been established in 1983. In 1993 the Third World Organization for Women's Science was created, with its Secretariat hosted by the Third World Academy of Sciences in Trieste.

Cooperative arrangements between centres in developing countries and international centres such as the International Centre for Science which is now being planned by various UN Agencies, will, we hope, ensure the requisite quality.

A FIVE-YEAR BLUEPRINT FOR SCIENCE AND TECHNOLOGY FOR THE DEVELOPING WORLD

If one were charged with developing a science and technology policy for a typical developing country of modest size, one would give importance to each of the following points:

(1)   Making sure that the high-level scientists and technologists in any given society know exactly what is expected of them. Their work for development should be looked after by the highest possible authorities in the land – if possible, by the rulers themselves. (Every country has a set of Merlins within their scientific communities capable of working, or at least supervising, miracles. However small their numbers may be, these men and women must have their morale built up. They must get the scientific infrastructure plus the equipment plus international contacts which they need to carry through their work. Reciprocally, they have to be told that they cannot afford to live in their ivory towers, that they must make themselves available to the public and that society will expect returns from them).

(2)   Carrying through the recommendations discussed above in respect of general science education, in particular at the secondary level.

(3)   Building up at the same time expertise in Classical Low Technologies which emphasize craftsmanship and fabrication.

(4)   Importing manufacturing technologies from abroad, taking care to ensure that every importation is supplemented by indigenous training.

(5)   Building up, as a matter of priority, comprehensive technological information centres.

(6)   Commissioning a comprehensive plan for Applied Sciences and for High Technology. (What one develops first depends upon a nation's priorities and could be in one or more of the following areas: agriculture, livestock, health, population, energy, local materials and minerals, environment, soil sciences and seismology, atmosphere and oceans, biotechnology, informatics – microelectronics and microphotonics plus new materials).

(7)   Finally, building up scientific and technological research within the universities. For this purpose, training programs should be instituted, both within the country and abroad, for cadres of scientists and technicians, so as to assure the critical size of local communities.

As for expenditure issues, one would need to spend a minimum of 4% plus 4% plus 8% = 16% of the educational budget respectively on Basic plus Applied Sciences plus Science-based High Technology.

What should be spent on training, development and research in the Classical Low Technology area? The short answer is as much as one may afford.

One minimal figure which has been suggested is worth repeating. It is UNESCO's famous 1% of GNP for *all* sciences, basic and applied, plus *all* technology, classical as well as high. On the average basis of 4% of GNP being spent on education by the South, with 16% of this for science and high technology, this works out at roughly 1/6:1/6:1/3:1/3 or 1% of GNP for basic and applied sciences versus classical low technology versus high technology.

Where would one get the necessary initial training? Clearly, here, one would have to rely on the universities and the institutes in the North, or on South-South collaborative programs, or on the United Nations Centres, for providing the training facilities.

For Basic Sciences, one may think of the IAEA and UNESCO-run International Centre for Theoretical Physics (ICTP) and the UNIDO-run International Centres for Genetic Engineering and Biotechnology (ICGEB) in India and Italy, or the International Centre for Science with its three new components, the International Centre for Earth Sciences and the Environment, the International Centre for Chemistry, Pure and Applied, and the International Centre for High Technology and New Materials, or the International Centre for Insect Physiology and Ecology (ICIPE) in Kenya, for the relevant basic disciplines.

For Applied Sciences, one would think of international centres comprising the World Bank promoted CGIAR Network, with the training component of these Centres enhanced. There are three centres devoted to research on tropical agriculture (in Colombia, India and Nigeria) a fourth (in Syria) concentrating on agriculture in arid zones, a fifth (in the Philippines) on cross-breeding of rice, and three on genetic improvement of cattle (in Ethiopia, Kenya and the Ivory Coast), plus the International Centre for the Potato (in Peru). In addition, there is the Centre (in Rome) for the conservation of genetic resources, one (in Holland) for the fostering of rural agricultural cooperation, a twelfth in Washington, D.C. for the study of nutrition, and finally, the world-famous International Maize and Wheat Improvement Centre (CIMMYT) in Mexico.

This group of 13 institutes commands a total of $250 million collected from donor countries by the World Bank. There is the hope that a similar set of at least twenty regional and national institutions may be created in three to five years for training and research in High Technology and for the Earth's Environment – particularly in Africa – with a similar measure of funding by the World Bank and other donor governments.

In conclusion, there are a number of special points which should be remembered in connection with the application of Science and Technology to Development. One must remember the long-term nature of Science and Technology as applied to development. We are not likely to see the benefits for a long time. The year 2000 would be a good year to aim at if we started in the early 1990s.

We also stress the necessity for saving on armaments and defence expenditures, at least for the South – 10% of the present defence budgets – and expending the funds thus saved for the enhancement of Science and Technology in the future.

11

East-West Medical Exchanges
and their Mutual Influence

Ma Kanwen

CHINESE MEDICINE AND THE WEST

The contacts between China and the Western world can be traced back to late in the 2nd century CE, when the general Zhang Qian was sent to Persia. However, little is known about whether Chinese medicine was introduced into the Western world at that time. Communication began to expand between China and the Arabian world, furthered by the Silk road. From the 7th and 8th centuries on, China had considerable interaction with Persia and Arabia, but it had very little direct knowledge of Europe before the Yuan dynasty in the 13th century.

Chinese medicines were probably introduced into the West through Persia and Arabia. According to the *Song Hui Yao*, in the 10th century, over fifty kinds of Chinese drugs were transported to Arabia from Canton.[1] Chinese medicines also reached the West through India, and from the 15th and 16th centuries on, through Portuguese merchants. Smilax's "China root" was in vogue in Europe. It was used by Charles V as a medicine for general health, even though Andreas Vesalius (1514-1564), the well known physician and reformer in anatomy, assessed its use less favourably.[2] But "China root" was used for treating a number of diseases, including syphilis. And the therapeutic properties of Chinese rhubarb were also known in Europe, as evidenced by the attempts of celebrated physician Hermann Boerhaave (1668-1738), to obtain rhubarb seeds.[3] Michael Boym, a Jesuit, in China in the 17th century, inserted material from Li Shizhen's 1590 *Compendium of Materia Medica* (*Ben Cao Gang Mu*), into his

---

[1] Ma Kanwen, "Historical Research in Chinese Medicine and Recent Developments in Western Countries", in *Lishi yu wenxian yanjiu ziliao* (published by the China Institute for the Historical Medicine and Medical Literature, Beijing, 1974), Vol. 4, p. 1.

[2] Andreas Vesalius, *Radicis Chinae Vsus* (Lyons: Sub Saito Coloniensi, 1547). See also, C.D. O'Malley, *Andreas Vesalius of Brussels* (Berkeley: University of California Press, 1964), chapter IX, "Letter on the China Root", pp. 207-217.

[3] Chinese Rhubarb did create a great sensation in the Western world. The best work that offers comprehensive sources on this subject so far is Clifford M. Foust, *Rhubarb, The Wondrous Drug* (New Jersey: Princeton University Press, 1992).

book *Flora Sinensis*, published in Vienna in 1656.[4] Such knowledge transfer meant that Li Shizhen's work was indirectly known to Darwin, who referred to the *Compendium of Materia Medica* as "ancient Chinese encyclopedias".[5] Knowledge about Chinese materia medica is also evident in other European books, such as Du Halde's *Description Géographique, Historique, Chronologique, Politique de l'Empire de la Chine et de la Tartarie Chinoise*, published in Paris in 1735.

Michael Boym also introduced into Europe the art of feeling the pulse in diagnosis. John Floyer (1649-1734), the eminent English physician, was so inspired by a translation of Boym's work that he devised a pulse watch, the earliest of its kind.[6] Acupuncture and moxibustion arrived in Europe in the 17th century and were studied and practised by a number of doctors.[7]

In the 18th century the Chinese method of variolation against smallpox, used longer in China than anywhere else, was introduced into England. Some members of the Royal family were inoculated.[8] While this process carried some risk, it was the only effective method of fighting against smallpox, which was rampant in many places throughout the world. Edward Jenner (1749-1816) tried innoculation in 1796. His epoch-making vaccination method may have been inspired by this Chinese technique of variolation.

However, during the early contacts between East and West, the introduction of Chinese medicine into the West did not follow any systematic pattern.

THE EARLY INTRODUCTION AND RE-INTRODUCTION OF WESTERN MEDICINE INTO CHINA

The 17th century saw the early introduction of Western medicine into China by the Jesuits. Jean Terrenz or Terrentius (1576-1630) compiled in Chinese (circa 1635) a small treatise on the structure of the human body, *Renshen shuogai*.[9] But because of the poor quality of the text and illustrations, and also because the material was confined to the Court, it exerted little influence. Later under Emperor Kangxi (1662-1722) interest in Western medicine grew when the Jesuits cured the Emperor of a malaria attack using Cinchona bark, and relieved his heart palpitation and a boil on his upper

---

[4] Michael Boym, *Flora Sinensis* (Vienna, 1656).

[5] C. Darwin, *The Variation of Animals and Plants Under Domestication* (London: John Murray, 1868), Vol. 11, Chapter XX, "Selection by Man (by the Ancients)", pp. 204-205.

[6] See J. Floyer, *The Physician's Pulse Watch* (London, 1707). In this book, "An extract of the Chinese Art of feeling the Pulse from Cleyer" is attached. But Floyer did not know that Cleyer was a plagiarist, who published Boym's work on Chinese pulse-taking under his own name.

[7] Gwei-Djen Lu et al, *Celestial Lancet* (Cambridge: Cambridge University Press, 1980), p. 270.

[8] Peter Razzell, *The Conquest of Smallpox – The Impact of Inoculation on Smallpox Mortality in Eighteenth Century Britain* (New Haven: Sussex, 1977), pp. 36-37, 48-49, 142-143; Derrick Baxby, "A Death from Inoculated Smallpox in the English Royal Family", in *Medical History*, Vol. 28, 1984, pp. 303-307.

[9] Fan Xing-zun, *Mingji xiyang chuanru zhi yixue* (Shanghai: China Medical History Society, 1943), pp. 17-18.

lip.[10] Following this, the Emperor ordered Father Joachim Bouvet to start collecting human anatomical charts. And later this task was taken up by Father Dominique Parennin, who translated into Manchu a text on anatomy and some medical subjects, probably between 1698 and 1722.[11] But the copies of this original text were very rare. Only three copies existed, and since these were also confined exclusively to the Court, their influence was again limited.

The real influence of Western medicine upon Chinese health work was not seen until the early 19th century, when China's feudal society was on the decline. By this time, Western medicine had undergone an unprecedted development, while the development of traditional Chinese medicine had stagnated, despite the splendid achievements of several thousand years of history.

During this period, China had no medical education in the modern sense, nor any official criterion for becoming a doctor. The medical profession was regarded in much the same way as that of the astrologer or fortune-teller. As in earlier centuries, medicine was taught chiefly through three means: through apprenticeship, teaching within the family or by self-instruction through reading medical texts. People could claim to be doctors by learning a few remedies or minor skills, from their families, from other doctors, or through the study of medical texts. Many literary men became versed in medicine, due to either dissatisfaction with their official careers or to concern over the health of their families. This was usually achieved through studying classic medical works which were easily available to the privileged. But because of the low social position of the medical profession, doctors considered it a disgrace to be regarded as "professional doctors", preferring instead to practice in the name of charity.

In summary, there were competent doctors of extensive learning and erudition, such as doctors who came from many generations of medical families, with rich clinical experiences and those who were proficient in particular specialties, but there were also those doctors with only a half-baked medical knowledge and those who were outright quacks. Although a number of open-minded doctors had doubts about the ancient medical classics and made efforts to discover a new approach to medicine, on the whole medicine during the Qing dynasty was dominated by adherence to the classics. There were no medical schools or colleges for ordinary people. For many generations medical training remained attached to the imperial medical institution, established exclusively for the service of the court.

THE INTRODUCTION OF THE SMALLPOX VACCINE TO CHINA

The first contribution modern Western medicine made to the Chinese people was the introduction of the smallpox vaccination in 1805, only nine years after its invention by

---

[10] Bai Jin (Joachim Bouvet, 1656-1730), *Kangxi di zhuan* Chinese translation by Ma Xuxiang (Beijing: Zhonghua shuju, 1980), pp. 230-231.

[11] J. B. de C. M. Saunders and Francis R. Lee, *The Manchu Anatomy and Its Historical Origin* (Taiwan: Li Ming Cultural Enterprise, 1981), "The Introduction", pp. 1-8.

the eminent English doctor, Edward Jenner. In the same year it was reported that a Spaniard, Don Francisco Xavier de Balmis, a Portuguese doctor, Domingos Jose Gomes, and a high court judge, Miguel de Arriaga, also introduced the technique of vaccination to Macao.[12] That same year, Alexander Pearson, surgeon to the East India Company in China, practiced vaccination among the local Chinese in Macao and Canton, and wrote a treatise entitled *The Extraordinary History of a New Method of Inoculating Practised in the Kingdom of England.* Pearson's treatise was translated into Chinese by George Staunton and published in Canton. From his reports to the National Vaccine Establishment, we know that the first people he vaccinated were from the poorer classes, and that the vaccination process was successful. The method he said, "sprang into favour amongst the Chinese, who though very conservative in their feelings, when once convinced of the benefit of any new method, take it up very readily and great numbers were brought to be operated on during the period of the raging smallpox in the course of the winter and spring months of 1805-1806".[13]

Very soon after, in 1806, Pearson trained some Chinese to be his assistants. Among them was Qiu Xi, then a 23-year old intellectual from Canton, who eventually became Pearson's principal assistant and the chief disseminator of the vaccination technique. Meanwhile, Pearson's work was also supported by the local authorities and the Hong merchants in Canton. In 1815, principal Hong merchants established a fund for the vaccination of the poor at any time, and opened a dispensary for this purpose in the Public Hall of the Hong merchants in Canton.

The spread of this new method to other parts of China was not easy. In many areas people still continued to use the old method of variolation. Zhou Chunxi, a noted literatus, lamented the difficulty of spreading the vaccination technique in his text *Yangdou shiyi* (*Removing doubts about foreign vaccination*):

> People usually get accustomed to those things which they often see, but feel strange about those things which they do not see often. This is natural and normal. It is particularly so in the case of the Western modern method of vaccination against smallpox. As in the past there was no such a method in our country, and people who live at the present period of time have never seen such a matter, and even those who are erudite and conversant with things past and present have never heard of nor ever seen it, I have mentioned in the Preface of my book that this method comes from Europe...People there pay much attention to literary studies and have delicate learning. The king there has set up schools widely. There are universities, secondary and primary schools. There are four departments in their universities and the King pays much attention to medicine...As for the foreign method of vaccination, which is a minor skill in medicine...there are only 10% of the people in our land who believe in it, and

---

[12] C. R. Boxer, "A Note on the Interaction of Portuguese and Chinese Medicine in Macao and Peking (16th-18th centuries)", in J. Z. Bowers et al (eds.), *Medicine and Society in China* (New York: Josiah Macy Jr. Foundation, 1974), p. 31.

[13] Wang and Wu, *History of Chinese Medicine* (Shanghai, China: National Quarantine Service, 1937), pp. 273-301.

90% of the people who still do not believe in it. This is because they are blinded by prejudice and ignorance... The foreign opium, which has brought untold troubles to our people, is still smoked by many people, while the vaccination method, which is also foreign, is considered harmful and avoided by many people with sneers. Alas, what a hopeless and stupid thing is this![14]

Despite difficulties, the practice of vaccination gradually developed, supported by the efforts of Western and local Chinese doctors, health workers and officials in various locations. Gradually, vaccination dispensaries were established in different regions of China. By the early 20th century, in addition to doctors trained in Western medicine, many open-minded native practitioners were trained to work in vaccination techniques. As a result, the traditional method of variolation was gradually replaced by that of vaccination. Needless to say, numerous Chinese benefitted from this new method, which can be seen as a deserved "feedback" to the Chinese people. We know that when Jenner was trying to spread his vaccination method, he was met with great hostility and opposition in England. He probably never expected that his invention would be so quickly accepted by Chinese people, and that it would play such an important role as a prelude to the re-introduction of Western medicine into China. The wholesale and systemic introduction of modern Western medicine into China did not begin until the arrival of more Western doctors, particularly Protestant medical missionaries, in the 19th century.

THE COMPILING AND PUBLISHING OF MEDICAL WORKS

The compilation and publication of medical books exerted a great influence on the development of Western medicine in China. Pearson's book on smallpox vaccination was a pioneering effort. Benjamin Hobson (1816-1873) was one of the first to realize the necessity and significance of publishing medical works in Chinese as a means of building up Western medical education in China. He arrived in Macao in 1839 and soon became an ardent advocate of modern medical education in China. He had several young Chinese students studying medicine under his care. But having tried in vain to establish a medical school in Hong Kong, he turned to the compilation of medical textbooks.[15] With the assistance of his Chinese collaborators, he compiled and published five books in Chinese on Western medicine and general science. The books were published in a beautiful wood-cut block printed form.

Among other early Western doctors who contributed much to the translation and compilation of medical works, the most outstanding were John Glasgow Kerr (1824-1901), John Dudgeon (1831-1901), and John Fryer (1830-1928). Kerr, of the American Presbyterian Mission, translated over twenty medical textbooks between

---

[14] Zhou Chun-xi, "*Yangdou shiyi*", in *Yinzhun niudou fangshu*, reprinted by Liu Kun, 1855.
[15] B. Hobson, *Report of the Hospital at Kum-li-fu in Canton for the Years 1848 and 1849* (London: Joseph Rogerson, 1849), p. 24.

1859 and 1886. These covered various branches of medicine and most were the first of their kind to appear in China. Dudgeon, a prolific writer of the London Missionary Society, completed a series of medical works while teaching at the *Tongwen* College and working at the missionary hospital in Beijing. His most influential work was a 16-volume book on anatomy, the *Quanti tongkao* in 1885. This represented not only the first systematic and comprehensive anatomical work ever published in China, but also the first modern Western medical work printed and published at the expense of the Chinese government. The publication's preface was contributed by several high officials of the Qing government.[16] A companion work on physiology soon followed. John Fryer was a British scholar who translated and compiled a total of 158 works on science and technology, as well as some in the social sciences. These were completed with the help of Chinese collaborators while he was working at the Jiangnan Arsenal. Nine of these books dealt directly with medicine and health, and one was the first text on forensic medicine to be published in China.

Before the appearance of the Chinese Medical Missionary Association and the China Missionary Medical Journal in 1887, the compilation and translation of medical works was usually done through individual efforts. Later a more organized approach to producing medical works began. Under the Association, in 1890, a Nomenclature Committee was formed to unify terminology. This was followed in 1905 by a Publication Committee to provide better organized translation and publication of medical works. Many medical missionaries, with the cooperation of Chinese doctors, made memorable contributions to China's modern medical literature.

The appearance of these modern medical works at this time exerted immense influence, not only upon those Chinese who wanted to study Western medicine, but also upon other intellectuals, particularly native traditional practitioners. Hobson's work serves as a telling example. As the first series of systematic modern medical textbooks ever published in China, these books created a sensation and became the most sought after medical works among interested Chinese. As soon as Hobson's first book on anatomy and physiology appeared, the whole volume was collected in the *Haishan xianguan congshu* (*Collection of Sea-Mountain Fairy House*), an encyclopedia of 56 volumes. The material was edited by Pan Shicheng, a noted Cantonese scholar, and published in 1851. This was the first time that a Western medical work had been included in a Chinese encyclopedia. Although Pan continued to adhere to traditional concepts, on the whole he exhibited a positive attitude toward the modern anatomy and physiology presented in Hobson's book. For the first time in China the expression "western medicine" (*xi yi*) appeared. Coined by Pan, the term is still in use today. It replaced the previous name for Western medicine as "medical learning of the extreme West" (*taixi yixue*).

Hobson's books on natural philosophy and natural history were particularly attractive to Chinese intellectuals who longed to obtain modern Western scientific knowledge. Two famous modern Chinese scientists, Xu Shou (1818-1884) and Hua

---

[16] *Quanti Tongkao*, prefaced by Rong Lu, Chung Hou, Bao Qi, 1885. This book is kept in the China Institute for the History of Medicine and Medical Literature, Beijing.

Hengfang (1883-1902) benefitted greatly from Hobson's work. They were so delighted to discover in it new scientific knowledge about chemistry, physics, engineering and other fields that they soon started to create scientific instruments and to perform experiments based on the descriptions given in Hobson's book. This led to the production of the first steamer in China.[17] In the period after the Jesuits had first brought Western scientific knowledge to China in the late 16th century, no modern Western scientific knowledge had been known to the Chinese, because of the later Qing policy of closing the country to foreign intellectual and cultural influences.

As a result, the response of the native Chinese doctors to Hobson's books was ardent and enthusiastic. In 1852, the year following the publication of Hobson's *Outline of Anatomy and Physiology*, Wang Shixiong (1808-1868), the famous Qing physician and specialist in febrile diseases, who came from a noted family of scholars and physicians, was in the process of re-editing *Jottings at the Chongqing Hall* (*Chongqing tang suibi*), the work of his grand-father, the noted physician Wang Xuequan.

In the preface to this re-edited work, Wang commented on Hobson's material, as follows:

> The world is differentiated into both ancient and modern, and is geographically also divided into home and abroad. The shape and complexion of mankind are also different. However, there are few differences in the function of men's internal organs and the circulation of the *Qi* and the blood...The Western doctor Hobson has recently published a book entitled *Quanti xinlun*, in which the brain is described as the main dominating organ, which controls man's consciousness and behaviour, and the spirit and intelligence of the body also rely upon it. Such a discussion is much more in detail than that of Terrentius' book".[18]

He went on further to say that according to Hobson's book, respiration was made by one exhaling and inhaling breaths, and that carbon dioxide was exhaled, and that by inhalation one received the living-air from heaven and earth. Therefore, if one held one's breath for a short while, one would feel very sick and restless, and would need to take a long breath until one felt restored.[19]

This provides the first evidence in China of a discussion of respiration according to modern physiology. It was also the earliest recorded acceptance of such knowledge by native Chinese physicians.

On the one hand Hobson's books provided new and modern medical knowledge for native physicians and practitioners, yet on the other hand, they produced a dilemma. Faced with the scientific evidence presented in Hobson's books Chinese

---

[17] J. Fryer, "Jiangnan zhizaoju fangyi yishu shilue, 1880", in Zhang Jinglu (ed.), *Zhongguo jindai shiliao chubian* (Shanghai Press, 1953, pp. 10-11).

[18] Wang Xuequan, *Chongqingtang suibi* (*Jottings at the Chongqing Hall*), originally printed in 1808, reprinted in *Qianzhai yixue congshu* (*Qianzhai's Collection of Medical Works*), Vol. 11, p. 17.

[19] *Ibid.*, p. 113.

physicians seemed convinced and willing to accept new ideas, but at the same time they had reservations. Lu Yitian, another noted physician of the time, exemplified this attitude in his book *Lenglu yihua* (*Deserted House Medical Jottings*), published in 1858:

> In the Western doctor Hobson's book (*Xiyi luelun*), we see a discussion of external illnesses in great detail but what is said about internal diseases is brief. The methods of cutting off flesh and amputating bones that it describes are such that Chinese doctors dare not try. Its methods of treating internal diseases are also different from those of Chinese doctors. For instance, the use of the tincture of arsenic in the treatment of malaria, extract of opium for cholera and camphor prepared in the form of tincture, all are absurd and contrary to Chinese methods".[20]

Lu's response to the use of a clock to count the beats of the pulse as described in Hobson's book, was to reserve judgement, saying: "As for the examination of the pulse, Western doctors use a clock to establish the pulse beat, taking advantage of the accuracy of the clock's movements. The book says that the Chinese way of using the doctor's respiration to count the patient's pulse is not as accurate as that of using a clock, for doctors' respiration may be different, either slow or fast, long or short".[21]

An interesting response to Hobson's *Outline of Anatomy and Physiology* is seen in the book *Zhongxi huitong yijing jinyi* (*Essence of Medical Classics in the Confluence of Chinese and Western Medicine*), published by Tang Zonghai, a Sichuan practitioner (1846-1897). In his book Tang adopted some Western medical ideas in order to elucidate traditional Chinese medicine, and to associate Chinese and Western medical practice. He adapted some illustrations from Hobson's book, such as those of the blocked vessels. However, he argued that Western anatomical study could provide only the methods of analysis, and lacked knowledge of the channels or meridians of the body. He went further to say that Westerners know only the shape and structure of the body, and not the functional activity of the vital spirit *qi*. He then concluded that each of the two medical systems had both strong and weak points. Tang has been considered by Chinese medical historians as one of the early major representatives of the medical sect of 19th century China which attempted to integrate Chinese and Western medicine and to elucidate Chinese medical theories in the light of Western medicine.

Tang Zonghai's approach was followed by a number of Chinese practitioners and physicians until recent years. One of Tang's active followers was Zhang Xichun (1860-1933), a native of Yanshan, Hebei province, who studied traditional Chinese medicine when a young man and Western medicine in his thirties. He advocated a way of integrating traditional Chinese medicine and Western medicine by taking the former as the main body or principal part, and assimilating to it the strong points of the latter. He was one of the strongest exemplars of those who made a bold attempt to integrate traditional Chinese medicine and Western medicine into one system, a project to which

[20] Lu Yitian, *Lenglu yihua* (*Deserted House Medical Jottings*) (Shanghai Health Press, 1958), p. 38.
[21] *Ibid.*

he devoted his whole life. In his *Preface to the Revised Edition of the Essence of Medical Classics in the Confluence of Chinese and Western Medicine*, in addition to mentioning Hobson's five books, Zhang expressed his views on traditional Chinese and Western medicine in the following way:

> Based on experiments, the Western doctor Hobson's five books give us a minute and comprehensive description of the human body. However, they mention nothing about the nature of the internal organs, nor about the mechanism and circulation of the vital spirit (*qi*) in the whole body. Therefore, we know that traditional Chinese and Western medicine each has weak points. If they can be comprehensively studied and integrated, and mutually supplemented, then medicine would be able to reach the peak of perfection".[22]

The viewpoint of Chinese physicians towards modern Western medicine, as expressed above, represents the influence of Hobson's work on Chinese medicine. This direction was first put forward by Wang Shixiong in 1852, clarified by Tang Zonghai in 1892, further described by Zhang Xichun in the early part of the 20th century, and later adopted by a number of Chinese practitioners. Subsequently the view that modern Western medicine was more minute and accurate in knowing the shape and structure of the human body but neglected the functions of the body became a commonplace assumption among many native Chinese physicians and practitioners. This provides evidence that native Chinese physicians openly recognized and accepted the fact that Western medicine had its strong points.

Hobson's books continued to enjoy popularity in China until the 1920s and 1930s. Deeply influenced by Hobson's works, Zhang Shanlei (1873-1934), (also called Zhang Shouyi) a well-known native physician of Shanghai, provided his students with Hobson's *Outline of Anatomy and Physiology* as a reference book when he was Director of the Zhejiang Lanxi School of Traditional Chinese Medicine in 1920. Among his many writings and publications was one entitled *Quanti xinlun shuzheng* (*Annotations on the Outline of Anatomy and Physiology*), which was published in Shanghai in 1935.

Hobson's books were reprinted several times by the Chinese, and foreign merchants in Shanghai expressed their approval of them by subscribing to a large new edition of the series at a cost of $2,000.[23] His works were also listed in the *Dongxi xue shulu* (*Bibliography of Eastern and Western Books*) (1899), an influential bibliographical work which lists the books dealing with Eastern and Western studies considered essential for Chinese readers. This prestigious bibliography was prefaced by Cai Yuanpei, the best known scholar and advocate of modern education at the time. In fact Hobson's books were so popular that in a 1898 edition the title of the whole

---

[22] Zhang Xicun, *Chongjiao zhongxi huitong yishu wuzhong, xu* [*Preface to the Revised Edition of the Essence of Medical Classics in the Confluence of Chinese and Western Medicine*] (*Guangyi shuju*, 1933).

[23] William Lockhart, *Medical Missionary in China* (London: Hurst and Blackett Pubications, 1861), p. 160.

series was described simply as *Five Books of Western Medicine* (*Xiyi wuzong*). This title was even further abbreviated by the Chinese to *Hobson's Five* (*Hexin Wuzong*).

TRAINING CHINESE ASSISTANTS AND RUNNING MEDICAL SCHOOLS

As mentioned earlier, Pearson pioneered the training of Chinese assistants. When the missionary hospitals opened, the need of trained Chinese assistants was urgently felt to cope with the load of hospital work and to spread modern medical knowledge. In 1887 the *China Medical Missionary Journal*, a newly published journal, issued an editorial affirming the potential of Chinese youth in studying modern medicine:

> From our experience, we believe that the bright Chinese youths, when properly trained, make as good students as are to be found anywhere; they are plodding, studious, very amenable to discipline, as a rule extremely quick at comprehension, and with the memory faculty remarkably developed. In fact, one might call them ideal students.[24]

It is interesting to note that in Dudgeon's 1864 annual report of work in the Peking Hospital, that among his Chinese pupils under training was a surgeon from the Imperial Medical Academy.

> During the summer, one of the Emperor's surgeons became a pupil in the hospital. He was one of 10 and had duty every 10th day. During the interval, he was in the habit of practising among the people, and giving them gratuitous advice and medicine. The surgeons attempt little, extracting teeth or opening abscesses exceed their skill. They have little knowledge of fractures and dislocations; their theories are absurd but their practice is occasionally correct. After a few months residence in the hospital, he received an appointment from the Mandarins to attend upon a large body of troops.[25]

In addition to training Chinese assistants by way of apprenticeship, attempts were made to found medical schools. Hobson was the first doctor to attempt to establish a medical college, but unfortunately his efforts failed. He was followed by Dr. John Kerr, who was more successful. In 1866, together with his Chinese collaborator Dr. Huang Kuan, Dr. Kerr started a small school with a three-year training program. In 1897 the program was extended to four years. This school formed the foundation for the later South China Medical College, established in 1904. During his many years of effort, Kerr trained upwards of 200 students.

Given the impossibility of teaching medicine single-handed, cooperation soon became the order of the day, and in due time missionary medical schools were founded.

---

[24] J. K. M., "Medical Education in China", in *The China Medical Missionary Journal*, Vol. 1, no. 3, 1887, p. 127.

[25] J. Dudgeon, *The Third Annual Report of the Peking Hospital* (Peking: James Ly and Co., 1865), p. 30.

Most resulted from the union of several missions. By 1909, 15 existing or prospective medical schools were operating under Christian influence.[26] By far the most active and influential was the Peking Union Medical College, which was the first medical college established in China through a collaboration between both British and American doctors, and with the cooperation of different mission societies. Dr. Thomas Cochrane, of the London Missionary Society, was the first dean of the college and played a large role in its foundation. He gained support from high officials of the Qing government, including the head eunuch, Lin Lianying, who was his patient, and who in turn influenced the Dowager Empress, Ci Xi. She contributed 10,000 taels to the college, while Chinese officials and the gentry added 1,600, and foreign residents offered 280. At the opening of this college, in February of 1906, Na Nuo, a member of the cabinet and head of the Ministry of Foreign Affairs,[27] presided and read an address of congratulations from the Dowager Empress. In the summer of the same year, the Qing government recognized the college. It was maintained by six missionary organizations until 1915, after which the Rockerfeller Foundation took over its support.

By the end of 1916, there were fourteen medical institutions controlled wholly or in part by missionary organizations. These included medical schools for women. Although the conditions of most of the medical schools founded by Westerners deteriorated because of a lack of funds and a shortage of teaching staff and facilities, the system of Western medical education exerted much influence upon the development of medical education in China.

One factor which aided the acceptance of Western medicine was the Westernization movement (*Yangwu yundong*) carried out during the reign of Emperor Tongzhi in the 1860s by comprador bureaucrats under the slogan of "self strengthening". The ultimate goal of this movement was the preservation of the feudal rule of the Qing dynasty. The idea was that in order to strengthen China, the Chinese needed to learn the superior teachings of the barbarians, to be able to control them. This movement was supported by the Emperor in the capital, and by such high officials as Zeng Guofan, Zuo Zongtang and Li Hongzhang in the provinces. From 1861 to 1895, a number of diplomatic and military modernization projects were launched because Western science and teachings, including medicine, were considered useful to the regime. Among the establishments was the formation of the *Tongwen* College (*Tongwen guan*) in Beijing in 1862, for the purpose of training foreign office interpreters. By 1872, medicine had been added to the college's curriculum, and Dudgeon was appointed Professor of Medicine.[28] This was the first time in China that a Western doctor had been employed as medical professor by a government-run institute. Although medicine was never a major focus at the college, its presence

---

[26] W. H. Jeffreys, "A Review of Medical Education in China", in *Chinese Medical Journal*, Vol. 23, No. 5, 1909, pp. 294-296.

[27] His name is wrongly recorded in some articles and books as Na Tong (Tung), for example, in E. J. Peill, "The New Union Medical College in Peking", in *The China Medical Missionary Journal*, Vol. 20, 1906, p. 123; and in Wang and Wu, *History of Chinese Medicine*, 1937, pp. 547 and 631.

[28] Zhu Youhuan (ed.), *Zhongguo jindai xuzhi shiliao* (Shanghai East China Normal University, 1983), Vol. 1, p. 41.

signified that for the first time Western medicine had permeated the Chinese imperial education and examination system.

Shortly after, as a result of the Westernization movement, and to a certain extent because of the superiority of Western medicine, the first medical college run by the Chinese government appeared. The story was that in 1878 Dr. John Kenneth Mackenzie of the London Missionary Society, while working in Tianjin with colleagues Dr. Andrew Irwin, Dr. Leonora Howard and a customs medical officer, cured the wife of the Viceroy, Li Hongzhang, while native doctors had failed to do so. Out of gratitude the Viceroy ordered that a temple near the government office be put at Mackenzie's disposal to allow him to open a dispensary. All expenses were defrayed by the viceroy. As a result a small medical school was opened in 1881, which was called in Chinese a *Yixue guan*. It was placed at Mackenzie's disposal and supported financially by the Viceroy.[29] Not only was this the first medical school supported by the Chinese government, but it also marked a further official recognition of Western medicine.

Meanwhile a new viewpoint put forward by one of the leaders of the Westernization Movement was becoming fashionable. The slogan "taking Chinese studies as the foundation, and Western studies for their practical use" (*zhongxue weiti, xixue weiyong*) was put forward by Zhang Zhidong (1837-1909), in his *Exhortation to Learning* (*Quanxue pian*), published in 1898. Zhang's views exerted a great deal of influence upon the thinking of the Chinese and accelerated the trend toward accepting Western science and technology.

During the upsurge of constitutional reform and modernization movements in the late 19th century, reformers and intellectuals emphasized the significance of medical education in building the Chinese nation, and firmly advocated the study and adoption of Western medicine. Zheng Guanying, a noted reformer, wrote that Western medicine had more advantages than traditional Chinese medicine, especially in surgery. He suggested that China should build different levels of hospitals in all regions of the country and recommended that, beginning with the Imperial Medical Academy, Western methods should be integrated with Chinese medicine.[30] At the time a popular point of view was that in order to build China into a powerful country, the Chinese race must first be strengthened, and in order to do this, Western medicine should be advocated and adopted by the nation's health workers.[31]

The Emperor Guangxu himself had been treated by Western medicine. His personal physician had been Dr. Thomas Cochrane of the London Missionary Society, and he had been attended by a French doctor from the French Embassy in Beijing.[32] The Emperor was also in favour of the constitutional reform and modernization

---

[29] J. Kenneth Mackenzie, "Viceroy's Hospital Medical School", in *The China Medical Missionary Journal*, Vol. 1, No. 3, 1887, pp. 100-106; H. Balme, *China and Modern Medicine: a study of medical missionary development* (London: United Council for Missionary Education, 1921), pp. 57-58.

[30] Zheng Guanying, *Shengshi weiyan*, "Yidao", Vol. 14, 1893.

[31] Liang Qichao, "Yixue shanhui xu", in *Yinbing shi wenji* (Shanghai zhonghua Shuju, 1932), Vol. 2, pp. 68 and 70.

[32] Cheng Keji et al, *Qingdai gongting yihua* (People's Literature Press, 1987), pp. 34-36.

movement, and as noted in a 1898 document he was involved in plans to establish a university in the capital, which was to have a department of hygiene and medicine.[33] This decision was warmly received and supported by many open-minded officials and intellectuals. In order to express support for this idea, an essay appeared in the *Zhixin Daily* stating that the reason Britain had become so strong was because it began by strengthening the race.[34] In appraising this measure, Liang Qichao published an article saying that putting Western medicine into Chinese medical education was a necessary policy for modernization.[35]

Meanwhile, in 1902, the *Tongwen* College was amalgamated into the newly established Capital University in Beijing. A year later the constitution of the university was drawn up under the care of Zhang Zhidong. In the university curriculum courses on traditional Chinese medicine were put first and Western medicine second. This was with a view to giving pride of place to Chinese learning with Western study as an essential subsidiary. In the same year, a medical institution consisting of two departments, medicine and materia medica, was established in the Capital University. Courses were provided on both Chinese and Western medicine and students were required to study for four years.

After the overthrow of the Qing dynasty in 1911 and the founding of the Republic of China, Chinese medical education entered a new stage. By this time, China already had her own doctors trained in Western medicine either abroad or at home, although the number was small. Some of them quickly became leading figures in the Chinese medical field and were keen on improving and developing modern medical education in China. Among them was Wu Liande (1879-1960), a Cambridge trained physician known as the "plague fighter". Wu's use of Western medicine in the fields of public health and preventative medicine in fighting the plague rampant in Northwest China from 1910 to 1911 deeply impressed the officials of the Qing government. In 1913, Wu Liande presented a memorial to the government on the improvement of Chinese medical education.[36] Influenced by this, the government issued that same year an edict permitting human dissection and encouraging the opening of Chinese medical schools along Western lines in various national and provincial centres. Statistics collected in 1932-33 indicate that there were twenty-seven medical schools in China with a total enrolment of 3,528 students. Four of these were supported by the national government, two by the army, five by the provinces, and sixteen by private means (fourteen of the latter were controlled wholly or in part by missionary organizations).[37]

As a result of the growth in new Chinese medical personnel, the National

---

[33] *Daqing dezong shilu* (Taibei: Huawen shuju, 1964), p. 3879.

[34] Zhu Youhuan (ed.), *Zhongguo jindai xuezhi shiliao* (Shanghai: East China Normal University Press, 1986), Vol. 2, p. 643.

[35] China Historical Society (ed.), *Zhongguo jindaishi ziliao congshu* (Shanghai: Shenzhou Guoguangshe, 1953), Series 8, "Wuxu bianfa", Vol. 2, p. 80.

[36] Wu Lien Teh, "Memorandum on Medical Education in China", in *The Chinese Medical Journal*, Vol. 28, No. 2, 1914, pp. 105-120.

[37] Lee Tao, "Some Statistics on Medical Schools in China for 1932-1933", in *The Chinese Medical Journal*, Vol. 47, 1933, pp. 1029-1039.

Medical Association was founded in 1915, with Dr. Yan Fuqing, a graduate of Harvard, as its first president. In the same year, the National Medical Journal appeared and by 1920, the membership of the National Medical Association reached 450 men and women, including some foreign doctors who had rendered some signal service to China. In 1928, the Ministry of Health was established in Nanjing, and in the following year the National Commission on Medical Education was constituted. In 1932, the China Medical Missionary Association was amalgamated with the Chinese Medical Association, and the National Medical Journal and the China Medical Missionary Journal amalgamated into the China Medical Journal. Chinese medical doctors made up the main body of the Association.

CONFLICT BETWEEN WESTERN AND TRADITIONAL CHINESE MEDICAL PRACTITIONERS

We have seen that since the early 19th century, when Western medicine was introduced into China on a large scale, the attitude of most Chinese towards Western medical knowledge, including officials, intellectuals and indigenous traditional practitioners, was fundamentally positive. Although, at first, there was suspicion and rumours about Western doctors, the process of acceptance began with Qiu Xi, Pearson's assistant and author of the *Brief Introduction to Vaccination Against Smallpox* (*Yin duo lue*). Qiu tried to integrate Western medical knowledge with Chinese medicine. He was succeeded by other Chinese indigenous practitioners, such as Wang Shixiong, Tang Zonghai and Zhang Xichun, who showed more or less willingness to accept new ways. By the turn of the century a growing awareness of Western medical knowledge convinced a few more traditional Chinese doctors of the value of Western medical knowledge. They began to see the strong points of Western medicine and realized the need to learn it. Some of them became devoted to the integration of traditional Chinese and Western medicine and this activity became a major trend among many individual doctors. Quite a few traditional doctors were keen to promote the spread of Western medicine. In 1904 Zhou Xuechao, a noted practitioner versed in both Chinese and Western medicine, founded a society in Shanghai for the study of Chinese and Western medicine, which published a journal entitled *Yixue bao*. This society was based on the model of a Western medical association and represented the first establishment in the field of traditional Chinese medicine. In the Journal's early volumes, most of the articles dealt with Western medicine and information on the drawbacks and malpractice of traditional doctors appeared frequently.

In the meantime more societies of traditional Chinese medicine continued to be founded throughout China by indigenous practitioners. Among them was the China Medical Association, founded in Shanghai in 1907 by Cai Xiaoxiang (1863-1913), Zhou Xuechao, Ding Fubao and others. Originally some doctors trained in Western medicine joined as members, but later a split occurred within this society because of a divergence of views. Indigenous practitioners disagreed on how to improve traditional

Chinese medicine and how at the same time to evaluate Western medicine. As a result, in 1910, the society was disbanded. By this time there were two fundamentally different schools of thought among the Chinese doctors. One was based on the slogan put forward by Zhang Zhidong, which advocated "taking Chinese learning as the foundation, and Western learning for its practical usefulness". This approach tried to reform traditional medicine by adapting Western medicine to it. The other position rejected an accommodation of Western medicine. It advocated the preservation of Chinese medicine and regarded any other approach as evidence of a slavish attitude towards Western medicine.

Early on, however, no controversies existed between doctors trained in traditional Chinese medicine and those trained in Western medicine. These only happened later in the 19th century during the large scale introduction of Western medicine into China. During this period, traditional Chinese medicine was devalued by some Chinese literati, by doctors trained in Western medicine and by Western doctors, including missionaries.

Yu Yue (1821-1906), a well-known scholar versed in Chinese classics and a prolific writer, had a close relationship with Zeng Guofan and Li Hongzhang, the leaders of the Westernization movement. In his essay, "On the Abolition of Chinese Medicine" (*Fei yi lun*), he described traditional Chinese medicine as no different from witchcraft.[38] This was the first direct attack on traditional Chinese medicine by a member of the Chinese literati. Another noted literatus, Wu Rulun (1840-1903), who had been the Chief Teacher of the Capital University, and also had close contact with Li Hongzhang, took the view that Western medicine was in many respects incomparably superior to Chinese medicine.[39]

Similar views were more often expressed by doctors trained in Western medicine. However, there were also people like Wu Liande who was able to see some of the positive aspects of traditional Chinese medicine. In the memorandum he presented to the Chinese government in 1913, he said:

> As is well known, many of the drugs used by native practitioners show excellent results in certain diseases and some of the methods of treatment used by them are satisfactory. But in the majority of cases, the treatment is purely empirical, and for these drugs and methods to give the greatest benefit they must be thoroughly investigated and their mode of action accurately ascertained.[40]

Some of the Western doctors in China during the 19th century had studied the history and theory of Chinese medicine and recognized that in the past Chinese medicine had made splendid achievements. It seemed to them that Chinese medicine

---

[38] Yu Yue, "Fei yi lun", in *Yu Lou zai cuan*, Vol. 45, circa 1890, pp. 1-9.

[39] Wu Rulun, *Tongchen wuxiansheng quanshu chi du*. See Chuan Hansheng, "Qingmo xiyang yixue chuanru shi Zhongguoren suochi de taidu", in *Shihua banyuekan*, Vol. 3, No. 12, 1936, pp. 47-49.

[40] Wu Lien Teh, "Memorandum on Medical Education in China", in *The Chinese Medical Journal*, Vol. 28, No. 2, 1914, p. 110.

must contain many correct and useful observations, in particular the action of medicaments commonly used by Chinese practitioners. Some of these doctors tried to use Chinese medicines in their hospital work. For example, Drs. Douthwaite and W. Wilson, both of the China Inland Mission, published material on the methods of purifying and utilizing many Chinese drugs, a process which considerably cut down their hospital expenses.[41] Dr. Joseph C. Thomason, the American missionary and historian of medical work who did much study on the history of Chinese materia medica, said:

> We have before us an undeveloped mine which only needs to be worked to yield us treasures of knowledge...We find then in China an exhaustless materia medica which must prove of great value to us as medical missionaries.[42]

Dr. E. V. Bretschneider, a physician to the Russian Embassy in China, undertook extensive studies on the history and circumstances of Chinese materia medica and published several valuable works on these subjects.[43] Dr. B. E. Read, the British scholar, published several volumes on the study and translation of Li Shizhen's great work *Ben Cao Gang Mu* (*The Compendium of Materia Medica*).[44] And through pharmacological studies at the Peking Union Medical College, the Chinese scholar Chen Ko-hui and American doctor C. F. Schmidt introduced ephedrine to Western medicine. Ephedrine is the active constituent of Chinese herb *Mahuang* (Ephedra sinica) and is an effective drug for the treatment of asthma.[45] In addition Dr. J. Cantlie, the second Dean of the Hong Kong Medical School succeeding Dr. P. Manson, gave positive comments on the benefit of acupuncture.[46]

Unfortunately, however, many western doctors in China looked down upon Chinese medicine. For example, talking about acupuncture, H. Jeffreys expressed an entirely different cast of mind from Cantlie. He said: "the surgical instrument best known to the Chinese is the deadly acupuncture needle, and I say 'deadly' with the full

[41] A. W. Douthwaite, "The Use of Native Drugs by Medical Missionaries", in *The China Medical Missionary Journal*, Vol. 4, No. 3, 1890, pp. 101-105.
[42] Joseph C. Thomason, "Chinese Materia Medica: Its Value to Medical Missionaries", in *The China Medical Missionary Journal*, Vol. 4, No. 3, 1890, pp. 115-119.
[43] E. V. Bretschneider's works include *Botanicon Sinicum*, which consists of three volumes. Volume 1 was published in London in 1882. Volumes 2 and 3 were published in Shanghai in 1892 and 1895. His *Early European Researchers into the Flora of China* was published in 1881 in Shanghai.
[44] B. E. Read translated several parts of the *Ben Cao Gang Mu*, including those on minerals and stones (1928), animal drugs (1931), avian drugs (1932), dragon and snake drugs (1933), medicinal plants (1935), turtle and shellfish drugs (1937), fish drugs (1939), and insect drugs (1941). He also published, among others, a book *Indigenous Drugs*, which contains 133 kinds of Chinese drugs (Shanghai, 1940).
[45] K. K. Chen, "Two Pharmacological Traditions: Notes from Experience", in *Annals Review of Pharmacology and Toxicology*, Vol. 21, 1981, pp. 1-6. See also K. K. Chen, "Half a Century of Ephedrine", in *American Journal of Chinese Medicine*, Vol. 2, No. 4, 1974, pp. 359-365.
[46] J. Cantlie, "'Needling' Painful Spots, as Practised by the Chinese", in *Journal of Tropical Medicine and Hygiene*, Feb. 1916. See also *The Chinese Medical Journal*, No. 6, 1916, pp. 410-413.

weight of the word".[47]   Apparently these doctors considered traditional Chinese medicine as absurd both in theory and practice. As Dudgeon said,

> Chinese medicine is generally supposed to contain nothing worthy of research. Its materia medica is judged by the list of disgusting substances contained in its pharmacopoeia; its medicine is ridiculed on account of its absurd doctrine of the pulse...[48]

Needless to say, such negative viewpoints towards traditional Chinese medicine put forward by a man such as Dudgeon, influenced many other Western doctors in China as well as abroad.

An inevitable conflict between doctors of traditional Chinese medicine and doctors trained in Western medicine was triggered by an event in 1911. At that time Wang Daxie, the Minister of Education, rejected traditional Chinese medicine as a part of the new medical curriculum. He said flatly, "Chinese medicine is utterly without any scientific basis".[49] In response and in order to regain the right to run schools for traditional Chinese medicine, a demonstration was organized by indigenous practitioners. Thus two opposite groups were formed in China, representing the two different medical systems, and sharp conflicts and heated debates ensued. Yu Yunxiu, a medical student returned from Japan, represented the side of the doctors trained in Western medicine. He published a series of articles, attacking traditional Chinese medicine, and tried to negate its theoretical base and its effectiveness in practice. He was also opposed to attempts to integrate Chinese and Western medicine or to keep Chinese medicine in the medical curriculum. In defence of their position, traditional doctors headed by men such as Yun Tiechao responded with a series of published articles.

Things went from bad to worse when a group of doctors trained in Western medicine and headed by Wang Qizhang and Yu Yunxiu started a movement to ban traditional Chinese medicine, using political pressure. In 1928, Wang presented a proposal along these lines to the National Education Conference. This was followed in 1929 by a more detailed submission sent to the Ministry of Health by Yu Yunxiu. On hearing that these proposals were being adopted by the authorities, the doctors of traditional Chinese medicine launched a nation-wide campaign against the government. Their demands included political equality and status with doctors trained in Western medicine, governmental support for the development of Chinese medicine, a legal right to run medical schools, financial support from the government to run traditional Chinese medical enterprises and the employment of traditional Chinese medical personnel in government institutions. Sadly for them, not one of these

---

[47] H. Jeffreys, "'Freely Ye Have Received!' Native Methods of Medical Practice in China, A Comparison", in *Chinese Medical Missionary Journal*, No. 3, 1906, p. 105.

[48] J. Dudgeon, *Report of the Peking Hospital for 1869*, p. 20.

[49] Zhen Zhiya et al, *Zhongguo yixue shi* (*The History of Chinese Medicine*) (Beijing: People's Health Press, 1991), p. 487.

demands was ever really achieved in over 30 years of struggle. Although traditional Chinese medicine still survives because it is deeply rooted in the non-elite sections of Chinese society, it was severely restrained following the 1928 proposals, and from that time Western medicine became the dominant medical system in China.

CONCLUSION

From the above account of medical exchange between China and the West, we see that before the 19th century, Chinese medicine had made contributions to the West. Western medical knowledge, chiefly anatomy, was first introduced into China in the 17th century by the Jesuits. However, Western ideas exerted little influence on Chinese medicine until the early 19th and 20th centuries, when Western medicine was formally reintroduced into China on a large scale and in a systematic way by Western doctors and scholars, most of whom were missionaries. This introduction coincided with an unprecedented development in Western medicine based on modern Western science and technology, whilst traditional Chinese medicine remained static and in a precarious position. Western doctors and scholars, chiefly medical missionaries, contributed much towards the reintroduction of Western medicine into China.

From the time that Pearson began the process until a fully functioning medical system came into being, tremendous change occurred. In the beginning, Western medicine was fundamentally well received by the Chinese in all walks of life. This acceptance was linked with and accelerated by the movements of Westernization, constitutional reform and modernization. As a result we see the birth and growth of China's own medical personnel trained in Western medicine. While Western medicine initially presented a dilemma for traditional Chinese practitioners, on seeing its merits, most adopted positive attitudes towards it. This contrasts with the approach taken by many Western doctors in China and Chinese doctors trained in Western medicine, who held negative attitudes towards traditional Chinese medicine.

However, prior to the 19th century, medical exchange had occurred between China and the West without conflicts. It appears that when these occurred in the early 20th century, they were due, to a great extent, to the wrong policy of Chinese authorities. Professional prejudice exhibited chiefly by the doctors trained in Western medicine, also played a role.

As for traditional Chinese doctors, they were in a defensive position. They were, to an extent, victims of faulty government policy and professional prejudice. While it was easy to fault the traditional practice of certain individual Chinese practitioners, a single practitioner cannot represent the professional level of all, for in China no unified criteria existed to determine or define a qualified practitioner.

Over the past thirty years or so in China, traditional Chinese medicine has been designated as a national cultural heritage. Ever since the 1950s official policy has encouraged the two medical systems to work together to develop and integrate the best of each and to offset their respective weaknesses. Many doctors receive training in both systems and doctors trained in Western medicine are encouraged to study traditional Chinese medicine. In 1955 the China Academy of Traditional Medicine was founded as one of the major research institutes affiliated with the Ministry of Health. Almost 30 years later in 1982, the development of traditional Chinese medicine and pharmacology was written into a new national constitution. One hundred and sixty-nine institutes carry out promising research and evaluation on the role of traditional Chinese medicine in the diagnosis, treatment and understanding of disease processes. Twenty-eight colleges for traditional Chinese medicine have been established for training traditional Chinese medical professionals.

Acupuncture is proven effective in treating more than 300 kinds of illness. Its ability to kill pain and its use as an analgesic in operations, including open-heart surgery, has aroused world-wide interest. Research on acupoints and the theories of channels of the human body have created new topics for the medical world. New drugs of high efficacy and low toxicity have been developed from medicinal herbs. For instance, an extract from the Qinghao, Artemisia apiacea, has proved effective in treating pernicious and cerebral malaria.

Encouraging results have come from combining the two systems of medicine in the treatment of some difficult conditions, such as haemolytic disease found in newborn babies, scleroderma and ectopic pregnancy. A controlled clinical study of 430 cases of acute myocardial infraction showed a death rate of 6.5% in cases treated with combined methods, 14.9% in cases treated with Western medicine alone, and no good results in cases treated only with traditional Chinese medicine. In cancer, combined methods have shown promise in prolonging life and reducing the side effects of radiation and chemotherapy. Some acute abdominal diseases, such as appendicitis, intestinal obstruction, and pancreatitis, when treated with combined methods, quite often do not require surgery. More than 5,000 fracture patients were saved from probable amputation in this way.

If one asks whether doctors trained in Western medicine find it difficult to accept traditional Chinese medicine, the answer generally is yes, at least in the beginning. The two have entirely different approaches. One is an ancient system imbued with characteristics of Chinese culture and philosophy. For historical reasons, traditional Chinese medicine was never able to dissect and experiment on the human body; actually the internal organs are understood as functional units rather than as solid structures. The traditional system puts emphasis on analyzing all the symptoms and signs of the patient, taking the body, mind and external environment as a whole. The objective is the patient and the internal causes of disease. Holism is its chief characteristic. In Western medicine, the objective is usually the specific disease, and its external causes. The Chinese approach is more flexible, and does not treat a patient from beginning to end according to one principle or prescription, but according to the patient's changing condition. If a case requires surgery, traditional Chinese medicine seeks to improve the patient's ability to resist the disease. Preventive medicine has always been emphasized.

However, traditional Chinese medicine can be too flexible and too general in diagnosis or judgement and it lacks objective parameters, sometimes relying too heavily on the real experience of the practitioner. Western medicine is usually more concrete in diagnosis and judgement, and utilizes all the available modern scientific and technological facilities. Pathogenic factors are more sharply defined. Treatment is often quicker, particularly in acute cases, and surgical interventions are effective. The weak points are that it relies too much on the methodology established by thinkers such as Bacon, Galileo and Descartes. As a result, the Western model of disease changed from a holistic to a biomedical one; disease is often viewed as something to be measured and quantified, a concept so dominant that it occasionally seems that unless the disease conforms to these strictures, no concrete diagnosis and judgement can be made. The social, psychological and behavioural factors of illness are thus often neglected.

In recent years, Chinese medicine has become a source of interest in many countries. An increasing number of doctors and experts in related fields have shown interest in the study of traditional Chinese medicine. What does traditional Chinese medicine offer to world medicine? In addition to its therapeutic measures, such as acupuncture and moxibustion, massage and other remedies already in use, its principles and theories, such as its holistic approach, and its method of treating certain kinds of diseases including chronic and degenerative illnesses, are worth studying. Traditional Chinese herbs are rich resources worthy of exploration. Compared with medicines made from chemical agents, they are comparatively cheap and convenient and have far fewer side effects, since most of them have been clinically tried for over 1,000 years. Some have been found to be good for enhancing the body's own resistance, and are of immunological significance, a fact that is valuable in preventive medicine.

Dr. E. Hume, the American doctor and founder of the Yale Medical School in Changsha, Hunan Province, who had worked together with a Chinese native practitioner on the study of Chinese medicine, concluded that Chinese medicine is

> ...a system of medical thought which is philosophical in conception, which has found truly illustrious examplars through the centuries, and which has evolved practical procedures of real value for both diagnosis and treatment. While the development of Greek and Arabian medicine formed, partly because of limited communication in the early days, the basis of European thought and teaching, the Chinese stream of medical thought, much older than the Greek and Arabian, was proving adequate to the needs of an eastern Asiatic civilization. We are only at the threshold of an adequate understanding of this development. It remains for the medical historian to press forward to explore the documents, still at hand for inquiry; and for the pharmacologist to explore the therapeutic values of the hundreds of substances in the P'en Ts'ao, so that the whole world of science may come to possess fuller knowledge of the Chinese Way in medicine.[50]

---

[50] E. Hume, *The Chinese Way in Medicine* (Baltimore: The John's Hopkins Press, 1940), p. 176.

A new stage of medical exchange between the East and West has begun. Medicine should not have national borders. Historical lessons are worth exploring. As an ancient and living medical system, I believe Chinese medicine can offer much, as long as proper attention is paid to it and as long as modern science and technology are applied to its exploration and research. Modern Western medicine, which is already rooted in the vast land of China, will also continue its progress and development.

12

Gigantic Peripheries: India and China in the International Knowledge System

Philip Altbach

At first glance, China and India seem to be well positioned for scientific leadership, and in fact they have achieved considerable success. They have relatively well-developed scientific infrastructures today, including scientific laboratories, universities, a network of scientific journals, and large numbers of scientists and researchers. India is, in fact, the Third World's scientific superpower in numbers of qualified scientists, and China is not far behind. Both have a long scientific tradition – dating back many centuries – in indigenous science and scholarship, and well over a century for Western-oriented science and higher education. Both have, in the years following World War II, promulgated scientific plans and have taken scientific development seriously.

Both countries have made particularly significant progress at the end of the 20th century. India has become a major force in computer software, based on its tradition of excellence in mathematics. It is now an exporter of information technology, and serves as a point of both technological innovation and service to information industries worldwide. India is also a producer of pharmaceutical products for both domestic and world markets. China has also made significant strides in applied scientific research in many fields. Both countries are nuclear powers and have a growing high-tech industrial base capable of producing sophisticated products, although they are not in general on the cutting edge of world technology.

This chapter has at its core a surprising contradiction: its basic argument is that the world's two largest countries, at least in terms of population, are now, and will remain for the foreseeable future relatively peripheral in international science and scholarship. They are, and will continue to be, influenced by scientific developments external to them. They will not have equal access to the major elements of scientific communication such as international scholarly journals and databases. In basic scientific research in most fields and disciplines, these two countries will remain behind the world leaders, and they will be dependent on ideas and discoveries from abroad.

Why must these two large and powerful countries be relegated to peripheral status in world science and technology? The truth is that world science is highly centralized, that its infrastructures are located in a small number of industrialized countries, that advanced science requires large investments of funds and highly sophisticated laboratories, and that top scientific personnel are concentrated in a small number of countries and at the key academic and research institutions within those countries. It takes a tremendous investment to break into the "major leagues" of world science, and it is unlikely that either China or India will have the resources to accomplish this.[1] It has been argued recently that the Internet and other new information technologies will democratize science, and make it easier for "have nots" to gain access to the latest innovations and develop more rapidly. While it is the case that knowledge travels ever more rapidly, the patterns of creation, ownership, and concentration show few signs of changing.

This is not to say that these two important countries cannot play a significant scientific role, or that science and research cannot help to contribute to national development. Both already play a role and have used science for development. By focusing on maintaining a scientific base, supporting scientific research and higher education, and ensuring that the best scientific personnel do not leave the country, scientific research can be sustained at a reasonable level.[2] By targeting specific areas of science as essential to national development and generously supporting these, it may be possible to build up world-class science in a few fields. China and India need to be realistic about their position in the world system of science and technology. By recognizing what is, and is not, possible, they can make the best use of indigenous potential and develop effective strategies for functioning in the world scientific system.

There are also distinctions to be made between the development of universities and of ancillary research capacity for internal purposes, and involvement in research at the international level. Both countries have built up large and differentiated academic systems that serve their domestic needs. Both countries have a number of universities as well as research facilities that approach or meet international standards. Advanced training in universities is necessary for expanding economies. Thus, the peripheral positions of these two countries in world research is not an argument against developing higher education. However, effective planning for higher education must take into account the nature of the international knowledge system and the place of the country in that system.

Countries cannot free themselves of the international knowledge system. Both the basic institutional structure of modern higher education and science and the intellectual underpinnings are Western in nature and have come to dominate the world. All contemporary universities are based on the Western model, regardless of their location.[3] No developing country has made a serious attempt to build a new university

---

[1] Robert M. May, "The Scientific Wealth of Nations", in *Science 275* (7 February 1997), pp. 793-796.

[2] Erik W. Thulstrup, *Improving the Quality of Research in Developing Country Universities* (Washington, D.C.: Education and Employment Division, Population and Human Resources Department, World Bank, 1992).

[3] There are a few non-Western academic institutions remaining, such as the Al-Azhar in Egypt, but these do not play a key role in modern scientific development. See also Philip G. Altbach and V. Selvaratnam (eds.), *From Dependence To Autonomy: the Development of Asian Universities*

model. Further, the scientific communications networks, journals, databases, and the like are also Western in orientation and controlled by the West.

This discussion has relevance to developing countries generally, since all have seen higher education as a central part of nation building, and many have stressed research as a function of higher education. The points made in this chapter apply to all developing countries, since all face similar problems in their efforts to build up scientific capacity and to work in the context of the world knowledge system. With a much smaller population and resource base than China or India, each developing country faces distinct circumstances, and their higher education and scientific development will be determined in considerable part by these realities. Many countries, such as most in sub-Saharan Africa, will find it impossible to build up a research infrastructure able to function at an international level, and universities will need to adjust to this reality. Others, such as the newly industrializing countries (NICs) of East Asia, do have the financial and personnel resources to build up a research base in selected areas.[4] However, many of the issues that affect China and India are also relevant for the NICs despite their greater wealth.

Adjusting to the realities of the international knowledge system is not solely a matter for the developing countries. Small industrialized nations or those outside the mainstream must survive in this context of limited resources due to size and position. Norway, for example, despite its high per capita income, must adjust its educational and scientific priorities to fit its place in the international knowledge system. Many Norwegian scholars obtain advanced degrees in other countries and use English as the language of scientific communication – and sometimes of teaching. The experiences of the largest and best developed of the Third World nations – China and India – provide relevant lessons for other countries.

THE INTERNATIONAL KNOWLEDGE SYSTEM

It is beyond the scope of this chapter to discuss the international knowledge system in detail, but we should look at some of the key elements of the system as they affect China and India.[5] By international knowledge system, we mean the people and institutions that create knowledge and the structures that communicate knowledge worldwide. There are, of course, many different kinds of knowledge. Our focus is on research-based scientific knowledge that is circulated internationally. This knowledge is both basic in that it relates to the advancement of the scientific disciplines and applied in that it is used for technological and industrial products and innovations. While the natural, engineering, and biomedical sciences are perhaps most central, we are also concerned

---

(Dordrecht, Netherlands: Kluwer, 1989).

[4] See Philip G. Altbach et al, *Scientific Development and Higher Education: The Case of Newly Industrializing Nations* (New York: Praeger, 1989).

[5] For a complete discussion of the knowledge system, see Philip G. Altbach, *The Knowledge Context: Comparative Perspectives on the Distribution of Knowledge* (Albany: State University of New York Press, 1987).

with the social sciences and even the humanities. The knowledge system affects all of the scholarly disciplines as well as applied fields. We are less concerned here with the areas of indigenous science and scholarship because these are not generally circulated internationally, although the example of acupuncture in China shows that there are some exceptions to this generalization. Fields such as religious studies, domestic history, music, and art have strong local roots and are much less dependent on external forces, but even these fields often look abroad for the latest methodological approaches or for scholarly legitimation in the West.

In the international knowledge system, the means of production and distribution are both centralized. The bulk of the world's research and development expenditures are made by a small number of industrialized countries. Developing nations, including China and India, account for under 10 percent of the world total. The United States, the European Union, and Japan dominate. Russia (the former Soviet Union), at one time a research power, is no longer very active in research at the international level. Both basic and applied research is dominated by the major industrialized countries. Basic science depends on funding from governmental sources, the existence of a large and well-trained university-based academic scientific community (or in a very few cases government-sponsored research laboratories), and a competitive scientific culture that stresses research productivity for career advancement and prestige. Increasingly, basic science requires expensive laboratories with the most up-to-date equipment and access to libraries and databases. Only the large, research-oriented universities in the industrialized countries offer these resources. Further, new interdisciplinary or subdisciplinary specialties are increasingly at the frontiers of science, and these tend to emerge in large and well-equipped academic institutions. Basic science also depends increasingly on networking – the personal and professional contacts that are helpful to scientific advancement. Being at the centre of scientific development is crucial to involvement in these informal networks.

The scientific communications system is also centralized and dominated by the research-producing nations. A few examples will indicate the elements of this network. While there are between 60,000 and 100,000 scientific journals worldwide, only about 3,000 are indexed by the Institute for Scientific Information, which keeps track of "significant", internationally circulated journal publications. Most of these influential journals appear in the major international scientific languages – predominantly English and to a lesser extent French and perhaps German and Spanish. These are the publications that communicate the significant discoveries in the scientific disciplines, are read by scholars and scientists throughout the world, and are cited by other scholars. Most of them are edited by senior scholars in the United States, Britain, and to a lesser extent Canada, Australia, and other major Western countries. These editors are the "gatekeepers" of science.[6] The norms and paradigms that are influential in the academic and scientific systems of the United States and the large industrialized

---

[6] Lewis Coser, "Publishers as Gatekeepers of Ideas", in *Annals of the American Academy of Political and Social Sciences 421* (September 1975), pp. 14-22.

countries dominate the world. Scholars in other parts of the world with different orientations find it difficult to get published in these international journals. Journals from other parts of the world are not often circulated internationally. The publishing system for books is quite similar. The recognized publishers and editors are located in the industrialized world, as are the main markets for books (as well as journals). English dominates international scholarly publishing. The most recent innovations in scientific communications, databases, and information networks are also located in the industrialized nations – especially in the United States. The nations that produce scientific research own the data networks, control what goes into them, and manufacture the hardware and software that permit these systems to work.

It is clear that developing countries are at a particular disadvantage. Not only are their scientific systems generally small and poorly equipped, they do not have easy access to the communications networks. They are, at best, consumers of knowledge. And it is often difficult even to obtain access to needed information because it is too expensive or utilizes high-tech networks that Third World nations do not have readily available. Third World scholars may not be able to write easily in English and may not have access to the latest fashions in science or scholarship. Thus, they tend to be excluded from the top journals and are not part of the "invisible college" of science that works through personal contacts, international conferences, seminars, and the like.[7] It is in this context of inequality and scarcity that even countries as large and powerful as India and China must function.

THE THIRD WORLD SCIENTIFIC SUPERPOWERS: INDIA AND CHINA

India and China both have large and relatively productive academic and scientific systems. Both have taken science and higher education seriously. Both see science and higher education as important to national development, and desire both to build research capability and harness it to technology and industry. The two countries exhibit many similarities and some differences. Together, China and India constitute close to one-third of the total population of the globe. This, in itself, is a significant factor because they are key consumers of scientific knowledge. Both countries have large and growing academic scientific systems. Both have increasingly sophisticated technology-based industries that seek to be linked to the global economy through trade and export.

China and India show some important similarities. The countries have made a significant commitment to higher education, but they enrol only a small proportion of the relevant age group. India enrols about 7 percent of the relevant age group, while about 5 percent attend postsecondary institutions in China. This compares with close to 80 percent in the United States, 40 percent in Japan, and around 20 to 40 percent in Western Europe. However, in the context of the developing countries, both India and

---

[7] See Diana Crane, *Invisible Colleges: Diffusion of Knowledge in Scientific Communities* (Chicago: University of Chicago Press, 1972).

China enrol a relatively high proportion – many countries in Africa, for example, have only 1 or 2 percent of the relevant age group in postsecondary education, although Latin America educates a much higher percentage, as do most of the rapidly developing economies of the Pacific Rim. South Korea enrols 50 percent and even the Philippines enrols 30 percent in postsecondary education.[8]

India has over 140 universities and 7,000 colleges, with 5,600,000 students in postsecondary education. It also has a large number of specialized postsecondary institutions – such as the internationally recognized Indian Institutes of Technology, several Institutes of Management, the Tata Institute of Fundamental Research, some of the undergraduate colleges, and others. India's higher education is highly differentiated, with the quality of teaching and research high at some of the apex universities and specialized academic and research institutions. However, the vast majority of undergraduate students in India's 7,000 colleges receive instruction that is well below international norms. India also has a network of government-funded research facilities in a range of disciplines, from atomic energy to coal technology.[9] In addition, Indian private industry has sponsored a few research laboratories in several fields such as silk technology and pharmaceuticals. In some fields, such as computer software development, India has a large and sophisticated research apparatus, both in some of the universities and research institutes and in the private sector. India also has one of the world's largest scientific communities – including researchers and postsecondary level teachers. It is often said that India ranks third in the world in terms of the number of scientists, after the United States and Russia.

China, similarly, has a large, differentiated, and complex academic and research system, with well over 1,000 colleges, universities, and other full-time institutions of higher education. More than half of this number are colleges of engineering and colleges of education. Only 4 percent are comprehensive universities, which have the highest prestige. There are 5 million undergraduates and over a quarter million graduate students in institutions of postsecondary education, as well as 189 doctoral granting universities.[10] China's higher education system has been rapidly expanding, with some private postsecondary institutions offering academic degrees. Like India, China's higher education system is highly differentiated, with a large number of institutions sponsored by provinces, cities, or other local authorities, which are often of moderate or low quality, and a small number of national universities, generally sponsored by the central government, at the top of the system. In recent years, the Chinese higher education has become more differentiated, with the central

[8] *Statistics are from Higher Education in Developing Countries: Peril and Promise* (Washington, D.C.: The World Bank, 2000).

[9] For recent analysis of Indian higher education, see Suma Chitnis and Philip G. Altbach (eds.), *Higher Education Reform in India: Experience and Perspectives* (New Delhi: Sage Publications, 1993), Moonis Raza, *Higher Education in India: Retrospect and Prospect* (New Delhi: Association of Indian Universities, 1991), and M. V. Mathur, R. K. Aurora, and M. Sogani (eds.), *Indian University System: Revitalization and Reform* (New Delhi: Wiley Easterm, 1994).

[10] For a discussion of recent developments in Chinese higher education, see Hubert O. Brown, "People's Republic of China", in *International Higher Education: An Encyclopedia*, P. G. Altbach (ed.) (New York: Garland Publishers, 1991), pp. 451-466.

government heavily investing in a small number of top universities intended to be "world class". In addition, China has a large number of research institutions in a variety of fields, some of which function at international levels of excellence. While Chinese science is somewhat less visible internationally than is Indian science, China has a large and active scientific community and a significant number of scientific journals, and it is rapidly catching up.[11] Chinese scientists have produced nuclear weapons and satellites. Except during the period of the Cultural Revolution in the 1960s, which was a devastating blow to science and higher education, China has emphasized scientific research and higher education as a part of its plans for modernization and development. Chinese higher education is undergoing significant change, as greater emphasis is placed on private initiative and funding, and links with industry are being encouraged.[12]

There are also some differences in the academic and scientific development of these two countries. India has permitted market forces and the private sector (although with considerable state subsidy) to determine the rate of growth of higher education. The large majority of Indian students attend private colleges that are subsidized by public funds and controlled, to an extent, by public authority. The Indian academic system has grown steadily – sometimes at a rate of close to 10 percent annually – for more than three decades, and efforts to control growth by government authority have largely failed.[13] Most agree that academic standards for the majority of students have declined in recent decades. There are massive problems of unemployment among college graduates. China, on the other hand, has tightly controlled higher education expansion. During several periods, most notably the Cultural Revolution in the 1960s, expansion was stopped. Indeed, at that time the entire academic system was closed for almost a decade, with disastrous consequences for higher education and research. Higher education in China has been rigidly planned by the central government, although the situation is now changing to some extent and provinces are playing a more active role in higher education development. In India, the majority of college and university students focus on the social sciences and humanities – despite unemployment of graduates in these fields – while China's planned academic development has emphasized engineering and science and, recently, the study of management, with a modest proportion in the social sciences.

While the legacy of foreign influences and colonialism is significant in both countries, the specific impacts have been quite different. The modern academic and research systems of both countries have Western roots, although both have rich ancient cultural and educational traditions. China's early Western-style academic development was influenced by Western missionaries and by modest government efforts to build a few universities. The language of instruction was Chinese, for the most part, and the

---

[11] Eugene Garfield, "Science in the Third World", in *Science Age* (October-November 1983), pp. 59-65.
[12] See Ruth Hayhoe, *China's Universities, 1895-1995: A Century of Cultural Conflict* (New York: Garland, 1996).
[13] Philip G. Altbach, "The Dilemma of Change in Indian Higher Education", in *Higher Education 26* (1993), pp. 3-20.

institutional models were American, German, French, and Japanese.[14] China's higher education development went through a number of quite distinct and disjointed phases, with significant disruptions during the war with Japan during the 1930s and 1940s and during the struggle between the Nationalists and Communists, which culminated in the establishment of the People's Republic of China in 1949. During the first phase of Communist rule, the Soviet academic and scientific model was introduced into China, displacing other influences.[15] This was followed by the break with the Soviet Union and the Cultural Revolution when higher education came to a complete halt, many academic and scientific facilities were damaged, and most scientists and scholars were forced to stop working. Since the 1970s, China has again been open to Western academic influences, with ever closer ties interrupted to some extent but not stopped by the Tiananmen Square incident in 1989.[16]

India, by contrast, was under British colonial rule for two centuries, achieving independence at approximately the same time as China's revolution. India's academic development proceeded without the disruptions that characterized China's. The British imposed an academic model, the University of London, and imposed the English language as the main medium of instruction and scholarship.[17] The colonial language and the colonial academic models remain, with some significant modifications, as the main features of the Indian academic system to the present. India's academic and intellectual ties have always been with the English-speaking Western countries, especially Britain and, in recent years, the United States. India's academic journals and books are published in English.

China's academic life has, since 1950, not only been tightly controlled in terms of academic growth and development, but also in terms of research focus and intellectual and ideological directions. India, by contrast, has had a significant measure of academic freedom and consistent contacts with the outside world. India's scientists and scholars, at least in the major universities and research laboratories, have long been a part of the international scientific community. At the same time, Indian higher education development has been guided more by market forces than by any effective planning. Chinese academics have had much less contact with the outside world, limited by the constraints of language, government policy, and funds, and only in the 1980s joined the international scientific community.

---

[14] Marianne Bastid, "Servitude or Liberation? The Introduction of Foreign Educational Practices and Systems to China from 1840 to the Present", in R. Hayhoe and M. Bastid (eds.), *China's Education and the Industrialized World* (Armonk, N.Y.: M. E. Sharpe, 1987), pp. 3-20.

[15] Ronald F. Price, "Convergence or Copying: China and the Soviet Union", in Hayhoe and Bastid (eds.), *China's Education and the Industrialized World*, 1987, pp. 158-83, and Leo A. Orleans, "Soviet Influence on China's Higher Education", in Hayhoe and Bastid (eds.), *China's Education and the Industrialized World*, 1987, pp. 184-198.

[16] Jurgen Henze, "Educational Modernization as a Search for Higher Efficiency", in Hayhoe and Bastid (eds.), *China's Education and the Industrialized World*, 1987, pp. 252-270.

[17] Eric Ashby, *Universities: British, Indian, African* (Cambridge: Harvard University Press, 1966). See also Aparna Basu, *The Growth of Education and Political Development in India, 1898-1920* (Delhi: Oxford University Press, 1974).

THE BRAIN DRAIN AND THE CHINESE AND INDIAN DIASPORAS

Large numbers of students and scholars from China and India have studied abroad – mainly in the industrialized nations of the West. Many remained overseas, while others returned home. In both cases, these foreign-educated Indians and Chinese have had a profound influence on the two countries. Foreign study is by no means a recent phenomenon. Students began going abroad in large numbers in the 19th century, and foreign-returned individuals played a great role in creating modern China and India. One need only mention Sun Yat-sen and Zhou Enlai as examples of Chinese who studied overseas and profoundly influenced modern China. Jawaharlal Nehru, B. R. Ambedekar, and many other Indians also studied overseas, mostly but not exclusively in England. It should be noted that these returnees not only bring foreign ideas back, they also reinterpret their own culture and society. For half a century, India has been one of the main "sending" countries among the developing nations. India has been among the top five countries sending students to the United States since the 1950s – it is likely that 200,000 Indians have earned academic degrees in the United States and probably a similar number in other countries over the past forty years.

China's foreign study experience has been somewhat different from that of India. Prior to the establishment of the People's Republic of China in 1950, the large majority of Chinese students studied in the West or in Japan. Between 1950 and the mid-1960s, most Chinese students went to the former Soviet Union – and the total numbers also decreased. After the Sino-Soviet split, the Soviet Union was no longer open to Chinese students. When China cut itself off from the outside world during the Cultural Revolution, virtually no students went abroad to study. However, beginning in the mid-1970s, when the country committed itself to the "four modernizations" and reopened the universities, students began studying abroad in unprecedented numbers. By the late 1980s, more than 25,000 students from China were studying in the United States, with perhaps an equal number enrolled in all other countries.[18] In 2000, almost 54,000 Chinese students were studying in the United States. China had overtaken India (with 42,300 students in the U.S.) as a major sender of overseas students. As is the case for India, a significant number of Chinese students have not returned home after completing their degrees. Non-return rates went up after the Tiananmen Square incident, when many Chinese students abroad became disillusioned with their government, and foreign countries, especially the United States, loosened immigration rules.

Foreign scholars are also of considerable importance in the process of knowledge transfer and intellectual contacts. A large number of established scholars from China and India have visited Western countries and Japan and have returned with ideas and orientations influenced by their sojourns abroad. For example, more than 13,200 foreign scholars from China were in the United States in the early 1990s and about 5,000 from India. Typically, foreign scholars are established academics who

---

[18] For a detailed discussion of the nuances of foreign contacts and foreign study in the Chinese context, see Ruth Hayhoe, *China's Universities and the Open Door* (Armonk, N.Y.: M. E. Sharpe, 1989).

remain abroad for periods ranging from a few months to several years, to pursue research. Many are sponsored by universities or other agencies in the industrialized nations (such as the Fulbright program in the United States or the DAAD [German Academic Exchange Service] in Germany).

What is important about foreign students and scholars in the context of this discussion of the academic and scientific development of China and India is that this very large group of individuals is profoundly influenced by their experiences abroad. They learn about science, research, and scholarship in the industrialized countries and bring this knowledge back with them. Their orientations to science and scholarship are shaped by what they learn abroad. Further, they are also frequently influenced by the academic models, the lifestyles, and perhaps the products and social ideas of the countries in which they study. Because of their expertise, and sometimes also because of the prestige of a foreign academic degree, these returned students and scholars frequently achieve positions of leadership in science, higher education, the arts, or in politics or business. All of this is inevitable. The flow of people who have been trained abroad is one element of the continuing set of relationships between China and India and the industrialized nations. There has been a significant brain drain from both China and India over the years. In one sense, this talent has been lost for the economic and social development of these countries. On the other hand, these populations serve as a point of ongoing contact and exchange.

Significant numbers of Chinese and Indians live outside of India and China. These populations are an important point of contact between India and China and the industrialized world. The full extent of Chinese and Indian populations living in the West is not clear, but they number in the millions. Many occupy positions in science, education, and the professions.[19] The number of Chinese and Indians holding academic posts in American universities is large, probably more than 10,000. Many of these scientists and scholars maintain contacts with colleagues in their countries of origin and frequently work in these countries.[20] They serve as consultants, visiting professors, and participate in conferences. In India, these people are called "nonresident Indians" and they constitute an important source of investment, knowledge, and contacts with the industrialized world. Similar populations of Chinese are equally engaged.[21] Chinese and Indian academics occupy especially important places in such fields as engineering, mathematics, and computer science in American universities.

There are also populations of Chinese and Indians settled in other parts of the world, and these groups are also very important to consider. Chinese living in Hong Kong and Taiwan are of special significance because of their wealth and high levels of scientific productivity. They are a source of knowledge, investment, and contacts with

---

[19] For an interesting general discussion of this theme, see Joel Kotkin, *Tribes: How Race, Religion and Identity Determine Success in the New Global Economy* (New York: Random House, 1993).

[20] Hyaeweol Choi, *An International Scientific Community: Asian Scholars in the United States* (Westport, Conn.: Praeger, 1995).

[21] Binod Khadria, "Migration of Human Capital to the United States", in *Economic and Political Weekly* (August 11, 1990), pp. 1784-1794.

the West and Japan. The economies as well as the scientific and academic systems of these two areas are also of importance to China in the long run. Other Chinese populations living in countries such as Singapore and Malaysia may also play a role. There are also established Indian populations settled in such regions as Southeast Asia, East Africa, and Guyana in Latin America, but these communities are less important in terms of India's international relationships.

Chinese and Indian populations settled abroad are sources of contact, ideas, and relationships with industrialized nations. Because they understand the home culture and society and because they speak the home language, they have special advantages. Many feel a sense of kinship as well. However, these populations are, in a sense, a source of continuing peripherality as well because they reinforce the importance of the ideas, products, and practices of the industrialized world. They are, rather, serving as points of access for foreign ideas, practices, and institutions. They are not, for the most part, reinterpreting Indian or Chinese traditions. From the perspective of this essay, these diasporas serve as a source of continuing peripherality. Their influence is considerable and very probably it is a positive one in terms of commerce, science, and industry. The Chinese and Indian diasporas are among the most important in the world because the groups are so large, well educated, and widely dispersed.

THE FUTURE

Because of their size and relatively high levels of scientific and educational accomplishments, India and China are active participants in the world knowledge system. Indeed, as the importance of these countries in world trade and commerce, they will be come increasingly important. Nonetheless, this participation will necessarily be unequal for many years. World science and scholarship will continue to be dominated by the West and Japan for the foreseeable future because of the reasons that have been discussed in this chapter. Thus, even India and China will, to a significant extent, remain peripheral in the world knowledge system. The industrialized nations simply have such large scientific infrastructures and spend so much on research and development that it is not possible for developing countries to catch up – even countries as large and scientifically advanced as China and India. Nor is it possible to opt out of the system – China tried this during the Cultural Revolution, to its great detriment.

The structural factors that have been discussed to a very large extent determine the place of a nation in the knowledge system. These factors are not only relevant to low per capita income countries. The wealthy nations of the Arabian Gulf, for example, also face a situation of peripherality. Their wealth does not permit them to play a central role in world science. In these cases – such as Kuwait and even Saudi Arabia – the problem is one of the size of the scientific and academic communities and the development of a culture of scientific research.[22] Even smaller highly industrialized

---

[22] Ali N. Alghafis, *Universities in Saudi Arabia: Their Role in Science, Technology and Development* (Lanham, Md: University Press of America, 1992). See also H. A. Al-Ebraheem and R. P.

nations with well-established academic traditions such as Norway or Finland find themselves in a peripheral position in the world academic system and must rely on research initiatives and publication outlets in the larger centres of academic power.

For the foreseeable future, India and China will depend on other countries for charting the basic direction of scientific research, for the means of obtaining information about the latest scientific developments, and to some extent for training in the most advanced scientific specialties. The basic paradigms of research will take place abroad and will necessarily affect the local scientific community. Scientific products, including the most advanced laboratory equipment, advanced computers, and of course, books and journals will continue to be imported. These products are not designed with China and India in mind, nor are they priced so that countries with a low per capita income can easily afford them. Training in some advanced scientific fields will also take place abroad. These are some of the elements of peripherality that will continue to affect science and higher education in China and India.

Nevertheless, these two countries have already achieved a certain level of scientific and academic independence, and they can continue to build on established strength and, by careful allocation of resources, achieve many of their academic and research and development goals. Indeed, in some areas, both countries have already made impressive progress, sometimes against major obstacles. Both countries have built up a significant capacity in military-related research and production and possess nuclear weapons and the means of delivering them. While Chinese and Indian technology in these areas does not meet world standards, it seems adequate for their purposes, and it has apparently mostly been developed indigenously.[23] This example is relevant for our broader discussion because it exemplifies the challenges, the opportunities, and the problems of targeted research. Both countries have invested considerable sums in military and nuclear research and development. They have, despite considerable problems and a lack of cooperation from the international scientific community, been able to build up capacity in this applied area.

China and India have the capacity to target specific areas of research for priority development. India has, for example, achieved considerable success in computer technology at all levels, from basic research building on India's long and distinguished research tradition in mathematics to applied areas such as software development. Significantly, Indian scientists work closely with colleagues abroad and are very much part of the international scientific community. Indians working abroad in this field, especially in the United States, have contributed significantly to India's development in computer science. These nonresident Indians have even invested in the Indian computer industry and have encouraged direct collaboration between firms in the United States and those in India. They have even helped to build up an Indian

Stevens, "Organization, Management and Academic Problems in the Arab University: The Kuwait University Experience", in *Higher Education 9* (1980), pp. 203-221.

[23] Not surprisingly, there is little discussion of military-related research in either China or India because of the national security implications involved. These comments are, therefore, based on general observation.

"Silicon Valley" in Bangalore as a centre for research and development in computer science and in applied computer applications. Much of the initiative for this development has come from the private sector, but the Indian government has also assisted by making research funds available and promoting work in this field. The late Prime Minister Rajiv Gandhi had a special interest in applied research and development generally, and in computer technology, in particular. There are other examples of successful targeting of research and the application of this research to development. India's successful "green revolution" dramatically improved agricultural production in the 1970s. This was done by a combination of using, and sometimes adapting, research developed in other countries – especially in this case by the International Rice Research Institute in the Philippines; applying this research to local needs in Indian scientific institutions; and then disseminating information and providing resources for the use of the new technologies. Similar examples can be provided for China.

One strategy available to China and India is targeting specific areas for intensive research and development investment. These areas are generally in fields that can directly benefit the economy and that build on existing strengths in the country. The strategy requires a coordinated effort among the academic and research communities, and the targeted industries or agencies, and the ability to ensure that research and development can be translated into applied products, innovations, or developments. However, it is also necessary to support a capacity for basic research as well because applied research cannot be built on a foundation lacking in a scientific community or appropriate infrastructures. Several of the Asian newly industrializing countries have successfully targeted applied research areas and have used these to support economic growth. Taiwan's support for a science-based industrial park at Hsinshu, and the links between several universities involved in the park and the Taiwanese computer industry, have yielded major success.[24] India has been more successful in building up basic scientific capacity through the large number of scientists working both in the universities and in government laboratories, many under the aegis of the Council of Scientific and Industrial Research, which is supposed to support and monitor applied research. However, the links between actual industrial and technological productivity and these scientific efforts are often not fully exploited. While China has a significant scientific infrastructure and strong ties among research institutions and industrial enterprises, it would seem that highly productive relationships between research and industry are less common, although recent policy initiatives have moved strongly in this direction.

Another aspect of the scientific role of these two countries, as well as several others such as the Philippines, is an active participation in a burgeoning world market for highly trained personnel. Many Chinese and Indians have emigration in mind as they complete their academic degrees at home, and as has been noted, large proportions of students from China and India do not return after completing their academic degrees

---

[24] H. Steve Hsieh, "University Education and Research in Taiwan", in P. Altbach (ed.), *Scientific Development and Higher Education*, 1989, pp. 177-213.

abroad. These expatriates often contribute to scientific development at home, and small numbers return to assume academic or research positions. The global marketplace for scientific talent, overall, works to the detriment of countries such as China and India, and there is little prospect of significantly reversing this trend.

India and China are tied to an international knowledge system that places them at a significant disadvantage, and it is virtually impossible for these two large and educationally well-developed Third World nations to achieve full parity and independence in this system. It is necessary to recognize the nature of the system and the realities that guide it. Nonetheless, it is possible for China and India, as well as many other Third World countries, to assess their scientific strengths carefully and to build on them. It is appropriate to conclude this discussion with ideas that may be useful to these two Third World scientific superpowers as they contemplate the use of research and development for national development:

- Scientific links and cooperation between China and India may significantly strengthen both countries. Political differences have kept them apart for many years, but with the end of the Cold War and other changes, it may be possible for these two countries to work together in areas of mutual scientific interest.
- Ensuring that at least a segment of the university system achieves international levels of teaching, research, and scholarship is crucial because applied research and development must have a base in domestic science. Careful choices of institutions, fields, and specialization can be made.
- Decentralization of decision making may be useful, especially in countries as large and complex as China and India. Initiative at the state or provincial levels, perhaps supported by central government funding, may yield results. Careful coordination between enterprises and academic and scientific institutions may be easier and more effective at a more decentralized level.
- At the same time that many decisions are decentralized, it may be useful, at the national or perhaps regional level, to target specific areas for research and development. Even countries as large as China and India cannot be strong in every scientific field.
- Cultivating the scientific diaspora is of importance because these scientists can be linked to the home country productively. This is especially important in the new global marketplace for scientific talent.
- Long-term linkages with academic and scientific institutions in other countries may be helpful in maintaining international contacts and access to the most current innovations and knowledge. These linkages may be largely in the West and Japan, but in some instances could be in the newly industrialized countries.
- Policies that encourage multinational companies with manufacturing or commercial facilities in the country to do some of their research and development in the country as well can help to build up infrastructures and

provide current scientific information that will be valuable to local industry. Multinational firms may also be encouraged or in some cases compelled to share some of their technologies.

Research, development, and science are linked not only to the higher education system but also to broader issues of industrial and trade policy, to the place of the country in the international world of science and scholarship, to ideas about the nature of research and higher education, and to the availability of intellectual freedom. While both China and India have built up impressive academic systems in the past half century and have also made considerable progress in industrial development, they have not pondered the interrelationships of these elements. The first step is to reach a clear and unemotional understanding of the nature and functioning of the world knowledge system. After that, it is possible to focus on how a nation that is not at the centre of scientific power can make the best possible use of its own academic and scientific resources. An important part of a successful strategy may be cooperation among countries that are in similar positions.

13

World Bank Transfer of Technology and Ideas to India and China

Earl Drake

INTRODUCTION

The World Bank has had a significant role in transferring modern technology, Western approaches to management, and market-based economic policies to the two most populous countries of the world. It has accomplished this by linking technology and policy change to concessional financing and by using a team of multinational professionals which has some empathy with local authorities. The most outstanding example has been the transformation of Indian agriculture from a basically subsistence system to a sector with marketable surpluses.

The Bank encountered similar problems in the two countries, such as huge and growing populations, mass poverty, lack of technical knowledge, skills and infrastructure, inadequate financial resources and vast regional differences. Despite this broad commonality, the record has been quite different in each.

The Bank has had some success in transferring technology and ideas to India because of the latter's long involvement with the Bank (45 years) and greater affinity for Western thought. However, the Bank was largely frustrated because much of the Indian economy remained mired in poverty, economic protectionism and inefficiency.

In the case of China, the Bank has only been involved since 1980 when it faced a more alien culture and ideology. Thus, the Bank's involvement has been cumulatively less tangible than in the case of India. Nevertheless, it has been pleasantly surprised at how quickly some sectors of the Chinese economy have adapted to new ideas.

This chapter has the limited aim of describing, from an historical perspective, the main successes and disappointments the World Bank has had in trying to realize its goal of introducing modern, Western, technology, ideas, management techniques and educational and other institutions in order to increase productivity and economic viability in India and China. It also describes and tries to explain the different reactions of India and China to the World Bank program. It does not attempt the enormous task of presenting a comprehensive report on all World Bank activities in those countries nor of evaluating their social, economic and cultural impact, much less of making a value judgement on whether India and China were wise in turning to the World Bank

215

for assistance.

THE WORLD BANK – ITS MANDATE, ORGANIZATION AND IMPORTANCE

In 1944, the major nations met at Bretton Woods to establish a post-war international financial system. They agreed to found the International Monetary Fund (IMF) and the International Bank for Reconstruction and Development, which became better known as the World Bank. Initially, the primary objective of the World Bank was to help finance the reconstruction of war-ravaged Europe and Japan. After European recovery was underway, attention shifted to economic problems in Asia, Latin America, and Africa, where new players were emerging on the world stage, many of them after suddenly graduating from colonial dependency with little preparation for coping with the complex responsibilities of full nationhood. Promoting their economic development became the mandate of the World Bank.

The World Bank is a multilateral, financial institution for the promotion of economic development. Each aspect of that definition requires some elaboration.

As a multilateral organization its membership is open to all governments which are prepared to accept its rules and responsibilities, as defined in its Articles of Agreement. It began operations in 1947 with only 45 members because the Soviet bloc members did not sign the Articles and, as yet, there were few independent nations outside Europe and the Americas. Today, almost every country in the word belongs. Unlike the United Nations however, all nations are not treated as equal in terms of voting rights. Voting power is based on the amount of money a country has contributed to the institution. At the beginning, the United States, as the paramount economic power at the end of the Second World War, completely dominated World Bank decisions. All Bank presidents have been American citizens. As other countries, like Japan and Germany, have gained economic power relative to the United States, American dominance has become less pronounced at the World Bank. Nevertheless, America and its G-7 Summit allies can still control 50% of the voting power at the Bank whenever they agree to work together through their representatives at the World Bank's Board of Directors. On the other hand, the Bank professional staff is highly international in terms of the number of nationalities represented and impressively competent in its professionalism because it is selected on the basis of merit. Although its financial power and senior management remain dominated by the major industrial countries, the World Bank is truly multilateral in terms of its staff, range of operations and international development ethos.

It is a financial institution because it borrows money in order to lend to member countries at a rate of interest fractionally higher than its cost of borrowing. It must ensure that its loans are financially sound in order to retain the confidence of its private sector bondholders and its rich member countries who have guaranteed the repayment of the bonds. The Bank also administers some concessional funds which are given to it by rich members for the benefit of countries too poor to repay its commercial-rate loans; these are known as International Development Association (IDA) credits. Nevertheless, even in the case of the "soft" IDA credits, all World Bank loan projects are conducted, not as a charity, but as a hard-headed, financial operation concerned about economic and financial rates of return. The size of these operations is enormous; by the end of the last fiscal year the World Bank had borrowed $85 billion and had extended to its members a cumulative total of $143 billion in bank loans, as well as $65 billion in IDA credits.[1]

The promotion of economic development is the principal purpose of the Bank. The Articles of Agreement do not permit the Bank's governing boards to take official note of political, human rights or commercial considerations, although obviously they do often informally affect members' attitudes. Staff members have been diligent in pursuing development goals and have won international recognition for the Bank as the premier development institution in the world in terms of size, impact and professionalism. Typically, staff members go far beyond ensuring that a loan will be repaid and spend a great deal of time with the host authorities on the project to ensure that development goals are identified, appropriate technology is transferred, local training programs are implemented and indigenous institutions are strengthened.

Given its great economic power, its pro-Western management and its need to be financially viable, the Bank has inevitably attracted criticism over the years. An extreme example is an Indian writer who concluded his book about India and the Bank as follows: "What are the achievements of the Bank in India? ... to integrate India in the world capitalist system so that international investors get a huge market for export of capital and technology to maximize their profits...the Bank acts as eyes and ears of international capital in India".[2] An illustration of a thoughtful and balanced critique, is a study by two Canadian scholars of an Indian forestry project which gave the Bank credit for being well-intentioned but documented Bank insensitivity toward problems of deforestation, environmental degradation, social forestry and indigenous people.[3]

In the field of formal education, when the Bank suddenly changed its emphasis to primary education, the most critical comments came from the beneficiary countries: "A typical complaint was the African finance minister who accused the Bank of casual arbitrariness in switching its lending priorities from higher to primary education, while his country remained indebted as a result of the now 'discredited' higher education loans. He was joined by other critics who attacked the arrogance of Bank officials in their dealings with borrowers, their failure to consult and to see things from the developing countries' perspective, and their simplistic views on how schools actually function and how educational change can be achieved and made more relevant to economic growth and equity. The World Bank succeeds in attracting both praise and damnation from all quarters – from all political perspectives and from all parts of the

---

[1] *The World Bank Annual Report 2000* (Washington).

[2] C. P. Bhambhri, *World Bank and India* (New Delhi: Vikas Publishing House, 1980), p. 128.

[3] R. S. Anderson and W. Huber, *The Hour Of The Fox: Tropical Forests, the World Bank, and Indigenous People in Central India* (Seattle: University of Washington Press, 1988).

world".[4]

But few critics of the Bank would deny that it has become far more than a mere multilateral forum and financial institution. Despite its undoubted shortcomings, most observers would agree that it has become the leading theorist, researcher, practitioner and advocate of transferring Western financial and capital resources and development concepts to less-developed countries in order to bring about economic and social progress. In the words of a western academic: "It has been instrumental in forging those policies that see education as a precursor to modernization. It has served as a major purveyor of western ideas about how education and the economy are, or should be, connected".[5] It is the combination of economic power, professional excellence, and the ability of many of its international staff to empathize with local problems, that has enabled the Bank to become a major vehicle for transferring modern technology and economic thinking to Asia.

THE BANK AND INDIA

India has been the Bank's largest borrower, with 322 loan projects dating back to 1949 and totalling $37 billion. Yet, relations have never been easy or automatic between the foremost development agency and this major developing country. The high point came in 1960, when the Bank took the lead on issues of great importance to India. First, it organized an international rescue operation to finance India's second five-year plan from balance-of-payments difficulties. I. G. Patel, special secretary in India's Ministry of Finance later wrote that the Bank-sponsored paper was "one of the most heart-warming documents in the annals of international relations".[6] That same year, the Bank, India, and Pakistan reached a difficult agreement on the Indus Waters Treaty which decided how those disputed waters would be shared between the two countries and be augmented by storage projects financed by the World Bank and its Western friends. The cordial atmosphere was such that India complimented the Bank President for yielding on one point "gracefully and magnanimously" and he, in turn, asked Prime Minister Nehru for "another manifestation of generosity and magnanimity on the part of India".[7] Underlining the historic importance of this agreement, Nehru then flew to Karachi and signed it together with President Ayub Khan of Pakistan, the World Bank and Western donor nations. It was the crowning achievement of the World Bank in negotiating Western financial and diplomatic support for the prickly, non-aligned, nation of India.

Transmitting Western ideas on economic policy and management practice was to prove much more contentious. India has always been willing to give high

---

[4] P. W. Jones, *World Bank Financing of Education* (London: Routledge 1992), p. xvi.
[5] *Ibid*, p. xiv.
[6] E. S. Mason and R. E. Asher, *The World Bank Since Bretton Woods* (Washington: Brookings Institution, 1973), p. 77.
[7] *Ibid.*, p. 625.

priority to economic development but it has also had very strong ideas of its own on what should be done.

These differences can be illustrated by what happened to a major Bank initiative on behalf of India. As mentioned above, the Bank mounted an international rescue effort to assist India with its balance-of-payments problems. Starting in 1958, the Bank formed the India Consortium. This group brought together annually all the major donor nations in order to have a critical review of India's development plan, secure sufficient pledges of aid, and coordinate programs and policies toward India. Initially, India was very grateful but that sentiment became moderated by some resentment as the Bank and donors began to use the Consortium to try levering India to change its policies. The Bank's official historians have commented ruefully: "The Bank as organizer and chairman of these groups serves as a middle man, and the middle man's lot is not necessarily a happy one...the Bank may find its power and influence enhanced by virtue of the fact that it is acting on behalf of others and not just on its own. The reverse is also true. It may become a lightning rod for resentment on the part of the recipient because of the pressure it has helped to mobilize, particularly if policy changes are made by the recipient but the quid pro quo in aid fails to materialize".[8]

Nor were bilateral relations between the Bank and India always smooth. On one occasion, the President of the Bank wrote privately to the Indian Government saying some pleasant things about its performance but adding: "I have the distinct impression that the potentialities of private enterprise are commonly underestimated in India and that its operations are subjected to unnecessary restrictions...I see a tendency toward this latter approach in your industrial policy". India retaliated by leaking portions of the letter to the press which responded with indignation, declaring that "India will little tolerate blackmail" and denouncing the "hidden threat" and "humiliating conditions".[9]

Underlying these arguments were two fundamental differences: the Bank wanted India to encourage the private sector as the best engine of economic growth while India wanted to emphasize the public sector as the best instrument of social justice; and the Bank encouraged India to lower all forms of protection and open the economy to the discipline of the international market place whereas India wanted to achieve economic self-sufficiency as a complement to the political independence it had recently won. Neither party was completely dogmatic on these points; the Bank was prepared to work within a socialist framework and the Indians to listen to and, occasionally, yield on using Western approaches to management and market research on individual projects. As a general rule however, the Bank has had only modest success in transmitting seminal ideas to India. The Bank has been frustrated in reaching most of its development objectives because much of the Indian economy remains mired in poverty, economic protectionism and inefficiency. Until very recently the prevailing economic views in India were socialism and autarky and they were

---

[8] *Ibid.*, p. 513.
[9] *Ibid.*, pp. 372-373.

difficult to reconcile with the Bank's prevailing market-based, global free-trade philosophy.

Neither Indian officials nor Bank staff displayed much interest in using Bank financing for formal education projects, and, indeed, the Indian side was adamantly opposed to Bank involvement in primary education until 1991. Where the Bank had its most positive response from India was in the establishment of institutions to deal with urban growth and, especially, in the transfer of technology in agriculture.

India was not prepared for the crisis caused by rapid growth in its urban population which now adds 7 million people to the cities annually. By the late 1960s, between a third and a half of the urban population was living in slum conditions without secure title to their land and with inadequate access to municipal services. The World Bank helped to strengthen the main organizations dealing with urban problems, notably the planning, development and financing agencies. For example, the Bank financed a program by the Calcutta Development Authority in the areas of water supply, sewerage and drainage, solid-waste collection and disposal, transport and housing. Over two million citizens benefitted from the project. The Bank then supported similar projects in other big cities and subsequently tried to adapt these results to fast-growing intermediate cities. Reflecting on the lessons learned by India and the Bank in the process, a Bank publication concluded: "One of the main lessons learned was the priority of strengthening institutions. Policy adjustments, changes in planning and design and improved cost recovery need to be accompanied (even preceded) by improved organization and financial management, program monitoring and evaluation and training. In recent projects, institutional programs have been initiated much earlier and are usually under way by the time a credit is approved".[10]

In the 1960s, India's huge agricultural sector was in distress as a result of population growth, low financial priority and a series of droughts. India was importing 10 to 12 million tons of foodgrains annually, a situation which could not be sustained. Approximately 80% of India's 650 million people lived in the countryside, where there was an average of one hectare of cultivated land for every three people and average per capita incomes below $200 a year. Until 1950, most farmers were dependent on rainfall to water their crops. The unpredictable monsoon rains seldom came at the right time for the farmer and usually brought too little or too much water. With alternating floods and droughts, the growing population faced unreliable food supplies. Malnutrition and even starvation was frequent. The remarkable story of how India and the World Bank collaborated to solve that staggering problem by instituting the "green revolution" is best told in the following passages from *IDA in Retrospect.*

> South Asia had the land, the labour, and the climate to feed itself. But four things were missing: schemes for water control; new farming technology and methods; adequate support services to help farmers apply these new methods; and sufficient capital. And these changes had to be nurtured and led by the right government policies.

---

[10] *IDA In Retrospect* (Washington: Oxford University Press,1982), p. 50.

In India as well as Pakistan, governments had deliberately depressed farm prices to provide the politically important urban population with cheap food, even though this discouraged farmers from producing more.

Changes began in 1964. A number of foreign experts working in India for the Rockefeller and Ford foundations began pressing the Indian government to import the high-yielding wheat varieties that had been developed by the International Maize and Wheat Improvement Center (CIMMYT) in Mexico and the rice varieties that had followed at the International Rice Research Institute (IRRI) in the Philippines. These new strains were highly responsive to fertilizers and good water control, and offered the potential for much greater yields. The Indian government decided that the potential of this technology far outweighed its risks.

The Bank was closely involved in this decision. It had carried out a massive study of Indian agriculture (and other key sectors) in close collaboration with the government of India. Although it was completed before the implications of the new high-yielding varieties were fully grasped, the report recommended the adoption of policies, programs, and institutions that became integral parts of the efforts to exploit the new technology. To underline its own commitment to these recommendations, the Bank offered very significant levels of assistance.[11]

Influenced by the Bank study, India set prices at which the government would purchase crops from farmers. The farmers were encouraged to grow more food by the favourable mixture of grain and fertilizer prices. A Food Corporation was created to buy up grain in the good years to store for the lean ones and to maintain comfortable stocks of rice and wheat. This discouraged hoarding and panic buying. IDA supported massive credit schemes to help farmers finance groundwater investments and mechanization. The Indian Council for Agricultural Research was strengthened and played a major role in adapting the imported seed technology for Indian use. Irrigation works and fertilizer factories were expanded.

An important element in the success of the green revolution was the training and support that farmers received from extension workers. In 1975, the Bank started large scale training programs for agricultural staff and building up a stronger extension service. It used the training-and-visit approach which is most effective in informing farmers of the latest technical developments, particularly about the latest generation of high-yielding varieties.

In India, IDA faced a unique opportunity to increase agricultural production by following up a scientific break-through and encouraging internal policy reforms. Its credits, which primarily supported on-farm irrigation investment, brought an additional 2 million hectares under irrigation, more than one-quarter of the total land

---

[11] *Ibid.*, pp. 43-44.

affected by groundwater development in the 1970s. Aided by effective institutions – the Agricultural Refinance and Development Corporation, commercial banks, and cooperative land banks – IDA was able to support the purchase by farmers of wells and pumpsets, which, when combined with new seeds and fertilizer, completed the highly successful package known as green-revolution technology. The result was a rapid and dramatic improvement in productivity...

India, which was the world's second largest cereal importer in 1966 and 1967, reached basic self-sufficiency toward the end of the 1970s. ...

In the words of [Agriculture Minister] Mr. Subramaniam: 'These were major innovations; to be fully implemented, they needed a tremendous amount of assured resource flows. It was at that time that the World Bank's President promised India this flow of concessional resources for a number of years. It was the marriage of scientific development, institutional support and IDA funding that contributed to the remarkable success of Indian agriculture'.[12]

The joint success in increasing wheat and rice production did not carry over to other parts of the economy. Some Bank projects in other sectors produced positive results but the Indian economy, as a whole, remained sluggish and unreceptive to the ideas and practices that were bringing dynamism to East and Southeast Asia. It was only in the early 1990s that a new Government of India began to show keen interest in new economic ideas but this had much more to do with local and international politics than World Bank activities. Nevertheless, the stage may have been set for a new era in Bank-India collaboration.

THE BANK AND CHINA

The Bank relationship with China has been quite different than with India. China joined the Bank much later than India; it has never had as intense and tempestuous a relationship with Bank management (although its relations with Bank Executive Directors representing Western member countries became strained over the Tiananmen tragedy in 1989); it never shared a dramatic technological partnership with the Bank like the "green revolution"; and it never allowed the Bank (or anyone else) to coordinate donor support for and criticism of its development performance. On the other hand, considering China's history of isolation from the world, secrecy about sharing information, and immersion in the doctrines of Marx and Mao, the Bank considers that it has had remarkable success in persuading some senior Chinese to adopt a few Western ideas on publicizing critical economic data, on the importance of institution-building and training and on introducing additional market elements to

---

[12] *Ibid.*, pp.45-46, 41.

improve the socialist economy.

The People's Republic of China entered the World Bank in 1980, succeeding the Government in Taiwan as the representative of China. In the subsequent decade it signed 99 loans and credits with the Bank totalling $10.8 billion. Unlike India, there have been no dramatic differences of opinion on policy or breakthroughs on transfer of technology; the Bank has, however, been pleasantly surprised at how quickly some parts of this alien Chinese system have adapted to new ideas and approaches. The major Chinese changes have been in opening up hitherto secret data; using modern equipment in universities; accepting training and technical assistance as part of technology transfer; and engaging in policy dialogue.

The first and most remarkable Bank influence has been on reducing slightly the deeply-ingrained Chinese resistance to sharing information. It is a condition of admission of any country to the IMF and World Bank that it makes available key economic and financial data. Beyond that, however, the Chinese leadership accepted a proposal from the first Bank mission that it prepare a major, comprehensive study of the Chinese economy. Its broad theme was an analysis of thirty years of development under Chinese socialism. Bank officials sensed that the release of basic data required for the study was painful for many Chinese whose State Secrecy legislation stipulates: "Do not ask about things that do not concern you and do not give information to people who do not need it". Gradually, the Bank was able to persuade key Chinese of the value not only of publishing statistics but also of using internationally-recognized categories for their compilations. In the past the Chinese had frequently used confusing Soviet definitions. For example, China had not measured gross domestic product (GDP) but net material product (NMP). A principal difference is that NMP does not include many services that are included in GDP. The change enabled Chinese officials to understand better the importance of services, like transport, tourism and repair services, in the economy and give greater attention to them. It also enabled China to compare itself to other countries and understand more clearly how they related to the world economy. Two veteran Sinologues concluded:

> With IMF demand for trade, currency, and credit data as a condition of membership, the government released information that previously had been unavailable not only to foreigners but to many Chinese as well. The two Bank studies also necessitated provision of substantial data that had previously been classified and kept within the bureaucracies concerned... The effect of this pressure to release data has not just been to make the Chinese system more transparent to external observers. Within China, more people have had access to data, and the principal beneficiaries have been economists in research institutes and universities. Partly as a result, they have become more involved in the policy process...[13]

The first Bank project also represented a major break-through for China

---

[13] H. K. Jacobson and Michel Oksenberg, *China's Participation in the IMF, the Word Bank, and GATT* (Ann Arbor: University of Michigan Press, 1990), p. 145.

because it involved higher education. This was the sector that had suffered most during the chaos and tragedy of the "Cultural Revolution" when classrooms and laboratories had been destroyed and teachers driven into the countryside and worse. Now Bank funds were used to assist 2,150 chemistry, physics, biology, computer science and engineering departments in 28 higher institutions. The aim was to improve the quality of graduate training and university management and increase the number of graduate students. Most of it was spent on books and equipment to strengthen educational laboratories, to upgrade analytical testing centres and to equip computer centres. The Bank streamlined its procedures and timetables in order to expedite this project because of the urgency of helping higher education. However, the Bank took enough time to insist on including two points over initial Chinese objections: the inclusion of biology as one of the sciences to be upgraded; and the earmarking of 20% of the loan for the training of university managers, rather than agree that it all be used for equipment.[14] Since then, China has gone on to borrow heavily from the Bank in order to strengthen over 120 universities in the basic sciences and technologies.

The third significant area of transferring ideas and practices came on the point just referred to above – the reluctant acceptance of training and technical assistance as an element of technology transfer. Initially, every Chinese Ministry tried to devote all the proceeds of Bank loans to the transfer of hardware. Equipment was a tangible sign of assets and modernity for the whole work unit and bestowed "face" on its leaders (even if it was only displayed in a glass case and never used properly because of the absence of a trained operator). Training would only benefit one lucky individual, inspire jealousy among his colleagues and possibly be lost if he defected from his sponsoring organization. The Bank insisted, however, as part of the efficient transfer of technology, in running training programs for middle-level managers throughout the bureaucracy. It sponsored joint research for economists from the Bank and from the Institute of Economics of the Chinese Academy of Social Sciences. Several Chinese officials praised the technical assistance from the Bank. One even wrote an appreciation of it: "With the Bank's assistance, we have come to understand that just importing equipment is not enough. Management is also important. So, the Bank insists that with very project, there must be a training component. This focus on how to manage a project is crucial. Previously, there had been much waste of material in capital construction projects, but foreign management techniques help us to reduce waste. With the World Bank approach, we would have avoided the errors we made [previously]".[15]

The last area of surprising collaboration was on policy dialogue. It began at the highest level, through discussions between the President of the Bank and Deng Xiaoping and Zhao Ziyang about China's aim to raise its per capita GNP to $800 by the year 2000. Agreement was reached that the World Bank should undertake a study of some of the key development issues that China would face and analyze opportunities for dealing with these issues in the light of international experience.

---

[14] *Ibid.*, pp. 111-112.
[15] *Ibid.*, p. 142.

This comprehensive report, and supporting studies on key sectors, put China's development and the choices it faced in a future perspective. It stressed the need to depart from the past emphasis on local self-sufficiency, to abandon local protectionism, and to move toward a broader orientation that would allow greater specialization within the country. It urged that greater reliance should be placed on market mechanisms based on the principles that prices should be determined by markets and that enterprises should be responsible for their profits and losses. This would involve, above all, price reform. The reports examined how the role of the state in the management of the economy would change, showing particularly how the emphasis in planning would shift from the short to the medium and long term. The report emphasized the need within higher education to recover from the effects of the Cultural Revolution and the need to make efficient use of energy. It laid out the case for greater emphasis on the development of the service sector. Lastly, it argued that the benefits gained through the development of China's socialist system – particularly the reduction of poverty and the relatively egalitarian distribution of income – could be preserved if the suggested changes were implemented.

The American sinologists, Jacobson and Oksenberg, studied the interaction between China and the Bank on policy questions and came to the following conclusions which I believe to be valid.

There could be no doubt that the opinions expressed in the second report and the reforms and Seventh Five-Year Plan converged. There has also been a coincidence between the recommendations advanced in the Bank's sectoral studies and Chinese policy.

The question is: What is cause and what is effect? Have World Bank officials actually affected the direction, pace, and details of Chinese development strategy? These are clearly politically sensitive question, and neither World Bank and IMF officials nor their Chinese partners from the premier down wished to project an image of extensive influence of foreigners over domestic policies.

Our extensive interviews suggest that the World Bank and IMF, while influential, have not been the source of the reform program which, after all, began before China's participation in them. Rather, there has been a convergence of views...

Zhao Ziyang and his advisers in effect elicited external views that were compatible with their thinking... The external advice has drawn upon and reinforced the predilections of the reformers and provided them with additional valuable evidence and argumentation to rebut their internal critics. In that sense, the visits by McNamara, Clausen, de Larosière, and Dunkel; the reports; and the annual meetings and consultations have increased the self-confidence of the reformers to persist in their course and to battle their bureaucratic opponents...

Above all, the changes that the World Bank and IMF suggested were compatible with internal trends. There was a convergence between the views of China's leaders and the international organizations concerning the measures necessary to sustain and accelerate growth. Further, the mode of World Bank and IMF operation was to engage in dialogue rather than to impose conditions, to convince rather than to demand. Confrontation did not occur over China's commitment to a socialist economy; rather there was a process of mutual education and mutual recognition that China's membership in the World Bank and Fund entailed a great challenge of incorporating a large, developing, planned commodity economy into these international organizations in ways that would not be disruptive.

A prerequisite for dialogue rather than dependence or confrontation and conflict is self-confidence and mutual respect. Our World Bank and IMF interviews stressed the importance of Chinese self-confidence. Possessing dignity, cultural pride, and a sense of place and having been tempered by the communist revolution, the Chinese officials with whom World Bank and Fund officials dealt were self-critical and willing to hear criticism.

Whatever its origins, Chinese self-confidence stands in sharp contrast, many Bank and Fund officials note, to the defensiveness and self-doubt of officials from many other developing countries. For instance, the World Bank has never been given permission to publish its country studies of India. China has welcomed critical analyses of its economic policies and far-reaching appraisals of the policy choices it faces and has quickly agreed that these should be made public.[16]

And what has happened since the crisis in Tiananmen Square in June 1989? For a time, it appeared that this productive relationship would be severed. Zhao Ziyang was removed from office and his chief World Bank collaborator was transferred away from China. The major Western shareholders forced the Bank to suspend all lending to China for a year. Yet, both Chinese and Bank officials kept calm, maintained their channels of communication, and waited for the political storm to blow over. Now Bank-China project lending is virtually back to normal. Sharing data, accepting training as part of technology transfer and engaging in economic policy dialogue have become the norm in Bank-China relations. This is a remarkable change, for which both sides deserve credit.

However, we should not be deluded into thinking that this represents a fundamental change in Chinese thinking which will automatically be extended to non-Bank relationships. This is an aberration from normal Chinese behaviour due almost entirely to their pragmatic ability to accommodate some whims of powerful foreigners, provided the adjustment is considered non-essential and the benefit to be extricated is of fundamental importance to China.

---

[16] *Ibid.*, pp. 140-155.

CONCLUSIONS

The Bank encountered many similarities in these two giant countries. Both were proud inheritors of ancient and great civilizations, with many sophisticated individuals among the ruling elites. Both faced enormous problems: huge and growing populations, mass poverty, inadequate financial resources, vast regional differences and shortages of the latest technical knowledge and equipment, modern management skills and economic infrastructure. Given all the similarities, how does one account for the different record in the two countries and what lessons for the future can the Bank and others draw from the Bank experience in the past?

I believe that the answer to the question about differences is threefold: the nature of the regimes; uneven expectations; and timing. The unpopular truth is that the Bank management preferred to deal with the authoritarian and centralized government of China (which could take unpopular decisions without fear of critical opposition parties and a free press) than with the quarrelsome, fractious, short-term, decentralized and democratic government of India. This may seem surprising if one assumes that the World Bank reflects the democratic political philosophy of its major shareholder governments. The truth is that World Bank management does not model itself on Western governments but on Western business corporations. The latter are authoritarian, hierarchical, undemocratic, secretive and ruthless in their manner of making decisions – just like China – and impatient of vacillating politicians worried about commitments which may affect their popularity with the electorate. For similar reasons, the Bank and India were faced with a crisis of expectation that they would agree on most points because they appeared to be similar in background and outlook; whereas no one assumed that the pro-Western, capitalist, World Bank would have anything in common with the alien and isolated regime in China.

Lastly, relations were greatly affected by the timing of their first encounters. The first Indian loans were negotiated when the Bank was still very dogmatic about the applicability of Western solutions to Asian problems and India, being very caught up in the anti-colonial struggles of the time, was insistent on all the appearances of economic and political independence from Western solutions. By the time China joined the Bank over thirty years later, the latter had become much more open-minded and experimental about adapting solutions to local economic, political and cultural circumstances. Moreover, the new Chinese leaders under Deng Xiaoping, who had just experienced the trauma of the Cultural Revolution and international isolation, were eager to modernize their economy through "opening to the outside world". The Bank and China were much more ready for each other in 1980 than the Bank and India had been in the early days.

What lessons can be learned for the future about transferring technology and knowledge? Beyond the broad observation that the Bank has been most successful where it has sent culturally-sensitive professionals to work with local entities who wanted change, I doubt that one can usefully draw many conclusions from the Bank experience that will be relevant to other relationships. The World Bank is unique in its combination of financial power, professional expertise, and multilateral character. Moreover, the two countries are unique among developing countries in the extent of their economic and military power and cultural self-assurance. They no longer have any fear of being dominated by the World Bank as an agent of unwanted economic imperialism. Now, they both see that the Bank can be useful as an adjunct to their own internal agencies which are pressing for modernization.

There are many people in India and China who worry that Western technology and economic ideas are being introduced too quickly without regard to the preservation of indigenous, cultural and moral values and ancient knowledge. To them, the Bank is sometimes seen as the source of the problem. They are wrong; the Bank is an agent of change but the roots of the problem are elsewhere and far more difficult to control.

14

Development as Transfer of Knowledge:
A View from Egypt

Samiha Sidhom Peterson

Theorists, policy makers, and practitioners of "development" have over the past four decades written and worked extensively in universities, government agencies and international institutions in formulating ideas, policies, and programs that eventually resulted in various forms of change in countries of the South. In spite of the numerous viewpoints regarding the outcome of such efforts, development input has been one of the significant frameworks for the transfer of knowledge between the North and South. Such a consideration is often missing in professional literature and policy analysis, and would enhance an understanding of the impact of efforts and programs aimed at bringing about societal change.

The end of World War II, and the initial efforts to restore War-ravaged Europe through the Marshall Plan, led the International community to embark on a parallel effort directed at the "Third World". Two major International challenges spurred this response from the North, namely: (a) the emergence of socialism as a viable alternative to economic systems, and (b) the pressure for economic change called forth by the newly independent countries of Latin America, Asia, and Africa. Socio-economic intervention through the transfer of knowledge therefore became a new medium for North/South relations.

The phenomena of social change has throughout history been explained by different theoretical orientations. Thus for example cyclical theories were used by the Ancient Greeks, Romans and Enlightenment Christians; while the Confucian tradition used the concepts of Yang and Yin as mediums for harmonious change towards the time of Great Happiness or the Original Golden Age. Ibn Khaldoun on the other hand, in explaining change in the Middle East, used a combination of dialectic and cyclical theories. Finally the 19th and 20th centuries were dominated by evolutionary thinking and evolutionary theories.[1]

The emergence of new paradigms for explaining social change can in effect be considered as part of the ongoing efforts to explain change. However these new

---

[1] Ingemar Fagerlind and Lawrence J. Saha, *Education and National Development: A Comparative Perspective* (New York: Pergamon Press, 1989), pp. 3-29.

paradigms were formulated within the social science tradition, and have therefore been used as a basis for research, for social policy and for various international initiatives. The new paradigms were given new conceptual frameworks such as "development theories", "modernization theories", "dependency theories", "World Systems theories", and "liberation theories". Although space and time will not allow a systematic analysis of each of these paradigms, it is still important to recognize that the ongoing debate within and between disciplines and paradigms has influenced North-South collaborative efforts.

The theoretical paradigms and the commitment of the international community towards enhancing the countries of the South consequently brought about a tradition of international aid which resulted in the development of bilateral and multilateral specialized agencies, primarily involved with the transfer of knowledge through development work. The names of these specialized agencies also reflected their general agenda and the rationale for their work. Thus for example the United States Agency for International Development (USAID), the Overseas Development Agency (British ODA), the Canadian International Development Agency (CIDA), The Inter-American Development Bank (IDB) and the United Nations Development Program (UNDP) are only a few of the many agencies which, as their names indicate, have been involved in international development work.

Considering the "development" paradigm briefly, we find that it has grown out of the Western evolutionary thinking, and initially focused on progress through stages towards a specific direction. Such a gradual approach was formulated by W.W. Rostow in his analysis of the stages of economic growth.[2] However, within that general framework there have been three main approaches that have influenced policies and programs of action, namely: (a) the Laissez Faire approach espoused time as an important variable for transferring societies from their underdeveloped to their developed stage – a repetition of the experience of the West; (b) the Government Planning Approach which perceived government intervention and planning as important mediums for changing society; and (c) the Growth with Equity approach, which concentrated on the distribution of the benefits of change to the poor.[3] In spite of these variations within and between various paradigms, individual practitioners involved in the transfer of knowledge usually refer to their work as development work rather than specify the specific paradigm influencing their work.

The impact of the tradition of "development" theories has influenced national and international programs of planned social change and has assumed that change was possible and desirable. In spite of numerous criticisms over the years and modification of the general emphasis on economic growth and stages of change, the general perspective of knowledge transfer and intervention is still dominant within the international community. Financial resources, technical input, transfer of technology

---

[2] W. W. Rostow, *The Stages of Economic Growth: A Non-Communist Manifesto* (Cambridge, England: Cambridge University Press, 1990).

[3] Charles K. Wilber, *The Political Economy of Development and Underdevelopment* (New York: Random House, 1988), pp. 4-14.

are still central to North-South relationships. In effect, such transfer is considered to be quite critical in a world that is increasingly being differentiated by the information and communications revolution.

In a recent monograph developed by the South Commission, and including distinguished participants from various countries of the South under the chairmanship of Julius Nyerere, the development experience, although perceived as an indicator of major change on behalf of the South that had been left with major post-colonial problems, was also considered to have some significant problems. These included the unequalizing pattern of development within countries; scientific and technological dependence on the North; neglect of the cultural dimensions; neglect of popular participation or democratization; corruption due to its potential relationship to centralization; and militarization.[4]

Involvement over the past three years with the Education Sector in Egypt, has in many ways highlighted the fact that transfer of knowledge for socio-economic change through bilateral and multilateral agreements is quite often influenced by a filtering process which constantly redefines the implications of development input. For analytic purposes the filtering and redefinition parameters for the transfer of knowledge will be briefly analyzed from a macro to micro level. Although the parameters are identified individually, in effect they operate within an interactive model. Charted on a continuum, these filtering parameters can be illustrated through the following figure:

Figure 14.1: A Model for Analysis of Development Input

MACRO LEVEL			MICRO LEVEL
INTERNATIONAL	NATIONAL	ORGANIZATIONAL	INDIVIDUAL
Debates-policies	donor/host policies	structure/culture policies	roles

Analysis of each of these parameters will clarify the ongoing filtering process and negotiation within the development framework. Examples from the Educational Sector in Egypt will primarily focus on the basic education phase.

THE INTERNATIONAL LEVEL

Formal education has since 1948 been addressed by the international community as a Human Right. Thus for example Article 26 of the Universal Declaration of Human Rights states:

---

[4] *Challenge to the South: Report of the South Commission* (Oxford: Oxford University Press, 1990), pp. 35-55.

(1)   Everyone has the right to education. Education shall be free, at least in the elementary and fundamental stages. Elementary education should be compulsory.

(2)   Education shall be directed to the full development of the human personality and to the strengthening of respect for human rights and fundamental freedoms. It shall promote understanding, tolerance and friendship among all nations, races, or religious groups, and shall further the activities of the United Nations for the maintenance of peace.

Although defined as a human right, the debate on the impact of education on socio-economic development started in the 1950s. Sociologists contended that there is a direct relationship between education and socio-economic development, in that it brings about change on an individual level which eventually promotes greater productivity and work efficiency. Thus education was defined as having a modernizing influence on values, beliefs and behaviour, and was considered to be a medium for developing a modern society.[5] The most radical perspective regarding the relationship of education and development is reflected through the writings of Brazilian educationist Paulo Freire, who perceived education as liberation, and development as a question of justice rather than wealth. Therefore, according to Freire, education is the medium through which the oppressed can be made aware of their oppression and can actively change their status from objects to subjects.[6]

In spite of the ongoing debates and various education initiatives in different parts of the world, the International community was confronted by the extensiveness of the problem as formulated in the World Declaration on Education for All. The preamble for the Declaration stated that:

– More than 100 million children, including at least 60 million girls, have no access to primary schools.
– More than 960 million adults, two-thirds of whom are women, are illiterate; and functional illiteracy is a significant problem in all countries, industrialized and developing;
– More than one-third of the world's adults have no access to printed knowledge, new skills and technologies that could improve the quality of their lives and help them shape, and adapt to, social and cultural change; and
– More than 100 million children and countless adults fail to complete basic education programs; millions more satisfy the attendance requirements but do not require essential knowledge and skills.[7]

---

[5] Fagerlind and Saha, *Education and National Development*, 1989, pp. 50-51.
[6] Paulo Freire, *Pedagogy of the Oppressed* (New York: Herder and Herder, 1972), p. 158.
[7] Sheila M. Haggis, *Education for All: Purpose and Context* (Monograph no. 1, Paris, UNESCO, 1991), p. 87.

Recognizing the extensiveness of the problem on an international level, the executive heads of UNESCO, UNICEF UNDP and the World Bank convened the "World Conference on Education for All – Meeting Basic Learning Needs", which was held in Jomtien, Thailand, 5-9 March 1990. The participation of 1500 individuals representing 155 countries, and 160 inter-governmental and non-governmental organizations as well as media representatives, resulted in the formal *World Declaration on Education for All* and *The Framework for Action to Meet Basic Learning Needs*. Leaders of the various countries who became signatories of the agreements, were therefore committed to addressing the problems of education both on the national level and within the international community.

The Jomtien Conference in effect had two main purposes, namely: extending basic education efforts and redirecting its objectives, content and methods of management in a way that would be beneficial for individual learners and society as a whole; and mobilizing the necessary resources to be used effectively towards the goal of basic education. Development input towards the education sector, with its definition as an international priority, was therefore expanded beyond national boundaries, and included international commitment by both countries of the North and the South. The transfer of knowledge through bilateral or multilateral organizations was therefore acknowledged as one of the potential components of educational reform. As stated in the World Declaration,

> ...The world community, including intergovernmental agencies and institutions, has an urgent responsibility to alleviate constraints that prevent some countries from achieving the goal of education for all.[8]

The World Education Forum which was held in Dakar, Senegal in 2000, brought 180 nation states to take stock of developments since the Jomtien meetings and identify forward looking strategies that would set clear operational goals to help the national and global community meet the basic learning needs of its citizens by the year 2015. Assessment of findings indicated that about 100 million primary school age children were still out of school, with 900 million adults who were still unable to read danger warnings or even sign their name. In addition quality issues continue to hamper many schools.

What then are the implications of these international forums for bridging the knowledge gap between and within countries, on even the elementary level of Education for All? It seems that the Dakar meetings provided one more opportunity for

–   Maintaining the momentum of defining the priority of education as a Human Right for all Citizens of the World, and continuing the reformulation of the parameters of that issue.

–   Reinforcing the critical role of Nation states and linking it to Global

---

[8] Sheila M. Haggis, *Education for All: Purpose and Context*, 1991, pp. 94-5.

partners.
– Mobilizing international financial support for bridging the financing gap to include both additional financial input agencies, NGO's, and other international donors.

While Education for All was considered critical on a global context, the "digital divide" has added another layer for the expanding divide associated with the transfer of knowledge. The expansion of digital related knowledge for individuals at the basic education phase will become a major global challenge that needs to go beyond initial literacy skills associated with Education for All.

THE NATIONAL LEVEL

Analysis of change in the educational sector has to be considered on a policy level, and through the perspectives of multiple national players. Central to the framework are the policies of the country that is actually initiating the reform efforts, in our case Egypt, and policies of bilateral countries which may be involved with the education sector in Egypt. Therefore potential transfer of knowledge is influenced by both policy guidelines.

Egypt over the past decade has increasingly given attention to the education sector and initiated numerous efforts for changing it. Having participated in Jomtien as part of this ongoing process, Egypt has expanded the need for educational reform from defining it as a sectoral reform effort to a national priority and national security issue. Considering Egypt's human resources to be its major resource, President Mubarak, the Cabinet, the People's Assembly and the Shoura Council (or Consultative Council) are presently defining the challenge as one that extends beyond the Ministry of Education or its specialized agencies, and in effect consider it to be a national challenge. As such they have allocated for the first time the largest budget ever to the educational sector, thus providing it with greatly needed resources.

The educational challenge for the Egyptian Government is presently both a quantity and quality issue. Defined as a human right and supported by the Egyptian Constitution the quantity challenge is exacerbated by the ongoing demographic increase in individuals to be served by this sector. Forty percent of the population is presently under 14 years of age, and 11 million of these children are registered in the basic education phase. This challenge is compounded by the Ministry of Education's systematic efforts at minimizing drop-out rates, and reaching non-registered children in the hamlets and countryside. The demographic realities imply increasing demands for adequate school buildings, and mobilizing sufficient resources for teachers and students, regardless of the physical location or economic background.

Quality issues on both the policy level and the reform implementation have focused on upgrading the delivery of education, and the educational environment. Special attention has therefore been given to curricular development; upgrading teacher performance; evaluation of students, teachers and administrators; classroom instruction; new goals for learning and instruction; and possibilities for life-long learning. Quality issues are considered to be multi-dimensional and interdependent.

Egypt has over the past decade continued to emphasize its responsibility towards its Education Reform Strategy and its commitment to Education for All. Assessment of Egypt's efforts, however, indicate some critical changes that reflect its commitment to address EFA goals. These include five main points.

The first is identifying human resources development as a national priority for all efforts, thus giving special care to Education, Health and Human Welfare issues. This priority was also supported by increased budget allocations to ensure the availability of adequate resources for various initiatives.

The second involves expanding the goal of Education for All Targets towards the new goal of Excellence For All. Initiated by the Government of Egypt and adopted by the Arab Ministers of Education in January 2000, this goal recognized the significance of quality education, the integration of new knowledge and new skills and the potential limitations for those who could not afford access to quality related opportunities. Development of human resources for Egypt implies a commitment to reach all its citizens in the basic education phase, and ensure that the education and knowledge bar is set high and is accessible to all.

The third is a matter of ensuring the integration of technology resources throughout the education system to include lifelong training for education managers, teachers and students. Moreover, technology as a medium for upgrading education in Egypt resulted in the initiation of a video conference system that has linked the twenty-seven governorates of the country. This system is presently used for both in-service teacher training and for ensuring that educational administrators are working towards the national goals for upgrading education. The use of technology for expanding the transfer of knowledge is also reflected in the new education satellite channels that are transmitting educational programs to students and schools throughout the country Likewise access to the internet has been emphasized to expand the potential framework for knowledge transfer for all students.

The fourth point is introducing an international in-service training opportunity for teachers. While costly, this initiative recognizes the significance of knowledge transfer which includes both the technical content and the culture of education that is associated with changes in our global community. This initiative has focused on 4-5 month training opportunities in various industrialized countries that include both internships in pre-university schools in the UK, the US, France, Japan, and Germany, in addition to upgrading expertise through various university related programs in the specific areas of knowledge. Initially the focus was on science, math and language teachers. This has expanded to include special education teachers, administrators and education counsellors. This initiative in effect recognizes the cultural dimension in the transfer of knowledge and is aiming to expand both the world view and skills of teachers who may have had very limited access to international opportunities.

' The fifth involves committing additional resources to education to continue an active strategy for enhancing access to education through an extensive school building program and providing the necessary resources for upgrading the quality of education. Increased allocations to education represent a national commitment to ensure that education opportunities will be available to all.

Egypt's educational policy is therefore formulated in context of its national reality, its internal challenges and dynamics, its place within the global community, and the international challenges before it. Although Egypt's commitment to reform the educational sector and to provide education for all is a priority, there is the realization that there is an increasing need for the transfer of appropriate knowledge and increased efforts at mobilizing resources. The emphasis on national priorities becomes a filtering process for any internal or external transfer of knowledge.

Within the international community the United States was at one time very active in providing input towards the basic education reform efforts. This assistance, which started about 20 years ago, included input towards the construction of schools; curriculum reform; testing and evaluation reform; educational planning; and education for the handicapped programs. National policies in Washington regarding United States development input are however subject to national foreign policy, which by extension defines its aid distribution policies, thus giving structure, pattern and justification for the pursuit of regional and global directives. In articulating the foreign policies, various Presidents have delineated the potential parameters of input for their administration.

A change in national policy towards development input quite often influences the actual activity of knowledge transfer and the matching of needs to inputs. Although the educational sector in Egypt has been capitalizing on its professionals for assistance with educational reform, United States input through the aforementioned activities was at one time central to expediting the process. However a change in US policy that was concerned with accountability for national funds to Congress, influenced United States input, and therefore has influenced the transfer of knowledge through this bilateral avenue. Thus for example the curriculum reform, which was initiated some years ago, was terminated at an earlier period than expected because directives from Washington changed the input from project related input to program input. Thus although the ongoing need for the transfer of knowledge through technical expertise is still significant, Washington's policies are influencing the input or transfer of knowledge through their funding restructuring.

FORMAL ORGANIZATIONS

Formal organizations which eventually become the implementers of international and national policies are quite often characterized by the same traits of complexity as large scale organizations. Thus in Weberian fashion, they are specialized, with a hierarchy of authority; are dominated by a complex set of rules and regulations; and have career oriented employees. In addition they quite often have a parallel informal structure that influences decision making. Rather than discuss the specific structures of organizations the chapter will briefly address some of the traits that influence the development experience. More specifically these include:

- Definition of Input as Interactive,
- Special Traits of International Organizations,
- Organizational Culture.

Definition of Input as Interactive

Development work is, by its very nature, based on an interactive model with different sets of expectations. The filtering process is a product of ongoing negotiations between two different structural and cultural units in society.

Development related work quite often includes a host country organization with multiple international counterpart organizations, each providing some input to the total work of the sector where change is taking place. This in effect was the case with the Ministry of Education in Egypt where USAID, CIDA, ODA through the British Council, UNICEF, UNDP and the World Bank are counterparts who over the years were involved with the Ministry of Education. Negotiating the implications of the input quite often meant:

- knowledge of a second language for ministry personnel;
- adequate understanding of the priorities and mode of work of the specific organizations with which work is being carried out;
- adequate understanding of overall Ministerial priorities;
- familiarity with international dialogue regarding the changes in education;
- an ability to work with different cycles of project funding;
- the authority to assist in the formulation of input to ensure complementary input from various organizations.

Special Traits of International Organizations

International agencies or organizations quite often have some special traits that influence their perception and development work. The following are examples of some of these traits:

- The practitioner arms of the major organizational policies quite often have an office within the society in which they are working. Thus in effect they are removed from the parent office such as Washington, the

Hague, London, Toronto where many of the policy decisions are made.

- Although their counterparts are often governmental agencies with similar traits of bureaucracies, the input of the international agency, which is generally project driven, is a small component of the overall responsibilities of the agency.
- Although representatives of donor countries are guests in the host country, the role is confounded by their role as donors. In societies where reciprocity is central to everyday interactions, the paradoxical expectations of being host and recipient influence the interactions and work context.
- The process of accountability, which is quite often organizational in international organizations, is counteracted by a host senior level (Minister of Education) involvement. Thus structurally there may be non-equal participants in the development process.

The Organizational Culture

The number of different agencies involved with the Ministry of Education in many ways reflects involvement with multiple working environments. International organizations, as a result of their own history, their priorities, their role definition and the scope of their input, create a cultural milieu which influences work and negotiation. Some of the important traits include:

- Rule and legal driven work which is tied to individual careers and accountability within an organization. Although rules are important in the Ministry of Education, networks play a significant role in carrying out work.
- Primarily paper oriented – with reports, memos, and studies for various components of their work. Although memorandums and minutes are important, in the Ministry, verbal commitments and communication are equally important.
- Specialized language and terminology which may be confusing for outsiders is common among various branches of the international organization in different geographic locations.
- Time and clock driven activities contrast with ongoing accommodation and negotiation of time commitments.
- A mode of transiency which implies that officers within the organization may change when newer opportunities come up, or when terms of appointment end, in contrast to Ministry personnel who may spend forty years in the host country as career personnel.

This list is just an attempt to communicate the cultural context of organizations involved in the transfer of knowledge. It influences both the output and the actual ongoing collaborative efforts between the donor organization and the host country.

THE INDIVIDUAL LEVEL

Individuals involved in development work are involved in their capacities as technical consultants, or organizational personnel. The transfer of knowledge is delivered by the multiple interactions among all the individuals involved.

Although international participants have specific terms of reference for their jobs, the implementation of these roles is quite often affected by

- – the career history of the individual,
- – their empathy towards their host country and their counterparts,
- – their interaction with their international colleagues,
- – the constraints of their work,
- – their ability to translate and transfer their expertise and/or their organizational role to their counterparts,
- – and their willingness to learn from their counterparts' interpretation of reality.

An often overlooked variable on an individual level is that negotiations which lead to the redefinition and filtering of the parameters for the transfer of knowledge may take place between two levels of expertise – the professional, whose work is considered in context of the professional and disciplinary expertise and the bureaucrat who is bound by the rules of the organization. What in effect happens is that the level of professional expertise may vary between the professional and the bureaucrat, and therefore may influence the formulation of input.

The individual role is quite significant in the process of filtering and transferring knowledge. Since it is at this stage that sustainability of change is enhanced, sustainability which is sometimes defined in institutional or financial terms, is in effect strengthened when the individuals who will continue the work after the development input understand the parameters of the input and define it as a beneficial change for the country.

SUMMARY

Development in this chapter was defined as a significant framework for the transfer of knowledge across cultures. Quite often it has primarily implied transfer of knowledge from the North to the South. However, the transfer of knowledge is not considered as occurring in a vacuum. Its context is sketched out in the analysis of four levels through which a filtering or redefinition process for development input takes place, namely: the international level, the national level, the organizational level and the individual level. Examples from the education sector were used at various junctures to clarify the implications of the discussion.

Part IV

Indigenous Knowledge
And Modern Education

15

Art, Technology and Knowledge Transfer

Ursula M. Franklin

It seemed only right that, at the end of this very rich conference, during which we discussed what was thought and written about knowledge and its transfer, we should also consider the evidence of knowledge from the point of view of what people did, rather than only of what they said or wrote.

Thus, in this chapter, we will look at the work of the artisans, who have left us tangible evidence of what they knew and did, evidence that is embedded in the artifacts they created and that can be studied today by means of modern laboratory techniques. We are fortunate that the tools of science have opened to the trained mind and the sympathetic eye another text to explore.

The authors of these texts are craftsmen and women, the artisans throughout time; it is their work that I will deal with here, as I try to focus on the multifaceted information that can be gleaned from the study of ancient artifacts as well as on the implication of this information for the transfer of knowledge within and across cultures

I will speak mainly as a physicist and a materials scientist, who studies the "texts" of people's work by using microscopes, employing chemical analyses or similar tools to ascertain details of materials composition, treatment and manufacturing. This is essentially an inquiry into the artisans' knowledge and their use of information available to them. Such studies can yield otherwise irretrievable cultural information.

Queries of this nature do not only ask how the ancient artisans applied their knowledge, but also why they would have chosen not to use certain other techniques, known and available to them. It is clear that technical and material resources do not necessarily determine artistic preference; there is always also habit, taste and cultural meaning.

The new insights that I want to emphasize may be arrived at as the result of scientific studies of similar types of artifacts from different cultures, such as, for instance bronze vessels from China, as well as those of Greece, India and Europe

Placing ourselves, in our mind's eye, in the position of those who made the objects, can give us a realistic feeling for the interaction of knowledge and experience in a given society and at a given time in history – the central theme of our conference.

By way of illustration I should mention that it was during my study of Chinese bronze casting technology that I realized how our technical studies could not only yield information on technical knowledge of individuals or groups, but would also provide vital information on social structures and processes.

In other words, it is not only the knowledge of the hand or the artisans' collective experience that we can recover through technical studies of ancient artifacts, but also crucial information on the division of labour, on the nature of resources and their uses, on the rhythms of time and production and the transfer of the technologies between particular crafts.

Production information of this kind, can be recovered particularly well from objects in metal – because metallic artifacts often resist the ravages of time better than other materials. It can also become relevant in the evaluation of textiles and other more fragile objects of similar contexts, since artisans may work in one material as well as in another

Just as there are libraries with important collections and expert scholars, there are now small groups of scientists in various countries who are dedicated to advancing this new area of interdisciplinary research into the technologies of different civilizations.

For instance, in China, wide ranging studies have been carried out by the Historical Metallurgy Group of the Beijing University of Iron and Steel Technology, technical studies that inform us about ancient production methods, the division of labour, process controls and importantly, management.

You may ask: "How does management come into the picture?" Let me explain: In most cultures, there are technologies in which the essential operational knowledge is concentrated in the hands and minds of relatively few individuals. These "masters" train apprentices and associates, turning over specific tasks to them, while remaining in control of their workshops.

But there also are technologies in which the necessary operational skills and expertise are derived from distinctly different crafts and specialities. Bringing such components together in order to produce material objects that incorporate all expertise requires not only technical know-how but co-ordination and oversight from those charged with the making of such objects.

Technical information on the division of labour, on craft specialization and standardization can help us to realize the profound impacts of technology on the structure of societies, be they ancient or modern.

Let me define at this point what I mean by the term *technology*. In the context of this paper, technology is practice, it is the way things are done. This definition allows us to de-couple the concept of technology from the notion of machines and devices and of things that go bump in the night. Technology is more than the sum of devices and instrumentalities. It is a system of social instructions; such instructions will use the available and acceptable tools, yet technology is much more than the sum of tools and materials.

The definition of technology offered here stresses the fact that there have always been technologies, practices that are handed on as the socially accepted way of doing something. This is why technological changes reveal change in the way members of a given civilization carry out their tasks at a certain historical time or in a particular place.

From this vantage point technology is more than an important economic parameter. In fact, it is one of the decisive factors that structure the life of any society. One realizes that the ways ordinary people work together are of fundamental social and cultural importance and that the scientific study of ancient artifacts allows us to reconstruct some of these ways in a very direct manner.

I would like to stress one particular facet of technology as "the way things are done around here" and it is this: Because technologies structure society in very profound ways, existing practices can and will determine the acceptance or rejection of new knowledge.

By the same token, technologies can define insider and outsider, the proper gender for a given task, the gendering of tools and their ownership. In terms of transfer of knowledge between cultures, the evidence of knowledge transferred is often signalled by changes in technologies.

Allow me now to come back to ancient Chinese bronzes, particularly those made during the Shang Dynasty (16th-11th century BCE). Because of their enduring medium, i.e. bronze, technical information about the division of labour and knowledge used in their production has been preserved within the objects.

As we learn to "read" the technological language of the artifact, it becomes clear that the bronzes were cast in a complex and characteristically Chinese process. The process involved a division of labour that continued throughout China's history. Its principles were transferred to both technical and social endeavours and profoundly structured Chinese society, its thought and its practice.

Although Roman production methods, in both metal and ceramics, showed similar divisions of labour, the technologies did not survive after the end of the Roman Empire and the breakdown of its social structures.

In Europe the "Chinese" division of labour occurs only after the Industrial Revolution – in fact the adoption of new and different manufacturing technologies *is* part of the "industrial revolution".

What, we may now ask, happened to knowledge and its transfer? From the technical evidence it is clear that as early as the Shang Dynasty, the Chinese divided labour by process rather than product.

In plain language this means that rather than one group of potters or metal workers specializing in making prestige objects and someone else and their assistants making the household stuff, Chinese workshops broke down the process of making objects into distinct stages such as preparation, purification and mixing of raw materials as well as various production stages. All stages had to be specified and carried out in such a way that the one stage, when completed, could become the beginning of the next. The stages had to be linked prescriptively. This sequential and linked way of production, in which one step has to fit into the next, then linked workers and their particular knowledge into a production activity, an activity that required for its success planning, order and compliance, so that work could be done properly.

Production activities of this kind cannot take place if those involved in it do not accept direction, management and control.

The archaeological record shows that the bronze and textile workshops of the Shang Dynasty must have been large and sophisticated establishments. Their products speak of workers well acculturated to prescriptive technologies, with their need for planning, order and supervision, as a way of doing things in which people are ordained to be assigned to tasks.

Keeping this early and continuous exposure to prescriptive technologies in mind, one can appreciate why the Confucian concept of *li* – the notion that there is always a right way of moral and practical conduct – is so deeply ingrained in the civilization of China.

Understanding the impact of the technology of work on the social fabric of the community is therefore crucial for the task of transferring knowledge within and between cultures.

Let me now summarize the burden of my argument, before extending it further:

(1)   I have tried to stress that within any given civilization, knowledge and culture are embedded not only in people and institutions, but also in "things", material objects that testify to what people have done and how they went about doing it.

(2)   Modern scientific studies can and have recovered such testaments. This research has yielded much substantive and structural information on the cultural facets of knowledge and understanding.

(3)   The technologies of ancient China are one, but by no means the only example of the social and cultural structuring of knowledge and its transfer.

I would like to give one more historical example, before turning to present-day considerations. It related to iron working in Europe and China. In many cultures the large scale use of iron is historically later than that of bronze. But since, as I hold, the acceptance or the rejection of new knowledge depends on the pattern of work and culture that has been laid down earlier, one can understand why China cast its iron the way it cast its bronze and it began doing so, producing large cast iron bells and statues before the Han Dynasties.

In Europe and in the classical world, on the other hand, other ways of working metals had evolved. Though iron and steel was forged and worked with considerable mastery (just think of the Damascene swords) the casting of iron did not become a production technique for metal objects until the 14th century. This was not, I would suggest, because it was not "known" that iron could be cast – and there is good evidence for this – but rather that casting iron objects just was not the appropriate thing to do.

There have been many occasions in the transfer of knowledge between East and West in which the receiving culture responded to the new knowledge with a "so what?"

Let me turn now to present-day opportunities and questions and ask: "how can the understanding of the past help us to deal well with the current tasks?"

This conference dealt, in many ways, with the needs of countries and cultures to adopt, accept and incorporate new knowledge. The applications of modern science and technology to such universal endeavours as commerce, war, public health and transportation, the reach of international influence and interaction has increased almost exponentially during the past century.

Today events and new developments impinge on countries that had been previously autonomous in the ways in which they dealt with their particular questions and problems. Increasingly nation states feel that it is necessary, in order to ensure their citizens a profitable position in the world, to find a profitable niche for their work in this new era of science-based technologies. Thus, the wish to transfer new knowledge into old and autonomous cultures has become acute and pressing.

Yet, if we believe – as I do – that technology both structures and restructures culture, then, we have to recognize that the new technologies pose threats to established cultures, be they East or West, North or South.

Throughout this conference, voices were raised in apprehension about the uncritical acceptance of new knowledge and new technologies. There have been voices saying that the new knowledge has to be filtered, through traditional values, through indigenous cultures and modified accordingly.

However, if one takes the view of technology that I do, namely that it is the way we do things that determines culture, then all traditional cultures, all ways of thinking about things may be threatened by the adoption of new global technologies and thus are at risk.

Across the world people have begun to do the same things in the same manner on the basis of the same knowledge. The burden of my argument, which I would have loved to make longer and more substantial, is that we need to be very careful in seeing whether we, as carriers of a particular culture, want to engage in facilitating a global techno-culture, something like a mono-culture in food production, focusing on one product, one type of variety. If we look at that all embracing techno-culture, we have to face the fact that traditional knowledge and traditional values may become merely ethnic decor and local colour, adorning the global techno-culture.

We must be cognisant of the fact that the acceptance of new knowledge, that comes enclosed and encapsulated in new technologies, will inevitably produce a new culture.

The question then is: How uniform a global civilization can the world stand, and how do we talk to each other about which technologies can and which should not be grafted on the trees of culture which we try to nurture.

ENDNOTES (Toronto, Spring 2001)

The opportunity of revisiting and editing this paper after nearly a decade is a privilege for which I am deeply thankful. I would still want to stress that

- – knowledge informs work
- – work structures and changes social relations and institutions
- – social relations and institutions are vital components of culture

Therefore if knowledge is transferred across cultural boundaries, resulting in new ways of working, then cultural changes are inevitable, including changes in the culture of education.

Yet, were I to address the conference today, I would emphasize much more, that working or learning together – whether in antiquity or in the present – involved two categories of knowledge:

One is the *explicit knowledge*, acquired and practiced through the task at hand (be it bronze casting or learning a foreign language). The other is the *implicit knowledge*, the skills of social understanding, acquired through the process of working together on a given task, the acculturation, I mentioned earlier.

The transfer of implicit knowledge is a complex social process. Its intricacy and importance may be greatly underrated because, historically, implicit knowledge was absorbed by ways of working and learning in a group. Yet, this "by the way" learning is the ongoing practicum of social skills, on which the cohesion of communities and cultures depends.

Mechanization and automation have dramatically changed the nature of work and the workplace during the past century. But it is the nature of the new global economy that has to concern us most. Not only have workshops and classrooms changed, often they have disappeared as locations of common endeavour. When students acquire information from the net, when workers are linked to workstations and monitored electronically, what happens to implicit knowledge?

When work and education becomes dispersed in space and time, what happens to social learning, to the personal experience of understanding and being understood? What will happen to cultures, to our common humanity?

16

On the Indigenousness of Chinese Pedagogy

Lu Jie

Chinese pedagogy has been a long time developing. Western pedagogy was first introduced into China 100 years ago. Since that time, Chinese pedagogy has experienced both "total Westernization" and "total Sovietization" (which introduced indiscriminately both the best and worst aspects of both these cultures.) Since the 1980s, however, Chinese pedagogy has come into its own. Nevertheless, there still exists in Chinese academic circles a strong Westernization thrust, which tends to incorporate into Chinese pedagogy a somewhat simplistic transplant of pedagogical trends and theories based on Western scientific knowledge.

Given the long and rich history of Chinese culture and learning, the country's indigenous knowledge in the liberal arts and social sciences, including pedagogy, should frame the future of the development of learning in China.

While the transformation of diverse cultures can motivate the evolution of a country's own learning and culture, ultimately the vitality of a culture is determined by a number of interrelated factors. Central among these are the richness of a country's own culture, the absorption of external cultures, and the working nature of the home society. Because the transformation and exchange of knowledge can add an important element to indigenous cultures, countries should remain open to international intercourse. The more opportunities for international communication through cultural exchange, the greater the understanding and ability to absorb appropriate outside cultures. This is important, given that the development of a nation's culture and pedagogy requires strong, indigenous roots blended with exotic ones. This is true for several reasons.

First, without an indigenous base it is impossible for countries to cope realistically within the context of their own culture, let alone the problems facing other nations. Take pedagogy as an example. On one hand, some general principles exist across the educational systems of different nations, but on the other hand, nations have specific and individual characteristics. For example, China has 1.2 billion people, of whom 300 million are studying in educational institutions. Of all the 300 million in educational institutions, 160 million are learners in or from rural areas (including county seats).[1] The situation in China is thus unique and quite different from Western countries.

Another factor is an on-going and unprecedented social transformation in which many distinctive issues arise, and many complicated conflicts occur. In the goals that this social transformation are reaching for, it is not only a matter of a transformation from traditional society to a modern industrialized society, but also from an economy characterized by a high degree of centralized planning to a market economy. In addition, China is a country whose modernization process occurred later than that of Western countries. The social transformation did not occur over the same period as the Western modernization process, but at a time when modern Western civilization had developed to a relatively mature level and its various crises and the malpractices that had arisen in its train were being rethought.

In the setting of globalization, China's social transformation is a component of a worldwide modernization process. For this reason, the primary historical social transformation mode from an agricultural civilization to an industrialized and then a post-industrial civilization has not followed this straightforward trajectory. The three types of social transformation are in fact occurring simultaneously and conflicts and contradictions are being generated, as a consequence of this. In China's on-going social transformation Chinese people have to make choices in the complicated context of a situation somewhere between tradition and modernity, modernity and post-modernity. The macro setting China finds itself in determines that Chinese pedagogy must develop in its own way rather than by imitating foreign education systems.

From a micro viewpoint, China is also a country with a long tradition of culture and education. Nurtured and edified by this culture, Chinese educators, learners and parents have come to formulate their own educational behaviour and models. Stressing the education of children is one of China's traditions. This tradition is expressed in the deep rooted beliefs of Chinese people today. Chinese people tend to connect the bringing-up and education of their offspring with the continuation or extension of their own lives, something which might be seen as a persisting national concept. Although it is driven by modern science and culture, the sense and conception of education among Chinese is nevertheless rooted in traditional Chinese culture. This results in intensely strong aspirations for education. It is common in China for parents to commit financial, human and time resources to education of their children, that go far beyond what they can actually afford. This passionate commitment to education constitutes a dynamic force for educational development in China.

In a sample survey of 800 people, 93% thought it an obligation of every citizen to support education, and fewer than 10% objected to this idea. Among all the issues that parents are concerned with, the education of their children is the first priority. At the same time this passion for education results in some special problems and what might even be described as educational misbehaviours. These include an obsession with ensuring that their children obtain higher education diplomas, efforts to have their

---

[1] *Zhongguo Jiaoyu Tongji Nianjian 1999* (Educational Statistics Yearbook of China 1999) (Beijing: Peoples Education Press, 2000).

children admitted for study in the best schools by any and all means available, all kinds of cramming programs for children, and heavy work burdens imposed upon children by teaching done at home. Chinese pedagogy must reflect these educational behaviours. The blind transplanting of the experiences and achievements of other countries into China will not explain or solve such basic educational problems in the Chinese context.

Second, China is a country with an ancient civilization more than 5000 years old, with a corresponding genetic heritage. External cultures introduced into China will be filtered automatically through this cultural heritage. It is the existence of strong indigenous cultures like China's that has illustrated the endurance of nationally recognized cultures. For example, in education the school of cultural educational philosophy is associated with Germany where it was formed, while the school of pragmatic pedagogy is associated with the United States.

The indigenous nature of Chinese culture is understandable, given the rich and valuable heritage of cultural education passed on to the Chinese people as descendants of the Yellow Emperor. Any attempt to replace this intrinsic culture with an exotic one can be seen to be detrimental to the development of a national culture and to the fostering of national dignity and self-confidence. This can be been as analogous to throwing away a large inheritance and begging in the streets. In modern times, a great variety of exotic educational theories have poured into China. In fact, almost all of the main schools of pedagogy have been introduced onto our country. But only a few of them, after undergoing a culturally sensitive review progress, have had any real influence on Chinese education. However, the educational ideas and theories of Tao Xingzhi and Chen Heqin are two typical examples of the integration of exotic pedagogy into indigenous cultures.

Finally, "indigenousness" is the road China must take if the country is to take its place in world learning and pedagogy. For a long time, the country was closed to international exchange. Now Chinese learning and pedagogy face the problem of finding a place in the arena of world learning. How can we ensure that our achievements are accepted in the context of international learning? How can we contribute to the development of world pedagogy? Some people may think that as long as we follow the concepts, theories, and approaches of Western pedagogy, we can gain acceptance. But the opposite is true. This tendency to learn and study through copying others is one of the key reasons why China has failed to establish a proper world position in international learning.

Mr. Yang Guoshu, a famous Taiwanese psychologist who has analyzed this problem in his book, *Research on Social and Behavioural Science in China*,[2] notes that while China and Chinese people are the object of study, the theories and concepts used are Western or reflect Western orientations. So while in daily life we are Chinese, in our studies we are Westerners, accepting and adopting Western concepts, theories, and approaches. Under such circumstances we are only able to ape Westerners at every step.

---

[2] Yang Guoshu & Wenchong, *Shehui ji Xingwei Kexue Yanjiu de Zhongguohua* (Research on Social and Behavioural Science in China) (Beijing: Institute for Nationalities Studies, Central Academy for Research, 1982).

In both the quantity and quality of our studies we cannot compare with Westerners. As a result, up to now we have failed to establish a position of importance in the field of social and behavioural sciences. This historical lesson serves to remind us that consistency with our origins is the only way for Chinese pedagogy to progress toward world status.

We need to pay more attention to the study of the educational problems in China, seek solutions, and develop a set of principles for Chinese education. Only then will we develop our own theoretical framework, approaches of study, and knowledge base, and so be able to contribute to and enrich the development of world knowledge. China is a country with 1.2 billion people, of whom 300 million are students. Given these statistics, the development of pedagogical principles and practical applications for China is in itself of international significance and represents a contribution to the human race. On the other hand, we must continue to study theories from other countries in order to broaden our knowledge. In conclusion, we must support indigenousness in the long run, but face the world with an open door.

From viewpoint of cultural psychology, the report submitted to UNESCO by the International Committee for Education in the 21st Century states that people today are in a dilemma. On one hand we are experiencing the process of globalization, while on the other hand we are seeking our cultural roots, with a view to keeping them alive.[3] Virtually it is a relationship of cause and effect. It is in the globalization process that the interaction, comparison and competition among different cultures occur and people with different cultural backgrounds experience cultures which are distinctive from their own. Realizing the great differences between them and their neighbours, people start to seek the roots of their own culture, or the indigenous foundations of their own society. There is also a trend for people in mixed cultural contexts to regard cultures different from their own as a threat and have a sense of homelessness or vagrancy. In this situation, people may ask such questions as "who am I?", "where do I come from?" or "where shall I go?", as they try to find their indigenous roots.

Tracing one's cultural roots is one of the features of the globalized world today. It is a rational awareness and also a kind of "cultural consciousness" as the famous Chinese anthropologist, Fei Xiaotong, has said. In education it is a cultural consciousness of education, generated in the frequent interaction between different cultures worldwide. What are the features of Chinese educational culture as it contributes to other main world cultures today? How is it formulated? In what ways is it expressed? What will it bring to us and what destination will it lead to? How can we make a sound evaluation of it? Cultural consciousness means that people in specific cultures are aware of their own culture. Only through rational thinking can a culture move forward from an unconscious or subconscious state to consciousness, from a passive, uncontrolled state to a purposeful sense of options, of creation and of construction. The phenomenon of "tracing one's roots" is a spiritual aspiration.

---

[3] Jacques Delors, "Education: the Necessary Utopia," in *Learning: The Treasure Within*, A Report to UNESCO of the International Commission on Education for the Twenty-first Century (Paris: UNESCO Publishing, 1998), p. 16.

At the threshold of the new century enormous change is going on worldwide. Every educational culture is changing, whether it is becoming more prosperous or declining. The purpose in rethinking the destination of Chinese pedagogy is to foster its development on the track of indigenousness. Only in this way can Chinese pedagogy be enormously revitalized.

17

Cultural Survival of Education in Iran

Fatemeh Bagherian

If a tree is transplanted from one place to another place where there is a different soil and environment, do we expect the tree to develop and bear fruit in exactly the same way as it would have in its original conditions? This metaphorical question illustrates the situation in Iran; not only with respect to the educational system but also in terms of the country's social, political, and economic systems.

With the "transplanting" of the Western education system to Iran came the expectations that this new system would flourish, contribute to development, and solve our existing socio-economic problems. But these expectations were not met. The new educational system did not evolve from within Iran's socio-cultural context but was imposed from the outside and was never integrated in any relevant way. The need for Western technological expertise is recognized. The question is, how can we develop a system of education that facilitates the transfer of Western knowledge and technology but, at the same time, maintains valuable cultural traditions?

This chapter concentrates on three points: first, the history of education in Iran; second, the establishment of Western education in Iran; and third, speculation as to what might be an appropriate educational system for combining Iran's traditional education with Western knowledge and technology.

HISTORICAL REFLECTIONS ON EDUCATION IN IRAN

Iranians share a common heritage through the Islamic culture. After the spread of Islam in the 7th century CE, science flourished. Although eminent scientists existed in Iran prior to the arrival of Islam, the aristocratic class had always held a monopoly on the area of science. Islamic teachings encouraged people to study eagerly; for example there are close to 700 verses in the Koran promoting further learning and thinking. The prophet, Mohammed said: "Seek knowledge even if you have to go to China", a very distant place at that time.

It is said that Mohammed would free war captives in exchange for their agreement to teach literacy to even a few Muslims. Inspired by Islamic ideas such as the importance of knowledge and social justice, the Muslims built a strong civilization and developed a significant body of knowledge during the period of the flowering of Islamic culture, from the ninth to the 13th century CE. This body of knowledge had a great effect on scientific development in Europe after the Middle Ages,[1] as discussed in chapter 7 by Len Berggren.

In Iran and other Muslim societies of this period, the educational system consisted of two levels: primary education (*maktab*) and higher education (*madrassa*). *Maktabs* were usually run by women in their own homes[2] and were widely distributed, even to villages. Girls and boys between the ages of seven and ten began their education in a *maktab* by reading and reciting the Koran. After completing one section of the Koran they studied Iranian literature.

Madrassas were established in the cities, usually in mosques. The schools were free, supported by the public and the government, and student accommodation and food was provided free. Students were allowed to select their teachers and courses according to their interests.[3]

Students were able to continue their study as long as they wished or were able. These schools did not offer degrees, but teachers confirmed that a student had completed a course through a recommendation that allowed students to become teachers. Students and teachers existed in interchangeable positions; both progressed in learning and kept well informed of current issues.

Because students selected their teachers freely, the quality of teaching determined who was qualified to be a teacher. Relations between students and teachers were not hierarchical but friendly, and communication was strong. At the same time, high respect was accorded to teachers who made their reputations based on their teaching as well as their morality.

A significant feature of these schools was the freedom for scientists to discuss any and all issues. And, because the schools were generally located in mosques, which are considered public places, the general public was welcome to attend classes and follow the discussions. Certain *madrassas* gained enormous reputations based on both their teachers and the facilities available, such as libraries and laboratories. For example, a famous library in Cairo had a collection of 1,600,000 books.[4]

After the 11th century when the Saljuqi dynasty came to power, the period of intense scientific activity and discovery which occurred in Muslim countries began to decline. The new dynasty represented an authoritarian attempt to control the people. The activity of the *madrassas* was limited, and freedom decreased in learning centres. A system of standardized schools was established in all parts of the country and salaried teachers were appointed.[5] Following this, the government gradually forbade

---

[1] J. Glubb, *The Lost Centuries: From the Muslim Empires to the Renaissance of Europe* (London, 1967).

[2] M. J. Fischer, *Iran, From Religious Dispute to Revolution* (Massachusetts: Harvard University Press, 1980).

[3] *Ibid.*

[4] M. Ja'fari, *Science from Islamic Aspects* (Tehran: industrial and scientific research center, 1982).

[5] J. Szyliowicz, *Education and Modernization in the Middle East* (London: Cornell University Press, 1973).

the learning of science and philosophy, and allowed only the study of religious science. This policy, along with the propagation of Sufism, discouraged people's motivation and resulted in a dramatic decline in the number and type of scientists.[6] Sufism embraces a fatalistic philosophy that encourages people to accept the present situation as their due. As a result, after the 12th century, no remarkable scientists appeared. This remained the case until the 14th century when the works of Ibn Khaldoun, father of sociology and the philosophy of history, became available.

Although the *madrassas* lost their creativity and were forced to concentrate on teaching religious science, the structure of the system remained: free education, including accommodation and a salary for teachers and students; an integration of teacher and student roles; strong relations between teachers and students; and free and open communication on the campus and with the general public.

THE WESTERNIZED EDUCATION SYSTEM IN IRAN

Familiarity with Western knowledge and technology began officially in the 16th century through diplomatic relations between Iran and European countries. Iranian students were occasionally sent by their government to Europe in order to learn about Western knowledge and technology. But the first serious attempt to establish a form of European education in Iran did not occur until the reign of Nasereddin Shah in the middle of the 19th century. Amir Kabir, a devoted vizier [prime minister], developed a technical college in order to be able to teach European technology in harmony with the traditional elements of Iranian culture.[7] His removal from government ended this approach.

It was under the Pahlavi dynasty that Western education was most widely imported into Iranian society. This regime established a standardized Western educational system in Iran in the early 20th century. Under the banner of modernization, Reza Shah, the founder of the Pahlavi dynasty, introduced a Western bureaucratic system. Large quantities of Western items were imported and sold cheaply; a step that ruined the handicraft industry in Iran. These "modern" policies ignored the cultural background of Iranian society and its traditional education system.

Subcultures and local languages have always existed in different parts of Iran. However in the new Westernized system all students were required to learn the same information. For example, a young child in a village school would read about hot dogs or eating dinner sitting around table, while no one in the village had ever heard of these things. But of the things that were part of their own lives, such as their local environment and traditional crafts, they learned almost nothing.

The problem was that the imported education system was originally created to fulfil the needs of a Western society; as a result when it was transplanted into Iranian

---

[6] M. Hairi, *The Early Encounters of the Iranian Thinkers with the Two-Sided Civilization of Western Bourgeoise* (Tehran: Amir Kabir, 1988).
[7] R. Arasteh, *Education and Social Awakening in Iran* (Leiden: E. J. Brill, 1962).

society it appeared like a weed transplanted to a fertile but fragile environment. This new type of education prepared high school students to study in universities or work in a bureaucratic organization but it did not teach them the skills appropriate to their social needs and realities. In addition, many students who wanted to go on to university, were not admitted because of space limitations. As a result, many found jobs in government, thus adding to a growing bureaucracy.

Those students who were successfully admitted into universities found that their new skills were often not in harmony with their social situation. This was especially true for students in the social sciences. For example, research methods studied in text books often bore no relationship to society and this mismatch of knowledge and application disillusioned both students and faculty. For example, an attitude questionnaire which might be appropriate in the West, was not appropriate in Iran where the fear of the security police and censorship negated the possibility of true expression.

SPECULATION AS TO AN APPROPRIATE EDUCATION SYSTEM

The original *madrassas* contained a number of positive aspects that are still in keeping with present day Iranian culture and society. An approach that combines some of these aspects with the present Iranian educational system could result in a combination of traditional applied aspects with new scientific and technological knowledge.

The following suggestions provide some examples of how this could be accomplished:

(1)   The capability of the traditional system to produce qualified teachers could be integrated in our present education system.

(2)   The flexibility of traditional schools that allowed students to choose their courses and teachers might be a valuable approach in the study of social sciences.

(3)   The traditional relationship between students and teachers could be reintroduced in our universities by providing living facilities for students and teachers at the same location.

(4)   Communication within the school and between school and society in our traditional education, if re-established in our present system, would enable students to do research related to current social needs and realities.

(5)   The tradition of opening classes to the public could bridge the gap between the academic community and society.

(6)   The reestablishment of the tradition of freedom of speech in the classes would encourage scientists to become more open-minded in their approach to research.

18

Social Justice Through Non-Formal Education and University Extension Education: An Indian Case Study

Renuka Narang

India is a vast country of over a billion people; 51.7 percent are male; 48.3 percent are female. One of the largest challenges facing the country is its high level of illiteracy. About one-third of the population is illiterate and the greatest disadvantage is faced by women; 24.15 percent of the male population is illiterate while the figure for women is 45.84 percent.[1]

This inequality in educational opportunity has led to economic and social disparity and the resulting need to address this situation through educational programs that promote a greater measure of social justice. What each individual requires is a minimum quality of life to sustain human dignity and a fair distribution of consumer goods along with the freedom and power necessary to participate in the democratic process and the nation's development.

This chapter describes the process whereby the Department of Adult and Continuing Education and Extension at the University of Mumbai worked to develop a non-formal community education program aimed at achieving greater social justice and being operationalized through the dimension of extension work within the university system. The model is a grassroots one focused on providing skills that would facilitate upward mobility in socio-economic terms for disadvantaged individuals through the provision of education in their local communities. An additional benefit has been the opportunity for university students working on the project to gain an appreciation of the richness and diversity of their indigenous local cultures.

The chapter begins with some background information on the evolution of continuing education and extension within the universities of India, with specific attention to the University of Mumbai. This is followed by an explanation of the conceptual model developed by the Department of Adult and Continuing Education and Extension as an outreach model of non-formal education. The next section covers the possibilities for implementing the conceptual model and the chapter concludes with

---

[1] The exact population figure for March 1, 2001 was 1,027,015,247. It is striking to note the improvement in both male and female literacy levels since the figures given in the first version of this paper in the early 1990s, with a reduction from 36.14 to 24.15 percent illiteracy for men, and from 60.58 to 45.84 percent illiteracy for women.

a discussion of the reality of operating an actual non-formal system.

BACKGROUND

Departments of Adult and Continuing Education and Extension were established in universities by the University Grants Commission in 1978. They were set up to activate extension work as the "third dimension" of the university system in a manner that would give extension an equal status with the other primary university functions of teaching and research. However, this has not occurred. Adult and Continuing Education and Extension units continue to struggle for parity within the formal education system. Despite this difficulty, these departments work to fulfil their mandate, which is defined as a two-way process between the university and the community by extending knowledge and other resources to the community and vice versa, also by establishing contact between the knowledge creators and socio-cultural realities. The aim of extension work is to optimally utilize the resources of Higher Education Institutions (HEIs) for meeting the educational needs of the common person and for ensuring that the students of the HEIs are sensitized to the socio-cultural realities of the world outside the classroom, particularly since barely 2% of the youth eventually gain access to the HEIs and tend to become elitist in their attitudes and approaches.

Thus within this context the several factors that were key to the design of the program for social justice at the University of Mumbai were as follows: the utilization of the participatory approach technique; the mobilization and involvement of the college teachers and students through the extension work projects; and the fact that there was an acute need for a non-formal stream of education which brought education within the reach of the common person.

At the University of Mumbai, three different sectors are involved in community outreach activities, yet each, so far, works independently of the others. The Board of Extramural Studies (BEMS) is a group of educators who create awareness among urban and rural people through series of lectures on topics such as health care, magic, superstition, etc. and through the conduct of short awareness programs/courses. The National Service Scheme (NSS) arranges for students to participate in community services such as tree plantation campaigns, blood donation camps, awareness programs about AIDS, literacy programs, etc. Under the NSS teachers are assigned an extension role. The third sector is the Department of Adult and Continuing Education and Extension (DACEE). This department earlier operated literacy programs, adult education centres as well as community education centres (known as *Jana Shikshan Nilayams*), continuing education courses and population education programs. Today it focuses on the provision of basic education programs with the assistance of the National Open School, continuing education for the community and the students, and population education programs. The field outreach programs are made possible with the assistance of university students who undertake project work as an optional part of their university studies.

In addition to the BEMS, NSS, and the DACEE sectors, other educational providers include the university's Academic Staff College, established to orient new teachers and update experienced teachers by including a component on extension work in its courses and the university's Institute of Distance Education which offers graduate and post-graduate degrees and diplomas through the distance education mode.

The efforts of all of these sectors have assisted a small number of community members and students, but the results have not been sufficiently widespread as to lead to social justice for a large number of the population.

THE CONCEPTUAL MODEL: THE UNIVERSITY OF MUMBAI'S NON-FORMAL EDUCATION PROGRAM

At the University of Mumbai, the Department of Adult and Continuing Education and Extension (DACEE) undertook the development of a systematic program for non-formal education in an effort to stimulate greater social justice through the reduction of illiteracy and the provision of basic education. The resources of the university were mobilized to this end. Figure 18.1 shows how the non-formal education stream was conceived as parallel to the formal education stream. The non-formal stream was developed conceptually to allow for the application of classroom knowledge by the students for the benefit of the community and to provide opportunities for illiterate and neo-literate citizens to learn at their own pace. The link between the basic education programs of the DACEE and the availability of distance mode undergraduate and postgraduate level education through the Institute of Distance Education provides the necessary channel to the possibility of further university education for those in local communities.

Through the non-formal stream an adult receives initial instruction through a basic education program or through a literacy class, which is delivered on a five-to-one basis, with one teacher for five students. This level acts as a stimulant, drawing the illiterate adult into the learning orbit. Once there, the adult can continue to receive education through the National Open School programs.

Figure 18.1: Parallel Structures of Non-Formal and Formal Education

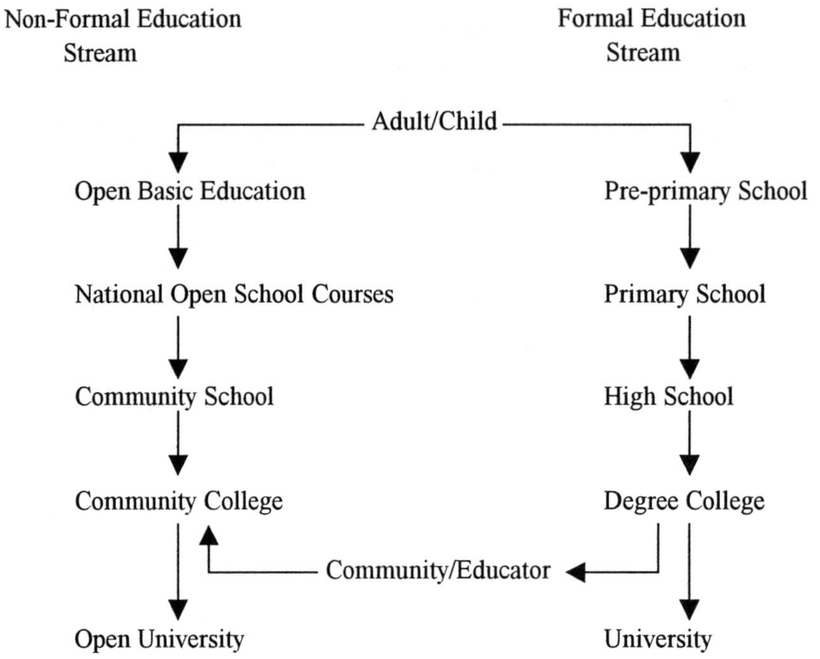

Non-Formal Education
Stream

Formal Education
Stream

—— Adult/Child ——

Open Basic Education

Pre-primary School

National Open School Courses

Primary School

Community School

High School

Community College

Degree College

—— Community/Educator ◄——

Open University

University

     Subsequent levels of advanced education are available through the National Open School or community schools, community colleges and degree education through the open university.

     Significant differences exist between the formal and non-formal systems. In the non-formal system students are older and learn at their own pace. The curriculum is learner defined and is focused on learning skills necessary for economic independence and upward socio-economic mobility and the empowerment required for the older students to participate in the political process. Both the content and the process reflect these values. Students may drop in and out of the system at any time. In contrast, the formal system requires 17 years of attendance to earn a university degree. Ideally mobility should exist between the two systems.

THE IMPLEMENTATION STRATEGY FOR THIS CONCEPTUAL MODEL

The Role of the University in the Non-formal Model

The role of the university in implementing a non-formal system of community education is to first ensure that a two-way exchange occurs between the application of the knowledge and the base of resources of the university to meet the needs of those in the community and the transfer back to the university of the socio-cultural realities of the communities. This involves an exchange process among student, teacher, and community member; each at some point acts as teacher and learner.

As noted earlier, a number of units in the university contribute to the delivery of community based education, but there are two key pillars on which the system is built. One is the incorporation into the foundation course of the undergraduate degree curriculum a component on adult and continuing education and extension work. In addition students may pursue community work or a field based project at the undergraduate and postgraduate level for which an additional academic credit is awarded. That is to say that there is a provision of a theoretical unit and a practical unit (project work) in the university curriculum. The other is the ruling by the University Grants Commission (UGC) that all extension programs be conducted in a specific community area adopted by the university department or by an affiliated college. These two factors have been core to the development of a relationship between the university, college and the community. The colleges subsequently adopted specific communities.

The work of five sectors within the university context, even though independent of each other, all involve delivering community based education in a co-ordinated manner: the Board of Extra Mural Studies, the National Service Scheme, the Department of Adult & Continuing Education & Extension and the Institute of Distance Education. The Academic Staff College is involved in the orientation of teachers to the Extension Dimension.

The Role of the College in the Conceptual Model

Theoretically, the role of the college is to link people in the community with students in formal degree classes through a Community Education Committee involving both the college and community members. It is the responsibility of this Committee to formulate educational plans for the continuing education of the community based on a needs survey. A Community Education Centre established for the community in the college provides support for the project and for other activities after the hours of formal instruction.

The immediate educational priority at the community level is to ensure the retention of children, especially girls, in school, and to foster the basic education of illiterate and neo-literate adults. At subsequent levels of more advanced education, the college plays a major role in conducting the courses of the National Open School and continuing education courses with the help of college students undertaking extension projects. This leads to the optimal utilization of the college's resources, including infrastructure, materials, knowledge and personnel. The work of the colleges is, in turn, supported by the Department of Adult and Continuing Education and Extension which has developed certificate courses for students and is currently developing a diploma course for teachers on how to carry out community education. Ultimately this might lead to bachelor and masters degrees in community education or in adult and continuing education and extension.

The Reality: Operating an Actual System

In 1989, the implementation of a non-formal model of community education began at the University of Mumbai and the process is ongoing. As a means of describing the operation of this sector of the university system, this concluding section in the chapter describes the characteristics of the system as seen at the college level.

A college adopts a community area around it of about 5,000 people. The principal of the college, assisted by teachers, has the responsibility of co-ordinating the program of studies and the student extension projects, involving the National Open School programs, continuing education and the Population Education Club. Each teacher has responsibility for fifty students engaged in extension projects. The principal and teachers are assisted by student managers – one for every twenty-five students. University students enrol in one of the over twenty-five available extension projects which include activities such as basic education classes, teaching children, conducting skill training courses, creating awareness about population issues and women's issues, etc. Student managers are encouraged to undergo a certificate course in project management. Students work for 120 hours in the community and maintain a journal documenting their experiences. At the end of the project they submit a project report for which the teacher submits a grade to the university for an award of 10 marks. The work of the students, student managers and the teachers-in-charge is supervised or monitored and evaluated by the field co-ordinators of the Department. In order to facilitate the involvement of a larger number of colleges, some colleges are identified as lead colleges and expected to co-ordinate the work of about five other colleges. Incidentally the University of Mumbai has over 300,000 students, over 300 affiliated colleges and over 35 teaching postgraduate departments.

In the initial years, from 1987 to 1997, the DACEE was treated as a miscellaneous scheme of the UGC and the extension work done by the students was treated as an optional co-curricular activity. The DACEE staff and program expenditures were wholly met by the UGC. However in 1994 a new University Act was passed in the state of Mahahrashtra, which led to the establishment of a Board of Adult and Continuing Education and Extension Services as a statutory authority of the university. The Director became an ex-officio member of the university senate. This recognition of the "Third Dimension of Extension" enhanced the status of the DACEE and swung it into the main stream of the academic life of the university. Further in 1997 when the State Government took over responsibility for the staff expenditures and the university began to meet the program expenditures, the DACEE gained both academic acceptance as well as permanency within the university system. The introduction of a participation charge for students registering for extension work brought financial self-sufficiency and stability to the DACEE.

Simultaneously efforts were made to achieve parity with the teaching and research functions of the university. First the DACEE was awarded the status of an "academic unit" which brought it out of the "non-teaching status" originally awarded to it. Eventually it was brought under the Faculty of Arts (Social Sciences) by an Ordinance (now awaiting final Government approval), which will give it the same status as a post-graduate teaching department. This provided the necessary stimulus to the DACEE to commence the development of a professional diploma or degree program in adult and continuing education and extension. Graduates of this program will provide the necessary human resources required to establish extension work on a continued and sustained basis in the university.

From 1995 the Department had also made efforts to establish a link with the National Open School (NOS), which offers distance mode courses at primary, secondary and higher secondary levels and whose programs have all the characteristics visualized for the non-formal education stream which was conceptualized by the DACEE in 1987. The provision of the NOS courses through college based study centres with the extension work students as teachers would make it possible for a college to conduct basic education school level programs for the community, also continuing education courses with national level certification. The NOS programs at the colleges are expected to commence in 2001.

The task that remains in 2001 is the integration of the extension work into the course requirements of the students at the undergraduate and the postgraduate levels, so that the provision of basic and continuing education as well as the creation of awareness about social issues among community members is carried out on a sustained basis by a college or postgraduate department. The last two tasks are to ensure that the NSS, BEMS and the DACEE work in a co-ordinated manner, so that the programs of all these units will lead to progress for the overall educational development of the community and ensure the establishment of permanent community education centres in colleges manned by qualified manpower.

The result will be the involvement of the university in an educational program for social justice and the exposure of university students to the rich cultural diversity of their local cultures. Stabilization of this new initiative in an attempt to make community education a permanent component of the university system offers not only the promise of greater social equity but also the means of assisting in the preservation of unique indigenous cultures through a wider awareness of their existence.

Part V

China's Influences
Past, Present and Future

19

An Ancient Bridge: the Influences of
the Arts of China on the West

Peter Swann

From the time of China's legendary beginnings in the third millennium BCE till Marco Polo's famous travels in the 13th century CE, the West possessed little knowledge of the East by direct contact. Nevertheless, China influenced the material and intellectual culture of the West during much of this time to a remarkable degree. The following touches on many of the ways by which China has directly affected Western culture, particularly from the Graeco-Roman period up to the present day. The chapter highlights a number of developments in Western taste in architecture, and in the decorative and applied arts as they relate to the influences particularly of Chinese goods and technology. It illustrates the fact that, long before the West could lay claim to any influence on the East, China was making its presence felt in many areas of Western material and intellectual culture.

The Romans of the ancient world had good reason to have a vague knowledge of a mystery-shrouded place in the Far East as a result of luxury items which reached Rome – in particular silk, the secrets of the production of which for centuries only the Chinese knew. It reached the West across the infamous, long, and dangerous Silk Road across central Asia, and this trade route formed the first tenuous bridge between Europe and the Far East. By the time silk had passed through many hands on its way to Rome, it had, of course, become very expensive, since there were many tolls to pay. Much subsequent history was taken up by Western efforts to circumvent those tolls and find a more reliable, more controllable, less expensive sea route to the East and back.

The Chinese could make silk in many varieties, both thick and heavy but also so fine that it was indeed diaphanous. Roman ladies discovered that even the heavier varieties could be taken apart and rewoven so that it too became diaphanous. These ladies, in an age as decadent as some might claim is ours, found it eminently suitable for making "see-through" garments. The outflow of gold to pay for this titillating fashion is said to have contributed economically to the fall of Rome. Never underestimate the power of women – or the dictates of fashion.

You will note that I used the word "Mystery" and indeed China was to remain thus shrouded for many, many centuries. Nobody believed Marco Polo's tall stories, written in a debtor's prison, about the splendours of the distant court of Kubilai Khan –

though Christopher Columbus took a well-notated copy with him on his famous voyages to discover the treasures of the East. "Mysterious" or "exotic" or "inscrutable" were to remain the adjectives applied to the area. And, of course, it was seen as the source of fabulous riches. From the East, too, came the expensive spices which made food as edible then as fashionable now. There were huge profits to be made from the spice trade. That is another story, but it does not concern us.

The other conception or misconception was that the East held some kind of arcane wisdom which a turbulent Europe had not acquired. At the end of the 19th century, the learned editor Max Müller entitled his great series of translations "The Wisdom of the East", and many of them have remained standard down to our own times. Even before that, in the 17th century, writers on philosophy and politics, notably in England and France, wrote enviously of what they imagined to be a far-off land, populous, peaceful and prosperous, and inspired by an even earlier writer, Aristotle, they wrote of a vast land ruled by sage kings and upright administrators. We still dream of this, even if, unlike the Chinese, we don't expect our civil servants to paint and write poetry. Remember that Thomas More wrote his *Utopia*, indeed coined the name, about 1615 CE soon after Western Roman Catholic missionaries had reached Eastern countries.

One of the great foundations of this land, or so it was believed, was that it was governed, not by untrustworthy, self-seeking politicians who would be hard-pressed to get a job anywhere else, but by learned academics of impeccable taste and integrity like us, I need hardly point out! We still think that to be an idea with considerable, if unrecognized, merit!

Of course, Marco Polo, nicknamed *"Il Milione"* from what everybody thought were his million lies about his extraordinary travels, was right in what he regarded as remarkable about China – its wealth and culture. Yet the Mongols he served for seventeen years, when they set out to conquer the world, brought such death, brutality and havoc right to the gates of Europe, that engrained in our collective consciousness is the idea of "the Yellow Peril". Not the Chinese or Japanese, you will note, but the Mongols, who devastated China as much as other parts of the known world. However, in doing so, these savage warriors also made their one and greatest contribution to world history – which was to bring East Asia into direct contact with Europe – thus initiating, building and securing, at least for a time, the bridge across which were to flow the many Chinese artistic and cultural achievements which have enriched us from the 13th and the 14th centuries onwards.

For instance, the Chinese were the first to discover the secrets of the manufacture of pure porcelain – one of the world's greatest cultural inventions – about a thousand years before the West did. The glories of the tenth to the 11th century Song dynasty ceramics, which Western connoisseurs did not really discover until this century, remain the inspiration of Western ceramic artists to this day. In shape, skill and delicacy of glaze they have never been surpassed. In any exhibition of modern ceramics, it is easy to pick out, on the one hand, those influenced by Chinese and also, though somewhat later in the 12th century, by Japanese ceramic traditions. The latter, on the one hand are strongly influenced by China, but on the other reflect their own traditions going back much earlier.

Even an early Chinese piece, such as the famous Ming celadon bowl presented to New College, Oxford in 1615 CE, was sufficiently valued in Tudor times to be given a costly ormolu mount. It belongs among the *"Cabinets of Curiosities"* of our earliest collectors which, in turn, are the ancestors of our great museums.

It is often said that trade follows the flag but with respect to the East, it was the flag which followed trade – particularly the trade in tea and porcelain. European ceramics were quite primitive when the first Chinese porcelain reached Europe which, together with tea, filled the holds of the merchantmen of the various East-India Companies – Portuguese, Dutch, French and British.

The Chinese, whose technical achievements, then as now, were matched only by their business acumen, were not slow to take advantage of this European appetite for their products. Literally millions of pieces were made for the European market, notably in the southern porcelain city of Jing-de-zhen, a city the size of Toronto with hundreds of factories devoted exclusively to the manufacture of porcelain. Ceramics are still made there. In the early 18th century it is estimated that England was importing no less than two million pieces a year, a forerunner of the export drives which seem to dominate our lives. The combination of luxury products and distant exotic places was irresistible to European nations whose visions, ambitions and greed were expanding exponentially.

Of course, the Chinese did not send their finest wares to the barbarians. These export-quality wares, though eagerly sought after in the West, were far inferior to the imperial wares which nobody in the West knew about. Recently, sunken ships have been discovered with their hold full of such export pieces. A recent sale at Sotheby's, Amsterdam, where buyers walked through a small warehouse filled with shelves of piled ceramic wares, gives an idea of the huge quantities recovered from just one ship. One type is still known as Kraak Porcelain named after the Dutch carricks which brought it. One of these was captured by the British, and its cargo inspired that country's enthusiasm and cupidity. The idea of Chinese technological superiority and artistic refinement, once established, was frequently reinforced.

Every European factory tried, eventually with success but sometimes in horrible taste, to imitate the Chinese. No European princely mansion, like Blenheim, and no Victorian house was complete without its examples of Chinese blue-and-white. And many of the decorations on them re-enforced the fantasies of Western thinkers and artists that China was a land of sensibilities far more delicate than ours. What cachet for an 18th century lady to have a Chinese vase in her boudoir – and equally so perhaps under her bed!

Consider the famous "Willow Pattern" which is still popular today. An ideal landscape with water, a pavilion, willow trees and a bridge, and a couple of lovers or birds. The story is an oft-repeated fairy tale of two lovers whose liaison so angered their disapproving parents that they fled their families, drowned and were changed into two birds – their spirits flying off to eternal happiness in some other less cruel world. This sad, sweet tale was irresistible, especially to sentimental Victorians.

I should add that as the trade bridge passed over the Middle East, the traffic along it stopped at various kingdoms. In these, in fact, some of the even finer imperial-quality wares found a resting place at the courts of Arab potentates. There, another myth was added, for Middle Eastern rulers had been convinced by some smart salesman that, if poisoned food was placed in Chinese vessels, they would either turn colour or crack.

Given the high level of domestic intrigue in those countries, Chinese celadon and "blue-and-white" became very much sought after and huge collections are still to be found there. It is interesting that traffic across the bridge went both ways in early times, for the use of cobalt blue mineral to decorate ceramics was first discovered and used in the Middle East (where, strangely enough, it was not developed) and then exported to China. By this time, the mineral, on account of its journey, was very expensive, but later, fortunately, the Chinese found their own ample sources.

In Europe, it was only a step from porcelain to a tremendous vogue for all things Chinese, especially in architecture, examples of which include the Chinese Palace at Drotningholm begun in 1763 CE, the garden landscape in Veitschocheim, Germany, and the mid-18th century ten-storied Pagoda in Kew Gardens, London, England. Of course, nothing is more evocative of the Orient, more quixotic than a pagoda. What an inspiration for the English builders of follies! We knew little or nothing of the real gardens of China or those of Japan which had been inspired by the Chinese. Only in the last few decades has true Japanese garden design begun to influence the West so strongly.

It was only a step from architecture to furniture which shared this happy mania. The most famous of mid-18th century designers was, of course, Thomas Chippendale – whose designs were most popular, and are still found in various derivatives and in countless copies. Again, we knew nothing of the splendid simplicity of Ming furniture, preferring the over-elaborate fussiness of later Chinese design. For the Victorians, the more detail, the more workmanship evident, the better. "My dear, just look at the carving..."

Occasionally the taste for designs thought to be Eastern ran riot, as in the Prince Regent's extravaganza in the Brighton Pavilion of the late 18th century. Here we see a wonderful pastiche, a fantastic muddle, a rich mine of ebullient misunderstanding which may offend those trained in the arts of China or Japan but which grows on one by its sheer exuberance and totally harmless folly. The British indeed have always loved their follies.

Through the centuries, Chinese porcelain in particular was a popular subject for artists in Italy, France, Holland, England and later in America. Mantegna, for example, would show a wise man from the East holding his offering to the infant Christ in a Chinese bowl. Scenes of people drinking tea from Chinese tea services were popular – and very proud they all look. A still-life, with exotic fruits in a kraak bowl, the Dutch found irresistible. Again, how much more challenging for a painter of a still life of flowers to show them in a Chinese vase. Not only in centuries past but also in modern times. Chinese porcelain would add allure to the obviously most virtuous family at tea, as well as to Whistler's model and mistress who dreamingly contemplates a Chinese vase. I am, of course, not suggesting that she was not also a model of virtue.

On another plane, a somewhat grim American mid-western family would gain some prestige by holding a Chinese bowl or teacup. Here, perhaps the symbolism is slightly more involved for these were the kind of worthy mid-westerners (or so I like to imagine) who contributed faithfully Sunday after Sunday to the chapel collections for the conversion of the unbelieving Chinese, thus contributing to an unrequited American love affair with China which lasted until the fall of Chiang Kai-shek. On the other hand, for those artists less interested in the lofty visions of sage governments or fairy-tale romances, the East, at least in their imagination, offered more worldly pleasures!

The peaceful, rustic designs which decorated the Chinese "blue and white" struck a chord in the European painters of romantic ruins in landscape. The fantasy was the same, just as false and artificial but totally irresistible. But from the Chinese, Western artists gained more than just wistful visions – they also absorbed the Chinese technique of moving perspective – something quite different from the scientific perspective they had been trying to represent.

Nowhere is this moving perspective more evident than in wall-paper where the repeat designs float as on a Chinese vase. Everybody knows that the Chinese invented paper, so this departure was perhaps only to be expected. Birds and particularly flowers, in which the Chinese were always most expert, were very suitable motifs, in turn reinforcing a Western interest in botany. We sometimes tend to forget how many flowers and fruits originated in China.

The misfortune in all of this trade from China was that the Chinese, in their conviction that their civilization was superior to any in the world, felt they needed nothing from the West to balance a trade which must go two ways. For the merchant princes of the East India Company, who were forced to pay the Chinese with bullion, this of course, was an intolerable situation and they were driven to come up with something the Chinese did want and they found this in opium. On this hangs a sad and shameful story which we, in our present drug-threatened state, can well appreciate. Unfortunately, we do not even get porcelain in exchange for our drug money!

Once European adventurers had opened the sea routes to the East, the story of the artistic bridge becomes increasingly fascinating and complex. If you were a wealthy man in the 18th century and wanted a set of porcelain for your dinner table, no matter how large, you could go along to the London offices of the East India Company where you would be shown a basic range of wares which you could order in any quantity you wished. If you then provided a book plate or a reproduction of your coat-of-arms, this could be added to the design you ordered and, in not much longer than it took for the ships to do the double journey, you would have your dinner service of far better quality than you could get in Europe and at a fraction of the cost.

In time the artistic influences often went both ways and the Chinese would sometimes decorate their porcelain after European patterns. However, since they had no experience of drawing from life, the results can only be described, as on occasion, "surprising". It must have been difficult for Chinese artists with their limited experience of depicting the slim boyish female form of the typical Chinese beauty, and never in the nude at that, to appreciate the more ample ideals of the West, either clothed or unclothed. Other scenes less fleshy were easier for the Chinese to depict. The Chinese were quick to oblige the Western market with designs and shapes from European tradition sent out to them – a Dutch gin bottle or bulb vase, a coffee pot and popular Biblical or historical scenes.

It was some time before the European factories learned how to make pure porcelain but, when they did, they began to produce "blue-and-white", and other wares in imitation of the Chinese in vast quantities. Every factory did this – particularly in Holland, Germany and England. Sometimes an English factory would import unpainted pieces and then decorate them in local taste. Sometimes the experiences of artists who visited China added to the fantasy. Who could resist the delicious, exotic vision of spending an hour or so haggling in a porcelain shop in a Canton bazaar? You will see that everything fitted in with the ideas of the Romantic movement. However, for most travellers, the reality of China was considerably less attractive than these whimsical visions of Cathay.

Eventually, everybody seems to have copied everybody else. The Japanese copied the Chinese and were in turn copied by, for example, Meissen or Worcester which in turn were sent back to China to be imitated. As European technology improved, it sometimes became difficult to distinguish one from the other. What I still find fascinating is to go into a store selling "China" and pick out the endless references to and derivations of designs originating in China. They would fill a large museum.

Other materials were equally exotic. Lacquer, for example, is an exclusively Eastern technique, originally from China, but sometimes known as japanning by its imitators and afficianados in the West. Again, the West knew nothing of the finest Chinese lacquer. These, wisely, the Chinese kept for themselves, certainly considering them too good for the barbarians. It was Japanese lacquer which exercised a greater appeal – with its typical oriental landscape motifs and richly gilt carvings.

By the early 18th century, the land bridge across Asia had, of course, long been by-passed by a sea route. The great East Indian trading companies established their trading posts in the south of China – at places like Canton (Guangzhou) whence came another great Chinese import – that of cloisonné and enamels. Canton enamels again abounded in flowers and birds or demure ladies engaged in charmingly feminine pursuits.

Indeed, the craze for the Chinese vision became a mania, and led one noble lord even to try to paint his cows blue to evoke a Chinese style blue-and-white landscape.

And so it went on, this trade-driven artistic exchange. To this day, along with the electric fans, slippers and ghastly knick-knacks, one can still find in the souvenir shops of Chinatowns everywhere, a ginger jar with a debased pattern of plum blossoms on cracked ice – the symbol of springtime – a very faint echo of an early 18th century original, as well as a pretty good blanc-de-chine Guan Yin (Goddess of Compassion), or an inexpensive garden seat which is worthy of a good home.

The whole genre often raises a smile – especially among those familiar with what they call the true arts of the East and not the so-called "debased" Western interpretations. But *Chinoiserie*, as much of it is called, is a genre in its own right, and it is one which has greatly enriched our lives and our homes, giving them colour and a vision, however false or fanciful, of a different and intriguing civilization. It is charming, often playful, and certainly harmless. But to deal adequately with the many influences from China would, I fear, lead me to out-do Marco Polo.

In some circumstances, fiction is stranger than truth. The famous early Jesuit missionary, Matteo Ricci, who had been restricted in his promenades to the south of China, was, after nineteen years, at last allowed to go to Beijing. There he informed his hosts of his great dream – to visit Cathay and he could not be convinced that he was, in fact, already there!

We all need our visions – whether they are of a London whose streets are paved with gold, or an America as was once depicted by Hollywood, or even some "Workers' Paradise". Perhaps we should look at *Chinoiserie* in the same light as the sanitized fairy-lands which Walt Disney has brought to life to the harmless delight of all.

Only in this century and relatively recently at that, have we begun to appreciate the deeper, spiritual springs of Chinese art which have flowed across this bridge to influence us and, of course, vice-versa. But that is another, equally complex story.

20

Chinese Influences
on the Enlightenment in Europe

Gregory Blue

INTRODUCTION

My aim in this chapter is to indicate in a general way some of the main areas in which scholars have found an impact of Chinese culture on Europe, especially in the early modern period. I should say at the outset that there is a large body of literature devoted to examining Sino-Western contacts at this time. In the present format I will only refer to a very limited amount of that literature and will touch only cursorily on a few of the aspects of the topic.

In line with my general aim I will employ a broad working definition of the Enlightenment, which is an historical category originally forged by German historians in the 19th century. It is used conventionally to refer to the century or so leading up to the French Revolution. More specifically, it is a label for the lively and contradictory intellectual movement, then current, which challenged religious authority and tradition and propounded the notion that reason, experience, and empirical evidence are the sole valid means for making judgments. This movement was largely animated by intellectuals independent of the universities, which in most European countries were still dominated by established Churches and scholastic thought. For that reason my topic is somewhat remote from the practical concerns of this conference in regard to exchanges between institutions of higher education. On the other hand, I hope it might have some relevance as an example of cultural interaction between China and the West. Like most periodization categories, the notion of the Enlightenment is fuzzy and has been subject to disagreement in terms of the exact time it is meant to cover. I shall use it here to refer to the late 17th century and the 18th century, a period in which there was a great profusion of information about China.

JESUIT SOURCES OF EARLY MODERN WESTERN KNOWLEDGE ABOUT CHINA

During this period information and ideas about China were in the first instance made available to the Western public through reports by several types of writers who had first-hand experience of the country or who served as spokesmen for those who had such experience. Such authors included religious missionaries, diplomats and merchants. Each of these groups naturally wrote with distinctive slants and for particular audiences. The missionaries, and especially the Jesuit missionaries, were by far the most important of these sources of information about China. The Jesuits, in the persons of Michele Ruggieri and Matteo Ricci, were given permission by Chinese officials to enter China in 1583, and Ricci was eventually allowed to establish an official residence for the Society of Jesus in Beijing in 1596. The Jesuit missionary strategy was aimed especially at winning over and converting the Chinese elite, including the Imperial officials and ultimately the Court, on the premise that the empire would become Catholic if the emperor were converted. In line with this, Jesuit missionaries were equipped with scientific skills meant to impress their hosts, and from the early 17th century down to the dissolution of the Society of Jesus in 1773, Jesuits held distinguished positions as scientific-technical experts in the Imperial bureaucracy.

Through their positions and connections, the Jesuit missionaries were well placed to send back to Europe detailed reports which were intended to inform the reading public about China and stimulate support for the missionary effort there. During the last half of the 17th century and the first half of the 18th they produced a steady stream of published accounts about the Middle Kingdom, accounts which ranged from general descriptions to specialized monographs, and which in several cases attained the status of contemporary "best sellers",[1] thus reflecting general interest in China at the time. In accord with the conventions for European travel literature at the time, the general accounts included discussions of a wide spectrum of topics including the location of the empire, the size of its territory and population, its wealth and productive resources, the fertility of the countryside and the prosperity of various cities and towns, the form of government, the classes of people, the empire's various sects, its social and economic institutions (which were generally praised), social manners and habits, the condition of the sciences and of the technical arts, the nature of the language, the networks of roads and canals, the native flora and fauna, etc. Specialized works were devoted especially to geography, history, politics, and military affairs, though many appeared on other topics as well. In addition, the Jesuits kept the West informed of new information regarding China in the *Lettres Edifiantes et Curieuses*, which appeared regularly in 34 volumes over the first three-quarters of the 18th century. It was primarily as a result of these Jesuit works that Voltaire could remark, not unrealistically, that by the mid-18th century more was known in Europe about China than about several

---

[1] From among the many excellent works written on the Jesuit literature on China only a few can be mentioned here. In particular, David E. Mungello, in *Curious Land. Jesuit Accommodation and the Origins of Sinology* (Honolulu, Hawaii, 1989), has given us a fine survey of the 17th century Jesuit literature, while Theodore Foss's dissertation provides a thorough examination of J. B. Du Halde's highly influential *Description géographique, historique, chronologique, politique de l'Empire de la Chine* (4 volumes, 1735). See Theodore Foss, *A Jesuit Encyclopedia for China*, 1979, (2 vols.). In addition, Etiemble's *L'Europe chinoise* (2 vols.) (Paris: Gallimard, 1988-89) includes discussion of various Jesuit views throughout.

European countries. It was because of the Jesuit Du Halde's services in thus making China known that Voltaire numbered him among the world's great authors.

CONDITIONS FOR EUROPEAN ADMIRATION OF CHINA

While the Jesuits and other sources of ideas and information about China provided a conduit through which Europe could learn about Chinese civilization, and European intellectual culture could be influenced by Chinese example, there were several important material conditions that can also be specified as facilitating Western admiration of China during the Enlightenment. One of these lay in the fact that China had not been conquered by a European power, and despite several proposals to do so it was simply not feasible for Europeans to invade and conquer the Chinese empire, as they had those of the Amerindians, or as they had taken over sultanates and small kingdoms in the Indian Ocean basin. This inability was the corollary of the fact that China was still comparatively strong, both economically and militarily, and was not in position of evident weakness *vis-à-vis* the West. To many Europeans the reported wealth and prosperity of China compared favourably to socio-economic conditions in Europe and in particular to those in Catholic Europe. This judgment was quite broadly accepted in the late 17th and early 18th centuries, and some notable European thinkers – such as the Physiocrats – continued to subscribe to it even in the second half of the 18th. Moreover, the impression of relative prosperity and order inside China was buttressed by the clear fact that in terms of international commodity trade China had had a strongly favourable balance of trade with the European powers since the European maritime expansion in the late 15th and early 16th centuries. China maintained that favourable balance through till the last decades of the 18th century, and it even grew as the volume of trade increased during the century, with the Chinese exporting products like silks, porcelain and tea for which Europeans trading companies were forced to exchange bullion to make up for their deficit in saleable goods – at least until they discovered the opium trade in the late 18th century.[2]

THE CONCEPT OF INFLUENCE AND SOME EARLY EXAMPLES

Theories of cultural diffusionism as current in historical and social scientific writing in the 19th and early 20th centuries have been criticized broadly for the assumption that civilization is produced by a few particularly clever peoples and then spread by those peoples' imposing "advanced" techniques and ideas on the remaining, less creative and

---

[2] Michael Greenberg, in *British Trade and the Opening of China 1800-1842* (Cambridge: Cambridge University Press, 1951), p. 6, observes that in the majority of trading seasons in the first two-thirds of the 18th century the ratio of bullion to British goods exported to Asia by the English East India Company did not exceed 10 to 1. China and India were the main absorbers of British funds.

intelligent parts of the human race in an essentially one-way educational process. The criticisms that such an assumption is culturally chauvinist and is linked to imperialist ideologies seem evident and justified to me. Valid questions can also often be raised about whether given "advanced" innovations are always beneficial, and to whom. It is furthermore becoming more and more clear that the success of transmissions of various forms of material and intellectual culture are not simply a matter of imposition, but that the exercise of options for creative acceptance by receiving groups, even in colonial conditions, are of crucial importance not only for the success of transmission, but also for further development of the innovations transmitted. However one of the premises of this chapter is that it would be wrong to jump from the discrediting of chauvinist forms of cultural diffusionism to rejection of the idea of any diffusion of culture. What I believe we need are less simplistic, more elaborated understandings of cross-cultural influences. Some, though not necessarily all, of these influences have the potential to contribute powerfully to the betterment of the human condition. In any case, to ignore cross-cultural transmissions is to ignore an extremely important aspect of global history.

Among early and beneficial transmissions one can number the spread of alphabetic languages in and from the Eastern Mediterranean and beyond in the first and second millennium before the Christian era, or the spread of Chinese characters in East Asia later on. Dissemination of several of the world's great religions likewise illustrates that the process of diffusion is a real, if highly complex, part of "the civilizing process". As regards relations between China and the West, Joseph Needham and others have shown the great scale and importance, in antiquity and in the Middle Ages, of the Westward transmission from China of a series of major technological innovations including several that Francis Bacon listed as showing the superiority of the knowledge of modern people over that of the European ancients: printing, gunpowder, silk technology and probably the magnetic compass.[3] One of the striking observations Needham has made concerning these innovations is that they had different and much more revolutionary effects in the baronial-feudal societies that adopted them than in the predominantly bureaucratic Chinese social order that gave rise to them. Even in the fields of science and mathematics it can be said that what the Jesuit missionaries took to Ming and Qing dynasty China was itself an outcome of earlier intercultural transmissions that had been critically appropriated and in turn further developed in Europe. As Donald Lach has written,

> While Clavius, Ricci's instructor in Europe, was making the calculations for the new Roman calendar, Ricci was calling for astronomers and mathematicians to be sent to Peking where there was a shortage of competent calendar makers. When the requested scientists finally arrived in the imperial Chinese capital, the "Western learning" they introduced was an arithmetic, algebra and trigonometry heavily indebted to India, and

---

[3] On Westward technological diffusion in antiquity and the Middle Ages, see for example Joseph Needham, *Science and Civilisation in China* (6 vols. in 15 pts. published to date) (Cambridge: Cambridge University Press, 1954ff), vol. 1, pp. 240ff.

an astronomy that possessed elements earlier derived from Hindu, Chinese and Arabic cosmologies.[4]

CHINESE INFLUENCES ON ENLIGHTENMENT MATERIAL CULTURE

Specifically Chinese influences on Europe were not limited to the pre-modern period, that is, to the period "before European world-hegemony", to take a phrase from the recent study by Janet Abu-Lughod. In fact in certain areas Chinese influence was more extensive in the 17th and 18th centuries, when knowledge of the country was rapidly increasing, than it ever had been before. This was less the case in the realms of technology and the natural sciences in which Chinese innovations had been of such great importance in earlier periods. In this area influence on Europe seems to have peaked with the 12th-14th century cluster of transmissions which included gunpowder and cast iron, important respectively in later European military expansion and industrial development. Thereafter, and especially from the 16th century, Europe increasingly made itself the centre of natural scientific and technological innovation.

Nevertheless Europeans still continued to value and search for useful knowledge and techniques developed by other societies throughout the early modern period, as can be seen for example from the aims of the early Royal Society in Britain. In this area as in others, the main sources of information about China were members of the Jesuit mission, with whom successive officials of the Royal Society and especially the French Academy of Sciences carried on detailed correspondence, for example concerning Chinese astronomical records. Jesuit published works on China also included as a matter of course not only assessments of the general state of the arts and sciences in China, but also accounts of particular techniques and bodies of information that were novel to European readers. Europeans were particularly keen to get knowledge regarding productive techniques in three areas in which the Chinese were more advanced, namely, the fabrication of porcelain, the processing of silk and the cultivation of tea. It was clearly no accident that porcelain, silk and tea were items that European countries were importing from China on a large scale. The acquisition of such knowledge was an essential part of import substitution programs in these sectors in the 17th and 18th centuries: in the Netherlands, Germany and later England in the ceramic sector; in France and Italy for silk manufacture; and in the eventual establishment of tea plantations in India by the British. At the same time, there was also much interest in and reporting about Chinese agriculture and agricultural policy, which was proposed as a model for Europe. Some sixty years ago the historian of agriculture Paul Leser suggested that Chinese and other East Asian influences were of considerable importance for the 18th century European agricultural revolution, a transformation that was a necessary condition for the industrial revolution of the late 18th and early 19th centuries. This position has been recently substantiated by Francesca Bray, who writes:

---

[4] Donald F. Lach, *Asia in the Making of Europe* (2 vols. in 5 pts. to date) (Chicago: University of Chicago Press, 1965ff), vol. 2, bk. 3, p. 415. See also Chapters 6 and 7 of this volume.

European mechanized cultivation and sowing methods ultimately derive from Chinese technology introduced to Europe in the 17th and 18th centuries. But the Asian prototypes are unrecognizable in the sophisticated and elaborate equipment of modern Western farms, or even of late 19th century enterprises.[5]

Mention must also be made of the fact that the late 17th and early 18th centuries were a period of great European interest in Chinese medicine, a system of medicine very different from the Western system in its theory and in practice, and one with comparable claims to therapeutic success.[6]

Finally, before leaving the topic of Chinese influences on Western material culture in the Enlightenment, it should of course be recalled that this period was one in which Chinese products and styles were avidly if often distortively incorporated into the life-styles and mental worlds of European polite society. Fervent attempts were made to approximate Chinese designs of buildings, gardens and furniture.[7] Items now so commonplace in the West as wallpaper and toilet paper were likewise established in Europe at this time, following Chinese usage.

Chinese influences on Europe in the period here under discussion were not only in the realm of material culture, however. They also affected the philosophy and abstract culture of the time. In order to understand how influence in this area came about, it is necessary first to turn once again to the missionaries and other Roman Catholic groups who provided Europe with so much material and discussion of Chinese civilization at the time.

THE RITES CONTROVERSY[8]

In almost all their works missionary writers concerned with China paid special attention to indigenous religions and schools of thought and to what the missionaries saw as the religious implications of Chinese civilization. While the Jesuits were

---

[5] Francesca Bray, "The Chinese Contribution to Europe's Agricultural Revolution: a Technology Transformed", in Li Guohao et al, *Explorations in the History of Science and Technology in China* (Shanghai: Shanghai Chinese Classics Publishing House, 1982), p. 632.

[6] See Lu Gwei-Djen & Joseph Needham, *Celestial Lancets: A History and Rationale of Acupuncture and Moxibustion* (Cambridge: Cambridge University Press, 1983) for an account on the Western reports of Chinese medicine at the time. See also Chapter 10 of this volume.

[7] See Hugh Honour, *Chinoiserie: The Vision of Cathay* New York: Dutton, 1961) and Oliver Impey, *Chinoiserie: The Impact of Oriental Styles on Western Art and Decoration* (London: Oxford University Press, 1977). See also Chapter 19 of this volume.

[8] The Rites Controversy has been examined by many authors. Among the most important treatments from my point of view are those of Virgile Pinot, *La Chine et la formation de l'esprit philosophique* (Paris: Geuthner, 1932), Ch. 2; A. H. Rowbotham, *Missionary and Mandarin. The Jesuits at the Court of China* (Berkeley, California: University of California Press, 1942), pp. 119-175; Etiemble, *L'Europe chinoise* (2 vols.) (Paris: Gallimard, 1988-89), chs. 19-21 which incorporated newly accessible material; René Etiemble, *Les Jésuites en Chine: La querelle des rites (1552-1773)* (Paris: Julliard, 1966); and Paul A. Rule, *K'ung-tzu or Confucius: The Jesuit Interpretation of Confucianism* (Sydney: Allen & Unwin, 1986), ch. 3.

intensely hostile to Buddhism and to Daoism, most of them followed Ricci in considering certain essential elements of Confucianism – such as Imperial and ancestral ceremonies, or rites – to be compatible with Christian belief, on the grounds that the Confucian practices were of a civil rather than religious nature. As Christians they also believed that mankind descended from Adam and Eve, and many argued that the wisdom of the Confucian moral doctrine transmitted through the elite, and consequently the success and longevity of the Chinese state, were the results of an initial divine message that had been preserved in diluted form in the Confucian classics from before the time of the separation of peoples. These Jesuits further maintained that, though most modern educated Chinese had been led into atheism, the Chinese classics contained references to the true God of the Old and New Testaments. Such notions meant in practice that the Jesuits could accept among their prospective converts certain Confucian beliefs and practices. These beliefs and practices were seen as needing purification and development in the light of the Christian message, but not as requiring Christian condemnation as idolatrous or superstitious. Indeed, the Christian message could be "accommodated" to Chinese thought so as to aid in conversion efforts.[9] This could have the opportune effect of not offending or shocking prospective converts through rejection of their entire belief-system, a system which was of course integrally bound up with the official state-ideology.

Such Jesuit ideas about Confucian practice were hotly debated by various enemies of the Jesuits within the Catholic Church, and most notably by the Jansenists and by non-Jesuit missionary groups who hoped to gain a stronger foothold in the vast China "mission-field". The Jansenists, the Dominicans and the Franciscans all had previous quarrels of some standing with the Jesuits, and in the last decades of the 17th century arguments concerning the Jesuit interpretation of Confucianism were added to these and were fanned into the heated "Chinese Rites controversy", so called because one of the questions in dispute was that of whether or not the Chinese Imperial and ancestral ceremonies were compatible with Christian belief. According to leaders of the missionaries to China who were not Jesuits, fundamental Confucian doctrine was either idolatrous or atheistic. The Chinese tradition contained no intimation of the one, true God. Confucian ceremonies were superstitious and were essentially opposed to the truths of Christianity. The Dominicans, the Franciscans and the members of the French Société des Missions Etrangères therefore argued that the Jesuits were theologically and morally lax, as well as politically opportunist, in practising an accommodationist conversion strategy in China. In 1701 the Faculty of Theology of the University of Paris ruled that crucial parts of the Jesuit interpretation of Confucianism in China generally were in error. This judgment regarding Chinese culture was upheld in subsequent years by successive popes and their representatives, who condemned the Chinese ceremonies as incompatible with Christian belief.

---

[9] This is a great simplification of the Jesuit position, which has been studied in detail in many works, among which one can especially recommend Paul Rule's *K'ung-tzu or Confucius?*, 1986, and René Etiemble's *Les Jésuites en Chine*, 1988-89.

RELIGION, POLITICS AND MORALITY

The Rites Controversy was carried on by the various contending parties in Roman Catholic officialdom as a battle over missionary strategy, but also more fundamentally as one over the character and integrity of Christian religion. In the broader culture, the different positions put forth in that debate were read as significant in still other ways. One of the first to make such critical readings was the French Calvinist philosopher Pierre Bayle, and I shall take Bayle's case as an example of the way in which Chinese influence could be exerted on Europe in the Enlightenment.[10] Even before the condemnation of the Jesuit ideas in 1700 Bayle had drawn on Chinese example in support of a number of his ideas. In 1685 Louis XIV had revoked the Edict of Nantes, the century-old proclamation that had ended the religious wars in France and brought the country civil peace. At the time, of course, religious doctrines were held with as much passion as political and economic ideas are now. Revocation meant renewed persecution of non-Catholic sects and the exile of considerable parts of the French intellectual elite and artisanate. The new hard-line policy was ordered by Louis, on the advice of his Jesuit counsellors, on the grounds that error in matters of religion could not be allowed. Since orthodox religion lay at the foundation of the State, heretical views contradicted the natural order and were politically subversive; those who held them had to be forced by their rulers to comply with accepted doctrine. In fact, most Calvinist churchmen at the time also accepted this policy, but maintained that it was their own sect's orthodoxy that needed to be imposed.

From the 1680s, Bayle, together with the English philosopher John Locke, developed a new position: they argued that the State should tolerate a variety of religious sects. Toleration was not actually totally new in practice – a considerable degree of toleration existed in the Netherlands and had done so in England during the Civil War; but the practice lacked theoretical justification, and this is what Locke and Bayle pioneered. In response to the notion that any state that adopted such a policy would be unstable, Bayle showed that in China, whose form of government had reputedly remained unchanged for thousands of years, three very different sects – Confucianism, Daoism and Buddhism – had long co-existed and been officially accepted by the Emperor. If toleration thus was practised in what was the world's largest and allegedly most prosperous society, could such a policy really be considered fundamentally unsound?

That was a forceful argument, deeply embarrassing to doctrinaire Christians intent on justifying the exclusive imposition of their creeds on their countrymen. The reported prosperity of China was commonly taken at the time as indicating the soundness of the principles according to which Chinese government was constituted.

---

[10] Fuller elaborations of Bayle's understanding and use of Chinese example, are given by Pinot, *La Chine et la Formation de l'esprit philosophique*, 1932, pp. 314ff; Etiemble, *L'Europe Chinoise*, 1988-89, vol. 1, e.g. pp. 222, 312ff & 354ff; and Basil Guy, *The French Image of China Before and After Voltaire* (Studies in Voltaire and the 18th Century, no. 21) (Geneva: Institut et Musée Voltaire, 1963), pp. 122ff.

The Chinese state appeared to be an enlightened absolute monarchy similar to those found in various European countries, and in the first place in France. Before 1700 such a positive assessment of the Chinese state was broadly shared, being held not only by the Jesuits, who argued for absolutism as an ideal, but also by missionaries such as Domingo Navarrete who belonged to other orders, and by "libertine" thinkers such as François Bernier and Sir William Temple. The praise which the Jesuits in particular bestowed on China was based on the same principle of ideal absolutism as that with which they justified the French monarchy, and their portrayal of China may be reasonably interpreted as part of a program to muster ideological support for the rule of the "Sun King".[11] Again, other people drew different conclusions from the Jesuit descriptions. Once again, the ideas of Bayle are of interest. Bayle observed that in the Rites Controversy the Jesuits had argued that, though most modern Chinese intellectuals were atheists, a small number had managed to preserve the ideas of true monotheistic religion from ancient times. The opponents of the Jesuits argued that the Chinese elite were all atheists.[12] Both sides agreed that the Chinese elite were overwhelmingly atheist. Since the Chinese intellectuals were generally reported to be highly moral, and the government they ran was judged benevolent and wise, Bayle concluded that a sound morality, including a political morality, is logically independent of belief in a transcendent God. This supported his previously held idea that the Christian Church was not the necessary foundation of an orderly society.

Though Bayle's idea of Chinese atheism was rejected by many later Enlightenment thinkers who were deists – and most notably by Voltaire – the principle of the separability of Church and state was one that held on and was generally accepted by those who considered themselves *"philosophes"*. For many of the *"philosophes"*, and most especially for Voltaire, China was particularly attractive because the ideas of Confucius constituted a sort of natural religion derived from reason and experience, one that put forward a clear practical morality and that never hardened into dogma, nor gained a heavy accretion of myth based on an allegedly special revelation.[13]

To restate: in the 17th and 18th centuries China was invoked as a model as European thinkers developed ideas like the distinction between morality and the Christian religion, the separation of Church and state, and the ideal of understanding human existence in terms of reason and experience. I would argue that the *"philosophes"* were essentially right in those analyses of China which they used to support these particular ideas. With these points in mind, I think one can fairly say that Chinese example was at the heart of the tendency towards secularization which constituted one of the main characteristics of the Enlightenment.

This is not to say that China was in all respects taken as a positive model by Enlightenment thinkers. For example, Montesquieu, whose ideas were of the utmost

---

[11] Pinot, *La Chine et la Formation de l'esprit philosophique*, 1932, p. 426.

[12] Alan Charles Kors *Atheism in France Volume I: The Orthodox Sources of Disbelief* (Princeton: Princeton University Press, 1990), pp. 160-177, examines the Rites Controversy and the place of Chinese example in the development of European atheism in the Enlightenment.

[13] I follow here the analysis of Pinot, *La Chine et la Formation de l'esprit philosophique*, 1932, pp. 425-28.

importance for the "philosophical" movement (and later for the American and French revolutions), strongly objected to Jesuit eulogies of China's government. He did so precisely because he saw them as apologies for the Bourbon absolutism which he found reprehensible. He was neither brash nor foolish enough to complain directly of his own ruling dynasty. He did however strongly criticize China by categorizing it generally (and thus abusively, in my opinion) as a despotism, the fundamental principle of which was fear. In this respect, China may be said to have served as a negative model for Montesquieu and for the many people who have since followed his analysis. Montesquieu's analysis of China as a despotism was immediately contested by other "*philosophes*" such as Voltaire and the economist Quesnay. The ensuing dispute over the possibility of "enlightened despotism" was one of the major controversies in the realm of political theory in the third quarter of the 18th century. Again we have a case of Chinese influence affecting the development of Western thought and practice through the prism of Western perceptions.

FINAL REMARKS

In bringing this chapter to a close I would like to draw two very general conclusions from the above discussions, and then make a final point.

The first conclusion is rather simple but I will state it anyway just because its opposite has been strongly held in the past. It is that Chinese civilization has historically influenced global civilization in important ways not only in ancient or medieval times, but also in the modern period.

The second relates to the fact that cross-cultural exchanges of ideas often lead to difficulties and dilemmas in the recipient society not foreseen by those responsible for the original transmissions. One of the upshots of this chapter is that by raising difficulties and dilemmas regarding fundamental traditions and values in European society in light of Chinese traditionist values, the Chinese example and influence on Europe contributed to the progressive transformation of European culture that we know as the Enlightenment.

Finally, I would like to note that, while I have been speaking throughout this chapter in terms of Chinese influence, I might alternatively have spoken often of Western appropriation of Chinese ideas and techniques. Perhaps this would not be appropriate when analyzing something like the fact that the balance of trade favourable to China in the 18th century influenced the emergence of criticism of the British East India Company. But in the cases I have considered in the last part of this chapter, influence and appropriation are two sides of the same coin. It should be pointed out, however, that in these cases appropriation did not entail exploitation. China cannot be said in any meaningful sense to have been exploited by the West before the end of the 18th or the beginning of the 19th century, even though by then Europe had probably already been the global hegemonic power for several centuries. The exploitation came only when the global economic and political balance of power had shifted still further in the West's favour, after the British gained predominance in India.

21

A Brief Overview of Sino-Western Exchange Past and Present

Li Bingde

From my perspective as a Chinese educationist, I would like to provide a thumbnail sketch of the development of intercultural exchange between China and the West. My comments may not be very revealing to experts in comparative cultural studies, but they may be of help to educators who desire a broader context in which to place educational exchange between China and the West.

It is my impression that China has long been open to external trends, and that China's relationship with other cultures has long influenced Chinese cultural development. This has been the main trend of the development of Chinese culture. However, the whole process of this development has been somewhat tortuous. The following account should demonstrate the interactive nature of Chinese cultural development, while undermining the view of an isolationist, static China.

FROM "HUNDREDS OF SCHOOLS COMPETING" TO THE CONTINUUM OF THIS SPIRIT OF OPENNESS (ABOUT 770 BCE — 1634 CE)

During the spring and Autumn Period (770—476 BCE) and that of the Warring Kingdoms (474—221 BCE), there were hundreds of academic schools competing with one another. The Logicians, Militarists, Daoists, Moists, Legalists and Confucianists all appeared on the stage of history during this time. They brought about a splendid phase in the history of Chinese cultural development. But, when the Warring Kingdoms came to an end, and China was unified, the Emperor Han Wudi, who reigned from 140 to 87 BCE, did not value this ethos of competing schools. He wished rather to promote the unity of people's thinking, employing one school of thought which he felt would help to consolidate his rule. So he declared all academic schools banned, except that of Confucianism.

Of course, the expectations of the throne and the prevailing thrust of cultural development are not always coincident. Contrary to Han Wudi's expectation, Confucianism failed to become the only defining ideology in China. Other schools of thought continued to prevail among the people, and new schools of thought were added to the mix. Buddhism was introduced from India during the Eastern Han Dynasty (24—220 CE). Islam and Christianity were introduced shortly thereafter.

Through much of the span of Chinese history, a range of ideologies were developed and embraced. The presence of a wide variety of worldviews has had a demonstrable effect on Chinese cultural development. The story of the development of science and technology in China is similar. Exchanges of science and technology between China and foreign countries have been active and of long standing. The British scholar Dr. Joseph Needham provides us with much historical evidence in this regard.

For example, among those responsible for scientific interchange was the Italian Jesuit missionary, Father Matteo Ricci. Father Ricci lived in Beijing in the beginning of the 17th century and worked with the assistance of Xu Guangqi to introduce Western science into China. Mr. Xu was a high official in charge of education in the Ming Dynasty (1368—1644 CE) The influence of their work among the educated Chinese was considerable, as noted in Chapter 20 of this volume.

The development of Chinese culture with its unique characteristics in fact owes a great deal to the existence of this atmosphere of competition among different academic schools. In spite of the dominance of Confucianism, it was still just one of the various schools. And even within Confucianism itself, there are also competing sub-schools. It is this tolerant and widely-embracing culture that promoted China's national power, and brought about the prosperity of the Han and Tang Dynasties, which in turn exerted a powerful influence on such neighbouring countries as Japan, Korea and Vietnam.

THE PERIOD OF CLOSING AND HALF OPENING THE DOOR (1644–1979)

The Period of a Closed Door

The Ming Dynasty fell to the Manchus soon after Father Matteo Ricci's cooperative work with Mr. Xu Guangqi, and was replaced by the Qing Dynasty (1644—1911 CE). When the Qing Dynasty began its rule of China, the country was very powerful with a solid national strength, and people lived a peaceful life. Therefore, several consecutive emperors became complacent, and with this came the self-impression that China was so rich and powerful it did not need to engage in exchanges with foreign countries, either economically or culturally. Due to this mentality, the imperial government adopted a closed door policy, which led to the stalemate of both economic and cultural development. At this time, on the other side of the globe, the Renaissance and the religious reforms associated with the Reformation were developing vigorously, having a great impact on the rise of science, and the transformation from a feudal agricultural society to an industrial capitalist society. With the development of capitalism, the West began to expand its influence around the world. Under such general circumstances in the international arena, the first Opium War exploded in 1840, and a series of wars followed it. The gates of China were forced open.

The Period of a Half Opened Door

With China's defeat in the Opium War and the series of wars that followed, the rulers of the Qing Dynasty were shocked, as if just awakening from a dream. However, they had not been awakened completely, but were still half awake. They only recognized the might of Western weaponry, which was produced from the advances that had been made in science and technology. This was the focus in terms of what Chinese people should learn from the West. As for other aspects of Western cultures, they were not on the list, and were not considered necessary for Chinese people to learn. As a result, the policy of "Chinese learning as the essence and Western learning for its usefulness" was stipulated and carried out, with a number of young people selected and sent to Europe, America and Japan to study. The government intended to have Chinese students learn Western science and technology, especially as these related to military considerations, but excluding any access to Western philosophy and political thought, because of the fear that the students would be influenced by ideas which were thought inimical to imperial rule.

The policy of "Chinese learning as the essence and Western learning for its usefulness" was of course designed to circumscribe cultural exchange, but it never actually worked. While learning about Western science and technology, Chinese students could not avoid learning about Western customs, religion, thought, and political institutions. The "essence" of Chinese learning could not be kept intact. Although constructed as a great dam to check the flood of Western ideas into China, the imperial education policy collapsed under the force of great waves rushing in from the West. The revolution of 1911, led by Dr. Sun Yat-sen, brought down the Qing Dynasty, and put an end to the fiction of the imperial cultural exchange policy. During the May 4th Movement of 1919, the Western concepts of democracy and science were greatly respected by educated Chinese. About this time, Marxism and Leninism also began to make their presence felt.

In 1949, upon the founding of the People's Republic of China, the country was once again closed to the West, but was wide open to the Soviet Union and to its satellite Eastern European countries. "Learn from the Soviet Union" was the slogan of this period.

In this brief account, we can see that from the mid-19th century till the 1980s, excepting the ten years of the Great Cultural Revolution (1966-1976), cultural influences from various foreign countries were introduced into China in abundance. At times, these influences delivered highly charged cultural shocks to traditional Chinese society. In only one and half centuries, Chinese scholars have imported, imitated and copied foreign cultures, often with no regard for the unique conditions of their own country. Before 1949, they copied the example of America and Europe; after that, they copied that of the Soviet Union. During all those years, borrowing and copying was the basis of the relationships they built with foreign cultures.

FOLLOWING A NEW ROUTE IN THE 1980s

With the end of the disaster of the so-called Cultural Revolution, Chinese people began to reflect on the past, and finally came to a new awakening. The awakening of this time was gained from two kinds of reflection.

One was reflection on the lessons learnt from the past. Although China has a culture of excellence with great vitality, it still needs to be improved to achieve continuous progress. On the one hand, the closed door policy and the half open door policy all were evidence of ignorance, which could only lead China to backwardness and disasters. On the other hand, however, blind and indiscriminate imitation and even copying of foreign cultures would not do any good to China either. China must follow a new route, entirely different from mere copying or harking back to the past.

The other kind of reflection was the inspiration obtained from facing up to reality and looking into the future. Chinese people have clearly seen that China is still a developing country, which is backward culturally, socially as well as economically. In order to regain a towering position among the nations of the world, China must seek rapid development in all areas, and manage to catch up. Also, as we view the world, we can identify an irresistible trend towards globalization, due to the progress of science and the development of the world economy. All human beings living in this global village must learn to coexist peacefully and make joint efforts to develop. Nevertheless, we should also see the multiplicity of world cultures. Economic globalization does not necessarily require uniformity among all cultures, as these two arenas are different but not contradictory to each other. As a matter of fact, due to the history and geographic locality of different countries and nations, a kind of cultural multiplicity is inevitable. Moreover, a mutual exchange among different cultures will enhance the understanding between different nations and regions, and further achieve common progress.

In summary, with the reflection on both the positive and negative lessons of the past, and the recognition of the current situation in world development, also the prospects of the future world, Chinese people have finally come to a clear realization that we must learn from foreign cultures and transform our own culture as well. The door must be open to the outside world. This is not only important for China's progress, but also for the sake of world peace and development. Only when China has achieved this, will she be able to make big strides forward, and also make greater contributions to world culture and human civilization. This has been identified as the new route China is determined to pursue, and China has already started on it.

EDUCATION AS A WINDOW OF CULTURAL DEVELOPMENT

I have just roughly sketched the history of the cultural development of China, in outlining the different periods mentioned above. I would like to further illustrate the history of this development through some examples from the evolution of educational thought.

What we mean by ancient Chinese culture is of course far more extensive than Confucianism alone. However, among the many schools, Confucianism was by far the most prominent, and indeed was the dominant ideology of China ever since the Western Han Dynasty. This is an obvious and indisputable fact to all of us. As the first great educator in the history of China, Confucius did make great contributions to Chinese education. Many of his ideas still have implications for today's education. We can still see the radiance of Confucius' ideas shining through many aspects of traditional Chinese culture. His followers, particularly those Confucian scholars of the Han, Tang and Song Dynasties, also contributed their own distinctive ideas to the development of Chinese educational thought and philosophy of teaching, from the perspective of the different sub-schools of Confucianism to which they belonged. All these contributions have been recorded in the history of Chinese education.

When the imperial examinations were abolished and modern schools were set up, the old educational system was destroyed and the traditional philosophy of education no longer had a significant influence. As a result, all kinds of foreign educational ideas were introduced, first from Japan, then from Europe and America. What was introduced from Japan was in fact based on European models, especially those in use in Germany. Chinese students of education learned about Johann Friedrich Herbart and other European educational thinkers via Japan. Later, scholars also went to England, France, Italy, Belgium, and Germany to learn European ideas directly. By the 1920s American influence on Chinese education had begun to grow rapidly. John Dewey came to China and gave lectures in Beijing, Nanjing and other cities from 1919 to 1921.

During the period of American influence, the exchange of ideas took place on many levels. Works by John Dewey, William Heard Kilpatrick, Edward Lee Thorndike and other American educationists were commonly used as textbooks for teacher training programs in many Chinese universities. Leading scholars of education in China, such as Hu Shi, Tao Xingzhi, Chen Heqin, Meng Xiancheng and Liao Shizheng traveled to the United States, some of them studying at Teachers' College, Columbia, where John Dewey taught. The project method, the Dalton Plan, the Winnetka Plan and other American schemes devised to improve education were experimented with in Nanjing, Shanghai and Beijing schools. By the 1930s, proponents of John Dewey's theories held sway in China. However, it was not true that educational thought from other countries did not exert any influence at this time. For example, I myself experimented with Ovide Decroly's teaching methods, which had been introduced, from Belgium, under the direction of my tutor, Professor Li Lianfang, in Kaifeng, Henan Province.

After 1949, the Soviet educational model was adopted. I.A. Kairov's works and that of other Soviet educationists were carefully translated into Chinese; Chinese educators and educational administrators were then made to follow Soviet pedagogical precepts strictly. In essence, China became the largest laboratory for the testing and application of Soviet educational theories, and of Kairov's theories in particular. The dominance of his thinking persisted for more than ten years before coming under severe criticism in the 1960s.

Certainly the history of borrowing and of copying foreign educational models shows that China has been open to the practices of the outside world. Closer scrutiny would show that the Chinese have been sincere in their efforts to learn from foreign experiences. Nonetheless, it must be concluded that simple borrowing and imitation cannot solve the practical problems with which we are confronted in the process of educating our people. A new road must be sought for the education enterprise in China. Beginning from the 1930s, there have been a few Chinese educators working toward a modernized system of education, which sought to probe some of these problems. For example, Yan Yangchu's experiments in Dingxian County, Hebei Province, Tao Xingzhi's experiments in Nanjing and Shanghai, and those of my own tutor Li Lianfang in Kaifeng, Henan Province, had a great impact on educational reform throughout the whole country. However, they were cut short by the military invasion of Japan, and the subsequent events.

Today, we are marching along the road whose signposts read: "Face modernization; face the world; and face the future".[1] These three exhortations reflect the particular situation and the practical requirements of China today. According to this policy China will and must learn from foreign countries. In the 1980s, numerous foreign educational authors, such as Jerome Bruner, Benjamin Bloom, Jean Piaget, L.V. Zankov and U.C. Barbansky, were translated into Chinese. In keeping with the reform policy, the Central Institute of Educational Research, as well as Beijing Normal University, East China Normal University, and Northeast Normal University began to publish periodicals on foreign education.

Chinese educators desire to learn from their foreign colleagues. In the process of learning, they are careful to keep the actual situation of China and its needs uppermost in their minds. Prior to learning from foreign countries, Chinese educators must have a thorough knowledge of their own country, including its history, geography, cultural traditions, and social and economic conditions. We are trying our best to combine positive aspects of foreign educational thought and experience with the unique characteristics of Chinese education in order to meet our practical needs. Since the country is very large and the population enormous, reforming its educational system can be an extremely challenging task. Hard and creative work, careful consideration, and the investigation and initiative of many are needed. It is a long and arduous journey that we have planned, but Chinese educators have already made a start. Educational innovations and experiments at all levels in the system and in all parts of the country are going on. There is a great army of university professors, schoolteachers, administrators, and researchers forging ahead, following the signposts towards modernization, the world and the future. Chinese educators are ready to give their all to this great cause, and they hope that their colleagues from various countries will support them in their efforts.

---

[1] This was an inscription written by Deng Xiaoping for the Jingshan School in Beijing in 1983. It came to be adopted as the main policy direction for education, and was affirmed in one of the most important reform documents, *The Decision of the Central Committee of the Communist Party of China on the Reform of the Educational Structure* (Beijing: Foreign Language Press, 1985).

22

Meeting Points of Transcultural Exchange - A Chinese View

Wang Fengxian

INTRODUCTION

This chapter addresses the impact of cross-cultural exchanges between China and the West on the process of the modernization of Chinese education. The discussion is divided into two major segments. The first section will describe periods of time in Chinese history which witnessed significant shifts in educational policies and practices based upon China's exposure to modern Western science and technology, distilling the wisdom and knowledge gained from these cross-cultural exchanges between East and West. The second section of the presentation will provide an overview of important issues to be considered in the study of knowledge transfers and cross-cultural exchanges.

The modernization of Chinese society is dependent upon the modernization of the Chinese education system which is instrumental in promoting and transmitting Chinese cultural values, science and technology. The process of modernizing Chinese education has been an integral part of past and contemporary Chinese history. In the course of history, educational modernization in China has been faced with the challenge of preserving Chinese culture, rooted in Confucian moral values, and integrating new Western knowledge with the existing wealth of cultural knowledge. Chinese and foreign cultures have had to be harmonized with each other to form a new integrated cultural system.

KNOWLEDGE TRANSFER BETWEEN CHINA AND THE WEST

The following account of four significant cross-cultural exchange periods between China and the West reveals how the transfer of knowledge has modified and enriched Chinese cultural and intellectual life. In the time period from the beginning of the Opium Wars in 1840 to 1880, the Chinese isolationist policy of closing China's borders to Western influences, coupled with the emphasis on conservatism and complacency in the political regime, was abandoned in favour of a new viewpoint. This viewpoint welcomed Western technological and military sophistication as a measure to consolidate feudalism, while maintaining the learning of traditional Chinese culture as the essence of the educational experience. Since ancient times, China stressed the importance of ethical and moral education in the training of government officials and citizens alike, with the underlying aim of consolidating and maintaining the feudal political system. However, the rumbles of the gunfire in the Opium War of 1840 shattered the illusion that the ancient Chinese feudal empire was invincible. The military superiority of foreign forces awakened the Chinese people from the dream of an invincible feudal empire and made them realize the futility of combating sophisticated armaments with broadswords, spears and royalism.

The Opium War led representatives of the feudal ruling class to advocate the reform of Chinese education. The recognition that Chinese learning could not stand up against powerful Western armies led to the open border policy which encouraged the transfer of military and technological knowledge from the West to China. This open door policy in the transfer of knowledge constituted a major ideological shift in the history of Chinese education. The new Westernization movement was represented by such leaders as Zeng Guofan[1], Li Hongzhang[2] and Zhang Zhidong.[3] This ideological movement proposed an integration of "Chinese learning" (referring to traditional Chinese teachings in moral and ethical principles) with Western military technology, languages, science and economy. This Westernization movement created a new awareness and sense of urgency on the part of Chinese educators of the need to reform and modernize education.

The second significant shift in educational policy towards increasing modernization occurred as a result of China's defeat in the Sino-Japanese War from 1895 to 1915. The Chinese people attributed their defeat in this war not to limitations in the educational system, which had incorporated the teaching of Western military technology, but rather to the corruption of the feudal government. Faced with this reality, bourgeois reformists including Kang Youwei[4], Liang Qichao[5], Tan Sitong[6] and Yan Fu[7] advocated a reform of the feudal government system. At the same time, they argued for the abolition of the imperial examination system, the further modernization of schools in terms of incorporating science and technology and the preservation of traditional ethical and moral values. The reformists were led by the notion that a change in the system of government represented a necessary prerequisite for the future

---

[1] Zeng Guofan, 1811-1871, local military leader, minister appointed by the Qing emperor.

[2] Li Hongzhang, 1823-1901, local warlord, leader of the Westernization movement in the late Qing dynasty.

[3] Zhang Zhidong, 1837-1909, representative of the Westernization movement, an official in charge of education in the late Qing.

[4] Kang Youwei, 1858-1927, one of the leaders of the constitutional reform and modernization movement of 1898 in the late Qing, a thinker and educator.

[5] Liang Qichao, 1837-1929, one of the leaders of the constitutional reform and modernization movement of 1898, a thinker and educator.

[6] Tan Sitong, 1865-1898, one of the members of the constitutional reform and modernization movement of 1898.

[7] Yan Fu, 1854-1921, Chinese modern thinker, translator, and educator.

modernization of Chinese education. Bourgeois democratic revolutionaries like Sun Yat-sen[8], Zhang Taiyan[9] and Cai Yuanpei[10] proposed that the feudal emperor be overthrown and a democratic system of governance be established, while the old Confucianist values be maintained as the foundation of Chinese life. Chinese educational reform and modernization came to a halt with the unsuccessful bourgeois revolution of 1911 which had attempted to institute a new political democratic regime. The failure to further modernize Chinese education at the end of the Revolution highlighted two salient questions regarding the transfer of knowledge between China and the West: The first question was how Western knowledge can be integrated and harmonized with ancient Chinese wisdom and knowledge. The second question leads to an inquiry into the complex interrelationships between the given political system of government and the educational system in China.

The third shift in Chinese education on the path towards greater modernization can be found in the May 4th Movement (1919) which focused on the emancipation of the individual person as an educational goal, the need for increased study of the sciences and the development of democracy. As the failed bourgeois revolution of 1911 curtailed successful educational reform, the May 4th Movement, led by a group of radical intellectuals including Chen Duxiu[11], Li Dazhao[12], and Lu Xun[13], proposed to critically examine the role of Chinese education and the need for modernization. The May 4th Movement was characterized by the subordination of Chinese values and morals to the adoption of Western educational learning. The Western educational knowledge to be taught in Chinese schools included Western science, democracy, art and the development of individuality. As Lu Xun pointed out: "All previous education in China was designed to make men into machines. Only the new Western literature and art was able to set the human individual free".[14] Mao Dun said, "The discovery of man, that is the development of individuality ...became the target of the May 4th Movement".[15]

However, the new conceptualization of educational content did not win the support of the large masses of Chinese people, but was confined to prominent radical intellectuals. The majority of Chinese who had been influenced by traditional moral and ethical principles were ill-prepared for and deeply disturbed by the complete denial of ancient Chinese education. They feared that China would be assimilated by Western

---

[8] Sun Yat-sen, 1866-1925, Chinese modern democratic revolutionary, interim president of the Republic of China.

[9] Zhang Taiyan, 1869-1936, Chinese modern thinker, democratic revolutionary.

[10] Cai Yuanpei, 1868-1940, Chinese modern democratic revolutionary, educator.

[11] Chen Duxiu, 1879-1942, Chinese modern thinker and educator, advocate of the new culture movement.

[12] Li Dazhao, 1889-1927, one of the creators of the Communist Party of China, educator.

[13] Lu Xun, 1881-1936, Chinese modern writer, thinker, revolutionary, educator.

[14] See Liu Funian (ed.), *Huigu yu tansuo: Ruogan jiaoyu lilun wenti* [Retrospection and Exploration: Some Questions of Educational Theories] (Shanghai: East China Normal University Press, 1991), p. 18.

[15] Mao Dun, "Guanyu Chuangzuo," [On Creative Work] in *Mao Dun quanji* [Collected Works of Mao Dun] (Beijing: People's Literature Press, 1991), Vol. 19, p. 266.

culture and in response, called on different people to promote the preservation of traditional Chinese values. This counter-educational movement against the radical reformers of May 4th, led to the establishment of the school of national quintessence, the school of electicism and the school of Neo-Confucianism.

The fourth major shift in educational thinking in China occurred in the thirty year time period between the May 4th Movement in 1919 and the founding of the People's Republic of China. Chinese culture and education became strongly influenced by Marxism, nationalism, science and the need to gear education to the common worker, peasant and soldier. The revolutionaries who proposed this model of educational reform included Mao Zedong, Chen Duxiu, Li Dazhao, Yun Daiying[16] and Yang Xianjiang.[17]

This fourth shift in educational thinking provided new blood to the treasure house of human culture, as it distinguished itself from the three reform movements in Chinese education portrayed earlier. While the previous educational reform movements were rooted in Western capitalist thought, the new reforms used Marxism and socialism as practised in Russia after the October Revolution as the primary reference points. The transfer of educational knowledge between Western Marxist and socialist regimes and China was facilitated by the fact that the societal conditions in these countries were similar to those experienced by China. The new ideas about Chinese education were welcomed by the national psyche of the people and found tacit approval.

Second, this new Marxist/socialist educational movement was coupled with the struggle to establish a democratic system of government under the leadership of the Communist Party of China. The reforms in each of these two societal segments - education and governance structures - were marked by practical progressive thinking. At the same time, these events led to the increasing politicization of Chinese education; the combination of ideology and educational thinking became a deep-seated salient phenomenon in the people's mind which not only replaced the slogan "Science and Democracy" of the May 4th Movement, but which was difficult to erase even in the economic construction period after the Liberation of 1949.

Third, this reform movement in education was spearheaded by workers, peasants and soldiers as opposed to radical intellectual thinkers. At the same time, quite a few intellectuals were "workerized, peasantized and revolutionized".

Fourth, the new educational thinking emerged during the period of the Chinese Civil War which led to a Chinese selective open door policy which favoured interaction among China and the USSR, as well as other countries under Marxist and socialist regimes.

The modernization of education in Western developed countries has had the benefit of being refined over an extended time period of 600 years, since the

---

[16] Yun Daiying, 1895-1931, one of the leaders of the early Chinese youth movement, a theorist of education, and a revolutionary martyr.

[17] Yang Xianjiang, 1895-1931, one of the leaders of the early Chinese youth movement, a theorist of education, editor and translator who died in Japan.

Renaissance. By contrast, Chinese educational reform can only be dated back to the Opium War of 1840. Thus, Chinese educational modernization will need to make increased efforts for reform in order to catch up with the educational thinking of the West.

ISSUES FOR CONSIDERATION IN CROSS-CULTURAL EXCHANGE

In the process of cross-cultural exchange two cultures merge with each other, or replenish each other, to form a new enriched culture, which incorporates new ideas of a foreign culture with those of a given traditional native culture. The development of any culture must rely on its own nativeness and adaptive soil as its "genes"; as long as this reliance on tradition and heritage is provided, cross-cultural exchanges can take root, bloom and provide "nutrition for the native culture". In this sense, the essence of cross-cultural exchanges between native and foreign cultures does not lie in imitating but in selecting specific aspects of the foreign culture, not in duplicating the foreign culture but in reconstructing a new integrated culture, not in assimilating but in absorbing new learning.

Furthermore, there is a need to emphasize the value of the diversity of human cultures. In fact, human cultures have never evolved into a single unified whole marked by the sameness of traditions, values and learning. Human cultures will always exist in different formations, places, times and strata in independence of one another. Human cultures will develop their own permeability to new ideas, inertia in creating change, unique patterns of transmitting values to the young, all in an effort to strive towards perfection and rejuvenation.

Cross-cultural exchanges between East and West should not only be focused on the transfer of scientific, technological advancements and material goods but should also lead to a dialogue about ethical and spiritual values of the great civilizations in the East and West.

The greatest obstacle to effective cross-cultural exchange is the separation of nations by war, conflict and entrenched political ideology which is impermeable to new ideas.

In China, Deng Xiaoping has had a remarkable vision for the modernization of China using cross-cultural exchanges between China and the West. In assessing the merit of these exchanges, the following criteria are applied: Will the exchange enhance the productive capacity of the Chinese workforce? Will the exchange lead to improvements in people's material standards of living? Will the exchange strengthen Chinese national cohesion? Will the transfer of knowledge promote a peaceful co-existence among nations?

CONCLUSION

Educational institutions, including colleges and universities, constitute ideal meeting places for the exchange of ideas and information. The universities are in a unique position to function as the bridge between cultures, as they have the necessary human and material infrastructure needed for the communication, transmission, preservation and storage of knowledge. The ability of the university to fulfil its mandate as a catalyst of cross-cultural exchange will of course depend on the socio-cultural-political context of the institutions of higher learning at a given period of time.

China strives to enhance the autonomy of universities and encourages cross-cultural exchanges. Thus, China is interested in organizing cooperative study projects with other nations, developing academic communications, exchanging students, teachers, professors and visiting scholars. Students who return to China after completing their education abroad form a crucial element in the process of Chinese modernization. They are the pioneers of cross-cultural exchange. In its cultural modernization process China is guided by the policy which "lets a hundred flowers blossom and a hundred schools of thought contend". In this process, China hopes to build a new enriched culture which is rooted in the traditional wisdom of the ages and which integrates new ideas with ancient Chinese culture.

23

A Bridge Rebuilt: Artistic Interchange
between China and the West in the 1980s

Ralph Croizier

The 20th century saw the first truly global interchange, or mixing of art from widely separated cultures. From this has arisen a sharp tension between the preservation of distinct cultural identities and the homogenization of art generally along lines of Western cultural hegemony. That larger question of global cultural diversity is the background to this essay, but the specific topic is the interchange between modern Western and Chinese art particularly in the decade of the 1980s. Investigating that topic should throw some light on the main theme of this volume – the role of institutions of higher learning in the cross cultural transmission of knowledge.

Supposedly art is more individualistic, less subject to institutions and institutional control than most other branches of knowledge. This is largely myth, for in the transmission of artistic influence between China and the modern West, especially the influence of Western art in China, modern institutions, usually art schools or academies rather than universities, have been very important.

From the beginning of the 20th century Western art had a place in the new foreign-type schools and universities set up for the purpose of introducing modern Western knowledge, especially science, to a China belatedly recognizing the need for fundamental change. Initially, the motivation was more practical than aesthetic. Western art was supposedly more realistic or "scientific" because, *inter alia*, it was based on fixed point perspective, careful handling of light and shadow, and accurate depiction of objects through *chiaroscuro*. Hence, to political as well as artistic reformers, it represented the spirit and techniques which China needed to survive in the modern world, and as a consequence, its drawing and painting styles were made part of the curriculum in the new schools.[1]

On the other side of the world, Chinese artists who went to the West, or in

---

[1] This process is described in Li Shusheng (ed.), *Zhongguo meishu tongshi* (Comprehensive History of Chinese Art), vol. 10 and Kao Mei-ch'ing, "China's Response to the West in Art, 1898-1937" (Ph.D. diss., Stanford University, 1972). The new edition of Michael Sullivan's pathbreaking survey of modern Chinese art, *Chinese Art in the Twentieth Century* (Berkeley: University of California Press, 1959), appeared under the title *Art and Artists in twentieth-century China* (Berkeley: University of California Press, 1996).

some cases Japan, almost always ended up enrolled in art schools. It may have been the casual attendance at the New York Art Students' League in the years before the revolution of 1911 by Sun Yat-sen's American-based secretary, the pioneer oil painter, Li Tiefu, or it may have been the rigorous degree program at *L'Ecole des Beaux Arts* in Paris of the early twenties taken by artists like Xu Beihong, Pan Yuliang and Fang Junbi. But, both in China and the West, formal art schools, rather than informal self-education or private discipleship, provided the main channel for the transmission of artistic techniques and mastery of materials so different from those of the native Chinese tradition.

Upon returning home these pioneers of Chinese oil painting and modern sculpture remained dependent on institutions, for, in the absence of any appreciable commercial market for Western art, they had to teach at government and private art schools in the major urban centres of China. Most of the "modern" schools were independent, although a few universities established art departments, notably National Peking University and later the National Central University in Nanking.

What kinds of Western art took root, however shallow, in China during the early part of this century? First, since the initial attraction of Western art was its allegedly realistic character, there was a strong strain of classicism or academic realism under the leadership of the Paris trained Xu Beihong. His attempts to translate the grand genre of Western history painting, already passé for over half a century in Europe, into a Chinese idiom, produced results which are best described as interesting in a pioneering cross-cultural context. Closely behind Xu and the other stylistic conservatives, came Chinese artists who were influenced by currents of 20th century European modernism – impressionism, post-impressionism, surrealism. They appealed to the demand for the newest and most modern from the West in a China desperate to modernize. Whether modernism in the arts equates with or leads to modernity in society and politics is, of course, another question. In many ways, the post-impressionists of pre-war Shanghai seem to have had the horse and the cart reversed.

The third type of Western artistic influence lay between or actually apart from the stylistic dispute between classicists and modernists. This influence informed China's politically committed "left-wing art movement", whose preferred technique was the raw, direct woodcut, which many European artists had used during troubled, war-torn times. The movement flourished initially in pre-war Shanghai, and was appropriated to the Communist Party cause in Yan'an during the Sino-Japanese War. Starting with strong modernist influences, especially from German expressionism, it was stylistically sanitized and adapted to Party line politics by 1949.

In this whole period, from before 1911 to mid-century, art was more than just pictures or decoration. It was a bridge for importing the ideas, values, and even institutions of Western culture. The Western style artists did not take over China. They remained vastly outnumbered by traditional style painters, and even among the foreign trained, many returned to the Chinese brush and ink. To a considerable extent, however, Western-style artists and the Western influenced intelligentsia set the agenda for change, both in art and in its wider social context. The new influences came from many sources – "schools" as diverse as classicism and expressionism, places as remote as Paris and Tokyo – but they all provided stimuli for change, often bewildering and confusing stimuli.

After 1949 the confusion stopped, at least on the surface. The Chinese Communist Party knew what it wanted from artists (socially and politically useful art), and knew what it did not want in art – any of the manifestations of the "bourgeois formalism" that from impressionism on dominated art in the "decadent West".

This meant that Soviet Socialist realism, in some ways compatible with the strain of French academic conservatism represented by Xu Beihong and his students, became the only approved source of foreign influence. There remained enormous tension between this brand of foreign realism and the native Chinese tradition of *guohua* (national painting) but, so long as Maoist orthodoxy prevailed, for thirty years all other Western influences were excluded.[2] This new isolationism reached its peak in the Cultural Revolution but then, in accordance with the ancient Daoist maxim of things reversing once an extreme is reached, China suddenly opened up in the late 1970s. Art once again became a bridge for cultural connections between East and West.

Unlike earlier periods when East Asian art had a considerable impact on Europe, the traffic flow across this artistic bridge has been mainly West to East in the 20th century. Recently, signs of more reciprocal exchanges have appeared, but most of this counter movement, Chinese art and especially Chinese artists going to Europe and America, is a phenomenon of the late 1990s. Certainly it is a significant development in the world of art when there are more Chinese artists (or artists of Chinese descent) in the 1999 Venice Biennale than those from any other country.[3] Still, before jumping to the conclusion that the West to East flow has been reversed or at least balanced, one should note that all these new art world celebrities work in modern or postmodern styles of Western origin. Moreover, this "internationalization of Chinese Art" is too recent a phenomenon for any confident assessment of its long term significance. It may be the beginning of a historic shift away from Western dominance towards a truly global postmodern art, or it may be just a market driven Western appropriation of the exotic "other".[4] It is too soon to tell about the 1990s. The eighties, however, now

[2] In the West, scholarly discussion of Chinese art in the Maoist period is rare. Ellen Johnston Laing, *The Winking Owl, Art in the People's Republic of China* (Berkeley: University of California Press, 1988), was the first substantial scholarly work. Julia Andrews, *Painters and Politics in the People's Republic of China, 1949-1979* (Berkeley: University of California Press, 1993) goes into much more detail on the connections between art and politics. Jerome Silbergeld, *Contradictions: Li Huasheng, Artistic Life and Cultural Politics in Socialist China* (Seattle: University of Washington Press, 1993) explores somewhat similar issues at the provincial level in Sichuan province. More general coverage is found in Michael Sullivan, *Art and Artists in twentieth-century China* (Berkeley: University of California Press, 1996). Chinese scholarship has been restrained by personal and political considerations. Zhang Shaoxia and Li Xiaoshan, *Zhongguo xiandai huihua shi* [*A History of Modern Chinese Painting*] (Nanjing: *Jiangsu meishu chuban she*, 1986) was a bold but restricted attempt to reappraise that period.

[3] Francesca dal Lago and Monica Dematté, "Chinese Art or the Venice Biennale" 1 and 2, in John Clark (ed.), *Chinese Art at the End of the Millennium*, Beijing: Chinese-art.com, 2000.

[4] In addition to the collection of essays from the internet site Chinese.art.com edited by John Clark, see

emerge quite clearly as another significant turning point in China's relations with the West and with Western art. It was that decade, beginning with the first post-Mao relaxation of political restraints in 1979 and ending with the Tiananmen crisis of 1989, that saw the East-West bridge in art rebuilt and this chapter concentrates on that period.

The outburst of new artistic activity in China during the 1980s has to be seen in relation to the sweeping political, economic, and social changes of "the reform decade". Two main factors are particularly relevant: one, the relaxation of Party ideological controls in order to enlist the intellectuals' active participation in Deng's modernization program; two, the "open country" policy aimed at hastening economic modernization through access to foreign capital, markets, and especially technology.

These two factors, internal liberalization and opening to external influences, were necessary but not sufficient causes for the remarkably rapid changes in art and the ready acceptance of Western influence. Much of the force behind that "new art tide" came from pent up demand for the new and foreign after thirty years of virtual isolation – a desire by older artists to rejoin the world, a stronger compulsion among younger artists to, in the words of a slogan current in the late eighties, "go to the world". This going out also meant welcoming in long proscribed currents of modern Western art.

Without attempting a systematic history of these eventful years, it may help to provide a rough chronological sketch. There were three main periods from the death of Mao to the spring of 1989, four if we include the aftermath of Tiananmen. First, in the late 1970s there was a revival of increasingly depoliticized traditional Chinese art, the rehabilitation of established masters persecuted during the Cultural Revolution, and cautious experimentation with the tamer forms of Western modernism. This cautious and controlled liberalization was overtaken by the assertive experimentation with hitherto banned Western styles by younger, unofficial artists such as the "Star Group" (*Xingxing*) during the "democracy movement" around 1979. In a sense they opened a gate to modern Western influences which, despite attempts by Party conservatives in the early 1980s to screen out "spiritual pollution", could not be closed again.

After 1985, the "new art tide" overwhelmed earlier Party strictures against entering "the three forbidden zones": abstraction, nudity, and socially critical art. Actually the young artists of China's self-proclaimed "avant-garde" circumvented the last restriction rather than directly confronting the Party on political grounds. Their modernist styles, abstract or surrealist, were indeed critical of the status quo but they were obscure enough that censors could not be sure exactly what was being said and, with the erosion of previous ideological certainties under the bombardment of Western cultural influences and economic reforms, they lacked the confidence to reimpose old restrictions. Aspects of Western modernism and post-modernism previously unimaginable in China – abstract painting, minimalist sculpture, full blown nudity, even conceptual and performance art – cropped up from Peking to Xiamen.

All this culminated in the first "Exhibition of Modern Art" opening at the

Gao Minglu (ed.), *Inside Out New Chinese Art* (New York: Asia Society, 1999) and, for the early nineties, Gao Minglu, *China's New Art Post-1989* (Hong Kong: Hanart, 1993).

National Gallery in Peking in January 1989. It brought together young artists and representative new works from all over China. It was closed the same day by the shot that was heard around Peking when the police objected to a young woman artist firing two pistol shots into her construction, "Dialogue", because "only then was it completed". The attendant publicity, the reopening and reclosing of the exhibition, made it a national event, and indeed, through the opening of China to foreign news media an international event. Six months later, political events brought an end to the reform decade and a remarkably open, creative, and chaotic era in the arts.

   The violent closure of the "reform decade" ended one period in the development of a new, Western-influenced Chinese art but did not erase the influence of what China had absorbed in that decade and would soon start to re-export to the West. But here the focus is on the seminal eighties and, because cross cultural influence is the theme of this volume, I will treat the developments between 1979 and 1989 according to sources or channels for transmitting Western influence rather than by artists or movements.

   The first channel of Western influence would be foreign visitors. They came in several categories directly relevant to art, although all foreign contact more or less influenced the climate in which the new art developed. There were the "China scholars" from the West, eager for first hand contact with the people and culture they had studied from an enforced distance for over a generation. Not many of them were interested in contemporary Chinese art and artists, but there were some exceptions. At the beginning of the reform era, the Chinese government invited Jerome Cohen, Harvard University specialist in commercial law to advise on the establishment of a legal system for doing international business. He soon established a Peking office for conducting Sino-American trade. His wife, Joan Cohen, was an art historian. At the centre of things in Peking she established personal contacts with younger, unofficial Chinese artists such as the Star group, encouraging, chronicling and supporting their experimentations with Western styles. She also provided them with Western contacts, (later she would introduce their works to New York), and with sources for modern Western art: books, reproduction volumes, art magazines. Through her writings – first in American art magazines and Hong Kong newspapers, then in her book *The New Chinese Painting, 1949-1986* – she introduced these artists to the West.[5] She was far and away the most important foreigner for the birth of the new, Western-influenced movement in Chinese art.

   But there were other foreign scholars too. Michael Sullivan visited China several times in the eighties renewing contacts with old artist friends from his days as British Cultural Attaché in Chungking during World War Two, and also meeting and reporting on some of the younger artists.[6] From Canada at least one other intellectual-cum-art historian, Ralph Croizier, visited Chinese art academies regularly

---

[5] Joan Lebold Cohen, *The New Chinese Painting, 1949-1986* (New York: Harry N. Abrams, 1987).

[6] At the beginning of the decade, the new art scene was discussed by Michael Sullivan, "Paint with a New Brush: Art in Post Mao China", in *China Briefing, 1980* (Boulder, Co.: Westview Press, 1989).

during the decade, sharing Western art books, slides, magazines, and meeting some of the important artists of the new generation.[7]

Probably such sources of Western interest and information were less important, certainly less inspiring, to Chinese artists than the visits of big name Western artists in the early and mid-eighties, figures like Robert Rauschenberg, George Segal, and the Canadian neo-realist Alex Colville. Even when they did not exhibit in China, they had both direct and indirect influence. So did modern artists of Chinese descent – Liu Guosong, who had pioneered semi-abstract Chinese landscape painting in Taiwan during the 1960s, and continues a modernist Chinese-Western synthesis while living in Hong Kong; Zao Wouki (Zhao Wuji), Paris-based abstract expressionist since the late 1940s, who has been for the new Western oriented generation, an inspiring example of a Chinese artist who has "made it" in the West in a Western medium.

And finally, for person-to-person sources of Western influence, there were the Western art students who started to attend schools in China at the end of the 1970s. There had been some foreign students at the Central Academy of Fine Arts before 1966 (pre-Cultural Revolution), but apparently no Americans or West Europeans. By 1978 or 1979, some Western students were being admitted to study Chinese art and art history at the two nationally established art academies – the Central Academy in Peking and the Zhejiang Academy in Hangzhou. As relations opened with the West, and the foreign exchange contribution of foreign students became more appreciated by academic institutions, which were increasingly dependent on self-financing, both these schools built residences for foreign students, opened "short-term" (usually summer) classes for foreigners, and encouraged more to pursue long-term study, even degree programs, in China. Peking and Hangzhou remained the most important centres for this artist-to-artist, student-to-student contact, but by the mid eighties provincial art academies were also trying to cash in on the foreign student trade. Unfortunately, by the late eighties, even before the Tiananmen Incident, rising costs in China combined with the diminishing novelty of studying in China had led to a decline in the number of foreign students, especially Americans.

The importance of this foreign student generation has yet to be assessed, but I think they formed one of the most important supports of that rebuilt bridge, for they introduced young Chinese to Western art, values, ways of thinking, and lifestyles, while bringing back something of Chinese art to the West. I will only cite one example of the exchange of people, ideas, and art. In the early eighties, Julia Andrews, art history graduate student from the University of California, Berkeley, was one of the first resident foreign students at the Central Academy. There she met the oil painting student, Han Xin, whom she subsequently married, and through him many of the important artists and art theorists of the new generation. In her own words, they "lured

---

[7] His contemporary view of the "new art tide" by the late 1980s is given in Ralph Croizier, "'Going to the World': Art and Culture on the Cosmopolitan Tide", in *China Briefing, 1989* (Boulder, Co.: Westview Press, 1989). The most comprehensive study of that period, by an insider, is Gao Minglu, *China's New Art Post-1989*, 1993; and Gao Minglu, *Inside Out New Chinese Art*, 1999.

me out of the Ming dynasty". The results of this have been beneficial to Western scholarship on modern Chinese art. Her book, *Painters and Politics in the People's Republic of China, 1949-1979*, appeared in 1993.[8] They have also been beneficial to art in the West where Han Xin has translated his strong academic training in Peking into a bold expressionistic examination of contemporary America. Finally, through her continued contact with artists and art critics in Peking, this example of unintended consequences in bringing together young Americans and Chinese has been beneficial to the entire modernist movement in Chinese art.

Not all contacts have been person-to-person. Art itself can speak directly to the receptive artist, perhaps most powerfully when the artist is confronted with original works of art. Such opportunities have always been rare for Chinese artists in China, but in the early 1980s some started to appear. A milestone, and a sensation at the time, was the 1982 exhibition of American art from the Boston Museum, in Peking and Shanghai. Originally, Chinese authorities tried to exclude modern abstract paintings, but capitulated to the Museum's insistence that it was either the complete exhibition or nothing. Young artists flocked to see the Pollocks and De Koonings. By the end of the eighties smaller scale exhibitions of most kinds of modern or contemporary Western art were almost commonplace.

All these channels of influence ran in one direction, from West to East. But before long, Chinese artists were joining the flood of students and more mature intellectuals going to the West for advanced study. At first most were expected to return home but by the end of the decade, especially among artists, returnees were the exception rather than the rule. The numbers can only be guessed at. Professor Zheng Shengtian, Director of an organization of Chinese artists in North America, "The International Institute for the Arts", estimates that including students as well as established artists, the number in North America might reach one thousand. His organization knows of almost five hundred practising Chinese artists in the United States and Canada. There are many more in Europe, especially France.

The development of these emigré artists outside of China is a paper, or a book, by itself. Here we are more concerned with their influence back in China, either as returnees or occasional visitors. It is a sad or ironic comment on Deng Xiaoping's modernization program that the artists who most benefitted from the relaxation of ideological control on the arts and the opening to the West – Yuan Yunsheng, Chen Danqing, Gu Wenda, Xu Bing and many others – have all been too politically alienated to further contribute to the development of modern art in China by returning home. The Shanghai painter, Chen Yifei, enjoying the patronage of the American oil magnate and New York gallery owner, Arnold Hammer, became one kind of influence by showing how commercially acceptable a technically competent and well connected Chinese realist could become by pandering to American middlebrow tastes for oriental exotica. He now maintains expensive apartments in Shanghai and New York – an international success story and a financial, though not stylistic, inspiration to many struggling young

---

[8] Julia Andrews, *Painters and Politics in the People's Republic of China, 1949-1979* (Berkeley: University of California Press, 1993).

Chinese artists.

The case I just mentioned, Chen Yifei, has one kind of institutional connection, Aramco Oil (Hammer's company), but that is not the kind of academic institution which the conference focused upon.[9] How important have university and art school connections been in facilitating this flow of artistic influences and talent between China and the West? We have touched on the leading art academies in China, separate institutions not connected with universities, and their pivotal role as centres for the new ferment in Chinese art and as a meeting place for Chinese and foreigners. The picture is not quite so clear on the other side of the world. Many Chinese artists have come to Western art schools or art departments within universities as visiting artists, if they are well known and well connected (usually through Western scholars visiting China), and as art students, if they are younger and unknown. Some of the visiting artists have stayed several years at a host institution, acclimatizing themselves to North American culture and the North American art world before setting themselves up as more or less successful independent artists. Yuan Yunsheng, leaving China for Harvard University after his nude murals in the new Peking airport were criticized, would be one example.

In this way North American universities, especially those with East Asia programs, have been important institutional links. Sometimes these have been regularized institution to institution exchanges between Chinese and North American schools usually funded from the American side by the university, a private foundation, or the government. Many more, especially younger artists and students, have found a number of ingenious financial solutions to become "self-paying" guests abroad.

In short, without the linkages, both personal and institutional, between North American and Chinese educational institutions, many Chinese artists still would have found their way to the West, inspired in varying degrees by artistic quest, cultural curiosity, financial gain, and alienation from their homeland. Some of the most interesting and potentially influential artists would not have reached the other shore if all these forces had not been at work. One thinks, for example, of the roles of Professor Bruce Parsons of York University in Ontario, Canada, and Peter Sells of the University of California at Berkeley in the United States, in bringing the endlessly innovative and controversial painter and performance artist, Gu Wenda, from the Zhejiang Academy of Fine Arts to Toronto, and then California.

So in the new era of Sino-Western artistic interflow, just as in the earlier pre-revolutionary period, educational institutions have been important, perhaps essential. They continue to be important in the nineties but less so as market forces (galleries, dealers, international exhibitions) have been the main propellant for Chinese artists' emergence on the world stage.

It probably is wise to forego any definitive judgement on the ultimate significance of this extraordinary period when, after thirty years of separation, China

---

[9] Nevertheless, ARCO has been instrumental in sponsoring two important exhibitions of new Chinese art at the Pacific Asia Museum in Pasadena, California. There are catalogues for both shows. *Beyond the Open Door* (Pacific Asia Museum, 1987) and *'I Don't Want to Play Cards with Cezanne'*, 1991. Both are well illustrated with informative essays.

reopened to the West and Western art. The legacy of the eighties is still being worked out in China and as part of a new global postmodern art. In some ways traffic on the bridge, its lanes widened by internet communication and global economics, is heavier than ever. But the initial excitement of its reopening, when a new generation of Chinese artists rediscovered modern art and reinvented modern Chinese art, is not likely to be matched again. The eighties were a special time.

24

The Concept of General Education
in Chinese Higher Education

Wang Yongquan
Li Manli

An early use of the term "general education" as applied to higher education appears in an 1829 article by A. S. Packard of Bowdoin College. In this article, Packard defends the common elements of the undergraduate curriculum in America (the classical, literary and scientific), and in particular, he defends the classical element, deeming it "general because of the scope of its subjects".[1] Since Packard's time, the concept of general education has developed. Different people have assigned different definitions to it, some of which even contradict each other.

In the past many sustained efforts have been made to develop a widely accepted definition of general education. In the 1930s, several scholarly groups which had a wide influence and were led by university presidents or higher education researchers made efforts to put forward a new definition of general education which could be widely recognized. Three different attempts, each specially organized, failed to achieve common ground.[2] In order to gain a good grasp of all of the connotations associated with the concept of general education, we have collected about 50 different articles and books, starting from the early 19th century, which might be seen as representative works on the subject of general education, and which contain the views of many distinguished scholars on the subject. For example, among them Arthur Levine suggests that "general education is the breadth component of the undergraduate curriculum, defined on an institution-wide or college-wide basis. It usually involves study in several subject areas and frequently seeks to provide a common undergraduate experience for all students at a particular institution".[3] He also says, "Liberal education is perhaps the most commonly used synonym for general education".[4] The "Harvard Redbook" of 1945 gave the following definition: "General education.... is used to

---

[1] See Russell Brown Thomas, *The Search for Common Learning: General Education, 1800-1960* (New York: McGraw-Hill, 1962), p. 13.

[2] L.T. Benezet, *General Education in the Progressive College* (New York: Arno Press and The New York Times, 1970), pp. 22-24.

[3] A. Levine, *Handbook on Undergraduate Curriculum* (San Francisco: Jossey-Bass, 1978), p. 525.

[4] *Ibid.* p. 528.

indicate that part of a student's whole education which looks first of all to his life as a responsible human being and citizen".[5]

In this chapter, we do not intend to offer a critique of these definitions. Rather, for the sake of stimulating discussion, we will use Max Weber's technique of the ideal type, and examine the nature, purpose and content of the concept, and so construct a tentative set of connotations of the term general education.[6] To use simple terms, and begin from the nature of the concept, it refers to one aspect of higher education, the non-specialist or non-professional aspect of education to which every university student needs to be exposed. The purpose of general education is to nurture in students a willingness to take active part in the life of society, to have a sense of social responsibility, and to become fully developed members of society and citizens of the country. The content of general education is very broad, non-professional and non-instrumental – a kind of foundation in terms of knowledge, skill and attitude.

This article will discuss the development of undergraduate general education in modern China, especially since the founding of the People's Republic of China, as well as problems associated with this development. Chinese social conditions, and the influence of Western culture and education, will serve as a backdrop for the discussion.

GENERAL EDUCATION IN CHINESE UNIVERSITIES AND COLLEGES IN DIFFERENT PERIODS OF HISTORY

Institutions of higher learning in China date back to Pi Yong and Pan Gong in the Western Zhou Dynasty which lasted from 1112 BCE to 771 BCE.[7] From this time up to the 19th century, Chinese higher education received little in the way of foreign influence, and at times denied such influence. Thus, only in the last century, has the Western philosophy and practice of liberal education become familiar to Chinese higher education circles.

The Period before the Revolution of 1911

Modern higher education in China started in the second half of the 19th century. At that time, the invasion of several world powers reduced China to a semi-colonial state. The powerful fleets and weapons of the colonizers created an interest among the Chinese in the knowledge system which produced such technology. The Chinese became curious about Western languages and literature, industry and commerce, finance and economics, law, military affairs, and education. Western style universities emerged in

---

[5] *Ibid.*, p. 603.
[6] Li Manli, *Tongshi Jiaoyu – Yizhong Daxue Jiaoyuguan* (General Education – A Viewpoint on University Education) (Beijing: Qinghua Daxue Chubanshe, 1999). pp. 10-17.
[7] See Zhang Ruifan, "Piyong and Pangong", in *Shanghai gaojiao yanjiu* (*Higher Education Research in Shanghai*), Vol. 2 (1985), pp. 107-114.

China as a result of these various interests. In 1898, the Metropolitan University, present-day Peking University, was the first such university to be set up by the central government. Around this time, Western churches in China also set up missionary universities. Many international exchanges of an educational nature were also conducted. Students were sent abroad, and professors from the West were invited to teach in China.

In 1902, the government of the Qing Dynasty promulgated the first regulations on university education in modern China – *The Regulations of the Metropolitan University made by Imperial Order*.[8] The regulations stated the aim of "setting the correct directions for students' development and training all-round persons",[9] on the basis of which, in 1906, more detailed aims were formulated. These were loyalty to the emperor, worship of Confucius, and the advocacy of patriotism, martialism, and pragmatism.[10] On the training of all-round persons, Zhang Baixi and others claimed in the 1903 *Essentials of the University Regulations* that whatever the students did later in life, whether they engaged in government work, agriculture, industry, or business, they should "love their country and be able to establish themselves".[11] They noted that these precepts were in accordance with Chinese educational tradition, and also based on the same principles in foreign schools where "moral education is allotted special attention (along with) intellectual and physical education".[12]

In China, the precept of an education producing well-rounded individuals was interpreted as liberal education or general education. There was, however, a difference between the Western and Chinese forms. *The University Regulations* issued by the government in 1903 stipulated that the university should consist of eight schools of learning – economics, law, literature, medicine, natural sciences, agriculture, industry, and business, and that each school should contain several departments. The *University Regulations* set the curriculum for each department. Each department taught specialized courses relating to the broader field of the school to which it was attached. Students did not take related courses in other departments, nor were they required by their university or school to take other non-departmental courses in common. The only exception was with respect to instruction of foreign languages, which accounted for twenty five per cent of overall teaching hours in schools of economics, business and literature.

By contrast, preparatory school regulations required that students had to study ethics, Chinese, a foreign language, physical education and other general education subjects such as history, geography, mathematics, physics, and chemistry before entering university. Even at the preparatory level, however, students were divided into

---

[8] See Shu Xincheng (ed.), *Zhongguo jindai jiaoyushi ziliao* (Reference Material on Modern Education History in China) (Beijing: People's Education Press, 1961), Vol. 2, pp. 549-566.

[9] *Ibid.*, p. 549.

[10] See Zhou Bangdao, *The First China Education Year Book* (Shanghai: Kaiming Book Co. Ltd., 1934), Part I, p. 1.

[11] Shu Xincheng, *Reference Material on Modern Educational History*, 1961, Vol. 1, p. 199.

[12] *Ibid.*, p. 10.

three groups according to the university departments they planned to enter. These divisions narrowed the scope of offerings depending on the students' future plans.

The differences between Chinese and Western forms of general education at this time are related to the fact that China was ultimately more influenced by Japan's higher education system than by the British and American systems. Japan's system was in essence a hybrid, which took much from Western notions of education, but emphasized specialization.

From 1911 to 1949

After the overthrow of imperial rule in 1911, the Ministry of Education declared in 1912 that the aim of education was to "emphasize moral education, supported by realistic education and military instruction"; it specified that the development of "moral integrity should be accompanied by aesthetic education".[13] This aim was formulated under the supervision of the well-known educationist, Cai Yuanpei, Minister of Education at the time. Cai Yuanpei pointed out that among the five aims put forward by the Qing government in 1906, loyalty to the emperor conflicted with the new republican system, and worship of Confucius violated the freedom of belief, therefore they should be abolished.

During frequent study tours in Germany, France and other Western nations, Cai came to be deeply influenced by Western educational philosophy. More than any other Chinese educationist, he transferred the Western ideal of liberal education to China. When he became president of Peking University, he stressed the development of individuality, advocated academic freedom along with interdisciplinary communication between liberal arts and sciences, and implemented the first elective and credit systems.

Under Cai's influence, Peking University prescribed common courses for undergraduate freshmen which included philosophy, history, science, sociology, and first and second foreign languages. These were to constitute fifty per cent of a freshman's credits. Five additional groups of courses with different emphases were offered as electives. Courses within these groups were meant to prepare students for their sophomore studies in particular departments. From their sophomore year onwards, students would take the required courses in their departments; they could, however, take related courses in other departments, and they continued to take first and second foreign language courses. Certainly, Cai's model, which was much copied by other universities in China, demonstrates a much greater emphasis on general education than had previously been the case in China.

From the 1920s onward, a different scheme than that of Cai Yuanpei prevailed. The emphasis shifted to practical and specialized courses because of the need to develop industry, and to conduct a war of resistance against the Japanese

---

[13] Shu Xincheng, *Reference Material on Modern Chinese Education History*, 1961, Vol. 1, p. 226.

invaders. In 1934, the government proposed that university education must focus on practical science, and it must "train students to master specialized knowledge and skills".[14] Thus, the development of liberal arts was restricted, and student funding in the liberal arts suffered. Many scholars raised objections about this turn of affairs. Critics, such as Mei Yiqi, President of Southwest Associated University at the time, maintained that specialized personnel without general education training could not meet the needs of society; even in training engineers, it was argued, "the most valuable training is general engineering training".[15] In 1938, the Ministry of Education, in response to such criticism, stipulated that freshmen should focus on basic courses, and did not have to belong to any specific department. In 1944, the Ministry's guidelines for undergraduate education were further altered to resemble the American system, where credits earned from general education courses constituted over forty per cent of the total required for graduation.

From 1949 through the Cultural Revolution

With the establishment of the People's Republic of China in 1949, higher education developed at an unprecedented pace. In 1952 and 1953, the Soviet Union's higher education system became the model for Chinese higher education. Accordingly, institutions of higher learning were restructured. In keeping with the Soviet model, and in response to rapid industrial growth, the restructuring required increased numbers of industrial personnel, more teacher training, the establishment of independent professional colleges, and the consolidation of universities.[16] After the restructuring, universities became institutions dedicated solely to the teaching of the humanities, the natural sciences and some of the social sciences. Departments within the universities became more specialized; physics, for example, was subdivided into numerous categories such as theoretical physics, solid state physics, and optics, with a different teaching plan for each. Enrolment, teaching and job assignments were all based on individual specialties, thus entrenching strict divisions within fields.

During this period of restructuring, the concept of liberal education was deemed impractical and obscure. There were the obvious and pressing demands of a growing industrial society, which liberal education did not seem to address. The restructured version of higher education was instituted to meet these demands.

When specialized education failed to meet all the requirements placed on it, increasing specialization was the response. Thus the number of specialties increased from 215 to 627 between 1953 and 1962. In 1963, the Ministry of Education intervened. It issued an official list of general specialties in universities and colleges,

---

[14] Zhou Bangdao, *The First China Education Yearbook*, 1934.

[15] Xiong Mingan, "Tentative Remarks on Mei Yiqi's Philosophy of Education", in *Shanghai gaojiao yanjiu*, No. 4, 1986, pp. 104-106.

[16] "Reform in Institutions of Higher Education Should Develop Steadily", *Renmin ribao (People's Daily)* Editorial, January 23, 1953.

which reduced the number of specialties to 432. This regulatory measure was not fully followed through however.

It should be noted that although higher education became increasingly specialized after 1949, there was a common curriculum. Instruction in Marxist theory, a foreign language and physical education were prescribed for all students; these three components constituted twenty to twenty-five per cent of the required hours for graduation. However, students in the humanities could not take courses in the sciences, nor could science students study humanities.

From 1976 to the Present Situation

After the Cultural Revolution a number of insights were gleaned with respect to education. Generally speaking, there had been too much emphasis on specialized education, specializations were overly narrow, and the organization of the curriculum was far too specialized. The training which students received could not enable them to adapt well to the rapidly changes needs of society, and also restricted their development as individuals.

In recognition of these considerations, the government made a number of reforms. It reduced the number of specializations and broadened their content. History, social sciences, natural sciences, aesthetics and ethics were added as electives to the core curriculum. Instead of twenty to twenty-five per cent, thirty per cent of an undergraduate's curriculum is now comprised of non-specialist courses. The core curriculum still includes instruction in Marxist theory, a foreign language, and physical education. However, students in the humanities are now encouraged to take courses in non-humanities areas, and students in mathematics and sciences are encouraged to study humanities. The precepts of general education are once again being taken seriously.[17]

Since the 1980s, China has been opening up to the outside world, and a significant mark of this new openness can be found in the active exchanges occurring in education. Numerous Chinese scholars have been visiting the West; experts in different fields have been invited to work and teach in China. It can be said that international academic exchange activities are flourishing. Once again, Western culture and education are considered sources of interest and influence in Chinese higher education circles.

---

[17] See for example the following articles: Xia Yulong, "Integration of Disciplines and General Education", in *Jiaoyu yanjiu* (*Educational Research*), No. 5, 1981, pp. 34-39; Wu Yanfu, "On the Issue of Students of Liberal Arts Studying Natural Sciences", in *Educational Research*, No. 8, 1981, pp. 48-52; Cai Keyong, "Reflections on General Education and Specialized Education", in *Gaodeng jiaoyu yanjiu* (*Higher Education Research*), No. 1, 1987, pp. 14-16; Wen Fuxiang, "Aims of Higher Engineering Education and Humanities and Social Sciences", in *Gaodeng jiaoyu xuebao* (*Journal of Higher Education*), No. 4, 1990, pp. 25-28; Li Hanru, "Reconsideration of Liberal Education and Specialized Education", in *Gaodeng gongcheng jiaoyu* (*Higher Engineering Education*), No. 1, 1990, pp. 35-38; Gu Yongcai, "Tentative Inquiry on the Curriculum of General Education", in *Nankai jiaoyu luntan* (*Nankai Education Forum*), No. 3, 1991, pp. 8-11.

In the early 1990s some imbalances still existed in aspects of higher education, the most important being the tendency to a very narrow definition of specializations, with overly narrow requirements, and a weak basis in foundation knowledge. This was addressed by broadening specializations, reducing the degree of concentration and strengthening the foundation. The particular concern that was addressed was the weakness in education in the humanities. Some universities took the initiative of providing students with more opportunities for studying the humanities as part of their reforms in teaching and learning. Two different types of keynote universities made an early start in these efforts. One type was that of comprehensive universities with a long history, and excellent traditions in the humanities. The other type was that of universities of science and technology, which were relatively weaker in the humanities. These two types of universities made experimental efforts which had the effect of stimulating the implementation of general education widely among higher institutions.

In September of 1995, national education agencies fully affirmed the educational reform ideas of these higher institutions, and actively promoted a campaign of "education for cultural quality" in universities.[18] The Ministry of Education selected 50 higher institutions as experimental sites for this work, calling on them to provide courses in the humanities, history, philosophy, fine arts and sciences, which were much broader in scope than those of the past. The purpose was to stimulate students' interest in aesthetics, raise their cultural level and the quality of their general understanding of the humanities and sciences. Over a period of three years and more, the work done at these experimental sites produced excellent results. This particular reform in higher institutions has aroused an enthusiastic response and been widely appreciated. The Ministry of Education has published a document, entitled "Some views on how to strengthen education in cultural quality for university students", in order to further develop this project. It has also established a national committee on education in cultural quality to guide the project. It has further decided to establish some bases in ordinary universities throughout the country which will be responsible for education in cultural quality. In order to realize this aim, there will be a campaign for upgrading the cultural quality of students, and teaching staff, as well as the cultural standards of universities. At the present time, many universities see this project, and the reforms in teaching and curriculum it calls for, as an area of priority in terms of their human and material resources.

SOME ISSUES CONCERNING GENERAL EDUCATION IN CHINA

When educational experiences from foreign countries are assimilated to help develop

---

[18] "Education for cultural quality" became an important concept which was widely debated in the late 1980s and early 1990s in China. According to Vice Minister of Education, Zhou Yuanqing's explanation, its main purpose was to deal with the inadequacies of higher education, particularly the evident weaknesses of humanities education. We see it as very close to the concept of general education.

one's own educational system, adaptation of these experiences takes place. This adaptation may not be conscious, but it seems inevitable. A natural process of integration, not duplication, will occur, because each country's needs and conditions are different. Even if duplication is the goal, some transformation of the replicated elements will occur. It can be predicted, therefore, that general education cannot and will not be the same in China as it is in the West. Just as Chinese general education, despite certain attempts, did not mirror that of the West in the first part of this century, it will not mirror that of the West in the present period. There is a tendency at the present time to exaggerate the usefulness of Western educational models. This must be watched, remembering that the formulation of a Chinese model of modern education is the goal.

The method for assimilating Western educational experience to a large extent involves tapping the understanding of exchange students. Exchange students are the main source of knowledge about Western education systems and academic subjects. It should be noted, however, that the majority of Chinese scholars visiting the West evaluate higher education based on their own academic activities abroad. They do not undertake major historical or comprehensive studies of the education which they receive. Their views are necessarily partial, and must be seen as such.

The tendency to emphasize specialized education has always existed in modern higher education in China, even though the express aim of education has most often been the training of well-rounded individuals. In pre-modern China, higher education emphasized the teaching of an extensive range of subjects and the training of various abilities. Though different in specific requirements, pre-modern higher education in China was in harmony with the spirit of Western liberal education. This being the case, why was there a turning away from a so-called liberal style education towards specialized education? The simple answer is in order to save the country from colonization and invasion. At the end of the Qing Dynasty, China had to develop industrial and military capabilities to match and counteract the military might of its colonizers. Similarly, in the 1930s and 1940s, China had to resist the forces of the Japanese invasion. After the founding of the People's Republic of China, China needed to effect rapid and massive industrialization in order to ensure its survival as an independent and economically viable socialist nation.

In relation to this last point, an emphasis on specialized education dovetailed with China's system of a planned state-run economy and bureaucracy. Students were enrolled in programs and assigned jobs on the basis of identifiable needs in the state-run system. Because employment was guaranteed, and there was no market for trained personnel, there was no need to prepare for changes in market demands. Students were expected to exit the education system fully trained for a specific job, and to be autonomous in that job. Given these constraints, specialized education was crucial.

In recent years, China has entered a period of major system reforms in terms of the economy and management, with a socialist market economy being gradually established, and an employment market emerging. Also in the global context the special feature of knowledge development lies in the fact that it does not emphasize the advancement of discrete disciplines, but rather new developments emerge on the basis of the integration of many disciplines and the interaction among them. Universities around the world are responding to the demands of this situation, and Chinese universities cannot be an exception to this. Following the overall changes in the nation's situation, higher education is experiencing profound reforms and transitions, and it is clear that general education will be given importance once again and be further developed.

How are we to estimate the situation of general education in Chinese universities at present, and the problems which it faces? On the one hand, all higher institutions now give importance to implementing general education, and virtually all have developed plans or guidelines for this purpose. Examples of these guidelines include an increase in humanities, fine arts and social science courses, plans to engineer the reading of great books, ideas on the nurturing of a campus culture with a broad and non-specialist focus.[19] All of these projects will have a very positive influence in terms of broadening students' knowledge and widening their horizons. On the other hand, however, these measures really only touch upon superficial aspects of general education and do not penetrate to the essence of the idea of general education. They have not been integrated into the overall process of higher education activities. Therefore we need further exploration, in order to link these ideas up to aspects of our national character, and to respond to the reform directions in the model of general education internationally.

All in all, the biggest problem facing China in implementing general education is that many people see it simply as a kind of concrete method or technique of education and do not view it as a radical principle or as an idea which should run through all of our educational activities. As a result general education becomes simply an additional set of activities that take place outside of the time devoted to specialist studies in a discipline or profession. We ought to establish a concept such that the strengthening of general education is not seen as a superficial change that is subordinate to the real demands of specialist higher education, but rather as a basic principle or theory underlying educational reform. Only in this way can we guarantee the formation of excellent personnel for the development of Chinese society in the information age and the age of the knowledge economy.

The recent swing toward the general education side of the pendulum has been accompanied by a reduction in the number of enrolments and job assignments related to the government's economic and social plans. Is there a link? Understanding cause and effect here is difficult. In the past, the necessity for specialized education seems to have occurred in times of threat. Perhaps an emphasis on general education is an

---

[19] Zhou Yuanqing, "Suzhi, suzhi jiaoyu, wenhua suzhi jiaoyu" (Quality, quality education and education in cultural quality), in *Qinghua daxue jiaoyu yanjiu* (Tsinghua University Education Research), No. 2, 2001, pp. 1-5; Li Manli, "Woguo dalu gaoxiao tongshi jiaoyu xianzhuang diaocha fenxi" (An analysis of a survey of the present conditions of general education in Chinese universities), in *Qinghua daxue jiaoyu yanjiu*, No. 2, 2001, pp. 128-136.

indication that more favourable circumstances prevail.

Whatever the case, one must resist the temptation to be too reductionist. In terms of the content of general education, China has always given importance to worldview education, humanistic perspectives and education in values and morality. China has also emphasized physical education and foreign languages. In addition it has stressed education in productive labour. There is no doubt that these elements will persist and be further developed with the future development of the concept of general education in China. But what other elements should be included in general education? How are we to enable students to develop basic knowledge and skill through their exposure to general education? What methods should we use? What aspects of the Western approach of establishing a core curriculum with some compulsory courses and some elective courses can we take as a reference point? These are all questions that need to be researched and solved. Just as in the past, we cannot simply borrow models mechanically from the West. In fact, general education in the West has had great differences in different social and historical periods. It is not simply an unchanging concept.[20]

What will be the status and contribution of general education in future within the information society? In the research of futurologists into the future trends of society in the coming years, there is one point that particularly merits our attention. Science and technology will become of ever more crucial importance to the knowledge economy. In face of this prediction, people will naturally raise the question of whether there is indeed any need for general education in the future society? It is extremely difficult to give an answer of either "yes" or "no" to this question. Our basic position is that we can affirm a general tendency for the future society, based on a knowledge economy, to make ever higher and higher demands for overall high quality in its people, rather than the opposite.

For this reason, if higher education takes the training of scientific and technical personnel as its main focus, it will be totally inadequate to provide simply a formation in scientific and technical knowledge. Broad knowledge, skills and qualities of character, including the ability to manage human relations, an attitude of cooperation and collaboration with others, positive motivation, skills of social interaction, an ability to observe and reflect on problems in a broad framework, the courage to take risks, and other holistic qualities are all viewed as specially important and necessary to the knowledge society. It may be true that specialist knowledge in the disciplines or professions are the most important aspect of higher education, but the integration of general education and specialist education is an essential aspect of higher education's adaptation to the future society, making possible the kinds of human

---

[20] A. Bloom, *The Closing of the American Mind* (New York: Simon and Schuster, 1987); E.L. Boyer, *College: The Undergraduate Experience in America* (Cambridge, Mass.: Harper and Row, 1987); J.G. Gaff, *General Education Today* (San Francisco: Jossey-Bass, 1983); R.M. Hutchins, *The Higher Learning in America* (New Haven: Yale University Press, 1967); P. Keller, *Getting at the Core: Curriculum Reform at Harvard* (Cambridge, Mass.: Harvard University Press, 1982); B. Thomas, *The Search for a Common Learning: General Education 1800-1960* (New York: McGraw-Hill, 1962).

development needed by the future society.[21]

CONCLUSIONS

Many problems confronting us today require an unprecedented understanding and linkage of the social and the scientific. Since the knowledge and methods of any one subject are often insufficient in the face of complex problems, we need to rely on multi- and cross-disciplinary practices to solve these problems. In order to do this, undergraduate education must be set up in such a way that it allows students to see problems in as broad a context as possible. Ideally, graduates of higher education should be able to communicate with experts in a number of different fields, and accommodate to rapid developments in their fields and in those of others.

Certain specific factors affect the nature of general education in China today. China's pursuit of a socialist market economy, and its policies of reform and openness are among these. The relatively low levels of economic, scientific and technological development are also factors. The lessons of the past are, of course, significant as well.

Given all these factors, general education in China is likely to consist of the following components: moral education; Chinese history and civilization; Western languages; mathematics and natural sciences; social sciences; physical education; aesthetics; and manual labour. A few comments about these components will help illustrate their links to the specific conditions and characteristics of China. With respect to moral education, students are required to develop an outlook on life and on the world which is healthy, noble and in harmony with their roles as Chinese citizens. The need to learn about China's history and culture has emerged to ensure that development occurs in relation to China's reality, and not in relation to some other nation's reality. Knowledge of Western languages is seen as an indispensable tool for learning from foreign experience, and is required more and more as higher education takes on concerns of an international nature. The study of mathematics and science by students of the humanities will help them to understand nature. Conversely, the study of social sciences will enable students of natural science, engineering, agriculture and medicine to understand society. Physical and aesthetic education are necessary complements to intellectual and moral education, and underline China's longstanding concern with the education of the whole person. Finally, manual work as part of general education will keep students from separating themselves from reality and from the masses. One may conclude that the emphasis here on several subjects, as well as on good citizenship, remains true to the definitions of general education invoked at the beginning of this paper.

---

[21] Wu Jisong, *Zhishi jingji* (The Knowledge Economy) (Beijing: Keji jishu chubanshe, 1998), pp. 32-33.

25

Lessons from the Chinese Academy

Ruth Hayhoe

This book has been about the dialogue among civilizations that has blossomed during the 1990s, after the end of the Cold War. The volume began with a series of challenges presented to the knowledge patterns which had become established in the Western university, and spread around the world over the recent two centuries of its colonial and postcolonial influence. This was followed by several rich expositions of the historical contributions of Eastern civilizations to the knowledge content and institutional patterns of modern higher education. The central section of the volume is taken up with analyses of some of the problems and imbalances that have arisen in the historical and contemporary process of knowledge transfer across cultures, also with ways in which these could be mitigated, through policy decisions and choices open to participants on both sides of the transfer process. This was followed by a set of papers discussing ways in which modern knowledge and modern institutions can retain and strengthen their links to the diverse indigenous cultures where they are located, thus fostering a healthy balance between openness to the global community and rootedness in local under-standing.

The final section of the volume has given close attention to Chinese civilization, and its interactions with the Western world, both historically and in the contemporary period. As explained in the introduction, our journey began with China and with a set of practical considerations arising out of educational exchange and collaboration. It is thus fitting that the volume should end with a focus on China. We have seen some of the rich contributions made by traditional Chinese science and arts to the world community, as well as the difficulties faced by Chinese scholars and thinkers in the modern period, when the roles were reversed and China found itself a recipient rather than a donor of advanced knowledge in science, technology, and even the arts. Both Chinese and Western perspectives on these interactions between China and the West are provided by the different contributors to this section.

The second last chapter, by Wang Yongquan and Li Manli, looked at the Chinese university and the ways in which its development over the 20th century was shaped by a sense of threat coming from external pressures. The most striking result of this was a tendency for knowledge to be organized into highly specialized categories, along lines related to specific national development goals. This went deeply against the grain of China's cultural and epistemological traditions, yet it was a logical necessity of late modernization, under considerable external threat. Only after the Cultural Revolution, Wang and Li suggest, did it become possible for Chinese universities to develop a coherent and integrative framework of knowledge in the curriculum. This represented a distillation of elements from China's own cultural traditions, and elements which Chinese scholars have selected from a range of Western influences introduced at different times over the century. This was the final chapter in our original volume, and might have been the final chapter in this new edition.

However, I was persuaded that this narrative account of the development of the European university, and of Chinese higher learning institutions, might complement Wang and Li's chapter, and add something to the concluding section of the volume. The purpose of the chapter is to look back in search of ways to understand the deep rooted differences in values and epistemological orientation in the two traditions. It is also to look forward and consider what the values and patterns of the Chinese academy might contribute to global higher education in future.

The narrative begins with the introduction of the European university, and its core values and knowledge patterns, to China in the early 17th century. The patterns of Chinese traditional higher learning institutions are then compared with those of the European university. The third phase of the narrative traces the development of four modern versions of the European university in the differing modernization contexts of Germany, France, the Soviet Union and the United States. In spite of differences in political ideology and socio-economic development, certain core values held in common continued to find expression in each of these modern versions of the university. The fourth phase of the narrative considers the evolution of modern universities in China, and the ways in which each of these Western models exerted an influence at different times over the century. The narrative concludes with some reflections on ways in which the values and patterns of China's rich scholarly traditions, which have finally been given space to reassert themselves in the modern Chinese context, may contribute to global higher education in the 21st century.

CORE VALUES OF THE EUROPEAN UNIVERSITY

The emergence of universities in 12th century Europe marked the end of the Dark Ages, and the beginnings of a renaissance of culture and knowledge that was to have a wide reaching impact around the globe. Although these early universities were essentially international institutions, open to scholars from all parts of Europe, it was several hundred years before the first contacts took place with scholarly institutions in China, which had developed over an even longer period. The Jesuit mission to China, which began in the 16th century, opened up channels for communication both ways,[1] and it was a Jesuit missionary from Italy who first provided a detailed introduction to the

---

[1] D.E. Mungello, *Curious Land: Jesuit Accommodation and the Origins of Sinology* (Honolulu: University of Hawaii Press, 1989).

university for Chinese readers.   In 1622 CE, Giulio Aleni published *A Summary of Western Learning* [*Xixue fan*] in Chinese.[2] In it he explained to Chinese scholars the character and achievements of the then 400-year-old universities of Europe. Naturally, his picture was informed by the patterns of Aristotelian and Thomistic thought that had shaped the university since its emergence in the 12th century. The focus was on knowledge and categories of knowledge, and his ability to use appropriate Chinese terminology in translating Western concepts showed his remarkable linguistic achievements and the understanding he had developed of the Chinese scholarly context.

Aleni depicted a hierarchical structure of knowledge in the university with the arts at its base, *philosophia* in the next tier, and the two professional fields of *medicina* and *leges* (laws) above this. At the apex of the structures was canon law, and supreme above all, *Theologia*. Aleni gave a detailed introduction to European knowledge achievements in each of these categories, showing how one led up to the next, and how *Theologia* integrated all other fields of knowledge, and gave meaning and direction to human life. The Chinese translation he chose for theology, the Heavenly Learning or *tianxue*, was particularly apt. "Without Heavenly Learning to show one the beginning and end of all things, the origin and destination of humankind, and the grave matters of life and death, all the human studies would be just like fireflies, unable to compare with the sun in the power of illumination", he commented.[3]

From this account, we can clearly recognize the institutions which had come to birth in Bologna, Paris and other medieval cities of Europe in the 12th century. A common curricular structure emerged over subsequent centuries, with faculties of arts, philosophy, medicine, law and theology. The core values of the university have often been identified as autonomy and academic freedom. Autonomy was protected by a set of structures derived from three important medieval institutions: the monastery, the guild and the church. From the monastery came the tradition of distance from the immediate demands of society and the pursuit of learning for its own sake and for the long term. From the guild came the pattern of a self regulating community of masters, the *universitas*, setting the standards as to who could enter as students, and regulating the life of the community by internally agreed criteria. From the church came a papal charter, granting all members of each university community the *ius ubique docendi*, the right to teach everywhere, and giving them protection from interference by local ecclesiastical or political authorities. In the early years, the most potent way of expressing resistance to such interference was simply *migratio*, a move to another city, or *cessatio*, a kind of medieval strike of all university members working in local religious or political institutions.

An institution had thus taken shape, the *studium*, which found independent ground between *imperium* and *sacerdotium*, the other great powers of medieval Europe.

---

[2] Bernard Hung-Kay Luk, "Aleni Introduces the Western Academic Tradition to Seventeenth Century China: A Study of the *Xixue Fan*", in Tiziana Lippiello and Roman Malek (eds.), *"Scholar from the West" Giulio Aleni S.J. (1582-1649) and the Dialogue between Christianity and China* (Brescia: Fondazione Civilta Bresciana and Sankt Augustin: the Monumenta Serica Institute, 1997), pp. 479-518.

[3] *Ibid.* pp. 509-510.

Academic freedom was protected by a far sighted Papal initiative, the university's charter, which protected scholars in debates over all kinds of questions, even those which were highly sensitive to local religious or political leaders. Theology put certain limits on the pursuit of knowledge, yet it also had an important integrative role, which contributed to the advancement of knowledge. The great British historian of the university, Hastings Rashdall, expressed this point in the following way: "Theology remained Queen of the Sciences, but a grander and nobler conception of theology arose.... Theology became not merely the Chinese mandarin's poring over sacred texts, but the architectonic science whose office it was to receive the results of all other sciences and combine them into an organic whole...."[4] Rashdall drew particular attention to the liberating role of the theologians of the University of Paris, who provided a context where religious and social disputes could be argued through on the basis of reason, rather than finding expression in the bloodshed which characterized the Inquisition in southern Europe.[5]

While specialism of knowledge was an important element in the university's tradition at this phase, it was moderated by the integrative role of theology, linking all knowledge to commonly-accepted ethical and spiritual directions. For this reason, the concept of "intellectual freedom" may better depict the medieval period than "academic freedom", which should be reserved for a later phase of the university's development. In this period, before the emergence of modern science, the issue of value neutrality had not yet arisen. All of the university's knowledge was to serve the moral and spiritual directions defined by theology.

CORE VALUES OF THE CHINESE ACADEMY

Let us now turn to the Chinese scholarly institutions and values which were predominant in the early 17th century. By an interesting coincidence, Chinese classical institutions of higher learning had also reached their definitive form in the 12th century, at around the same time as the universities in Europe came into being. This was largely due to the emergence of Song neo-Confucianism as the dominant form of scholarship, and the work of several great scholars, most notable among them Zhu Xi. In 1190 CE Zhu had standardized the canon of knowledge used in the imperial examination system in the form of Four Books and Five Classics, a canon that was to persist up until the end of the last imperial dynasty, the Qing, in the early 20th century. The formal pole of traditional Chinese higher learning, imperial institutions at capital, provincial and prefectural levels which administered the civil service examinations, had reached institutional forms that were relatively stable – the *taixue,* the *guozijian,* the Hanlin academy. In addition, Zhu Xi made important contributions to the emergence of

[4] Hastings Rashdall, *The Universities of Europe in the Middle Ages* (Oxford: Oxford University Press, 1969), Vol. III, p. 442.
[5] Hastings Rashdall, *The Universities of Europe in the Middle Ages* (Oxford: Clarendon Press, 1936), Vol. 1, pp. 548-549.

non-formal scholarly institutions, the academies or *shuyuan,* which grew up from libraries and Buddhist monasteries in quiet rural settings where scholarship could be pursued outside the ambit of the imperial bureaucracy and its examination system.

Four major divisions of knowledge dominated the Chinese traditional curriculum, from the 12th century up to the late 19th century: the classical canon and commentaries (*jing*), history and related subjects (*shi*), philosophy (*zi*) and the arts, or belles lettres (*ji*). "This system was based on the Confucian approach to scholarship – the Classics express the Way in words, history in deeds, while philosophers and literary artists illustrate various other aspects of the Way".[6] In his introduction to the European university, Aleni had noted that these four knowledge categories all fell into the category of arts, at the base of the curriculum in the European university. In fact, studies in medicine, law, engineering and agricultural sciences had also long been developed in China, though they were not regarded as high status knowledge, nor were they tested in the imperial examinations. Rather they were treated as technical knowledge, to be regulated and supervised by scholar officials in order to serve the common good.

China's traditional curriculum was not characterized by the same degree of hierarchy as has been noted above in the European curriculum, where theology was the reigning science, responsible to regulate and integrate all other subjects. For Chinese scholars, "the transcendant and the mundane were complementary parts of a universe that was an organic unity".[7] There was no theology as such, but rather a commitment to the independence and integrity of the moral self, and forms of self-cultivation that would awaken, extend, and actualize the goodness immanent in one's nature.

The structure of traditional higher learning in China was shaped by the imperial examination system, which allowed the Emperor to select scholar officials to administer imperial rule from all parts of the empire through a meritocratic system of study. The content of knowledge to be examined was regulated by the Hanlin Academy, and the examinations focused on the Four Books and Five Classics. The administration of the examinations was under the Board of Rites, which was responsible for education offices at prefectural and provincial level where aspiring scholars were registered to take part and move up through several levels of examination, before reaching the capital and palace examinations. Those who were successful in this exacting progression became scholar officials within the imperial system, with a close network between successful examinees and the scholar officials who examined them, also among candidates selected in the same year. In many ways it was a more influential community than that of the students and masters of the European university.

The Hanlin Academy could not be described as having the autonomy enjoyed by the university. However, it exercised a scholarly monopoly over the whole empire as an integral part of the imperial bureaucracy.[8] Only those who mastered the standards of knowledge it set could serve as administrators of the empire. The Jesuits of the 17th

---

[6] Bernard Luk, "Aleni Introduces the Western Academic Tradition to Seventeenth Century China", 1997, p. 486

[7] *Ibid.* pp. 511-512.

[8] Adam Liu Yuan-ching, *The Hanlin Academy 1644-1850* (Connecticut: Archon Books, 1981).

century were impressed by the remarkable way in which scholarship was recognized and rewarded in China, and one admiring British visitor of the 19th century described China in the following way: "The whole of China may be said to resemble one vast university which is governed by the scholars who have been educated within its walls".[9]

Members of the Hanlin Academy, and of the wider scholar-official bureaucracy, did not enjoy the kinds of intellectual freedom valued by scholars within the European university, yet they had a remarkable level of intellectual authority. This extended even to the responsibility of remonstrating with the Emperor himself, if his policies or actions were seen to be out of line with the truths of the classical texts. The absence of the tension between *imperium* and *sacerdotium* which Rashdall noted in Europe meant a degree of integration between spiritual and political authority quite different from the European scene. In addition, the economic influence of the merchant city and of guilds of craftsmen was relatively modest in China, where medieval cities remained rather bureaucratic in composition.[10]

At the opposite pole to the Hanlin Academy, with its remarkable degree of intellectual authority and the scholarly domination it exercised throughout the empire, were the informal academies or *shuyuan*. These were locally based, often located in remote areas and originally associated with libraries and Buddhist monasteries. There scholar-officials who fell out of favour with the Emperor, or who did not wish to serve a new dynasty at a time of transition, gathered to pursue research and reflection in a community around a library. The content of study in these *shuyuan* tended to be broader than that represented in the canon for the imperial examinations, often including Buddhist, Daoist and other heterodox works. The patterns of study were largely informal, with one leading scholar often acting as *shanzhang* or master of the academy, and mentoring a large number of younger scholars in their own individual regime of study. These were often centres of lively debate, including criticism of the imperial government, also places were new knowledge could be debated and integrated into traditional canons.[11]

The autonomy enjoyed by these *shuyuan* was considerable at certain periods of time, but in times of crisis or political change the tendency was for imperial authority to seek to coopt them into the service of the examination system, or force them to close down, because they were potential centres of political dissent. It was thus a fragile autonomy, never benefitting from the protection which the papal charter provided to European universities, nor able to build an independent community of scholars which extended throughout the empire. Similarly the intellectual freedom they enjoyed at certain times was wide-ranging, and important to the revitalization of scholarship, yet

---

[9] Quoted in Teng Ssu-yu, "Chinese Influence on the Western Examination System", in *Harvard Journal of Asiatic Studies*, Vol. 7, No. 4, 1942, p. 290.

[10] William Rowe, *Hankow: Commerce and Society in a Chinese City, 1796-1889* (Stanford: Stanford University Press, 1984); William Rowe, *Hankow: Conflict and Community in a Chinese City, 1796-1895* (Stanford: Stanford University Press, 1989). These two volumes provide a rich and textured challenge to the longstanding Weberian thesis about the bureaucratic nature of the Chinese city, yet they do not entirely negate it.

[11] John Meskill, *Academies in Ming China* (Tuscon, Arizona: University of Arizona Press, 1982).

it was vulnerable to imperial suppression at other times.

The core values and patterns of the Chinese academy were thus quite distinct from those of the European university. Chinese scholars enjoyed a remarkable degree of intellectual authority and the capacity to dominate the empire in their role as officials, yet their institutions of independent scholarly learning had a somewhat fragile intellectual freedom and a fragmented local autonomy. Structurally, there was no clear dividing line between political power and scholarly knowledge, but rather an ongoing creative tension between an informal locus of power rooted in the integrity of the scholar qua scholar and a formal locus of power in the recognized status of the scholar qua official. Epistemologically, there was no single discipline, such as theology, which ruled all subordinate disciplines, integrating them into an agreed moral and spiritual direction. Rather the four areas of knowledge, classics, history, philosophy and literature, all supported the scholars' task of self-cultivation and the life-time pursuit of virtue and spiritual fulfilment.

The role of scholar officials within the imperial government was to ensure that all scientific, technical and professional knowledge was developed in ways that served society's greater good, while pure scholars in the *shuyuan* exercised a critical scrutiny over the government from a distance, ensuring both the continuity and ongoing revitalization of the canon. This set of patterns was successful in fostering a scientifically rich civilization, admired both in the region and from afar, up to the mid to late 18th century.[12]

The one point of confluence between the Chinese academy and the European university, as they took form in the 12th century, was the exclusion of women from formal participation in scholarship. It is a remarkable historical coincidence that this seems to have happened at the same period in both civilizations. In the case of Europe, David Noble has documented the process whereby women became excluded from intellectual life at the time universities were first established, due to the dominant role of a celibate clergy. This stood in striking contrast to an earlier period when women abbesses and scholars had played a visible role in church institutions.[13] The best example is, perhaps, Hildegard of Bingen, whose scholarly treatises on cosmology, ethics, and medicine, together with her extensive correspondence with several popes and monarchs on topics of scholarly and social importance, had put her in the mainstream of scholarship in the period shortly before the emergence of universities.[14]

In the case of China, the Tang dynasty, 698-907 CE, had been a period of remarkable openness in Chinese culture. Buddhism, introduced earlier from India, had reinforced certain liberating Daoist ideas from China's own philosophical heritage, and women found themselves able to play an active role in religion and scholarship,

---

[12] Joseph Needham, *The Shorter Science and Civilization in China*, edited by Colin Ronan (Cambridge: Cambridge University Press, 1978).

[13] David Noble, *A World Without Women: The Christian Clerical Culture of Western Science* (New York: Alfred Knopf, 1992).

[14] Peter Dronke, *Women Writers of the Middle Ages* (Cambridge: Cambridge University Press, 1984), pp. 144-150.

particularly through the opportunities provided by Buddhist nunneries.[15] In the 12th century, however, the great neo-Confucian scholar, Zhu Xi, had taken a stand against Buddhism in the restoration of Confucian philosophy to prominence. This had included laying down clearly circumscribed duties and study tasks for women within the family, and strongly discouraging women from taking up religious or scholarly roles as Buddhist nuns.[16]

Nevertheless, the patterns of knowledge that persisted within neo-Confucian philosophy were less alien to women than the increasing specialism and the embrace of value neutrality which came to characterize the European university's development. A revisionist historical approach to women's history in China has recently uncovered some of the ways in which women scholars subsequently developed active roles as itinerant teachers, and in the publication of poetry and scholarly works, in settings they organized for themselves, particularly in the prosperous region of southern Jiangsu and Zhejiang provinces.[17]

In the 16th and 17th centuries, China was widely regarded as a model for Europe.[18] This was not only for the achievements of traditional science in areas such as agriculture and engineering, but also for its tolerance of religious difference, and the secular character of the state, as Gregory Blue has convincingly argued in chapter 20 of this volume. Its porcelain, furniture, silk wallpaper, architectural styles and other aesthetic treasures were also exceedingly popular in Europe, as evident in Peter Swann's lively account in chapter 19. Over this period, China enjoyed a favourable balance of trade with Europe importing silver for its porcelain, silks and teas, until the British turned this around through the Opium Trade.

The development of modern science and the industrial revolution in Europe was to change this situation fundamentally, leaving China in a position of back-wardness and vulnerability by the late 18th and early 19th centuries. Many scholars have speculated over the question of why modern science developed only in Europe, not in China or any of the other Eastern societies, which had contributed so significantly to the rich heritage of traditional science.[19] That question goes beyond the scope of this chapter. Nevertheless, as we compare university and academy, it is important to remember that the European university has not always been regarded by historians as the leading institution in the scientific revolution. Alternative institutions, such as academies of science, also played an important role.

Still, the university became the intellectual institution most closely associated

[15] Kathryn Tsai, "The Chinese Buddhist Monastic Order for Women: The First Two Centuries", in Richard Guisso and Stanley Johannesen (eds.), Women in China: Current Directions in Historical Scholarship (Lewiston, New York: Edwin Mellen Press, 1981), pp. 1-20.

[16] Bettine Birge, "Chu Hsi and Women's Education", in W.T. de Bary and J. Chaffee, Neo-Confucian Education: The Formative Stage (Berkeley: University of California Press, 1989), pp. 325-367.

[17] Dorothy Koh, Teachers of the Inner Chambers: Women and Culture in Seventeenth Century China (Berkeley: University of California Press, 1995).

[18] L.A. Maverick, China: A Model for Europe (San Antonio, Texas: Paul Anderson Co., 1946).

[19] In chapter 7 of this volume, Len Berggren emphasized the point that medieval Islam made active and important contributions to the sciences it had adopted from Greece, and described some of its fine scientific achievements.

with the modernization process. By virtue of its perceived importance for successful modernization, it was transplanted to almost every society throughout the globe, no matter what had been their traditional approach to higher learning. This was done either through colonialism or by the proactive efforts of modernizers in countries such as China, Japan and Thailand.[20]

FOUR MODERN VERSIONS OF THE WESTERN UNIVERSITY

The patterns of the modern university that developed in Germany, France, the Soviet Union and the United States, set widely emulated models for both capitalist and socialist modernization processes. The focus in this part of the narrative will be on these four cases, since these were the models that had the greatest impact on China over the 20th century, as its leaders sought first to join the capitalist world under the Nationalist regime and then to join the socialist world under a Communist system. The core values of autonomy and academic freedom were maintained and transformed in different ways in these four distinctive contexts.

The University of Berlin, founded by Wilhelm von Humboldt in 1810, had the greatest influence worldwide in the 19th and early 20th centuries.[21] Under this model, philosophy replaced theology as queen of the sciences, and academic freedom, both the freedom to teach, *Lehrfreiheit,* and the freedom to learn, *Lernfreiheit,* was maintained in a relatively autocratic state. University scholars dedicated themselves to the advancement of theoretical knowledge in the basic disciplines of the arts and sciences, and largely refrained from direct interference into the political life of the state.[22] While the traditional professions of medicine and law remained within the university, new applied professions such as engineering and commerce were developed in separate *Technischen Hochschulen* which were closely allied with government and industry's efforts at economic modernization.[23]

The autonomy of the university was protected by the state on a principle similar to that of the Papal protection of the medieval university's autonomy, in the belief that the advancement of basic theoretical knowledge was of ultimate importance to the health of the state. Thus university scholars enjoyed considerable prestige and social influence as civil servants, yet largely refrained from direct involvement in political or social action. The flowering of scholarship in 19th century Germany, in both the pure and applied sciences and such areas as literature, history, philosophy and the arts, attests to the strengths of this model. It produced kinds of knowledge that had

---

[20] P. Altbach and V. Selvaratnam (eds.), *From Dependence to Autonomy: The Development of Asian Universities* (London: Kluwer, 1989).

[21] Wilhelm von Humboldt, "On the Spirit and the Organisational Framework of Intellectual Institutions", in *Minerva*, Vol. 8, April, 1970, pp. 242-250.

[22] Fritz Ringer, *The Decline of the German Mandarinate* (Cambridge, Mass.: 1969), especially chapters 1-3.

[23] Isolde Guenther, "A Study of the Evolution of the German Technische Hochschule", unpublished PhD thesis, University of London Institute of Education, 1972.

practical application to economic modernization tasks, yet also maintained space for any question, no matter how fundamental, to be raised and debated within the university.

However, the inability of the university to stand up to the rise of Hitler and his fascist agenda in the 20th century has raised deep questions about the adequacy of moral and spiritual knowledge in the university, which have been addressed by scholars such as Frederic Lilge, in *The Abuse of Learning*.[24]   The Kantian distinction between fact and value freed scientific and social enquiry from the constraints of theology, and allowed philosophy to become an arbiter and integrator of all kinds of knowledge while leaving the ethical directions of society open to democratic debate.[25] Weber's famous essay "Science as a Vocation" gives a vivid picture of both the possibilities and constraints of a university knowledge which was called on to be neutral in terms of spiritual, ethical or political direction.[26] The academic freedom of the university was somehow predicated on a value neutrality, which made it difficult to deal effectively with a challenge such as fascism. Weber's principled refusal to deal with the substance of moral or spiritual issues was a characteristic of academic freedom in the modern German university that distinguished it from the intellectual freedom identified earlier in the medieval university.

The evolution of modern universities in France took quite a different form than in Germany, with academic freedom becoming associated with a high degree of specialization of knowledge, and the scholar viewed primarily as a *spécialiste* or *scientifique*. Traditional universities were abolished around the time of the French Revolution, and the Napoleonic system which replaced them early in the 19th century was characterized by a rational distribution of traditional faculties of medicine, law, arts and sciences in each *académie* or academic district of the country, headed up by a university council in Paris which gave direction to the whole system. New fields of knowledge such as engineering, commerce and administration, necessary to the modernizing state, were placed in *grandes écoles* which had higher prestige than the universities and opened direct access into leading positions in the civil service.[27] The famous *concours*, for the selection of an elite of future civil servants in these institutions had been inspired by aspects of the Chinese civil service examinations.[28]

The strength of the French version of the modern university lay in its un-compromising rationalism and secularism, and the ways in which specialist knowledge in traditional disciplines and professions, as well as new applied fields, served the

---

[24] Frederic Lilge, *The Abuse of Learning: The Failure of the German University* (New York: McMillan and Co., 1948).

[25] Paulsen, Friedrich, *Immanuel Kant* (London: John Nimmo, 1902), describes Kant's achievement in this way: "This gives to knowledge what belongs to it – the entire world of phenomena for free investigation; it conserves, on the other hand, to faith the eternal right to the interpretation of life and the world from the standpoint of value". (p. 6).

[26] Max Weber, "Science as a Vocation", in H. H. Gerth and C. Wright Mills, *From Max Weber: Essays in Sociology* (New York: Oxford University Press, 1967).

[27] Frederick Artz, *The Development of Technical Education in France 1500-1850* (Cambridge Mass, and London, England: The Society for the History of Technology and MIT Press, 1968).

[28] Teng Ssu-yu, "Chinese Influence on the Western Examination System", 1942.

modernizing state. In terms of autonomy, the university has been described as *l'Etat enseignant,* claiming the right to regulate all aspects of education, not in subservience to successive governments but in loyalty to the long-term interests of the state.[29] Academic freedom was associated with the highly specialized nature of modern knowledge, and the demands of the scholar specialist, rather than with pure theoretical knowledge, as in the case of Germany.[30] Wang Yongquan and Li Manli have shown why this approach to modern higher education was appealing to a China under external threat, both in the 1930s and in the 1950s.

The Soviet model of the university owed a great deal historically to the influence of both France and Germany, but French patterns of increasing specialization of knowledge came to characterize it most strongly.[31] After the Russian revolution of 1917, a new socialist system of higher education was established with a certain number of major universities under the ministry of higher education, including polytechnical universities similar to the French model of the *école polytechnique,* and comprehensive universities close to the model of the University of Berlin. In addition, a large number of specialized institutions in specific fields of engineering, industry, health and agriculture functioned under specialist ministries of the Soviet government. This system took the specialization of knowledge to an extreme, as it endeavoured to provide higher training for an increasing cohort of the population in ways that could fit precisely into the nation's macro economic development needs.[32]

Given the highly centralized and controlling nature of the Soviet state, one would assume that the values of autonomy and academic freedom could not survive in such a system. In fact, however, the leadership recognized the need for specialist knowledge at a very advanced level in the natural sciences and engineering, and provided a degree of freedom to the scientific community that far exceeded that enjoyed by ordinary citizens. This specialist knowledge was integrated into a unified perspective by the Marxist-Leninist teachings, which also made a clear connection between scientific analysis and the moral political directions of state and society. The Marxist dialectic provided ground, in theory at least, for unitary moral and political directions for state and society. Its role had some similarities to that of theology as queen of the sciences in the medieval university, though it turned out to be more arbitrary and repressive.[33] In retrospect, the collapse of the Soviet state has shown how tenuous were the links between fact and value, and how much outright repression on the part of the state they sanctioned.

The final case for reflection is the American university model, which had its origins in the patterns of the college, inherited from Britain and closely linked to

---

[29] Pascale Gruson, *L'Etat Enseignant* (Paris: Mouton, 1978).

[30] *Ibid.* p. 91.

[31] William Johnson, *Russia's Educational Heritage* (Pittsburgh, Pennsylvania: Carnegie Press, 1950), especially chapter 3.

[32] Nicholas Dewitt, *Soviet Professional Manpower* (Washington, D.C.: National Science Foundation, 1955); Alexander Korol, *Soviet Education for Science and Technology* (New York: John Wiley and Sons, and the Technology Press of MIT, 1957).

[33] L.G. Churchward, *The Soviet Intelligentsia* (London: Routledge and Kegan Paul, 1973).

Protestant Christianity. The early American colleges were small communities of scholars, dominated by young men planning to enter the ministry in local Protestant churches. There was little science or professionalism, rather a focus on general knowledge in the arts and in practical subjects, as needed for service to the local community, with the moral directions set by Christian theology.[34] The development of science in 19th century America, and the strong influence of the German university model upon the emergence of graduate schools, brought about important changes in the American university. A system emerged, whereby undergraduate education remained broad and liberal, with efforts to ensure that all students were exposed to the arts, social sciences and natural sciences, whereas graduate education integrated teaching and research in basic sciences, humanities and the traditional and new professions.

The colleges had had little autonomy, as their governing boards were dominated by members of the local religious and political community. However, universities began to gain autonomy in the late 19th century, with the development of basic scientific research and the emergence of specialist disciplines. Still, the struggle for academic freedom, in the face of strong religious opposition to the teaching of controversial topics, such as evolutionary theory, presented a remarkable contrast to Germany, where academic freedom flowered under a relatively autocratic government. This situation may also have been linked to the dominance of a philosophy of pragmatism and problem solving, in both social and natural science, reflected in the work of philosophers such as Charles Peirce, William James and John Dewey. The dualism between theory and practice, fact and value, that shaped the European university, proved less acceptable in America.[35]

American scholars were struggling for a broader intellectual freedom, one might argue, rather than the academic freedom associated with pure theory and highly specialized disciplines of knowledge in the European context. They could not easily detach themselves from pressing political and social concerns nor abandon the forms of integrated knowledge that had characterized the early colleges. For this reason, the American university model had a certain attraction for Chinese scholars, given core values of scholarship which never tolerated narrow specialism and viewed all knowledge as infused with values and judged by its effectiveness in practice.[36] This point comes across in Wang Yongquan and Li Manli's reflections on the concept of

---

[34] Richard Hofstadter and Walter Metzger, *The Development of Academic Freedom in the United States* (New York and London: Columbia University Press, 1955).

[35] Joseph Ben-David, *American Higher Education: Directions Old and New* (New York: McGraw Hill Book Co., 1972), p. 75 gives the following explanation: "The assumption...that it was not the task of the college to provide moral guidance to its students, and that the students had to be treated as responsible adults and left to their own devices did not fit the American situation. It did not quite fit the situation in Germany and the other countries in Europe from which the idea was copied either, but it fitted the United States situation least of all. The political and moral order of American society, as was shown by de Tocqueville, was based on the moral authority of local communities and religious groups, and not on the ideal of a self-directing moral personality, or the authority of a national elite serving as a model for everybody".

[36] David L. Hall and Roger Ames, *The Democracy of the Dead: Dewey, Confucius and the Hope for Democracy in China* (Chicago and Lasalle, Illinois: Open Court, 1999).

general education in Chinese universities in chapter 24.

There are striking commonalities among these four versions of the Western university, rooted in the core values of the medieval university they inherited. There are also important differences, which affected greatly the ways in which they interacted with Chinese higher education over the 20th century. One point shared by all four was the fact that women had been largely excluded from their development up to the 19th century. The approaches to knowledge and institutional organization had come from a predominantly male world of science and scholarship. At the time of the university's greatest triumph, when it was being transplanted to all parts of the world as an essential agent of modernization, women were just beginning their long struggle, first for equal access to the university as students, then as professors.[37]

Once accepted within the university, women began to look at structures of knowledge and patterns of governance, and realize how alien these were to their ways of knowing and interaction.[38] Scholars such as Sandra Harding[39] and Carolyn Merchant[40] have critiqued the linear and mechanistic character of its rationalism; its espousal of a dualism of facts and values as a solution to the need for freedom of scientific inquiry; its concern with objectivity and the resultant isolation of the subject from the objects under scrutiny; its embrace of metaphors drawn from the mining of natural resources and subjugation of "irrational" forces in nature. Recently these concerns have been given wider attention in a critical literature on universities by scholars such as Bruce Wilshire[41] and Mark Schwehn,[42] who have focused on the inadequacy of the university's epistemological patterns and institutional structures for dealing effectively with moral and spiritual questions.

In the opening chapter of this book, Hans Weiler has identified a series of major challenges to entrenched patterns of knowledge in the Western university, and this narrative has perhaps given some insight into the ways in which they had become entrenched, and the deep roots that have rendered them resistant to change. Clearly, they played a vital role in the process of modernization, yet they have made it difficult for the university to deal effectively with some of the important cultural, spiritual and environmental challenges arising in that process.

Hopefully this narrative also sets a context for readers to see the university as

---

[37] Suzanne Stiver Lie and Virginia O'Leary, *Storming the Tower: Women in the Academic World* (New York: Kogan Page, 1990).

[38] M.F. Belenky, B.M. Clinchy, N.R. Goldberger, and J.M. Tarule, *Women's Ways of Knowing* (New York: Basic Books, 1986).

[39] Sandra Harding, *The Science Question in Feminism* (Ithaca, New York: Cornell University Press, 1986); Sandra Harding, *Feminist Epistemology: Social Science Issues* (Bloomington, Indiana: Indiana University Press, 1987); Sandra Harding, *Whose Science? Whose Knowledge? Thinking from Women's Lives* (Ithaca, New York: Cornell University Press, 1991).

[40] Carolyn Merchant, *The Death of Nature: Women, Ecology and the Scientific Revolution* (San Francisco: Harper and Row, 1980).

[41] Bruce Wilshire, *The Moral Collapse of the University: Professionalism, Purity and Alienation* (Albany: State University of New York Press, 1990), p. xxiii.

[42] Mark Schwehn, *Exiles from Eden: Religion and the Academic Life in America* (New York: Oxford University Press, 1993), p. 40.

a product of its time and civilization, and to appreciate some of the rich possibilities coming from other civilizations which might transform universities in the 21st century.

Various contributors to this volume have opened up a wide range of reflections on this subject: Ji Shuli, in his depiction of Sinic science, Al Zeera in her alternative Islamic paradigm for the social sciences and Kirkness and Barnhardt, in their comments on the heritage of spiritual understanding which First Nations young people would like to bring into the university community, among others.

The narrative now continues with an overview of the development of modern universities in China, showing some of the conflicts that arose as distinctive Western versions of the university were transplanted into a Chinese cultural and epistemological environment. Only toward the end of a century of experimentation and change have universities emerged in China that are able to combine features of their own cultural heritage with patterns introduced from abroad. These institutions may have an important contribution to offer to global dialogue on higher education in the 21st century.

MODERN CHINESE UNIVERSITIES IN A CENTURY OF CONFLICT

Modern universities emerged in China under conditions entirely different from those prevailing in Europe and North America in the early 20th century. A long and proud tradition of academies and civil service examinations was abolished in 1905, as the last imperial dynasty, the Qing, faced collapse and the revolution that was to end the dynasty in 1911 became imminent. The decision to create universities along Western lines was a matter of national survival, in times of great difficulty. Many of those leading this development had qualified for political or educational office within the traditional imperial knowledge system. In contrast to the atmosphere of confidence and even triumphalism that prevailed in Europe of the time, their mood was close to despair, as they saw China falling farther and farther behind the Western powers.

Several of the progressive Chinese intellectuals who led China's early universities were active feminists. Some had come to believe that since Chinese women had suffered humiliation for centuries in traditional Chinese society they would best be able to understand the sense of humiliation and powerlessness they experienced in a world dominated by imperialist powers. One wrote the first history of Chinese women.[43] Women thus entered modern Chinese universities as students under circumstances where they faced less opposition than their Western sisters had done. One might also argue that they found themselves in a less alien environment, since the patterns of knowledge associated with modern science and industrialism, introduced to the Chinese context from abroad, had not penetrated deeply into the culture. The

---

[43] Chen Dongyuan, *Zhongguo funu shenghuoshi* (A History of Women's Lives)(Shanghai: Commercial Press, 1928). See pp. 366-68 for discussion of an article written by Chen Duxiu, in *Xin Qingnian* (New Youth) in 1916, where he made the point that Chinese women could best understand the sense of oppression that Chinese men then felt in the face of global imperialist pressures.

persistence of holistic and integrative patterns of knowledge from China's academy tradition in the emerging modern universities made them places where men and women together addressed the intellectual, moral and spiritual tasks of developing new forms of knowledge that could contribute to modernization and national salvation.

We have noted earlier that four versions of the Western university had the most significant influence in modern China – the German, French, American and Soviet – at different time periods. This brief overview will focus on Peking University, showing how it was shaped first on a German model, then modified through influences coming from the progressive traditions of the *shuyuan*, as well as the American university model. Our narrative will begin with Cai Yuanpei, a kind of modern Chinese counterpart to Giulio Aleni, in his comprehensive knowledge of the academic philosophy and institutional patterns of the German and French university traditions.

Born in 1868, Cai Yuanpei gained a thorough grounding in Chinese classical scholarship through study in a traditional *shuyuan*. He also took the civil service examinations, achieving the highest honour as Hanlin Academician in 1892.[44] His first guide and mentor in Western academic traditions was a former Chinese Jesuit, Ma Xiangbo, who taught him Latin and philosophy while he was a teacher in the Nanyang Public Institute, one of China's first modern higher institutions.[45] Subsequently, he spent two lengthy periods in Europe, from 1906 to 1911, and from 1912 to 1917, studying in the universities of Leipzig and Berlin, also helping to foster a Sino-French university in Lyons, France.[46]

His influence on Chinese higher education can be seen most strikingly in the ways in which he reformed Peking University between 1917 and 1923, when he became its Chancellor on return from his second stay in Europe. Convinced that autonomy and academic freedom, close to the German model, were essential to the development of modern scholarship in China, he reorganized the university's style of government to ensure that professors rather than government officials should rule the university (*jiaoshou zhixiao*). He appointed scholars of the highest standing who represented many divergent points of view, in order to encourage lively debates. The phrase he used for academic freedom (*jianrong bingbao*), conveyed a sense of all ideas being tolerated and allowed to compete for attention.[47] It was actually closer to the concept of intellectual freedom, as one can see from the following self-written inscription from his memoirs.

---

[44] William Duiker, *Ts'ai Yuan-p'ei: Educator of Modern China* (University Park and London: Pennsylvania State University Press, 1977).

[45] Lu Yongling, "Standing Between Two Worlds: Ma Xiangbo's Educational Thought and Practice", in R. Hayhoe and Y. Lu (eds.), *Ma Xiangbo and the Mind of Modern China* (New York: M.E. Sharpe, 1996), pp. 158-159.

[46] R. Hayhoe, "Catholics and Socialists: The Paradox of French Educational Interaction with China", in R. Hayhoe and M. Bastid (eds.), *China's Education and the Industrialised World: Studies in Cultural Transfer* (New York: M.E. Sharpe, Toronto: OISE Press, 1987), pp. 109-112.

[47] Document 58, "Ts'ai Yuan-p'ei's policy for Peking University", in John Fairbank and Teng Ssu-yu, *China's Response to the West: A Documentary Survey 1839-1923* (Cambridge: Harvard University Press, 1954) pp. 238-239.

I am open to all scholarly theories and incorporate learning from diverse sources, according to the general standards of the universities of all nations and abiding by the principles of freedom of thought. Regardless of which school of thought, if their words are logical, those who maintain them have reason, and they have not yet met the fate of being naturally eliminated, and even if they are mutually contradictory, I will still allow them to develop freely.[48]

Along the lines of the German tradition, Cai adhered to the notion that pure theoretical knowledge should be separated from practical and applied fields. He reformed the university curriculum, moving engineering and law to other specialist institutions, and focusing on basic disciplines in the arts and sciences. Philosophy and psychology were viewed as the integrating disciplines to which all students should be exposed. Deeply concerned with moral issues, Cai saw them as intimately connected to aesthetics, rather than to either state Confucian beliefs or other religions. He believed that moral direction for society would come out of intellectual debates that spurred both self-cultivation and social advancement, in a broad Confucian mode. The spirit could be nurtured through a revitalization of aesthetics, from literature to the visual arts. An agnostic himself, Cai favoured tolerance of all religions, and had great respect for his Roman Catholic mentor, Ma Xiangbo, who was known for opposing any concept of a state religion.[49]

Cai's commitment to the advancement of pure theoretical knowledge in the university, following the German model, meant that he encouraged some distance from political activism on the part of university scholars. When the lively debates he had fostered among scholars of different persuasions erupted in the May 4th movement of 1919, he supported the commitment to revolutionary change in the cultural and literary areas, but opposed political activism on the part of students. Deeply troubled by what he perceived as the university's direct involvement in politics, he resigned his chancellorship in protest, asking the students to refrain from political action and commit their efforts to longer term social development.[50]

Cai had been a strong advocate of women's education from an early period. In 1902, he had founded a patriotic girls' school, and as minister of education in 1912, he had promoted coeducation and improvements for women's education. In 1920, he opened Peking University to women students, the first government supported university to do so in modern China. When he became minister of education again in 1928, he gave priority to removing barriers to women's education at all levels.[51]

Cai was also a great admirer of the French model of the university, seeing its leadership over the whole education system as important in protecting schools from

---

[48] Wen Rumin, Zhao Weimin (eds.), *Peking University* (Beijing: Peking University press, 1998), p. 27.
[49] Ma Xiangbo, "Should a Head of State preside over religious ceremonies?", in R. Hayhoe and Y. Lu, *Ma Xiangbo and the Mind of Modern China*, 1996, pp. 241-252.
[50] Cai Yuanpei, *Cai Yuanpei xuanji* (Selected writings of Cai Yuanpei) (Beijing: Zhonghua shuju, 1959), p. 98. See also Duiker, *Ts'ai Yuan-p'ei: Educator of Modern China*, 1977, pp. 69-74.
[51] Duiker, *Ts'ai Yuan-p'ei: Educator of Modern China*, 1977, pp. 10, 64-5.

political manipulation.[52]   As Minister of Education, he tried to introduce the French pattern of university districts, with all schools in each major district under the guidance of the university.[53] When this failed, he established the Academica Sinica as a high level and independent centre of scholarship for the whole country, inspired to some degree by the *Académie Française*. Earlier, in the 1920s, he had helped to create the *Université Sino-française* with campuses in Beijing, Shanghai and Lyons, France.

As Chinese universities developed during the 1920s and 1930s, the other major influence was the American. One of the influential scholars whom Cai appointed as Dean of Arts at Peking University in the mid 1920s was Hu Shi, an American educated philosopher. He believed that the scholarly community should dedicate itself to identifying and solving problems in the economic, social and political spheres, and thus serve China's long-term development. Moral and political direction would arise from broad social debate, and could not be pre-determined, either by a revival of state Confucian values or by a modern "ism" such as Marxism.[54]

During his years as Dean of Arts at Peking University, Hu Shi supported Cai in the development of a research institute for national studies, which was dedicated to a critical interpretation and assessment of China's classical literature, philosophy, history and canons. Students and professors worked independently, according to their own timetable, in the spirit of the traditional *shuyuan*. Beijing's other major university, Tsinghua, invited Hu to design a similar research institute, where four of China's greatest scholars in history and humanities were appointed as tutors. The focus of their work was on an integration of scholarship and ethics, in developing a critical understanding of China's classical knowledge, and applying this to contemporary issues of social and political development.[55]

Among the new universities and colleges established between the 1911 revolution and the Japanese invasion in 1937, there were public and private institutions, national, provincial and local, over 100, with a wide variety of models and types. The political chaos of the warlord years, and the limited capability of the Nationalist government established in 1928, meant that the main constraints on their development were economic. Generally, American influences tended to be strong, but there were significant European influences as well. Of particular interest are the 16 Christian universities, developed by missionaries from North America, which were involved in social development projects, agricultural renewal, medicine, education and even

---

[52] R. Hayhoe, "Catholics and Socialists", 1987, pp. 109-112.

[53] Allen Linden, "Politics and Education in Nationalist China: The Case of the University Council 1927-1928", in *Journal of Asian Studies*, Vol. 27, No. 4, August, 1968.

[54] Hu Shi, "The Significance of the New Thought", Document 62 in Fairbank and Teng, *China's Response to the West*, 1954, pp. 252-5. See also Jerome Grieder, *Hu Shih and the Chinese Renaissance* (Cambridge, Mass.: Harvard University Press, 1970).

[55] Ding Gang, "The Shuyuan and the Development of Chinese universities in the early twentieth century", in R. Hayhoe and J. Pan (eds.) *East-West Dialogue in Knowledge and Higher Education* (New York: M.E. Sharpe, 1996), pp. 218-244. Hu Shi was later to serve as Ambassador of the Republic of China to the United States, from 1938 to 1942, and as the last president of Peking University under the Nationalist regime, after it returned to Beijing in 1945.

famine relief, in some cases.[56] As early as 1928, a Chinese woman who held a doctorate in chemistry from the United States, Dr. Wu Yifang, became president of one of these, Ginling Women's College.

Generally these institutions shared the spirit of liberalism first fostered at Peking University by Cai Yuanpei and further developed by Hu Shi and many other American returned scholars. The conflict between scholarship and political activism which had so concerned Cai at Peking University, gradually found resolution in an increasing emphasis on applied knowledge that could make a practical difference in social, economic and even political terms.[57]

During the Sino-Japanese War, from 1937 to 1945, Peking University, Tsinghua University and the private Nankai University were combined to form the Southwest Associated University (*Lianda*), and continued to function throughout the war in the remote southwestern city of Kunming, close to Burma. The vitality and outstanding scholarly standards of this institution, functioning under the most difficult of circumstances, illustrates the enormous potential of a melding of values from the German and American academic traditions with aspects of the Chinese traditional *shuyuan*. John Israel's recent history of *Lianda*, provides copious information on the richness of its intellectual life, as Chinese traditional literature, history and philosophy were rethought in terms of the dilemmas of modernization and war, as Western style social sciences were adapted to Chinese social and economic realities, and as the scholarly community took up the role of both academy and university. The quality of research in basic sciences, under extremely difficult and restrictive circumstances, was also remarkable. Two later Nobel-prize-winning physicists had their initial university education there. In addition, considerable work was also done in engineering, including a focus on aeronautical engineering needed for the war-time effort.

Physical distance from the war-time capital of Chongqing, and the protection of a provincial governor who was not easily controlled by the Nationalist Party, assured the university considerable autonomy. The focus on basic research in theoretical fields gradually shifted to a greater and greater concern to do teaching and research related to practical issues of national development and even national survival. In a moving way, Israel charts the shift from a pure liberal approach to knowledge, that might be associated with academic freedom, to a more contextualized one that fits better with the concept of intellectual freedom:

> In sharing poverty for the sake of education, faculty members and students felt drawn to each other, and a sense of community emerged. It was more akin to that of the traditional *shuyuan*, than to that of the status-conscious universities of pre-war days. The existence of a 'vital, upbeat, creative spiritual life' was a matter of pride and

---

[56] Jessie Lutz, *China and the Christian Colleges* (Ithaca, New York and London: Cornell University Press, 1971).

[57] Yeh Wen-hsin, *The Alienated Academy: Culture and Politics in Republican China 1919-1937* (Cambridge, Mass: Council on East Asian Studies, Harvard University, 1990) gives a detailed and contoured picture of the development of universities over this period.

satisfaction for those who survived the mid-war Lianda years.[58]

The combined strength of progressive Chinese, European and American scholarly values made this an oasis of cultural, social and scientific thought within a desert of war-time devastation.

The political and economic crises that succeeded the Sino-Japanese War were such that a gradualist approach to social and economic change   gave way to all out revolution under the leadership of the Communist Party. In some ways, it was no surprise that Marxism-Leninism should have gained wider and wider support in China with China's urgent concern to be able to stand up to external aggression. There was also great appeal in its confident assertion of a set of moral-political directions made certain by a unified modern science.

The establishment of a People's Republic that could finally stand up in the world, in 1949, was a moment of great importance. Many Chinese university scholars had welcomed the revolution, hoping universities could contribute to a rapid socialist modernization process, while still maintaining the role of critical reflection necessary to an authentic modern cultural identity. Among them was Ma Xulun, a philosopher and the first minister of higher education after 1949, Ma Yinchu, a distinguished economist and graduate of Columbia University, who was appointed president of Peking University, and Liang Shuming, sometimes called the last Confucian for his tenacious belief in Confucian self-strengthening.[59] Given that Mao Zedong himself had been a great admirer of the *shuyuan* tradition,[60] they believed the best features of Western patterns introduced over recent decades could be combined with progressive features of the *shuyuan* to serve China's socialist construction.

Tragically, however, the opposite occurred, triggering a set of conflicts that reverberated up to the 1980s. In their hurry to achieve socialist construction within a decade, the new leadership invited Soviet experts to mastermind a total overhaul of the higher education system along Soviet lines.[61] This resulted in a huge number of highly specialist institutions under specific ministries, a small number of so-called comprehensive universities, which had departments only in basic humanities and sciences, and polytechnical universities mainly focusing on the engineering sciences. All of the universities which had evolved over the first half of the century were thoroughly restructured to fit into the new system-wide configuration. The system was, in turn, integrated into a process of nation-wide manpower planning for five-year periods.[62]

---

[58] John Israel, *Lianda: A Chinese University in War and Revolution* (Stanford, California: Stanford University Press, 1998), pp. 331-332.

[59] Guy Alitto, *The Last Confucian: Liang Shu-ming and the Chinese Dilemma of Modernity* (Berkeley: University of California Press, 1986), especially pp. 322-324.

[60] Ding Gang, "The Shuyuan and the Development of Chinese Universities", 1996, pp. 235-237.

[61] Deborah Kaple, "Soviet Advisors in China in the 1950s", in Odd Arne Westad (ed.), *Brothers in Arms: The Rise and Fall of the Sino-Soviet Alliance 1945-1963* (Washington, D.C.: Woodrow Wilson Centre Press and Stanford: Stanford University Press, 1998), pp. 117-140.

[62] R. Hayhoe, *China's Universities 1895-1995: A Century of Cultural Conflict* (Hong Kong: Comparative Education Research Centre, The University of Hong Kong, 1999), chapter 4.

The intellectual authority and monopoly of knowledge-power that had characterized the traditional civil service examination system now came to shape the new socialist system. People's University was created as "our very first modern university" intended to lead the new system by educating "the cadres who will serve the people", according to Liu Shaoqi, China's state premier. Under it were institutes of political science and law in each region which were described as "of the quality of a political training class". Supporting People's University at the regional level, their task was "to destroy China's old ideology and old organizations".[63] Liu was the author of a highly influential volume entitled "How to be a good Communist", which laid out a program of self-cultivation for loyal Party members in terms replete with classical references that emphasized discipline and obedience.[64]

People's University was set up with only eight departments: finance, trade, economic planning, cooperatives, factory management, law, diplomacy, and Russian. It was placed at the apex of the new higher education system, with the task of leading the training of cadres to manage the whole socialist system. The sciences and other fields were to be left to subordinate institutions, since Liu had proclaimed that bourgeois science was not really different from proletarian science in his speech at the university's opening on October 3, 1950.[65] In effect, People's University was to become a new style Hanlin academy, arbitrating the canons of ideologically correct knowledge, and dominating the teaching of political theory and all other social science fields. It appeared that two deep concerns could be met at the same time in this Soviet model of modern higher education – to catch up with the developed world through training specialists for rapid modernization, and to have a commonly shared set of moral-political directions which could replace traditional Confucianism.

In terms of the first concern, remarkable achievements in economic development were made in the 1950s, as a modern higher education system was finally spread throughout China's hinterland, in a realization of Cai Yuanpei's dream of French style university districts. There was also a growing representation of women in higher education, including a relatively large ratio in the basic and engineering sciences, which dominated enrolments.

In terms of the second concern, however, the apparent link between scientific analysis and moral-political development provided by Marxism-Leninism soon gave way to destructive intra-party power struggles, in which Mao's radical vision for social transformation came into direct conflict with Liu's Soviet-oriented approach. The conflicts that ensued in the educational revolutions of 1958 and 1966 were deeply destructive, especially for the intellectual community. In certain ways, the Soviet style

---

[63] Liu Shaoqi, "Speech at the Ceremonial Meeting for the School-Opening of Chinese People's University", in Union Research Institute (ed.), *Collected Works of Liu Shao'ch'i 1945-1957* (Kowloon: Union Research Institute, 1969), pp. 235, 236.

[64] Liu Shaoqi, "How to be a good Communist", in Union Research Institute (ed.), *Collected Works of Liu Shao'ch'i Before 1944* (Kowloon: Union Research Institute, 1969), First version, 1939, pp. 151-218, Revised version, 1964, pp. 219-283.

[65] Liu Shaoqi, "Speech at the Ceremonial Meeting for the School-Opening of People's University", 1969, pp. 237-238.

university of the 1950s had values and patterns that harked back to the medieval university of Europe. Marxism-Leninism had replaced theology as queen of the sciences, proclaiming its authority on the basis of a unified science of history. Liu Shaoqi's confidence in this "truth" had a similar ring to that of Aleni in proclaiming the truth of theology in the early 1600s. All other knowledge areas were clearly subordinate to its authority, giving it a position parallel to the narrow versions of state Confucianism which had been used by a succession of emperors for the suppression of dissent.

Sadly, Marxism Leninism did not have the flexibility of theology, nor could it tolerate open debate. Thus intense conflict escalated between those in the party following the Soviet road and radicals supporting Mao's vision for China's socialist development. The conflicts could not be contained within reasoned debate, either in or outside the new university system, but broke into open and violent conflict, culminating in the Cultural Revolution of 1966. The dream of clear moral and political directions, and a prosperous and unified modern socialist state, failed. It was a dream emanating from a science fundamentally rooted in the European enlightenment, and linked back in certain ways to the earlier role of theology in European scholarly thought.

Only in the early 1980s, when Deng Xiaoping declared China would open its doors to modernization, the world and the future, could the rich experience of modern university building in the pre-1949 period be recovered, and reforms be undertaken that have allowed diverse influences from the outside to interact with new developments in China's higher education. It is also only most recently that scholars within China have been able to join their voices with a large Chinese diaspora which has undertaken to introduce a "Confucian project" in dialogue with western critics of the Enlightenment project such as Juergen Habermas.[66]

One event in the two decades since China opened up to the world has demonstrated most vividly the degree to which the rich legacy of a century of experimentation with European and American models of the university has remained alive, in spite of determined efforts to destroy both ideology and organizations in the early 1950s. That is the famous democracy movement of 1989, which culminated in the tragic events of June 4th. It is not surprising that the movement started at Peking University, where intellectual freedom had been institutionalized 70 years earlier by Cai Yuanpei, and where the May 4th tradition of cultural transformation and social advancement through critical debate and the tolerance of all views had never been wiped out.

There are many other evidences in the rich intellectual life of contemporary China of the heritage of a melding of China's progressive traditions of the *shuyuan* with dimensions of the European and American university model developed over the century. Most recently, there has been a strong movement towards a restructuring of the Chinese university through large-scale mergers, that would integrate the various fields of knowledge, which had been separated under the Soviet system. Medical and agricultural universities are being merged with comprehensive universities, sometimes in a

---

[66] Tu Wei-ming, "Toward a Third Epoch of Confucian Humanism", in Tu Wei-ming, *The Way, Learning and Politics* (Albany: State University of New York Press, 1993), pp. 141-159.

reversal of history, as narrowly specialist institutions that had been separated out from universities in the Soviet-inspired reorganization of 1952, are reunited into their original intellectual home. [67]   Tsinghua University, designated a polytechnical university in 1952 and deprived of its departments in humanities and social sciences, has now re-established a centre for integrated studies of Chinese philosophy and thought which aspires to recapture its past glory, while Peking University has regained its lost faculty of medicine.

To what degree do China's universities now enjoy autonomy, and intellectual freedom, such that they may be a vehicle for communicating China's rich civilizational heritage to the global community? There are certainly continuing constraints, related to the political system, yet the celebration of the 100th anniversary of Peking University on May 4th, 1998, signified the new status enjoyed by major universities within China and in the global community. The event was held in the Great Hall of the People and over 100 university presidents from major universities around the world came to pay their respects. This was the first time in modern history that the whole of the Chinese Communist leadership, every member of the Party's influential Politbureau, sat through a ceremony in honour of its premier intellectual institution. In the speech given by Communist Party Chairman Jiang Zemin for this occasion, the central phrase was "Science and Education to Revitalize the Nation", and the leading role of major universities in China's next phase of development was clearly acknowledged.

The other point that is noteworthy in contemporary Chinese higher education is that women now participate more fully than ever before, with 48% of university teachers under 30 and 36% of all teaching staff being women in 1998. [68] Women's more integrative and cross-disciplinary approaches to knowledge are increasingly finding their way into curriculum development, and women are in the forefront of new approaches to disciplines such as sociology and anthropology. [69] Also the number of women scholars in fields such as basic sciences and engineering are relatively high, by global standards, due to the fact that women were strongly encouraged to enter these fields in the 1950s. As the Chinese university enters into more and more extensive dialogue with universities in the global arena, it is in a situation where women as well as men are active interlocutors.

LESSONS FROM THE CHINESE ACADEMY

This chapter has traced the first contacts between the European university and the Chinese academy, then sketched out contrasts between the institutional patterns, organization of knowledge and core values in the two traditions. It has then outlined the

---

[67] For a few examples, see R. Hayhoe *China's Universities 1895-1995*, 1999, pp. 259-260.
[68] Department of Planning and Development, Ministry of Education, People's Republic of China, *Educational Statistics Yearbook of China 1998* (Beijing: People's Education Press, 1999), p. 32.
[69] Christina Gilmartin, G. Hershatter. L. Rofel and T. White (eds.) *Engendering China* (Cambridge, Mass: Harvard University Press, 1994).

ways in which the European university transformed itself in four differing modern contexts, while still maintaining core values of autonomy and academic freedom. Despite the remarkable successes of the modernization process, the university's tendency towards increasing specialization, a dualism in epistemology and value neutrality has given it certain limitations in dealing with the moral and political dilemmas of the 20th century. The ways in which the four Western versions of the university exerted their influence on modern Chinese higher draws attention to the issue of values and the relationship between moral-political, spiritual and academic knowledge. The simple conclusion which I would like to try and elaborate here, is that there are lessons we may be able to learn from elements in the epistemology and institutional patterns of the Chinese academy that have persisted or re-asserted themselves in modern Chinese universities which could enhance the capacity of the university to deal responsibly with the challenges of the 21st century.

With the increasing plethora of information that is part of the internet age, and the remarkable possibilities of modern scientific knowledge in fields such as genetics to transform fundamental elements of human life, the choices open to human decision multiply. What is the university's role in moral decision-making? How can it help us to judge what is of ultimate value in the masses of information readily available? Can it offer guidance for the pursuit of spiritual development amid a world whose material structures and patterns are increasingly transparent? There is much in Christianity and Judaism, also in Western philosophy, which addresses these questions, yet the epistemological orientation and institutional patterns of the university have not always facilitated this type of inquiry. It may thus be worthwhile considering how China's traditions of the academy and its philosophy of Confucianism could enrich the university and enhance its capacity in this area. The focus in this chapter has been on China, but the traditions of other Eastern civilizations also have much to contribute, as we have seen earlier in this volume.

The American philosopher, Robert Cummings Neville, noted at a conference in 1998 that "for the first time in history it is possible for any self-conscious participant in a world-wide philosophical culture to speak of Confucianism in the same breath with Platonism and Aristotelianism, phenomenology and analytic philosophy as a phi-losophy from which to learn and perhaps to inhabit and extend". The entry of Confucianism into the world culture of philosophy is an historic moment, made possible by scholars from the Chinese diaspora such as Tu Weiming. Neville notes that "world society will never be civilized until a genuine world culture is developed that respects the diverse cultures and harmonizes them to make crucial response to such issues as care for the environment, distributive justice and the meaning of human life in the cosmos".[70]

While noting that social sciences in the West have tended to be "lame and stumbling over normative matters". Neville suggests the possible redemptive value of Confucianism. He calls attention to "a profound Confucian tradition of more than two

---

[70] Robert Cummings Neville, "Tu Wei-ming's Neo-Confucianism", in the *International Review of Chinese Philosophy and Religion*, Vol. 5, 2000, pp. 163, 169.

millennia that reflects on the differences between civilized and barbaric rituals, between better norms for personal and social life and worse ones, between better conventions and worse ones".[71] He notes how this may overcome the dualism that has tended to be prevalent in Western social sciences: "Western ethical theory has tended to focus on individual acts and the principles or goals of such actions; Western political and social theory has focused on actual historical institutions and social structures. Ritual conventions lie between these two and embrace much of what is normative in both".[72] "A new Confucian theory of ritual convention as constitutive of humanity in both personal and social dimensions provides an even more effective approach to norms in an age of pluralism, social disintegration and conflict".[73]

The leading figure in introducing Confucianism to a wider global community over recent decades, Tu Wei-ming, has depicted the dilemma of the Enlightenment in terms of a set of values of instrumental rationality, individual liberty, calculated self-interest, material progress and rights consciousness. He suggests that these have made possible remarkable prosperity yet, at the same time, disturbing social and environmental problems. In a recent volume on Confucianism and the environment, Tu gives the following succinct summary of the process and relationships of learning within Confucianism, which he views as a response to this dilemma of the Enlightenment:

> The Confucian way is a way of learning to be human. Learning to be human in the Confucian spirit is to engage oneself in a ceaseless, unending process of creative self-transformation..... The purpose of learning is always understood as being for the sake of the self, but the self is never an isolated individual (an island); rather it is a centre of relationships (a flowing stream). The self as a centre of relationships is a dynamic open system rather than a closed static structure. Therefore, mutuality be-tween self and community, harmony between human species and nature, and con-tinuous communication with Heaven are defining characteristics and supreme values in the human project.[74]

These values of connectedness and integration have long been associated with women's ways of knowing on both sides of the globe. It may therefore be appropriate to conclude with some thoughts from a distinguished woman sociologist, living and working in China, who brings a uniquely feminist angle to the view of how Chinese scholarship may contribute to the global community:

> The birth and development of women's studies itself is a kind of "revolution" against traditional scolasticism....Women's sensitivity, sympathetic nature and excellence in

---

[71] *Ibid.* p. 187.

[72] *Ibid.* p. 188.

[73] *Ibid.* p. 190.

[74] Tu Wei-ming, "Beyond the Enlightenment Mentality", in Mary Evelyn Tucker and John Berthrong (eds.), *Confucianism and Ecology: The Interrelation of Heaven, Earth and Humans* (Cambridge, Mass.: Harvard University Centre for the Study of World Religions, distributed by Harvard University Press, 1998), pp. 13-14.

listening attentively to others' opinions, their desire to avoid and resolve conflict as well as their intuition about and experience in the world, the ease with which women connect to one another, their courage in earnestly practising what they advocate all bring a special vigour to women's studies..... Contemporary Western sociology, with its advocacy of precise science and technology and dry mathematics, can offer scant help to women's studies. Anthropology, by contrast, with its attention to cultural difference, its in-depth inquiry into the rich and varied lives of different peoples, and its simple and unadorned theory, methods and results, is worthy of study and use.....[75]

What is the main lesson to be learned from the Chinese academy? Above all else, I would suggest, it is a restoration of a sense of connectedness, between theory and practice, fact and value, individual and community, institution and political-social-natural context. The core values of the European university, autonomy and academic freedom, were of crucial importance to the emergence of modern science and industrialism. Yet the institutionalization of these separations has given Western universities great difficulty in dealing with modern crises in value, from fascism to environmental destruction. By contrast the Chinese world of scholarship, both in terms of institutional structure and epistemological tendency, has been more fluid, less absolute in the lines it drew to separate itself from the natural environment, the political system, and religious authority. This may have made it more vulnerable to conflict, as seen in the modern history of Chinese universities, yet it has also been less prepared to relinquish moral, political and spiritual responsibility and engagement. Its values of intellectual freedom and a kind of scholarly localism, even fragmentation, have linked it closely to local social, political and spiritual struggles. It could not rise above, but had to be immanent in its environment.

---

[75] *Ibid.* p. 78.

Bibliography

Abu-Lughod, Janet L., *Before European Hegemony: the World System A.D. 1250-1350* (New York: Oxford University Press, 1989).

Adorno, Theodor W. et al, *The Positivist Dispute in German Sociology* (London: Heinemann, 1976).

Ake, Claude, *Social Science as Imperialism: A Theory of Political Development* (Ibadan, Nigeria: Ibadan University Press, 1979).

Al Faruqi, I. and Nasseef, A. (eds.), *Social and Natural Sciences: The Islamic Perspective* (Jeddah: King Abdul Aziz University, 1981).

Al Faruqi, I., *Tawhid: Its Relevance for Thought and Life* (Malaysia: Polygraphic Press, 1983).

Al Faruqi, I., *The Cultural Atlas of Islam* (New York: MacMillan, 1986).

Al Zeera, Z., "Evaluation of the Orientation Program at the University of Bahrain: A Sociocultural Perspective" (unpublished Ph.D. thesis, University of Toronto, 1990).

Alatas, Syed Hussein, "The Captive Mind and Creative Development", in *International Social Science Journal* Vol. 26, No. 4, 1976, pp. 691-700

Al-Ebraheem, H.A. and Stevens, R.P., "Organization, Management and Academic Problems in the Arab University: The Kuwait University Experience", in *Higher Education*, No. 9 (1980), pp. 203-221.

Alghafis, Ali N., *Universities in Saudi Arabia: Their Role in Science, Technology and Development* (Lanham, MD: University Press of America, 1992).

Alitto, Guy, *The Last Confucian: Liang Shu-ming and the Chinese Dilemma of Modernity* (Berkeley: University of California Press, 1986).

Allen, Garth et al, *Community Education: An Agenda for Educational Reform* (Milton Keynes: Open University Press, 1985).

Altbach, Philip G., *Comparative Higher Education: Knowledge, the University and Development* (Hong Kong: Comparative Education Research Centre, The University of Hong Kong, 1998).

Altbach, P. and Selvaratnam, V. (eds.), *From Dependence to Autonomy: The Development of Asian Universities* (London and Dordrecht: Kluwer, 1989).

Altbach, Philip G. et al, *Scientific Development and Higher Education: The Case of Newly Industrializing Nations* (New York: Praeger, 1989).

Altbach, Philip G., "The Dilemma of Change in Indian Higher Education", in *Higher Education*, Vol. 26, No. 1 (1993), pp. 3-20.

Altbach, Philip G., *The Knowledge Context: Comparative Perspectives on the Distribution of Knowledge* (Albany: State University of New York Press, 1987).

Alvares, Claude, "Science, Colonialism and Violence: A Luddite View", in Ashis

Nandy (ed.), *Science, Hegemony and Violence: A Requiem for Modernity* (Delhi: Oxford University Press, 1988).

American Indian Higher Education Consortium (AIHEC), *Tribal Colleges: An Introduction* (Washington, D.C.: Institute for Higher Education Policy, 2000).

Amir, S.M., "Scientific Research in Muslim Countries", M.A.K. Lodhi (ed.), in *Islamization of Attitudes and Practices in Science and Technology* (USA: International Institute of Islamic Thought and Association of Muslim Scientists and Engineers, 1989), pp. 15-20.

Anderson, R.S. and Huber, W., *The Hour of the Fox: Tropical Forests, the World Bank, and Indigenous People in Central India* (Seattle: University of Washington Press, 1988).

Andrews, Julia, *Painters and Politics in the People's Republic of China, 1949-1979* (Berkeley: University of California Press, 1993).

Apel, Karl-Otto, *Understanding and Explanation: A Transcendental-Pragmatic Perspective* (Cambridge, MA: The MIT Press, 1984).

Arasteh, R., *Education and Social Awakening in Iran* (Leiden: E.J. Brill, 1962).

Archibald, J., "Coyote's Story About Orality and Literacy", in *Canadian Journal of Native Education*, Vol. 17, No. 2, 1990, pp. 66-81.

Armstrong, R., Kennedy, J., & Oberle, P.R., *University Education and Economic Well-Being: Indian Achievement and Prospectus* (Ottawa: Indian and Northern Affairs Canada, 1990).

Arnove, R., "Introduction: Reframing Comparative Education: The Dialectic of the Global and the Local", in Robert Arnove and Carlos Alberto Torres (eds.), *Comparative Education: The Dialectic of the Global and the Local* (Lanham, Boulder, New York, Oxford: Rowman and Littlefield Publishers, 1999), pp. 1-23.

Artz, Frederick, *The Development of Technical Education in France 1500-1850* (Cambridge, Mass, and London, England: The Society for the History of Technology and MIT Press, 1968).

Ashby, Eric, *Universities: British, Indian, African* (Cambridge: Harvard University Press, 1966).

Bacon, Francis, "Novun Organum, Aphorism 129", in Francis Bacon, *Advancement of Learning and Novun Organum* (New York: The Colonial Press, 1899).

Bacon, Francis, "Advancement of Learning", in Joseph Devey (eds.), *The Physical and Metaphysical Works of Lord Bacon* (London: Bell and Sons, 1911), Bk II, Ch. II.

Bai, Jin (Joachim Bouvet), *Kangxi di zhuan* (Beijing: Zhonghua shuju, 1980).

Balme, Harold, *China and Modern Medicine: A Study of Medical Missionary Development* (London: United Council for Missionary Education, 1921).

Barber, Benjamin, *Strong Democracy: Participatory Politics for a New Age* (Berkeley: University of California Press, 1984).

Barnhardt, Ray, "Higher Education in the Fourth World: Indigenous People Take Control", *Tribal College: Journal of American Indian Higher Education*, 1991, Autumn.

Barnhardt, Ray, *Domestication of the Ivory Tower: Institutional Adaptation to*

Cultural Distance (Fairbanks, AK: University of Alaska Fairbanks, 1986).

Barthes, Roland, *Writing Degree Zero* (Boston: Beacon, 1970).

Bastid, Marianne, "Servitude or Liberation? The Introduction of Foreign Educational Practices and Systems to China from 1840 to the Present", in R. Hayhoe and M. Bastid (eds.), *China's Education and the Industrialised World: Studies in Cultural Transfer* (Armonk, N.Y.: M.E. Sharpe, 1987), pp. 3-20.

Basu, A., *The Growth of Education and Political Development in India, 1898-1920* (Delhi: Oxford University Press, 1974).

Bauman, Zygmunt, "Life-world and Expertise: Social Production of Dependency", in Nico Stehr and Richard V. Ericson (eds.), *The Culture and Power of Knowledge: Inquiries into Contemporary Societies* (Berlin/New York: de Gruyter, 1992), pp.81-106.

Bauman, Zygmunt, *Modernity and Ambivalence* (Cambridge: Polity Press, 1991).

Baumer, F.L., *Modern European Thought: Continuity and Change in Ideas, 1600-1950* (New York, Macmillan Publishing Company, 1977).

Beaty, J., & Chiste, K.B., University Preparation for Native American Students: Theory and Application, in *Journal of American Indian Education*, Vol. 26, No. 1, 1986, pp. 6-13.

Belenky, Mary Field, Clinchy, B.M., Goldberger, N.R. and Tarule, J.M., *Women's Ways of Knowing* (New York: Basic Books, 1986).

Ben-David, Joseph, *American Higher Education: Directions Old and New* (New York: McGraw Hill Book Co., 1972).

Benezet, L.T., *General Education in the Progressive College* (New York: Arno Press and The New York Times, 1970).

Benoit, Paul, "La Théologie au XIII? Siècle: une science pas comme les autres", in Michael Serres, *Eléments d'histoire des sciences* (Paris: Bordas, 1989).

Berger, P., Berger, B., & Kneller, H., *The Homeless Mind: Modernization and Consciousness* (New York: Random House, 1973).

Berger, Peter L. and Luckmann, Thomas, *The Social Construction of Reality: A Treatise in the Sociology of Knowledge* (Garden City, NJ: Anchor Books, 1967).

Berggren, J.Len, "Medieval Islamic Methods for Drawing Azimuth Circles on the Astrolabe", in *Centaurus*, Vol. 34, 1991, pp. 309-344.

Berggren, J.Len, *Episodes in the Mathematics of Medieval Islam* (New York and Heidelberg: Springer Verlag, 1986).

Berkeley, Bishop George, *Three Dialogues between Hylas and Philonous* (Cleveland: World Publishing Co., 1963).

Bhabha, Homi K., *The Location of Culture* (London/ New York: Routledge and Kegan Paul, 1994).

Bhambhri, C.P., *World Bank and India* (New Delhi: Vikas Publishing House, 1980).

Birge, Bettine, "Chu Hsi and Women's Education", in W.T. de Bary and J. Chaffee, *Neo-Confucian Education: The Formative Stage* (Berkeley: University of California Press, 1989), pp. 325-367.

Blomstrom, Magnus and Hettne, Björn (eds.), *Development theory in transition: The dependency debate and beyond* (London: Zed Books, 1984).

Bloom, A., *The Closing of the American Mind* (New York: Simon and Schuster, 1987).

Blyden, Edward W., *Christianity, Islam and the Negro Race* (London: W.B. Whittingham & Co., 1888, reprinted by Edinburgh University Press, 1967).

Bohr, Niels, *Atomic Physics and Human Knowledge* (New York: Wiley, 1958).

Boner, Alice, Sarma, Sadasiva Rath and Baumer, Bettina, *Vastusutra Upanisad* (Delhi: Motilal Banarsidass, 1982).

Borda, Fals, "The Challenge of Action Research", in *Development*, 1981, No. 1, pp. 55-61.

Bosse, Hans, *Verwaltete Unterentwicklung: Funktionen und Verwertung der Bildungsforschung in der staatlichen Entwicklungspolitik* (Frankfurt: Suhrkamp, 1978).

Boulding, Elise, "Cultural Perspectives on Development: The Relevance of Sociology and Anthropology", in *Alternatives*, Vol. 14, 1989, pp. 107-122.

Boxer, C.R., "A Note on the Interaction of Portuguese and Chinese Medicine in Macao and Peking (16th – 18th centuries)", in J.Z. Bowers et al (eds.), *Medicine and Society in China*, (New York: Josiah Macy Jr. Foundation, 1974).

Boyd, Dwight and Pan, Julia, *Women and Minorities as Educational Change Agents* (Toronto: Department of Theory and Policy Studies in Education, OISE/UT, 2001).

Boyer, E.L., *College: The Undergraduate Experience in America* (Cambridge, Mass.: Harper and Row, 1987).

Boyer, P., *Tribal Colleges: Shaping the Future of Native America* (Princeton, NJ: The Carnegie Foundation for the Advancement of Teaching, Princeton University Press, 1989).

Boym, Michael, *Flora Sinensis* (Vienna, 1656).

Brandt, Willy, *Common Crisis: North-South: Cooperation for World Recovery/The Brandt Commission* (Cambridge, Mass.: MIT Press, 1983).

Bray, Francesca, "The Chinese Contribution to Europe's Agricultural Revolution: a Technology Transformed", in Li Guohao et al, *Explorations in the History of Science and Technology in China* (Shanghai: Shanghai Chinese Classics Publishing House, 1982).

Brenkman, John, *Culture and Domination* (Ithaca NY: Cornell University Press, 1987).

Brokensha, David et al, *Indigenous Knowledge Systems and Development* (Lanham, MD: University Press of America, 1980).

Brown, Hubert O., "People's Republic of China", in P.G. Altbach (ed.), *International Higher Education: An Encyclopedia* (New York: Garland Publishers, 1991), pp. 451-466.

Butt, N., *Science and Muslim Societies* (London: Grey Seal, 1991).

Cai, Keyong, "Reflections on General Education and Specialized Education", in *Gaodeng jiaoyu yanjiu* (*Higher Education Research*), No. 1, 1987, pp. 14-16.

Cai, Yuanpei, *Cai Yuanpei xuanji* (Selected writings of Cai Yuanpei) (Beijing:

Zhonghua shuju, 1959).

Cantlie, J., "Needling Painful Spots, as Practised by the Chinese", in *Journal of Tropical Medicine and Hygiene,* February, 1916.

Carter, D.J. and Wilson, R., *Minorities in Higher Education 1996-7: Fifteenth Annual Status Report* (Washington, D.C.: American Council on Education, 1997).

Cartwright, Nancy, *How the Laws of Physics Lie* (Oxford: Clarendon Press, 1983).

Casanova, Pablo Gonzalez, *The Fallacy of Social Science Research: A Critical Examination and New Qualitative Model* (New York: Pergamon, 1981).

Castells, Manuel, "High Technology, World Development, and the Structural Transformation: The Trends and the Debate", in *Alternatives,* Vol. 11, 1986, pp. 297-343.

Challenge of Education: A Policy Perspective, Publication No. 1517 (New Delhi: Ministry of Education, 1986).

Challenge to the South: Report of the South Commission (Oxford: Oxford University Press, 1990).

Chambers, R., *Rural Development: Putting the Last First* (New York: Longman, 1983).

Chan, W.T. (trans.), *Instructions for Practical Living and Other Neo-Confucian Writings* (New York: Columbia University Press, 1963).

Charlton, Sue Ellen, *Women in Third World Development* (Boulder: Westview, 1984).

Chen, Dongyuan, *Zhongguo funu shenghuoshi* (A History of Women's Lives) (Shanghai: Commercial Press, 1928).

Chen, K.K., "Half a Century of Ephedrine", in *American Journal of Chinese Medicine,* Vol. 2, No. 4, 1974, pp. 359-365.

Chen, K.K., "Two Pharmacological Traditions: Notes from Experience", in *Annals Review of Pharmacology and Toxicology,* Vol. 21, 1981, pp. 1-6.

Chen, Yiyun, "Out of the Traditional Halls of Academe: Exploring New Avenues for Research on Women", translated by S. Katherine Campbell, in C. Gilmartin et al, (eds.), *Engendering China* (Cambridge, Mass.: Harvard University Press, 1994).

Cheng, Keji et al, *Qingdai gongting yihua* (People's Literature Press, 1987).

Childers, E.B., "Amnesia and Antagonism" in Farish A. Noor (ed.), *Terrorising the Truth: The Shaping of Contemporary Images of Islam and Muslims in Media, Politics and Culture* (Penang, Malaysia: Just World Trust, 1997), pp. 123-149.

China Historical Society (ed.), *Zhongguo jindaishi ziliao congshu* (Shanghai: Shenzhou Guoguangshe, 1953), Series 8, "Wuxu bianfa", Vol. 2.

Chitnis, Suma and Altbach, Philip G. (eds.), *Higher Education Reform in India: Experience and Perspectives* (New Delhi: Sage Publications, 1993).

Choi, Hyaeweol, *An International Scientific Community: Asian Scholars in the United States* (Westport, Conn.: Praeger, 1995).

Chrisjohn, R.D., & Mrochuk, M.L., *First Nations House of Learning Program Evaluation Report* (Vancouver, B.C.: First Nations House of Learning, University of British Columbia, 1990).

Chuan, H.S., "Qingmo xiyang yixue chuanru shi Zhongguoren suochi de taidu", in

Shihua banyuekan, Vol. 3, No. 12, 1936, pp. 47-49.

Churchward, L.G., *The Soviet Intelligentsia* (London: Routledge and Kegan Paul, 1973).

Cohen, Joan Lebold, *The New Chinese Painting, 1949-1986* (New York: Harry N. Abrams, 1987).

Colebrooke, H.T., *Algebra, with Arithmetic and Mensuration, from the Sanscrit of Brahmegupta and Bhascara* (London: John Murray, 1817).

Connor, P., *Oriental Architecture in the West* (London: Thames and Hudson, 1979).

Conway, Jill K. et al (eds.), *Learning About Women: Gender, Politics, and Power* (Ann Arbor: University of Michigan Press, 1987).

Coser, Lewis, "Publishers as Gatekeepers of Ideas", in *Annals of the American Academy of Political and Social Sciences,* No. 421 (September 1975), pp. 14-22.

Crane, Diana, *Invisible Colleges: Diffusion of Knowledge in Scientific Communities* (Chicago: University of Chicago Press, 1972).

Croizier, Ralph, "'Going to the World': Art and Culture on the Cosmopolitan Tide", in *China Briefing, 1989* (Boulder, Co.: Westview Press, 1989).

Crossley, J.N. and Henry, A.S., "Thus Spake al-Khwarizmi: A Translation of the Text of Cambridge University Library Ms. li.Vi.5", in *Historia Mathematica,* Vol. 17, 1990, pp. 103-131.

Crossman, C., *The Decorative Arts of the China Trade* (Woodbridge, Suffolk: Antique Collector's Club, 1991).

Crozier, Michel J. et al, *The Crisis of Democracy: Report on the Governability of Democracies to the Trilateral Commission* (New York: New York University Press, 1975).

Dal Lago, Francesca & Dematté, Monica, "Chinese Art or the Venice Biennale" 1 and 2, in John Clark, (ed.), *Chinese Art at the End of the Millennium* (Beijing: Chinese-art.com, 2000).

Dallal, A., "Science, Medicine and Technology: The Making of a Scientific Culture", in John L. Esposito (ed.), *The Oxford History of Islam* (Oxford: Oxford University Press, 1999), pp. 155-213.

Dallmayr, Fred R. and McCarthy, Thomas A., *Understanding and Social Inquiry* (Notre Dame: University of Notre Dame Press, 1977).

Dantzig, Tobias, *Number: the Language of Science* (New York: Macmillan and Co., 1954).

Darwin, C., *The Variation of Animals and Plants Under Domestication* (London, John Murray, 1868).

Deleuze, Gilles and Guattari, Félix, *A Thousand Plateaus: Capitalism and Schizophrenia* (Minneapolis: University of Minnesota Press, 1987).

Delors, Jacques et al (eds.), *Learning: The Treasure Within,* Report to UNESCO of the International Commission on Education for the Twenty-First Century (Paris: UNESCO Publishing, 1998).

Dewitt, Nicholas, *Soviet Professional Manpower* (Washington, D.C.: National Science Foundation, 1955).

Ding, Gang, "The Shuyuan and the Development of Chinese universities in the early twentieth century", in R. Hayhoe and J. Pan (eds.), *East-West Dialogue in Knowledge and Higher Education* (New York: M.E. Sharpe, 1996), pp. 218-244.

Douthwaite, A.W., "The Use of Native Drugs by Medical Missionaries", in *The China Medical Missionary Journal,* Vol. 4, No. 3, 1890, pp. 101-105.

Dronke, Peter, *Women Writers of the Middle Ages* (Cambridge: Cambridge University Press, 1984).

Du Halde, J.B., *Description Géographique, Historique, Chronologique, Politique de l'Empire de la Chine* (Paris, 1735).

DuBois, Marc, "The Governance of the Third World: A Foucauldian Perspective on Power Relations in Development", in *Alternatives,* Vol. 16, 1991, pp. 1-30.

Duiker, William, *Ts'ai Yuan-p'ei: Educator of Modern China* (University Park and London: Pennsylvania State University Press, 1977).

Eaton, C., "Man" in S.H. Nasr (ed.), *Islamic Spirituality* (New York: Crossroad, 1987).

Edelman, Murray, *Political Language: Words That Succeed and Policies That Fail* (New York: Academic Press, 1977).

Ellul, Jacques, *The Technological Society* (New York: Knopf, 1967).

Enriquez, V.G., "Towards Cross-cultural Knowledge through Cross-indigenous Methods and Perspectives", in J. L. M. Binniei-Dawson, G. H. Blowers and R. Hoosain (eds.), *Perspectives in Asian Cross-cultural Psychology* (Lisse, Netherlands: Swets and Zeithinger, B. V., 1981), pp. 29-41.

Escobar, Arturo, "Discourse and Power in Development: Michel Foucault and the Relevance of his Work to the Third World", in *Alternatives,* Vol. 10, 1984-85, pp. 377-400.

Etiemble, René, *Les Jésuites en Chine: La querelle des rites (1552-1773)* (Paris: Julliard, 1966).

Etiemble, René, *L'Europe chinoise* (2 vols.) (Paris: Gallimard, 1988-89)

Fagerlind, Ingemar & Saha, Lawrence J., *Education and National Development: A Comparative Perspective (*New York: Pergamon Press, 1989).

Fairbank, John and Teng,. Ssu-yu, *China's Response to the West: A Documentary Survey 1839-1923* (Cambridge: Harvard University Press, 1954).

Fan Xing-zun, *Mingji xiyang chuanru zhi yixue* (Shanghai: China Medical History Society, 1943).

Farganis, Sondra, *Social Reconstruction of the Feminine Character* (Totowa, NJ: Rowman and Littlefield, 1986).

Fay, Brian, *Critical Social Science: Liberation and its Limits* (Ithaca: Cornell University Press, 1987).

Fei Xiaotong, Li Anguo, *Zhongguo wenhua yu xinshiji de shehuixue renleixue – Fei Xiaotong, Li Yiyuan duihualu* (Chinese Culture and Social Anthropology in the New Century) (Beijing: Transaction of Beijing University, 6th Issue, 1998).

Feyerabend, Paul K., *Against method: outline of an anarchistic theory of knowledge* (London : Verso, 1978).

Fischer, M.J., *Iran, From Religious Dispute to Revolution* (Massachusetts: Harvard

University Press, 1980).

Floyer, J., *The Physician's Pulse Watch* (London, 1707).

Foss, Theodore, *A Jesuit Encyclopedia for China*, 1979, 2 vols.

Foucault, Michel, *Power / Knowledge: Selected Interviews and Other Writings, 1972-1977* (New York: Pantheon, 1980).

Foucault, Michel, *The Archeology of Knowledge* (New York: Pantheon, 1972).

Foucault, Michel, *The Order of Things: An Archeology of the Human Sciences* (New York: Pantheon, 1971).

Foust, Clifford M., *Rhubarb, The Wondrous Drug* (New Jersey, Princeton University Press, 1992).

Franklin, Ursula M., "All is not well in the House of Technology", in *Transactions of the Royal Society of Canada*, Sixth Series, Vol. VIII, 1997, pp. 22-33.

Franklin, Ursula M., "Bronze and other Metals in early China", in David N. Keightley (ed.), *The Origin of Chinese Civilization*" (Berkeley: University of California Press, 1983), pp. 279-299

Franklin, Ursula M., "Issues of Access to Justice raised by Modern Technology", in *Windsor Yearbook of Access to Justice*, Vol. XIV, 1994, pp. 243-254.

Franklin, Ursula M., "Personally happy and publicly useful", in *Our Schools/Ourselves*, Vol. 9, Nr. 4, Toronto, 1998, pp. 81-97.

Franklin, Ursula M., *An Examination of Prehistoric Copper Technology and Copper Sources in Western Arctic and Subarctic North America* (Minerva Series, Monograph Nr.100, National Museums of Canada, Ottawa, 1981).

Franklin, Ursula M., *Every Tool shapes the Task; Communities and the Information Highway* (Vancouver: Chapbook, Lazara Press, 1996).

Franklin, Ursula M., *Knowledge Reconsidered: A Feminist Overview* (Ottawa: Canadian Research Institute for the Advancement of Women, 1984).

Franklin, Ursula M., *The Real World of Technology* (Toronto: House of Anansi Press, 1999, second and enlarged edition) (first published by CBC Enterprises, Toronto, 1990).

Franklin, Ursula M., *Will Women Change Technology or Will Technology Change Women?* (Ottawa: Canadian Research Institute for the Advancement of Women, 1985).

Franklin, Ursula M., with J. Berthrong and Alan Chan, "Metallurgy, Cosmology, Knowledge; the Chinese Experience", in *The Journal of Chinese Philosophy*, No.12, 1985, pp. 333-369.

Freire, Paulo, *Pedagogy of the Oppressed* (New York: Herder and Herder, 1972).

Friedman, Thomas L., *The Lexus and the Olive Tree* (New York: Farrar Straus Giroux, 1999, republished by Anchor Books, New York, 2000).

Fries, J., *The American Indian in Higher Education, 1975-76 to 1984-85* (Washington, D.C.: Office of Educational Research and Improvement, U.S. Department of Education, 1987).

Fryer, J., "Jiangnan zhizaoju fangyi yishu shilue, 1880", in Zhang Jinglu (ed.), *Zhongguo jindai shiliao chubian*, (Shanghai Press, 1953), pp. 10-11.

Fuller, Steve, *The Governance of Science: Ideology and the Future of the Open Society* (Buckingham: Open University Press, 2000).

Gadamer, Hans-Georg, *Reason in the Age of Science* (Cambridge, MA: MIT Press, 1981).

Gaff, J.G., *General Education Today* (San Francisco: Jossey-Bass, 1983).

Gao, Minglu (ed.), *China's New Art Post-1989* (Hong Kong: Hanart, 1993).

Gao, Minglu (ed.), *Inside Out New Chinese Art* (New York: Asia Society, 1999).

Garfield, Eugene, "Science in the Third World", in *Science Age* (October-November 1983), pp. 59-65.

Geertz, Clifford, "'From the Native's Point View': On the Nature of Anthropological Understanding", in R. A. Scheweder and R. A. Levire (eds.), *Cultural Theory: Essays on Mind, Self, and Emotion* (Cambridge: Cambridge University Press, 1984), pp. 133-136.

Geertz, Clifford, "Blurred Genres: The Refiguration of Social Thought", in Clifford Geertz, *Local Knowledge: Further Essays in Interpretive Anthropology* (New York: Basic Books, 1983), pp. 19-35.

Gilmartin, C., Hershatter, G., Rofel, L. and White, T. (eds.), *Engendering China* (Cambridge, Mass: Harvard University Press, 1994).

Giroux, H., "Border Pedagogy in the Age of Postmodernism", in *Journal of Education*, Vol. 170, No. 3, 1988, pp. 162-181.

Gleick, James, *Chaos: Making a New Science* (New York: Viking, 1987).

Glubb, J., *The Lost Centuries: From the Muslim Empires to the Renaissance of Europe* (London, 1967).

Goodby, M. and Lockett, T., *Oriental Expressions: The Influence of the Orient on British Ceramics* (Stoke on Trent: The Northern Ceramic Society, 1989).

Goodman, Sharon and Graddol, Denise, *Redesigning English: New Texts, New Identification* (London and New York: Routledge, 1996).

Goody, J., "Alternative Paths to Knowledge in Oral and Literate Cultures", in D. Tannen (ed.), *Spoken and Written Language: Exploring Orality and Literacy* (Norwood, NJ: Ablex Publishing Corporation, 1982).

Gouldner, Alvin W., *The Coming Crisis of Western Sociology* (New York: Basic Books, 1970).

Gran, Guy, "Beyond African Famines: Whose Knowledge Matters?", in *Alternatives*, Vol. 11, 1986, pp. 275-296.

Greenberg, Michael, *British Trade and the Opening of China 1800-1842* (Cambridge: Cambridge University Press, 1951).

Greenblatt, Stephen, *Marvelous Possessions. The Wonder of the New World* (Oxford: Clarendon Press, 1991).

Greene, J., "Three Views on the Nature and Role of Knowledge in Social Science" in E. Guba (ed.), *The Paradigm Dialogue* (New York: Sage Publications, Inc., 1990)

Gruson, Pascale, *L'Etat Enseignant* (Paris: Mouton, 1978).

Gu, Yongcai, "Tentative Inquiry on the Curriculum of General Education", in *Nankai* jiaoyu luntan (Nankai Education Forum), No. 3, 1991, pp. 8-11.

Guadilla, Carmen Garcia, "Globalization, Regional Integration, and Higher Education in Latin America" (Keynote paper at the Conference on Globalization and Higher Education: Views from the South, Cape Town, South Africa, March 27-29, 2001)

Guadilla, Carmen Garcia, Produccion y Transferencia de Paradigmas Teoricos en la Investigacion Socio-Educativa (Caracas: Tropykos, 1987).

Guba, E., "The Alternative Paradigm Dialogue", in E. Guba (ed.), The Paradigm Dialogue (Newbury Park: Sage Publications, 1990), pp.17-27.

Guenther, Isolde, "A Study of the Evolution of the German Technische Hochschule", unpublished PhD thesis, University of London Institute of Education, 1972.

Guy, Basil, The French Image of China Before and After Voltaire (Studies in Voltaire and the 18th Century, no. 21) (Geneva: Institut et Musée Voltaire, 1963).

Habermas, Jürgen, Knowledge and Human Interests (Boston: Beacon, 1971).

Habermas, Jürgen, Die neue Unübersichtlichkeit (Frankfurt: Suhrkamp, 1985).

Habermas, Jürgen, Die postnationale Konstellation – Politische Essays (Frankfurt/Main: Suhrkamp, 1998).

Habermas, Jürgen, Knowledge and Human Interests (London: Heineman, 1978).

Habermas, Jürgen, Legitimation Crisis (Boston: Beacon, 1975).

Haggis, Sheila M., Education for All: Purpose and Context (Paris, UNESCO: Monograph no. 1, 1991).

Hairi, M., The Early Encounters of the Iranian Thinkers with the Two-Sided Civilization of Western Bourgeoise (Tehran: Amir Kabir, 1988).

Hall, David L. and Ames, Roger, The Democracy of the Dead: Dewey, Confucius and the Hope for Democracy in China (Chicago and Lasalle, Illinois: Open Court, 1999).

Hamarneh, Sami K., "The Life Sciences," in John R. Hayes (ed.), The Genius of Arabic Civilization (New York: New York University Press, 1975), pp. 173-202.

Hampton, E., "Toward a Redefinition of American Indian/Alaska Native Education" (Doctoral Dissertation. Harvard University, 1988).

Harding, Sandra, Feminist Epistemology: Social Science Issues (Bloomington, Indiana: Indiana University Press, 1987).

Harding, Sandra, The Science Question in Feminism (Ithaca, New York: Cornell University Press, 1986).

Harding, Sandra, Whose Science? Whose Knowledge? Thinking from Women's Lives (Ithaca, New York: Cornell University Press, 1991).

Harley, J.B. and Woodward, D., The History of Cartography, Vol. 2: Cartography in the Traditional Islamic and South Asian Societies (Chicago: University of Chicago Press, 1992).

Harrington, J., "Education System Forces Alien Values on Natives", in The Ubyssey, Vol. 73, No. 36, 1991, p. 4.

Hartner, W., "Al-Battānī", in C. C. Gillespie (ed.), Dictionary of Scientific Biography, Vol. I (New York: Charles Scribner's Sons, 1970), pp. 507-516.

Hayhoe, R. and Pan, J. (eds.), East West Dialogue in Knowledge and Higher Education

(New York: M.E. Sharpe, 1996).

Hayhoe, R. et al (eds.), *Knowledge Across Cultures: Universities East and West* (Wuhan: Hubei Education Press, and Toronto: OISE Press, 1993).

Hayhoe, Ruth, "Redeeming Modernity", in *Comparative Education Review*, Vol. 44, No. 4, 2000, pp. 423-439.

Hayhoe, Ruth, "Catholics and Socialists: The Paradox of French Educational Interaction with China", in R. Hayhoe and M. Bastid (eds.), *China's Education and the Industralised World: Studies in Cultural Transfer* (New York: M.E. Sharpe, Toronto: OISE Press, 1987), pp. 109-112.

Hayhoe, Ruth, *China's Universities and the Open Door* (Armonk, N.Y.: M.E. Sharpe, 1989).

Hayhoe, Ruth, *China's Universities, 1895-1995: A Century of Cultural Conflict* (New York: Garland Publishers, 1996; Hong Kong: Comparative Education Research Centre, University of Hong Kong, 1999).

Heisenberg, Werner, *Physics and Philosophy* (New York: Harper Torchbooks, 1962).

Henze, Jürgen, "Educational Modernization as a Search for Higher Efficiency", in Hayhoe, R. and Bastid, M. (eds.), *China's Education and the Industrialised World:Studies in Cultural Transfer* (New York: M.E. Sharpe, 1987), pp. 252-270.

Herrera, Amilcar O., "The Generation of Technologies in Rural Areas", in *World Development,* Vol. 9, 1981, pp. 21-35.

Hettne, Björn, "Transcending the European Model of Peace and Development", in *Alternatives* Vol. 10, 1985, pp. 453-476.

Higher Education in Developing Countries: Peril and Promise (Washington, D.C.: The World Bank, 2000).

Hill, Donald R., "Mechanical Technology," in John R. Hayes (ed.), *The Genius of Arabic Civilization* (New York: New York University Press, 1975), pp. 203-220.

Hobson, B., *Report of the Hospital at Kum-li-fu in Canton for the Years 1848 and 1849* (London: Joseph Rogerson, 1849).

Hofstadter, Richard and Metzger, Walter, *The Development of Academic Freedom in the United States* (New York and London: Columbia University Press, 1955).

Honour, Hugh, *Chinoiserie: The Vision of Cathay* (New York: Dutton, 1961).

Horgan, John, "Quantum Philosophy", in *Scientific American*, July, 1992.

Hountondji, Paulin J., *African Philosophy: Myth and Reality* (Bloomington: Indiana University Press, 1983).

Howard, D. and Ayers, J., *China for the West: Chinese Porcelain & other Decorative Arts for Export* (New York: Sotheby Park Bernet, 1978).

Howard, D.S., *Chinese Armorial Porcelain* (London: Faber Publications, 1974).

Hsieh, H. Steve, "University Education and Research in Taiwan", in Altbach, P.G. (ed.), *Scientific Development and Higher Education: The Case of Newly Industrializing Nations* (New York: Praeger, 1989), pp. 177-213.

Hu, Shih, "The Significance of the New Thought", Document 62 in J. Fairbank and Teng Ssu-yu (eds.), *China's Response to the West: A Documentary Survey* (Cambridge: Harvard University Press, 1954), pp. 252-255.

Hume, E., *The Chinese Way in Medicine* (Baltimore: The John's Hopkins Press, 1940).

Huntington, S., "The Clash of Civilizations?", in *Foreign Affairs*, Vol. 72, No. 3, 1993.

Hutchins, R.M., *The Higher Learning in America* (New Haven: Yale University Press, 1967).

Ibn Khaldun, *The Muqaddimah: An Introduction to History*, translated by Franz Rosenthal (Princeton: Princeton University Press, 1958).

IDA in Retrospect (Washington: Oxford University Press,1982).

Impey, Oliver, *Chinoiserie: the Impact of Oriental Styles on Western Art and Decoration* (New York: C. Scribner's Sons, and London: Oxford University Press, 1977).

Inayatullah, Sohail and Gidley, Jennifer (eds.), *The University in Transformation: Global Perspectives on the Futures of the University* (Westport, CT: Bergin & Garvey, 2000).

Indian and Northern Affairs Canada (INAC), *Postsecondary Education for Status Indians and Inuit* (Ottawa, Ontario: Indian and Northern Affairs Canada, 2000).

Investment in Education: The Report of the Commission on Post-School Certificate and Higher Education in Nigeria (Lagos: Federal Ministry of Education, 1960).

Israel, John, *Lianda: A Chinese University in War and Revolution* (Stanford, California: Stanford University Press, 1998).

Ja'fari, M., *Science from Islamic Aspects* (Tehran: Industrial and Scientific Research Centre, 1982).

Jacobson, H.K. and Oksenberg, M., *China's Participation in the IMF, the World Bank, and GATT* (Ann Arbor: University of Michigan Press, 1990).

Jayawardene, S.A., "The Influence of Practical Arithmetics on the Algebra of Rafael Bombell", in *Isis*, Vol. 64, 1973, pp. 510-523.

Jeffreys, W.H., "'Freely Ye Have Received!' Native Methods of Medical Practice in China, A Comparison", in *Chinese Medical Missionary Journal*, No. 3, 1906.

Jeffreys, W.H., "A Review of Medical Education in China", in *Chinese Medical Journal*, Vol. 23, No. 5, 1909, pp. 294-296.

Jenyns, S. and Watson, W., *Chinese Art II* (Oxford: Phaidon, 1981).

Jin Yaoji (Ambrose King), "Xiandaixing, quanqiuhua yu Huaren jiaoyu" (Modernity, Globalization and the Education of Chinese People), in Lu Jie (ed.), *Huaren-jiaoyu: Minzu Wenhua Chuantong de Quanqiu Zhanwang* (Education of Chinese: The Global Prospect of National Cultural Tradition) (Nanjing: Nanjing Normal University Press, 1998), pp. 1-14.

Jinadu, L. Adele, *The social sciences and development in Africa: Ethiopia, Mozambique, Tanzania and Zimbabwe* (SAREC Report R1: 1985) (Stockholm: SAREC, 1985).

Johnson, William, *Russia's Educational Heritage* (Pittsburgh, Pennsylvania: Carnegie Press, 1950).

Jones, P.W., *World Bank Financing of Education* (London: Routledge, 1992).

Joseph, G.G., *The Crest of the Peacock* (London: Tauris and Co., 1991).

Kao, Mei-ch'ing, "China's Response to the West in Art, 1898-1937" (Ph.D. diss.,

Stanford University, 1972).

Kaple, Deborah, "Soviet Advisors in China in the 1950s", in Odd Arne Westad (ed.), *Brothers in Arms: The Rise and Fall of the Sino-Soviet Alliance 1945-1963* (Washington, D.C.: Woodrow Wilson Centre Press and Stanford: Stanford University Press, 1998), pp. 117-140.

Keller, P., *Getting at the Core: Curriculum Reform at Harvard* (Cambridge, Mass.: Harvard University Press, 1982).

Kennedy, E.S. et al, *Studies in the Islamic Exact Sciences* (Beirut: American University of Beirut, 1983).

Kennedy, E.S., "The Arabic Heritage in the Exact Sciences", in *Al-Abhāth*, Vol. 23, 1970, pp. 327-344. (Reprinted in E. S. Kennedy, et al., *Studies in the Islamic Exact Sciences*, 1983, cited above.)

Kennedy, E.S., "The History of Trigonometry: An Overview", in *Historical Topics for the Mathematics Classroom: 31st Yearbook of the National Council of Teachers of Mathematics*. (Reprinted in E. S. Kennedy *et al*, *Studies in the Islamic Exact Sciences*, 1983, cited above.)

Khadria, Binod, "Migration of Human Capital to the United States", in *Economic and Political Weekly* (August 11, 1990), pp. 1784-1794.

King, D. A., *Islamic Mathematical Astronomy* (London: Variorum Reprints, 1986).

King, K., "Two Key Fragmentations" (paper presented at Capri Conference, 1989).

Kirkness, V., *First Nations House of Learning, 1990-91 Calendar* (Vancouver, B.C.: University of British Columbia, 1990).

Koh, Dorothy, *Teachers of the Inner Chambers: Women and Culture in Seventeenth Century China* (Berkeley: University of California Press, 1995).

Korol, Alexander, *Soviet Education for Science and Technology* (New York: John Wiley and Sons, and the Technology Press of MIT, 1957).

Kors, Alan Charles, *Atheism in France*, Volume I: *The Orthodox Sources of Disbelief* (Princeton: Princeton University Press, 1990).

Kothari, Rajni, "On Humane Governance", in *Alternatives,* Vol. 12, 1987, pp. 277-290.

Kotkin, Joel, *Tribes: How Race, Religion and Identity Determine Success in the New Global Economy* (New York: Random House, 1993).

Kramrisch, Stella, *The Hindu Temple,* 2 vols. (Delhi: Motilal Banarsidass, 1946).

Kuhn, Thomas S., *The Structure of Scientific Revolutions,* 2nd ed. (Chicago: The University of Chicago Press, 1970). (First edition, 1964)

Lach, Donald F., *Asia in the Making of Europe* (2 vols. in 5 pts.) (Chicago: University of Chicago Press, 1965ff).

Lackner, Michael und Werner, Michael, Der *cultural turn* in den Humanwissenschaften. *Area Studies* im Auf-oder Abwind des Kulturalismus? (Schriftenreihe *"Suchprozesse für innovative Fragestellungen in der Wissenschaft"*, hrsg. vom Programmbeirat der Werner Reimers Konferenzen, Heft Nr. 2) (Bad Homburg: Werner Reimers Stiftung, 1999).

Laing, Ellen Johnston, *The Winking Owl, Art in the People's Republic of China*

(Berkeley: University of California Press, 1988).

Langgulung, H., "Ibn Sina as an Educationist", in *The Islamic Quarterly,* Vol. 32, No. 2, 1988.

Laudan, Larry, *Progress and Its Problems: Towards a Theory of Scientific Growth* (Berkeley: University of California Press, 1977).

Lee, Tao, "Some Statistics on Medical Schools in China for 1932-1933", in *The Chinese Medical Journal,* Vol. 47, 1933, pp. 1029-1039.

Lenk, Hans (ed.), *Zur Kritik der wissenschaftlichen Rationalität* (Freiburg: Alber, 1986).

Lepenies, Wolf, *Benimm und Erkenntnis – Über die notwendige Rückkehr der Werte in die Wissenschaften. Die Sozialwissenschaften nach dem Ende der Geschichte. Zwei Vorträge* (Frankfurt/Main: Suhrkamp, 1997).

Lepenies, Wolf, *Between Literature and Science: The Rise of Sociology* (Cambridge: Cambridge University Press, 1988).

Levine, A., *Handbook on Undergraduate Curriculum* (San Francisco: Jossey-Bass, 1978).

Lewis, Bernard, "Other People's History", in *American Scholar,* Vol. 59, No. 3, 1990, pp. 397-405.

Li, Hanru, "Reconsideration of Liberal Education and Specialized Education", in *Gaodeng gongcheng jiaoyu (Higher Engineering Education),* No. 1, 1990, pp. 35-38.

Li Manli, "Woguo dalu gaoxiao tongshi jiaoyu xianzhuang diaocha fenxi" (An analysis of a survey of the present conditions of general education in Chinese universities), in *Qinghua daxue jiaoyu yanjiu (Tsinghua University Education Research),* No. 2, 2001, pp. 128-136.

Li Manli, *Tongshi Jiaoyu – Yizhong Daxue Jiaoyuguan* (General Education – A Viewpoint on University Education) (Beijing: Qinghua Daxue Chubanshe, 1999).

Li Yiyuan, Yang Guoshu, Wenchong, *Collection of Essays on Modernization and Indigenousness in China* (Taibei, Taiwan: Laurel Crown, 1985).

Li, Yan and Du, Shiran, *Chinese Mathematics, A Concise History* (Oxford: Clarendon Press, 1987).

Liang, Qichao, "Yixue shanhui xu", in *Yinbing shi wenji,* Vol. 2 (Shanghai Zhonghua Shuju, 1932).

Lie, Suzanne Stiver and O'Leary, Virginnia, *Storming the Tower: Women in the Academic World* (New York: Kogan Page, 1990).

Lilge, Frederic, *The Abuse of Learning: The Failure of the German University* (New York: McMillan and Co., 1948).

Lincoln, Y. and Guba, E., *Effective Evaluation* (San Francisco: Jossey-Bass, 1985).

Linden, Allen, "Politics and Education in Nationalist China: The Case of the University Council 1927-1928", in *Journal of Asian Studies,* Vol. 27, No. 4, August, 1968.

Liu, Funian (ed.), *Huigu yu tansuo: Ruogan jiaoyu lilun wenti (Retrospection and Exploration: Some Questions of Educational Theories)* (Shanghai: East China

Normal University Press, 1991).

Liu, Shaoqi, *Collected Works of Liu Shao-ch'i 1945-1957* (Kowloon: Union Research Institute, 1969).

Liu, Shaoqi, *Collected Works of Liu Shao-ch'i Before 1944* (Kowloon: Union Research Institute, 1969).

Liu, Yuan-ching, Adam, *The Hanlin Academy 1644-1850* (Connecticut: Archon Books, 1981).

Lockhart, William, *Medical Missionary in China* (London: Hurst and Blackett Publications, 1861).

Lu, Gwei-Djen & Needham, Joseph, *Celestial Lancets: A History and Rationale of Acupuncture and Moxibustion* (Cambridge: Cambridge University Press, 1983).

Lu, Gwei-Djen et al, *Celestial Lancet* (Cambridge: Cambridge University Press, 1980).

Lu, Jie (ed.), *Education of Chinese: The Global Prospect of National Cultural Tradition* (Huaren jiaoyu: minzu wenhua chuantong de quanqiu zhanwang) (Nanjing: Nanjing shifan daxue chubanshe, 1999).

Lu, Yitian, *Lenglu yihua (Deserted House Medical Jottings)* (Shanghai Health Press, 1958).

Lu, Yongling, "Standing Between Two Worlds: Ma Xiangbo's Educational Thought and Practice", in R. Hayhoe and Y. Lu (eds.), *Ma Xiangbo and the Mind of Modern China* (New York: M.E. Sharpe, 1996), pp. 158-159.

Luk, Bernard Hung-kay, "Aleni Introduces the Western Academic Tradition to Seventeenth Century China: A Study of the Xixue Fan", in Tiziana Lippiello and Roman Malek (eds.), *Scholar from the West, Giulio Aleni S.J. (1582-1649) and the Dialogue between Christianity and China* (Brescia: Fondazione Civilta Bresciana and Sankt Augustin: the Monumenta Serica Institute, 1997), pp. 479-518.

Lutz, Jessie, *China and the Christian Colleges* (Ithaca, New York and London: Cornell University Press, 1971).

Lyotard, Jean-François, *The Postmodern Condition: A Report on Knowledge* (Minneapolis: University of Minnesota Press, 1984).

Ma, Kanwen, "Historical Research in Chinese Medicine and Recent Developments in Western Countries", in *Lishi yu wenxian yanjiu ziliao* (Beijing: China Institute for the Historical Medicine and Medical Literature, 1974), Vol. 4, p. 1.

Ma, Xiangbo, "Should a Head of State preside over religious ceremonies?", in R. Hayhoe and Y. Lu (eds.), *Ma Xiangbo and the Mind of Modern China* (New York: M.E. Sharpe, 1996), pp. 241-252.

Macdonell, A.A., *A History of Sanskrit Literature* (New York: Haskell House, 1968).

Mackenzie, J. Kenneth, "Viceroy's Hospital Medical School", in *The China Medical Missionary Journal*, Vol. 1, No. 3, 1887, pp. 100-106.

Mackenzie, J. Kenneth, "Medical Education in China", in *The China Medical Missionary Journal*, Vol. 1, No. 3, 1887.

Mahdi, M., "The New Wisdom: Synthesis of Philosophy and Mysticism", *Encyclopedia Britannica*, (1987).

Mao, Dun, "Guanyu Chuangzuo" (On Creative Work), *Mao Dun quanji (Collected*

Works of Mao Dun) (Beijing: People's Literature Press, 1991), Vol. 19.

Marcuse, Herbert, *One-Dimensional Man: Studies in the Ideology of Advanced Industrial Society* (Boston: Beacon, 1964).

Mason, E.S. and Asher, R.E., *The World Bank Since Bretton Woods* (Washington: Brookings Institution, 1973).

Mathur, M.V., Aurora, R.K. and Sogani, M. (eds.), *Indian University System: Revitalization and Reform* (New Delhi: Wiley Easterm, 1994).

Mattelart, Armand, *Transnationals and the Third World: The Struggle for Culture* (South Hadley, MA: Bergin and Garvey, 1983).

Maverick, L.A., *China: A Model for Europe* (San Antonio, Texas: Paul Anderson Co., 1946).

May, Robert, "The Scientific Wealth of Nations", in *Science,* No. 275 (7 February 1997), pp. 793-796.

Mazrui, Ali A. and Mazrui, Alamin M., "The Digital Revolution and the New Reformation: Doctrine and Gender in Islam", in *Harvard International Review*, Vol. xxxii, No. 1, Spring, 2001, pp. 52-55.

Mazrui, Ali A. and Mazrui, Alamin M., *The Power of Babel: Language and Governance in Africa's Experience* (Oxford, England: James Currey and Chicago: University of Chicago Press, 1998).

Mazrui, Ali A. and Tidy, Michael, *Nationalism and New States in Africa* (Nairobi, Kenya: Heinemann Educational Books, 1984).

Mazrui, Ali A., "Islam and Western Values", in *Foreign Affairs*, Vol. 76, No.5, 1997, pp. 118-132.

Mazrui, Ali A., "The African University as a Multinational Corporation: Problems of Penetration and Dependency", in *Harvard Educational Review,* Vol. 45, No. 2, May 1975, pp.191-210.

Mazrui, Ali A., *A World Federation of Cultures: An African Perspective* (New York: The Free Press, 1976).

Mazrui, Ali A., *Africa's International Relations* (London: Heinemann and Boulder, Colorado: Westview Press, 1977, subsequently reprinted).

Mazrui, Ali A., *Cultural Forces in World Politics* (London: James Currey and Portsmouth, New Hampshire: Heinemann, 1990).

Mazrui, Ali A., *Political Values and the Educated Class in Africa* (London: Heinemann Educational Books and Berkeley: University of California Press, 1978, subsequently reprinted).

Mazrui, Ali A., *The Political Sociology of the English Language* (The Hague: Mouton, Co., 1975).

Mazrui, Ali A., *Towards a Pax Africana* (London: Weidenfeld and Nicholson and Chicago: University of Chicago press, 1967).

Merchant, Carolyn, *The Death of Nature: Women, Ecology and the Scientific Revolution* (San Francisco: Harper and Row, 1980).

Meskill, John, *Academies in Ming China* (Tuscon, Arizona: University of Arizona Press, 1982).

Ministry of Human Resource Development, Government of India, *An Encyclopedia of Indian Adult Education, National Literacy Mission* (New Delhi: Government of India, 1999).

Mohanty, Chandra ,"Under Western Eyes: Feminist Scholarship and Colonial Discourses", in *Boundary Two*, Vol. 12, No. 2 and Vol. 13, No. 1, Spring/Fall 1984, pp. 333-357.

Mukherjee, R.N., "Background to the Discovery of the Symbol for Zero", in *Indian Journal for the History of Science*, Vol. 12, 1977, pp. 225-231.

Mungello, D.E., *Curious Land: Jesuit Accommodation and the Origins of Sinology* (Honolulu: University of Hawaii Press, 1989).

Murata, S., "Masculine-Feminine Complementary in the Spiritual Psychology of Islam", in *The Islamic Quartery*, Vol. 33, No. 3, 1989.

Murdoch, J., "Euclid: Transmission of the *Elements*", in C. C. Gillespie (ed.), *Dictionary of Scientific Biography*, Vol. 4 (New York: Charles Scribner's Sons, 1971), pp. 437-459.

Murray, A., *Reason and Society in the Middle Ages* (Oxford: Clarendon Press, 1978).

Nandy, Ashis, "From Outside the Imperium: Gandhi's Cultural Critique of the West", in *Alternatives*, Vol. 7, 1981, pp. 171-194.

Nandy, Ashis, "Recovery of Indigenous Knowledge and Dissenting Futures of the University", in Sohail Inayatullah and Jennifer Gidley (eds.), The University in Transformation: Global Perspectives on the Futures of the University (Westport, CT: Bergin & Garvey, 2000), pp. 115-123.

Nandy, Ashis, "Shamans, Savages and the Wilderness: On the Audibility of Dissent and the Future of Civilizations", in *Alternatives*, Vol. 14, 1989, pp. 263-277.

Nandy, Ashis, "The Traditions of Technology", in *Alternatives*, Vol. 4, 1978-79, pp. 371-385.

Nasr, S.H. (ed.), *Islamic Spirituality* (New York: Crossroad, 1987).

National Policy on Education, Publication No. 1539 (New Delhi: Ministry of Human Resource Development, Department of Education, 1986).

Needham, Joseph, *Science and Civilisation in China* (6 vols. in 15 pts.) (Cambridge: Cambridge University Press, 1954ff).

Needham, Joseph, *The Shorter Science and Civilization in China*, edited by Colin Roman (Cambridge: Cambridge University Press, 1978).

Neville, Robert Cummings, "Tu Wei-ming's Neo-Confucianism", in *The International Review of Chinese Philosophy and Religion*, Vol. 5, 2000, pp. 163, 169.

New Guidelines on Adult and Continuing Education and Extension Programmes in Universities and Colleges, 1988 (New Delhi: University Grants Committee, 1988).

Newton-Smith, W.H., "The Rationality of Science: Why Bother" in W.H. Newton-Smith and T.J. Jiang (eds.), *Popper in China* (London: Routledge, 1992).

Nicholson, N., *Great Houses of Britain* (London: Spring Books, 1978).

Nicola Valley Institute of Technology, 1990-91 Calendar (Merritt, B.C.: NVIT, 1990).

Nietzsche, Friedrich, *Beyond Good and Evil,* trans. Danto, A.C., *Nietzsche as Philosopher* (New York: Macmillan, 1968).

Noble, David, *A World Without Women: The Christian Clerical Culture of Western Science* (New York: Alfred Knopf, 1992).

Nowotny, Helga et al, *The New Production of Knowledge: The Dynamics of Science and Research in Contemporary Societies* (London: Sage, 1994).

O'Donnell, Guillermo, Schmitter, Philippe C. and Whitehead, Laurence (eds.), *Transitions from Authoritarian Rule: Prospects for Democracy* (Baltimore: Johns Hopkins Press, 1986).

O'Malley, C.D., *Andreas Vesalius of Brussels* (Berkeley: University of California Press, 1964).

Orleans, L.A., "Soviet Influence on China's Higher Education", in R. Hayhoe and M. Bastid (eds.), *China's Education and the Industrialised World: Studies in Cultural Transfer* (New York: M.E. Sharpe, 1987), pp. 184-198

Parsons, Talcott, "Value-Freedom and Objectivity", in Fred R. Dallmayr and Thomas A. McCarthy, *Understanding and Social Inquiry* (Notre Dame: University of Notre Dame Press, 1977), pp. 56-65.

Pateman, Carole, *Participation and Democratic Theory* (Cambridge: Cambridge University Press, 1970).

Pateman, Carole, *The Sexual Contract* (Stanford: Stanford University Press, 1988).

Paulsen, Friedrich, *Immanuel Kant* (London: John Nimmo, 1902).

Paulston, R.G. and Liebman, M., "Social Cartography: A New Metaphor/Tool for Comparative Studies", in Rolland G. Paulston (ed.), *Social Cartography: Mapping Ways of Seeing Social and Educational Change* (New York and London: Garland Publishing, 2000), pp. 7-28.

Pavel, D.M., Skinner, R.R., Farris, E., Calahan, M., Tippiconnic, J. and Stein, W., *American Indians and Alaska Natives in Postsecondary Education* (Washington, D.C.: National Center for Education Statistics, 1998).

Peterson, G., Hayhoe, R. and Lu, Y.L. (eds.), *Education, Culture and Identity in Twentieth Century China* (Ann Arbor: University of Michigan Press, 2001).

Pinot, Virgile, *La Chine et la formation de l'esprit philosophique* (Paris: Geuthner, 1932).

Polanyi, Michael, "The Growth of Science in Society", in William R. Coulson & Carl R. Rogers (eds.), *Man and the Science of Man* (Columbus, Ohio: Charles E. Merrill, 1968).

Popkewitz, T., "Whose Future? Whose Past? Notes on Critical Theory and Methodology" in E. Guba (ed.), *The Paradigm Dialogue* (New York: Sage Publications, Inc., 1990)

Popper, Karl, *Conjectures and Refutations* (New York: Harper & Row, 1963).

Popper, Karl, *The Logic of Scientific Discovery* (London: Hutchinson, 1959).

Pottinger, R., "Disjunction to Higher Education: American Indian Students in the Southwest", *Anthropology and Education Quarterly*, Vol. 20, No. 4, 1989, pp. 326-344.

Price, Ronald, "Convergence or Copying: China and the Soviet Union", in Hayhoe, R. and Bastid, M. (eds.), *China's Education and the Industrialised World: Studies in Cultural Transfer* (New York: M.E. Sharpe, 1987), pp. 158-183.

Provincial Advisory Committee, *First Nations Access to Post-secondary Education in British Columbia* (Victoria, B.C.: Ministry of Advanced Education, Training and Technology, Government of British Columbia, 1990).

Putnam, Hilary, *The Many Faces of Realism: The Paul Carus Lectures* (La Salle, IL: Open Court, 1987).

Rahnema, Majid with Victoria Bawtree (Hrsg.), *The Post-Development Reader* (London: ZED Books, 1997).

Rajagopal, P., "Meaning through Geometry: Temple Design in Medieval India" (paper presented to the Canadian Society for the History and Philosophy of Mathematics at the University of Prince Edward Island, Charlottetown, May 1992).

Rajagopal, P., "Practical and Commercial Problems in Indian Mathematics", in *Arhat Vachana*, No. 4, 1992, pp. 55-70.

Rajagopal, P., "The Sthananga Sutra Programme in Indian Mathematics", in *Arhat Vachana*, No. 3, 1991, pp. 1-8.

Rashdall, Hastings, *The Universities of Europe in the Middle Ages* (Oxford: Clarendon Press, 1936ff.), 3 vols.

Ray, A., *English Delftware Tiles* (London: Faber and Faber, 1973).

Raza, Moonis, *Higher Education in India: Retrospect and Prospect* (New Delhi: Association of Indian Universities, 1991).

Razzell, Peter, *The Conquest of Smallpox – The Impact of Inoculation on Smallpox Mortality in Eighteenth Century Britain* (New Haven: Sussex, 1977).

Ree, Harry, *Educator Extraordinary: the Life and Achievement of Henry Morris, 1889-1961* (London: Peter Owen Ltd., 1973).

"Reform in Institutions of Higher Education Should Develop Steadily", in *Renmin ribao (People's Daily)* Editorial, January 23, 1953.

Reyhner, J. and Dodd, J., "Factors Affecting the Retention of American Indian and Alaska Native students in Higher Education" (Paper presented at the Expanding Minority Opportunities: First Annual National Conference) (Tempe, AZ: Arizona State University, 1995).

Ricci, David M., *The Tragedy of Political Science: Politics, Scholarship, and Democracy* (New Haven: Yale University Press, 1984).

Rinaldi, M., *Kraak Porcelain: A Moment in the History of Trade* (London: Bamboo, 1989).

Ringer, Fritz, *The Decline of the German Mandarinate* (Cambridge, Mass, 1969).

Robertson, Roland, "Globalization: Timespace and Homogeneity: Heterogeneity", in M. Featherstone, S. Lash, R. Robertson, (eds.) *Global Modernities* (London: Sage Publications, 1995), pp. 25-44.

Robinson, F., "Technology and Religious Change: Islam and the Impact of Print", Inaugural Lecture given on March 4, 1992, at Royal Holloway and Bedford New College as Professor of the History of South Asia, University of London. See

Modern Asian Studies, Vol. 27, No.1, 1993, pp. 229-251.

Rogers, Carl, "Some Thoughts Regarding the Current Presuppositions of the Behavorial Sciences", in William R. Coulson & Carl R. Rogers (eds.), *Man and the Science of Man* (Columbus, Ohio: Charles E. Merrill, 1968).

Rostow, W.W., *The Stages of Economic Growth: A Non-Communist Manifesto* (Cambridge, England: Cambridge University Press, 1990).

Roth, Paul A., *Meaning and Method in the Social Sciences: A Case for Methodological Pluralism* (Ithaca NY: Cornell University Press, 1987).

Rouse, J., *Knowledge and Power* (Ithaca, N.Y.: Cornell University Press, 1987).

Rowbotham, A. H., *Missionary and Mandarin. The Jesuits at the Court of China* (Berkeley, California: University of California Press, 1942).

Rowe, William, *Hankow: Commerce and Society in a Chinese City, 1796-1889* (Stanford: Stanford University Press, 1984).

Rowe, William, *Hankow: Conflict and Community in a Chinese City, 1796-1895* (Stanford: Stanford University Press, 1989).

Rule, Paul A., *K'ung-tzu or Confucius: The Jesuit Interpretation of Confucianism* (Sydney: Allen & Unwin, 1986).

Rust, V.D., "From Modern to Postmodern Ways of Seeing Social and Educational Change", in Rolland G. Paulston (ed.), *Social Cartography: Mapping Ways of Seeing Social and Educational Change* (New York and London: Garland Publishing, 2000), pp. 29-51.

Sabra, A.I., "The Exact Sciences", in John R. Hayes (ed.), *The Genius of Arabic Civilization* (New York: New York University Press, 1975, pp. 149-172.

Sabra, A.I., *The Optics of Ibn al-Haytham*, Parts I and II (London: The Warburg Institute,1989).

Sachs, W. (ed.), *The Development Dictionary* (London: Zed Books, 1992).

Said, Edward W., *Reflections on Exile and other Essays* (Cambridge, MA: Harvard University Press, 2000).

Said, Edward W., *The World, the Text, and the Critic* (Cambridge: Harvard University Press, 1983).

Saidan, A.S., *The Arithmetic of Al-Uqlidisi* (Boston D. Reidel Publishing Co., 1978).

Salam, Abdus, "Higher Education and Development", in *Higher Education in Europe*, Vol. 11, No.3, 1986, pp. 7-12.

Salam, Abdus, *Ideal and Realities: Selected Essays of Abdus Salam* (World Scientific, 1989).

Salam, Abdus, *Science in the Third World* (Edinburgh University Press, 1989).

Salam, Abdus, *Supergravities in Diverse Dimensions* (North Holland: Elsevier Science, 1989).

Salam, Abdus, *Unification of Fundamental Forces: The First of the 1988 Dirac Memorial Lectures* (Cambridge University Press, 1990).

Sarton, George, *A History of Science* (New York: Norton, 1970).

Saunders, C.M. and Lee, Francis R., *The Manchu Anatomy and Its Historical Origin* (Taiwan: Li Ming Cultural Enterprise, 1981).

Schlipp, P.A. (ed.), *Albert Einstein: Philosopher Scientist* (Evanston: Library of Living Philosophers, 1949).

Schöfthaler, Traugott and Goldschmidt, Dietrich (eds.), *Soziale Struktur und Vernunft: Jean Piagets Modell entwickelten Denkens in der Diskussion kulturvergleichender Forschung* (Frankfurt: Suhrkamp, 1985).

Schwehn, Mark, *Exiles from Eden: Religion and the Academic Life in America* (New York: Oxford University Press, 1993).

Scollon, R., & Scollon, S., *Narrative Literacy and Face in Interethnic Communication* (Norwood, NJ: Ablex Publishing Corporation, 1981).

Scollon, R., *Human Knowledge and the Institution's Knowledge: Communication Patterns and Retention in a Public University* (Center for Cross-Cultural Studies, University of Alaska Fairbanks, 1981).

Seshadri, C.V. and Balaji V., *Towards a New Science of Agriculture* (Madras, MCRC), undated.

Sharif, M., *A History of Muslim Philosophy* (Wiesbaden, Germany: Otto Harrassowitz, 1963).

Sheth, D.L., "Alternative Development as Political Practice", in *Alternatives*, Vol. 12, 1987, pp. 155-171.

Shu, Xincheng (ed.), *Zhongguo jindai jiaoyushi ziliao* (Reference Material on Modern Education History in China) (Beijing: People's Education Press, 1961), 2 vols.

Shukla, K.S., *The Patiganita of Sridharacarya* (Lucknow: Department of Mathematics and Astronomy, Lucknow University, 1959).

Silbergeld, Jerome, *Contradictions: Li Huasheng, Artistic Life and Cultural Politics in Socialist China* (Seattle: University of Washington Press, 1993).

Snow, Jon. "All the News that Fits on Screen", in *The Guardian* (London), Sept 19, 1995.

Staal, Frits, *Agni: The Vedic Ritual of the Fire Altar*, 2 vols. (Berkeley: Asian Humanities Press, 1983).

Staudt, Kathleen, *Women, Foreign Assistance, and Advocacy Administration* (New York: Praeger, 1985).

Steele, R., *The Earliest Arithmetics in English* (Oxford: Oxford University Press, 1922).

Stehr, Nico and Ericson, Richard V., *The Culture and Power of Knowledge: Inquiries into Contemporary Societies* (Berlin/New York: de Gruyter, 1992).

Stehr, Nico, *Wissen und Wirtschaften: Die gesellschaftlichen Grundlagen der modernen Ökonomie* (Frankfurt/Main: Suhrkamp, 2001).

Stromquist, Nelly P., *Action Research: A New Sociological Approach* (Ottawa: IDRC, 1982).

Sullivan, Michael, "Paint with a New Brush: Art in Post Mao China", in *China Briefing, 1980* (Boulder, Co.: Westview Press, 1989).

Sullivan, Michael, *Art and Artists of twentieth-century China* (Berkeley: University of California Press, 1996).

Sullivan, Michael, *Chinese Art in the Twentieth Century* (Berkeley: University of

California Press, 1959).

Sutton, Margaret, "Social Sciences and Ordinary Understanding: Coming to Terms with Tourism in Bali" (Unpublished Ph.D. dissertation) (Stanford, CA: Stanford University, 1991).

Swann, Peter, *2,000 Years of Japanese Art* (with Yukio Yashiro) (New York: H.N. Abrams, 1958).

Swann, Peter, *A Concise History of Japanese Art* (New York and Tokyo: Kodansha International, 1979).

Swann, Peter, *An Introduction to the Arts in Japan* (New York: Praeger, 1958).

Swann, Peter, *Chinese Monumental Art* (New York: Viking Press, 1963).

Swann, Peter, *Chinese Painting* (New York: Universe Books, 1958).

Swann, Peter, *Hokusai* (London: Faber and Faber, 1959).

Swann, Peter, *Japan* (London: Methuen, 1966).

Swetz, Frank J., *Capitalism and Arithmetic* (La Salle: Open Court, 1987).

Szyliowicz, J. *Education and Modernization in the Middle East* (London: Cornell University Press, 1973).

Teng, Ssu-yu, "Chinese Influence on the Western Examination System", in *Harvard Journal of Asiatic Studies*, Vol. 7, No. 4, 1942, p. 290.

Teynac, F., Nolot, P. and Vivien, J.D., *Wallpaper – A History* (London: Thames and Hudson, 1982).

The World Bank Annual Report 2000, (Washington).

Thomas, Russell Brown, *The Search for Common Learning: General Education, 1800-1960* (New York: McGraw-Hill, 1962)

Thomason, Joseph C., "Chinese Materia Medica: Its Value to Medical Missionaries", in *The China Medical Missionary Journal*, Vol. 4, No. 3, 1890, pp. 115-119.

Thompson, John B., *Critical Hermeneutics: A Study in the Thought of Paul Ricoeur and Jürgen Habermas* (Cambridge: Cambridge University Press, 1981).

Thulstrup, Erik W., *Improving the Quality of Research in Developing Country Universities* (Washington, D.C.: Education and Employment Division, Population and Human Resources Department, World Bank, 1992).

Tichane, R., *Ching-te-chen: Views of a Porcelain City* (Painted Post, N.Y.: New York Institute of Glaze Research, 1983).

Tierney, W.G., "The College Experience of Native Americans: A Critical Analysis", in L. Weis, & M. Fine (eds.), *Silenced Voices: Class, Race and Gender in United States Schools* (Albany, NY: State University of New York Press, 1993).

Tierney, W.G., *Official Encouragement. Institutional Discouragement: Minorities in Academe – The Native American Experience* (Norwood, N.J.: Ablex Publishing Corp., 1992).

Toomer, G., *Ptolemy's Almagest* (New York: Springer-Verlag, 1984),

Tsai, Kathryn, "The Chinese Buddhist Monastic Order for Women: The First Two Centuries", in Richard Guisso and Stanley Johannesen (eds.), *Women in China: Current Directions in Historical Scholarship* (Lewiston, New York: Edwin Mellen Press, 1981), pp. 1-20.

Tu, Wei-ming, "Beyond the Enlightenment Mentality", in Mary Evelyn Tucker and John Berthrong, *Confucianism and Ecology: The Interrelation of Heaven, Earth and Humans* (Cambridge, Mass.: Harvard University Centre for the Study of World Religions, distributed by Harvard University Press, 1998), pp. 13-14.

Tu, Wei-ming, "Toward a Third Epoch of Confucian Humanism", in Tu Wei-ming, *The Way, Learning and Politics* (Albany: State University of New York Press, 1993), pp. 141-159.

UNESCO, *Continuing Education: New Policies and Directions, APPEAL Training Materials for Continuing Education Personnel [ALTP-CE]* (Bangkok: Principal Regional Office for Asia and the Pacific, UNESCO, 1993).

UNESCO: http://www.unesco.org/dialogue2001/en/background.htm.

University Grants Commission, *Guidelines for Department / Centre for Adult and Continuing Education, Extension Work and Field Outreach* (New Delhi:University Grants Commission, 1997).

University System and Extension as the Third Dimension, A Report of the Review Committee Appointed by the University Grants Commission (New Delhi: University Grants Commission, 1987).

Van Der Waerden, B.J., "Pell's Equation in Greek and Hindu Mathematics", in *Russian Mathematical Surveys*, Vol. 31, 1976, pp. 210-225.

Van Egmond, Warren, *The Commercial Revolution and the Beginnings of Western Mathematics in Renaissance Florence, 1300-1500* (Bloomington: Indiana University, 1976).

Vesalius, Andreas, *Radicis Chinae Vsus* (Lyons: Sub Saito Coloniensi, 1547).

Visvanathan, Shiv "On the Annals of the Laboratory State", in Ashis Nandy (ed.), *Science, Hegemony and Violence: A Requiem for Modernity* (Delhi: Oxford University Press, 1988).

Vogel, K., *Mohammed ibn Musa Alchwarizmi's Algorismus, Das Fruehste Lehrbuch zum Rechnen mit Indischen Ziffern* (Aalen Osnabrueck: Zeller, 1963).

von Humboldt, Wilhelm, "On the Spirit and the Organisational Framework of Intellectual Institutions", in *Minerva*, Vol. 8, April, 1970, pp. 242-250.

Wang and Wu, *History of Chinese Medicine* (Shanghai, China: National Quarantine Service, 1937).

Wang, Xuequan, *Chongqingtang suibi (Jottings at the Chongqing Hall)*, originally printed in 1808, reprinted in *Qianzhai yixue congshu (Qianzhai's Collection of Medical Works)*, Vol. 11.

Weber, Max, "Science as a Vocation", in H.H. Gerth and C. Wright Mills, *From Max Weber: Essays in Sociology* (New York: Oxford University Press, 1967).

Weber, Max, *The Protestant Ethic and the Spirit of Capitalism* (New York: C. Scribner, 1958).

Weiler, Hans N., "Continuity and Change in U.S. Higher Education: Challenges to the Established Order of Knowledge Production", in *Zeitschrift für internationale erziehungs- und sozialwissenschaftliche Forschung* Vol. 7, No. 1, 1990, pp. 1-15.

Weiler, Hans N., "Die Produktion von Wissen und die Legitimation der Macht: Zur

politischen Ökonomie des internationalen Forschungssystems", in Walter Sülberg (ed.), *Demokratisierung und Partizipation im Entwicklungsprozess*
(Frankfurt: IKO, 1988), pp. 17-38.

Weiler, Hans N., "Legalization, Expertise, and Participation: Strategies of
Compensatory Legitimation in Educational Policy", in *Comparative Education
Review*, Vol. 27, No. 2, June 1983, pp. 259-277.

Weiler, Hans N., "Technology and Politics in the Production of Knowledge: Some
Notes on a New World Bank Initiative to Build Educational Research Capacity in
Developing Countries", in *NORRAG News* No. 10, July 1991, pp. 19-23; in
Spanish: "La Tecnología y las Política en la Producción de Conocimiento: ciertos
comentarios acerca de una nueva iniciativa del Banco Mundial para establecer la
capacidad de investigación en educación en los países en desarollo", in *Educación
Superior y Sociedad*, Vol. 2, No. 2, 1991, pp. 42-46.

Weiler, Hans N., "The International Politics of Knowledge Production and the Future
of Higher Education", in Gustavo López Ospina (ed.), *New Contexts and Perspectives* (Caracas: UNESCO/CRESALC, 1992), pp. 33-51; in Spanish: "La
Política Internacional de la Producción del Conocimiento y el Futuro de la
Educación Superior", in Gustavo López Ospina (ed.), *Nuevos Contextos y Per-
spectivas* (Caracas: UNESCO/CRESALC, 1991), pp. 33-56.

Weiler, Hans N., "The Political Dilemmas of Foreign Study", in *Comparative
Education Review* Vol. 28, No. 2, May 1984, pp. 168-179; also in Elinor G.
Barber, Philip G. Altbach, and Robert G. Myers (eds.), *Bridges to Knowledge:
Foreign Students in Comparative Perspective* (Chicago: University of Chicago
Press, 1984), pp. 184-195.

Weiler, Hans N., "Wissen und Herrschaft in einer Welt der Konflikte: Die politische
Ökonomie der internationalen Wissensproduktion und die Rolle der UNESCO",
in Peter Haungs et al (eds.), *CIVITAS – Widmungen für Bernhard Vogel zum 60.
Geburtstag* (Paderborn: Schöningh, 1992), pp.649-659.

Weiler, Hans N., "Wissen und Politik als international vermittelte Beziehung", in Peter
A. Döring (ed.), *Der Neubeginn im Wandel der Zeit: In Memoriam Erwin Stein*
(Frankfurt/Main: Deutsches Institut für Internationale Pädagogische Forschung,
1995), pp. 129-137.

Weiler, Hans N., *Wissen und Macht in einer Welt der Konflikte: Zur Politik der
Wissensproduktion* (Berlin: Böll-Stiftung, in press)

Wen, Fuxiang, "Aims of Higher Engineering Education and Humanities and Social
Sciences", in *Gaodeng jiaoyu xuebao (Journal of Higher Education)*, No. 4, 1990,
pp. 25-28.

Wen, Rumin and Zhao, Weimin (eds.), *Peking University* (Beijing: Peking University
Press, 1998).

Wilber, Charles K., *The Political Economy of Development and Underdevelopment*
(New York: Random House, 1988).

Wilshire, Bruce, *The Moral Collapse of the University: Professionalism, Purity and
Alienation* (Albany: State University of New York Press, 1990).

Winch, Peter, *The Idea of a Social Science and its Relation to Philosophy* (London: Routledge and Kegan Paul, 1958).

Wu Jisong, *Zhishi jingji* (The Knowledge Economy) (Beijing: Keji jishu chubanshe, 1998).

Wu, Lien Teh, "Memorandum on Medical Education in China", in *The Chinese Medical Journal*, Vol. 28, No. 2, 1914, pp. 105-120.

Wu, Yanfu, "On the Issue of Students of Liberal Arts Studying Natural Sciences", in *Jiauyu yanjiu (Educational Research)*, No. 8, 1981, pp. 48-52.

Xia, Yulong, "Integration of Disciplines and General Education", in *Jiaoyu yanjiu (Educational Research)*, No. 5, 1981, pp. 34-39.

Xiong, Mingan, "Tentative Remarks on Mei Yiqi's Philosophy of Education", in *Shanghai gaojiao yanjiu (Higher Education Research in Shanghai)*, No. 4, 1986, pp. 104-106.

Yang Guoshu & Wenchong, *Shehui ji xingwei kexue yanjiu de Zhongguohua* (Research on Social and Behavioural Science in China) (Beijing: Institute for Nationalities Studies, Central Academy for Research, 1982).

Yang Zhongfang, "Xiandaihua, Quanqiuhua Shi Yu Bentuhua Duili Dema? – Shilun Xiandaihua Yanjiu de Bentuhua" (Modernization, Globalization and Indigenousness: Are they in conflict?), in *Sociology Study*, 1st Issue, Beijing, 1999.

Yeh, Wen-hsin, *The Alienated Academy: Culture and Politics in Republican China 1919-1937* (Cambridge, Mass.: Council on East Asian Studies, Harvard University, 1990).

Youshchkevitch, A.P., *Les mathématiques arabes (VIIIe – XVe siècles)*, Trans. Cazenave, M. and Jaouiche, K. (Paris: J. Vrin, 1976).

Zhang, Ruifan, "Piyong and Pangong", in *Shanghai gaojiao yanjiu (Higher Education Research in Shanghai)*, Vol. 2 (1985), pp. 107-114.

Zhang, Shaoxia & Li, Xiaoshan, *Zhongguo xiandai huihua shi* (A History of Modern Chinese Painting), (Nanjing: Jiangsu meishu chuban she, 1986).

Zhang, Xicun, *Chongjiao zhongxi huitong yishu wuzhong, xu (Preface to the revised edition of the Essence of Medical Classics in the Confluence of Chinese and Western Medicine)*(Guangyi shuju, 1933).

Zhen, Zhiya et al, *Zhongguo yixue shi (The History of Chinese Medicine)* (Beijing: People's Health Press, 1991).

Zhou Yuanqing, "Suzhi, suzhi jiaoyu, wenhua suzhi jiaoyu" (Quality, quality education and education in cultural quality), in *Qinghua daxue jiaoyu yanjiu (Tsinghua University Education Research)*, No. 2, 2001, pp. 1-5.

Zhou, Bangdao, *The First China Education Yearbook* (Shanghai: Kaiming Book Co. Ltd., 1934).

Zhu, Youhuan (ed.), *Zhongguo jindai xuezhi shiliao* (Shanghai: Shanghai East China Normal University Press, 1983, 1986), 2 vols.

Index

Aboriginal peoples. *See* First Nations
(Canada)
Abraham Ecchellensis, 129
Abu Abd Allah Malik, 99
Abu-Lughod, Janet, 281
Abū Sa'd, 136
Abū Sahl al-Kūhī, 129, 130–1
The Abuse of Learning, 332
Academic freedom. *See also* Universities
American universities, 334
China, and autonomy of *shuyuan*, 328–9
as core value in Western universities,
325–6
French universities, 332–3
At Southwest Associated University
(Lianda) during Sino-Japanese
War, 340–1
Soviet universities, for scientific com-
munity, 333
in traditional German universities, 331–2
Academica Sinica, 339
Achebe, Chinua, 31
Adelard of Bath, 128, 133
Africa
contending cultures, and ethnic conflicts,
93–4
education, proposed strategies for change,
97
higher education, enrolment in, 204
indigenous agricultural knowledge of, 31,
37
languages, lack of post-graduate studies
in, 95
universities
African academic tradition of, 95
and legacy of colonialism, 94, 95
Western education, and role of women in,
96–7
Agriculture
as applied science, 165
Chinese, European interest in, 281–2
India, and foreign assistance, 211, 215,
220–2

indigenous, as less destructive of environment, 49
research, in Third World, 165
Akbar (Emperor), 108
Ake, Claude, 26
Al Azhar University (Cairo), 94, 95
al-Battānī, 133, 134
al-Bīrūnī, 132–3, 163
Al Faruqi, 62–3
al-Fazari, 119, 121
Al Ghazali, 70
al-Idrisi, 132
al-Khwarīzmī, Muhammad ibn Mūsā, 113,
119–20, 124, 133, 163
al-Kindi, 135
al-Mamun (Caliph), 119
al-Mansur (Caliph), 119
al-Uqlidisi, 121
Alatas, Syed, 26
Aleni, Giulio, 325, 327, 337
Alexander de Villa Dei, 120
Algebra. *See* Mathematics
Algeria, pro-democracy movement in, 94
Algorismus vulgaris (Common algorism),
120
Algorithms. *See* Mathematics
Alhazen. *See Ibn al-Haytham*
Ali b. Isa, 131
Almagest, 132, 133
Alvares, Claude, 50
Amir Kabir, 257
The Anatomy of Female Power, 96
Andrews, Julia, 306–7
Apel, Karl-Otto, 28
Apollonius of Perga, 129
Archibald, Jo-ann, 84
Archimedes, 129, 130, 163
Aristotle, 60, 163, 164
Arithmetic. *See* Mathematics
Arriaga, Miguel de, 180
Art, Chinese
under Chinese Communist Party, 302,
303